Pioneering AI and Data Technologies for Next-Gen Security, IoT, and Smart Ecosystems

Ferdin Joe John Joseph
Thai-Nichi Institute of Technology, Thailand

Karthikeyan Chinnusamy
Veritas, USA

Joseph Jeganathan
University of Bahrain, Bahrain

Ahmed J. Obaid
University of Kufa, Iraq

S. Suman Rajest
Dhaanish Ahmed College of Engineering, India

IGI Global
Scientific Publishing
Publishing Tomorrow's Research Today

Vice President of Editorial	Melissa Wagner
Director of Acquisitions	Mikaela Felty
Director of Book Development	Jocelynn Hessler
Production Manager	Mike Brehm
Cover Design	Jose Rosado

Published in the United States of America by
IGI Global Scientific Publishing
701 East Chocolate Avenue
Hershey, PA, 17033, USA
Tel: 717-533-8845
Fax: 717-533-7115
Website: https://www.igi-global.com E-mail: cust@igi-global.com

Library of Congress Cataloging-in-Publication Data

Names: Joseph, Ferdin Joe John, 1987- editor | Chinnusamy, Karthikeyan, 1973- editor | Jeganathan, Joseph, 1980- editor | Obaid, Ahmed J. (Ahmed Jabbar) editor | Rajest, S. Suman, 1988- editor
Title: Pioneering AI and data technologies for next-gen security, IoT, and smart ecosystems / edited by: Ferdin Joe John Joseph, Karthikeyan Chinnusamy, Joseph Jeganathan, Ahmed J. Obaid, S. Suman Rajest.
Description: Hershey PA : IGI Global Scientific Publishing, [2026] | Includes bibliographical references.
Identifiers: LCCN 2025024332 (print) | LCCN 2025024333 (ebook) | ISBN 9798337346724 hardcover | ISBN 9798337346731 paperback | ISBN 9798337346748 ebook
Subjects: LCSH: Artificial intelligence--Industrial applications
Classification: LCC TA347.A78 P56 2026 (print) | LCC TA347.A78 (ebook)
LC record available at https://lccn.loc.gov/2025024332
LC ebook record available at https://lccn.loc.gov/2025024333
British Cataloguing in Publication Data
A Cataloguing in Publication record for this book is available from the British Library.

Table of Contents

Detailed Table of Contents

Mobile cloud computing, also known as MCC, has become increasingly popular among users of high-speed mobile devices. Users face dangers to their privacy and security due to several factors, including the growing number of subscribers to MCC and the possibility of unauthorized access to user data. Within the realm of conventional research, efforts are made to construct a safe model to maintain the data in MCC. There are a number of difficulties and gaps in MCC that represent severe dangers to security policy despite the fact that it provides modeling for a variety of architectures. The purpose of this research article is to offer an attribute-based encryption (ABE) system as a means of mitigating the effects of such problems. By facilitating data separation and storage in cloud servers, the ABE solution contributes to the facilitation of white-box traceability and facilitates direct refurbishment.

Wireless Sensor Networks (WSNs) have permeated various domains, such as industrial automation, healthcare, and environmental monitoring, due to their ability to effectively collect and communicate data in diverse environments. The reliability

This chapter focuses on improving the existing monitoring system's ability to detect and prevent disruptive behaviours, which is critical given the growing public safety concerns. Recognizing patterns connected with potential threats, inappropriate behavior, and security issues can be challenging in many scenarios. The proposed approach of integrating attention mechanisms into image processing is suggested as a solution to detect suspicious activities. By employing this novel methodology, the model is optimized, and the design language is simplified, thereby ensuring enhanced precision in surveillance. The principal aim of the framework is to augment the model's sensitivity to significant temporal and spatial variables. A Convolutional Neural Network powers it with attention elements that are strategically positioned. To improve activity detection and public safety, the suggested approach places a higher value on refining classification than employing complex language.

SAR photography has great potential for remote sensing, especially ship identification. This study discusses revolutionary SAR picture interpretation advances, including ship recognition methods and uses beyond maritime surveillance. We explain SAR technology and ship identification issues such as clutter, noise, and environmental variability. We suggest novel solutions using machine learning and signal processing advances. We investigate CNNs, RNNs, and deep learning architectures for robust ship detection in SAR images. We also study adaptive filtering and wavelet transforms to improve detection accuracy and eliminate false alarms. SAR picture interpretation has applications beyond ship detection, as this study discusses. These include disaster management, environmental monitoring, and maritime security, demonstrating SAR technology's versatility in meeting varied social needs. Sentinel-1 and TerraSAR-X are public SAR image interpretation datasets that inform our analysis.

The chapter presents a new hybrid intrusion detection framework that combines LSTM networks with gradient-boosting techniques. The approach presented in this study utilizes two prominent datasets, namely CICIDS2018 and CICIDS2017. The main objective is to improve the precision and reliability of intrusion detection in systems. This is achieved by capturing temporal dependencies in network traffic data and improving predictive performance by implementing boosting algorithms. The datasets are subjected to a thorough preprocessing process involving cleaning, normalization, and feature selection. This guarantees that the input for the model is of the highest quality. The LSTM component functions as the central element, extracting complex patterns and relationships from sequential data. The predictions generated by the LSTM model are refined by gradient boosting algorithms, which utilize their ensemble learning capabilities to improve overall performance.

Due to the development of the "Internet of Things (IoT)," a huge quantity of data is transferred to the cloud architecture. As a consequence, expenses and storage charges are associated with cloud servers. Storage capacity can be enhanced by implementing a deduplication technique to spot duplicate information. Both cryptography and deduplication are carried out using the full hash values of the information chunks. The deduplication systems are vulnerable to file threats. So, we developed an effective optimal key-based deduplication model. The proposed model uses attributes including filename, size, block name, size, type of file, and data pattern for deduplication. The "Long Short-Term Memory (LSTM)" model is introduced for effective deduplication performance. The LSTM model separates the attributes and deduplicated attributes once the data file is not duplicated. Once it is proved that the data are deduplicated, the edge node (client) enciphers the data by

IWSNs are necessary for smart manufacturing because they allow the continuous monitoring and control of resources. However, their susceptibility to cyber threats requires enhancing efficient and effective IDS systems. The proposed work introduces a newly developed approach based on ML and DL techniques to achieve efficient intrusion detection in IWSNs. The framework offers feature extraction using higher-order features and dominant Eigenspace to enhance the detection accuracy while maintaining enhanced computational time and selecting adaptive thresholds. The performance analysis against benchmark datasets shows a high level of effectiveness with a detection accuracy of 99.2%, precision of 97.9%, recall ratio of 98.3%, and F1 Score of 98.1%. Moreover, the experimental results show a decreased detection delay and improved resource efficiency, making the system ideal for real-time applications in smart manufacturing systems. However, the proposed framework is superior to the previous solutions in terms of accuracy and required time.

Intelligent surveillance systems are crucial for monitoring densely populated areas for a wide range of applications, including security and crowd control. The primary objective of this study is to use wireless sensing technologies in order to identify and analyze the actions of subspecies inside various habitats. The suggested system utilizes sophisticated machine learning algorithms to differentiate and evaluate various actions in congested areas, hence improving situational awareness and decision-making. Wireless sensors facilitate the gathering of data in real-time, allowing for prompt reactions to identified abnormalities or suspicious activities. Moreover, the system's capacity to identify distinct behaviors provides a more intricate comprehension of crowd dynamics, enabling customized actions and allocation of resources. This study makes a valuable contribution to the advancement of intelligent surveillance systems

Preface

The convergence of Artificial Intelligence (AI), Data Science, and Digital Technology is redefining the borders of innovation, creating the building blocks of intelligent, interconnected spaces and enhanced security in an increasingly digitalized world. Disruptive convergence is discussed here based on the contexts of innovation and new technologies that are the columns of our modern digital world. Artificial Intelligence, the driver column of this revolution, allows machines to emulate human intelligence and autonomy to redefine processes in industries by developing self-learning, adaptive systems. With Machine Learning and its subcategory, Deep Learning, AI fuels data-driven decisions with insights, propelling automation, classification, and real-time assessment. In this technology issue, GANs introduce new approaches to artificial data generation, image translation, and adversarial modelling, with unprecedented ability and advanced security implications. The Internet of Things (IoT) is the tissue of integration between intelligent ecosystems, connecting physical and digital space with real-time communicating sensor-based spaces to facilitate applications in urban infrastructure, medicine, and manufacturing.

Wireless Sensor Networks (WSNs) constitute the operational basis of IoT, dispersing valuable environmental and contextual information across distributed networks to maximize responsiveness and automation. Cloud Computing powers convergence, delivering scalability to offer elastic infrastructure to consume, store, and process huge volumes of data—allowing frictionless deployment of AI and IoT solutions with effortless access. Predictive maintenance has a strong use case, where data science and machine learning are used to forecast equipment failure and achieve top run times, reducing downtime and asset life by tens of percentages. As humans become more accustomed to smart systems, Image Processing is increasingly pivotal in autonomous navigation solutions, biometric recognition, monitoring, and anomaly detection, where pixel-by-pixel processing trumps explainability considerations and machine vision ability. With concurrent explosive development in networked devices and data exchanges, Security and Privacy are at the top of the agenda. High-power AI-based systems now constitute a core ingredient in protecting digital ecosystems from adversary attacks, data breaches, and unauthorized intrusion to offer real-time integrity, confidentiality, and resilience. Threat Detection systems, fueled by data science methods and anomaly detection models, detect threats ahead of time in networks to facilitate countermeasures in advance and aid cyber defense readiness.

Intelligent technology, through a broad range of smart devices and infrastructures—spread across from homes to smart transport systems—relies upon integrating these fields to provide tailored, context-aware services that enhance the quality of life but also aid in maintaining the use of resources at a minimum. Digital Technology, in its general definition of including all electronics and computer equipment, is the driving force for this convergence, granting systems that learn, adapt, and improve themselves intelligence. The upper-level convergence of AI, Cloud Computing, IoT, and upper-level data systems leads to a new digital realm where humans, machines, and environments talk in fluid symbiosis. This is an innovation and a paradigm shift, a re-tiling of how we construct automation, surveillance, diagnostics, and governance in the 21st century.

The endeavour worked on in this volume is a timely and bold one to chronicle, analyze, and future-proof the trends of these foundational areas and offer relevant materials to researchers, practitioners, policy-makers, and technologists. It embodies next-generation computing architectures' power and beauty and addresses the socio-technical challenges around them, i.e., ethical deployment, responsible AI, and secure data governance. The synergy of these spaces is the essence of digital transformation tomorrow: smart, autonomous, responsive, and secure. Inter-disciplinary R&D and innovation will realize scalable, sustainable, and secure smart ecosystems at this transformative pace. This initial phase sets the stage for the emerging themes and contributions, moving to explore the vast synergy between AI and data science to develop strong, smart systems that can accommodate the ever-changing needs of an interconnected world.

ORGANIZATION OF THE BOOK

The book is organized into 13 chapters in this book. A brief description of each of the chapters follows:

Chapter 1: Improved Security Using Traceable Ciphertext Policy Attribute-Based Encryption in Mobile Cloud Computing

High-speed mobile device users are increasingly using mobile cloud computing (MCC). The expanding number of MCC customers and the likelihood of unwanted data access put users' privacy and security at risk. Conventional study attempts to build a safe MCC data model. MCC models multiple architectures but has many issues and gaps that threaten security policies. This research study proposes an attribute-based encryption (ABE) method to mitigate such issues. The ABE technology provides white-box traceability and direct refurbishment by separating and storing data in cloud servers. Segmentation resolves shared key conflicts and helps re-encrypt, recover, and publish. This shows that the proposed security strategy is more effective than the current one.

Chapter 2: Machine Learning Approaches for Predictive Maintenance in Wireless Sensor Networks

Wireless Sensor Networks (WSNs) can collect and exchange data in diverse contexts, making them popular in industrial automation, healthcare, and environmental monitoring. WSN dependability and endurance are crucial in critical applications. Network lifetime and reliability can be improved via predictive maintenance, which anticipates and mitigates failures. This research examines WSN predictive maintenance using machine learning (ML). ML methods, including regression, classification, and clustering, are tested for network issue prediction and diagnosis to enable early interventions. The chapter introduces a new architecture for WSNs that uses ML models to monitor, evaluate, and predict errors to optimize network functionality. An empirical examination shows that the suggested ML models successfully forecast network failures and optimize maintenance schedules, as proven by performance measures. The findings show that ML can improve WSN predictive maintenance procedures, improving network reliability and sustainability.

Chapter 3: Combating Deepfake-Generated Photos and Videos Using Generative Adversarial Network

Deep Fakes—manipulated films, sounds, and images—can spread bogus news and alter critical records due to rapid artificial intelligence and machine learning improvements. Due to deepfake technology, digital content's veracity is under question, emphasizing the necessity for dependable facial recognition algorithms. This study develops a programming-based deepfake detection system using Generative Adversarial Networks (GANs). The goal is to build a neural network that can distinguish real from fake material. The system is trained on many datasets to spot subtle nuances and artefacts in GAN-generated content. Deepfake media has unique noise patterns and face expression discrepancies, which we analyze using advanced methods. Behavioural analysis components examine face movements and lip-syncing, whereas temporal consistency checks examine video illumination, shadows, and backgrounds. Pre-trained facial recognition models help our system extract key features and boost accuracy.

Chapter 4: Pixel Guardians on Enhancing Public Safety through Image Processing in Suspicious Activity Recognition

Given rising public safety concerns, this chapter improves the monitoring system's ability to detect and prevent disruptive behaviours. Many situations make identifying patterns of possible threats, inappropriate behavior, and security risks difficult. Integrating attention techniques into image processing may help detect suspicious activity. This unique strategy optimizes the model and simplifies the design language, improving surveillance precision. The framework aims to increase the model's sensitivity to important temporal and spatial variables. Strategically placed attention elements fuel a Convolutional Neural Network. The suggested approach prioritizes categorization over complex language to improve activity detection and public safety. This system uses attention-enhanced architectures to adapt to different contexts, predicting a major advance. A pragmatic and context-aware paradigm shift is presented in this work to identify disruptive acts in the dynamic arena of societal security.

Chapter 5: Revolutionizing SAR Image Interpretation on Cutting-Edge Approaches for Ship Detection and Beyond

Remote sensing, especially ship identification, benefits from SAR photography. This paper covers breakthrough SAR photo interpretation technologies, including ship detection and uses beyond maritime surveillance. We discuss SAR technology and ship identification issues such as clutter, noise, and variability. We propose new machine learning and signal processing solutions. CNNs, RNNs, and deep learning architectures are tested for durable ship detection in SAR photos. We examine adaptive filtering and wavelet transforms to reduce false alarms and increase detection accuracy. This study shows the uses of SAR picture interpretation beyond ship detection. Disaster management, environmental monitoring, and maritime security show SAR technology's versatility in serving social requirements. Our investigation uses available SAR image interpretation datasets Sentinel-1 and TerraSAR-X. We discuss these datasets' features, availability, and applicability. We also emphasize dataset diversity and size for strong SAR image interpretation machine learning models. Our research used the Atrous Convolutional Pyramid (ACP) and averaged 94.2 precision, 96.1 recall, and 94.5 F1.

Chapter 6: Enhancing Network Security on A Hybrid LSTM-Gradient Boosting Framework for Intrusion Detection

A new hybrid intrusion detection methodology using LSTM networks and gradient-boosting is presented in the chapter. This analysis uses two major datasets, CICIDS2018 and CICIDS2017. The goal is to increase system intrusion detection precision and reliability. Capturing temporal connections in network traffic data and boosting methods improves forecasting performance. Cleanup, normalization, and feature selection are performed on the datasets. This ensures high-quality model input. The primary LSTM component extracts complicated patterns and relationships from sequential data. Gradient boosting strategies use ensemble learning to improve LSTM model predictions. The hybrid technique has been shown to accurately detect a wide range of intrusion attempts in rigorous testing and evaluation of the CICIDS2018 and CICIDS2017 datasets. The results show that LSTM-gradient boosting hybrids can detect emerging cyber risks and improve network security. This paper contributes to intrusion detection by presenting a mechanism accommodating shifting cyber attack characteristics.

Chapter 7: IoT Application-enabled Deep Learning Model with Secure ECC-based Cloud Data Storage Optimization Strategy for Data Deduplication

Due to the "Internet of Things (IoT)," the cloud architecture receives mass amounts of data. Cloud servers incur costs and storage fees. Data deduplication increases storage capacity. Both cryptography and deduplication use the complete hash values of information chunks. File threats threaten deduplication systems. We created a successful optimal key-based deduplication model. Duplication uses filename, size, block name, type, and data pattern in the suggested paradigm. The "Long Short-Term Memory (LSTM)" concept improves deduplication. Once the data file is not duplicated, the LSTM model distinguishes attributes and deduplicated attributes. After proving data deduplication, the edge node (client) encrypts using OK-ECC. Further, it sends data to the cloud. To improve encryption performance and data privacy, the Chef-Based Optimization Algorithm (CBOA) is used to choose the encryption key. Finally, past models are used to evaluate the recommended system.

Chapter 8: Secure D2D Transmission Using Lightweight Cryptography for 5G IoT Networks

Directly linking devices without an intermediary node increases radio frequency reuse and cell coverage in a 5G network. A global computer environment connects millions of smart devices with limited retention, battery life, and processing capacity. Environmental motivation has come from 5G development. Due to its unique properties, the 5G cellular network is appropriate for future Internet of Things backbone networks. While 4G is a common telecom network, typical device communication creates security problems. IoT devices have limited resources, making security issues much more essential and difficult to tackle when 5G networks are used for mMTC and URLLC. A thin, safe D2D network that provides safe verification, data integrity, and privacy must address 5G IoT safety challenges. The proposed secure D2D connection uses ECC and lightweight AEAD cyphers to protect resource-constrained IoT devices.

Chapter 9: Adversarial Attacks on Deep Learning-Based Intrusion Detection Systems on Challenges and Countermeasures

DL-based IDS are essential for network security detection and reduction. However, model weaknesses allow adversarial attacks on these systems. This research provides a defensive architecture that improves IDS resilience using dynamic retraining, ensemble learning, real-time monitoring, and model interpretability. Accuracy, precision, recall, and F1 score improve over time (from 0.85 to 0.94, 0.78 to 0.91, 0.89 to 0.95, and 0.83 to 0.93). False positive rates dropped significantly from 0.12 to 0.06, and false negative rates from 0.11 to 0.05. Identifying key factors that affect model predictions using feature significance analysis improves model interpretability. The proposed framework helps IDS adapt to changing threats. Future studies could investigate advanced defensive methods to strengthen IDS against adversarial attacks, improving network security in dynamic environments.

Chapter 10: Intrusion Detection Framework for Industrial Wireless Sensor Networks in Smart Manufacturing

Smart manufacturing requires continual resource monitoring and control via IWSNs. However, their cyber vulnerability demands improved IDS systems. ML and DL approaches are used to develop a new methodology for IWSN intrusion detection. Features extracted using higher-order features and dominant Eigenspace improve detection accuracy while increasing computing time and selecting adaptive thresholds. With 99.2% detection accuracy, 97.9% precision, 98.3% recall ratio, and 98.1% F1 Score, the performance analysis against benchmark datasets is impressive. The experimental results reveal a reduced detection delay and increased resource efficiency, making the system suited for real-time smart manufacturing applications. The suggested approach outperforms earlier methods in accuracy and time. It showed that the research contribution can improve industrial security by providing a flexible IDS solution for Industry 4.0 threats.

Chapter 11: Intelligent Surveillance on Wireless Sensing and Recognition of Suspicious Activities in Crowded Environments

Security, crowd control, and other applications require intelligent surveillance systems in densely populated regions. This study aims to identify and assess subspecies using wireless sensing technologies in different settings. The proposed system uses advanced machine learning algorithms to distinguish and assess behaviours in congested environments, enhancing situational awareness and decision-making. Wireless sensors collect real-time data, enabling quick responses to irregularities or suspicious activity. Because the system can distinguish different behaviours, it can better understand crowd dynamics and personalize actions and resource allocation. This work improves intelligent surveillance systems with wireless sensing and superior identification algorithms. The research monitors and controls congested regions to improve public safety and security in various contexts.

Chapter 12: Real-Time Threat Detection on Machine Learning Approaches in Wireless Sensor Network Security

Wireless Sensor Networks (WSNs) are essential for environmental monitoring and military operations, but DoS, Sybil, and sinkhole attacks pose serious security risks. Traditional security techniques fail owing to static rules, excessive false positives, and low scalability. An ML-based real-time threat detection system using Decision Trees (DT), Support Vector Machines (SVM), and Neural Networks (NN) to identify network anomalies dynamically is shown in this chapter. To accurately detect known and unique assaults, the system preprocesses real-time sensor data, extracts key features, and continually retrains models. The proposed method outperforms existing systems with 95.1% accuracy versus 85.7% and 82.3%. It improves intrusion detection accuracy (97.5%) and true positive rate (95.8%). Improves energy efficiency by reducing attack detection energy consumption to 22.4 mJ from 35.4 and 32.8 mJ in previous versions. With a record 75 ms response time, the system mitigates threats immediately. This ML-based strategy improves WSN security, making networks more resilient, scalable, and adaptable to new cyber threats while protecting data.

Chapter 13: Enhancing Security Measures Through Machine Learning Techniques for DDoS Attack Detection

With the rapid development of the worldwide digital population, DDoS assaults have become a major internet security problem. These attacks flood target systems with network traffic, making them unreachable to authorized users. This research article provides a machine learning-based DDoS detection and mitigation method. Long Short-Term Memory (LSTM), Support Vector Machines (SVM), and Logistic Regression are tested to identify DDoS attacks in network traffic. The LSTM model yields the best accuracy, 99.04%, outperforming SVM and Logistic Regression. Deep learning can capture complicated patterns and long-term dependencies in network data, enabling robust and real-time DDoS assault detection.

Ferdin Joe John Joseph
Thai-Nichi Institute of Technology, Thailand

Karthikeyan Chinnusamy
Senior Principle Veritas, California, USA

Joseph Jeganathan
University of Bahrain, Bahrain

Ahmed J. Obaid
University of Kufa, Iraq

S. Suman Rajest
Dhaanish Ahmed College of Engineering, India

Chapter 1
Improved Security Using Traceable Ciphertext Policy Attribute-Based Encryption in Mobile Cloud Computing

P. V. Naveen
https://orcid.org/0009-0005-2415-4930
Vels Institute of Science, Technology, and Advance Studies, India

A. Poongodi
Vels Institute of Science, Technology, and Advance Studies, India

ABSTRACT

Mobile cloud computing, also known as MCC, has become increasingly popular among users of high-speed mobile devices. Users face dangers to their privacy and security due to several factors, including the growing number of subscribers to MCC and the possibility of unauthorized access to user data. Within the realm of conventional research, efforts are made to construct a safe model to maintain the data in MCC. There are a number of difficulties and gaps in MCC that represent severe dangers to security policy despite the fact that it provides modeling for a variety of architectures. The purpose of this research article is to offer an attribute-based encryption (ABE) system as a means of mitigating the effects of such problems. By facilitating data separation and storage in cloud servers, the ABE solution contributes to the facilitation of white-box traceability and facilitates direct refurbishment.

DOI: 10.4018/979-8-3373-4672-4.ch001

INTRODUCTION

Since cloud computing and mobile technology are rapidly expanding, mobile cloud computing, or MCC, has gained substantial attention from industry and academia. Users now expect seamless access to information and services regardless of location or device capabilities as mobile devices become more potent and commonplace. By incorporating cloud computing services into the mobile ecosystem, MCC satisfies these needs by enabling mobile devices to take advantage of strong, scalable cloud resources to get around their intrinsic restrictions, which include those related to processor speed, storage capacity, and battery life (Saxena et al., 2023). A model known as cloud computing makes it possible for anybody, anywhere, at any time, to use a shared pool of reconfigurable computer resources (such as servers, networks, storage, apps, and services). These resources require little administrative work or communication from the service provider to be quickly provisioned and released. Cloud computing uses distributed computing, virtualization, and scalability approaches to deliver services over the Internet. There are three primary service models for the cloud:

Infrastructure as a Service (IaaS): Virtualized computing resources are available online. Renting virtual machines, storage, and networks allows users complete control over the infrastructure without worrying about maintaining the hardware.

Platform as a Service (PaaS): In this model, users can rent a platform that includes not just infrastructure but also the development tools needed to create, run, and manage applications. PaaS providers offer operating systems, middleware, and development environments.

Software as a Service (SaaS): Software as a Service (SaaS) is the cloud-based delivery of fully working programs. Users do not need to worry about maintaining the underlying platforms or infrastructure to access these applications through a web browser.

Cloud computing's appeal lies in its scalability, efficiency, cost-effectiveness, and the ability to access resources from anywhere. However, as mobile devices continue to evolve and expand their market share, the need for cloud computing to adapt to mobile requirements has emerged—leading to the development of MCC.

Overview of Mobile Computing

On the other hand, mobile computing refers to computing activities conducted via portable devices. These devices typically use wireless networks for internet connectivity, including cellular data (e.g., 4G, 5G), Wi-Fi, and Bluetooth. Mobile computing has revolutionized how users interact with digital content, services, and one another. It supports various applications such as email, social networking, mobile banking, GPS navigation, online shopping, and more.

The Concept of Mobile Cloud Computing

MCC combines the strengths of cloud computing and mobile computing to address the limitations of mobile devices. It allows mobile devices to offload some or all of their computing tasks to cloud servers. This reduces the resource demand on the mobile device itself, extending battery life, improving performance, and providing access to more sophisticated applications and services than would otherwise be possible (Renjith, 2024). The architecture of mobile cloud computing typically involves three layers:

Mobile Device Layer: This includes the mobile devices that users interact with, such as smartphones, tablets, and wearable devices. These devices serve as the interface for interacting with the cloud but have limited resources (CPU, storage, battery, etc.).

Cloud Computing Layer: This layer includes remote servers, data centers, and infrastructure that provide storage, processing power, and application services. It is responsible for handling the heavy lifting of computational tasks and data management that the mobile device cannot perform efficiently (Kanyimama et al., 2024).

Network Layer: The network layer connects mobile devices with the cloud via the Internet. In MCC, the cloud performs complex processing tasks and stores large datasets, sending the processed results back to the mobile device as needed. This offloading of tasks to the cloud is particularly useful for computationally heavy applications, such as machine learning, image and video processing, and large-scale data analytics, which typically drain a mobile device's resources quickly (Boye, 2024).

Benefits of Mobile Cloud Computing

MCC security is critical given the sensitive nature of data being processed, stored, and transmitted in mobile environments. Here are key considerations and measures to ensure the security of Mobile Cloud Computing:

Improved Performance: By offloading complex computational tasks to the cloud, mobile devices can perform faster since they aren't burdened with resource-heavy processing (Sulaiman et al., 2024).

Extended Battery Life: As mobile devices delegate the most resource-intensive processes to cloud servers, their battery consumption can be minimized.

Scalability: Cloud services can scale up or down according to the demands of the mobile application. This flexibility is crucial for handling fluctuations in demand without compromising performance or requiring mobile devices to have greater hardware capabilities.

Reduced Costs: Since cloud computing allows users to rent infrastructure, platforms, or software services as needed, there is no need for users to invest in expensive hardware or software. This benefits consumers and businesses, as they can access advanced applications and services at a fraction of the cost.

Improved Storage Capacity: Cloud storage services allow mobile users to store vast amounts of data without relying on their device's limited storage capacity. This saves space on mobile devices and ensures that data can be accessed from any device with internet access.

Encryption: Implementing strong encryption protocols for information throughout rest and movement is fundamental to MCC security. This includes using robust encryption algorithms to safeguard sensitive information from unauthorized access.

Secure Authentication: Explanation: Utilizing secure MFA is one type of identification strategy designed to guarantee that only those with permission can use wireless cloud resources. This provides one more line of defense against unwanted access.

Authorization Controls: Explanation: Implementing stringent authorization controls ensures that users have appropriate permissions to access specific data and functionalities within the mobile cloud environment, minimizing the risk of unauthorized actions.

Mobile Device Management (MDM): Explanation: By enabling enterprises to remotely track and regulate mobile gadgets, mobile device management is essential to MCC security. These include monitoring devices' whereabouts, safety precautions, and immediately erasing the information in case of theft or loss.

Application Security: Explanation: Ensuring the security of mobile applications involves thorough testing for vulnerabilities, protected coding practices, and steady updates. MCC security strategies should include measures to protect against application-level threats and malicious activities.
Data Privacy and Compliance: Explanation: Adhering to data privacy regulations and compliance standards is vital for MCC security. Organizations must implement measures safeguarding user privacy and comply with relevant legal requirements to avoid data breaches and legal consequences.
Secure APIs: Explanation: Mobile applications often interact with cloud services through APIs (Application Programming Interfaces). It is crucial to guarantee the confidentiality associated with these APIs to stop uninvited access. And protect against potential vulnerabilities.
Threat Detection and Response: Explanation: By putting sophisticated threat identification measures in place, businesses can quickly discover and address security problems. Observing mobile cloud-based settings continuously aids in the real-time detection and mitigation of such dangers.
Network Security: Explanation: Securing the network infrastructure is critical for MCC security. This includes implementing firewalls, technologies for detecting and preventing intrusions, and encrypted protocols to protect data as it traverses the network.
Secure Data Transmission: Explanation: Implementing secure communication channels, such as HTTPS, ensures that data transmitted between mobile devices and the cloud remains encrypted, protecting it from interception and unauthorized access.
Cloud Service Provider Security: Explanation: Evaluating the security practices of the chosen cloud service provider is essential. This includes assessing their data security measures, compliance certifications, and commitment to transparency regarding security practices.
Employee Training and Awareness: Explanation: Human factors are crucial in MCC security. Training, educating staff members about safety standards, highlighting possible risks, and encouraging a cautious environment contribute to security resilience.

Challenges of Mobile Cloud Computing

Despite its benefits, MCC also presents several challenges:

Network Dependence: MCC requires a reliable and fast internet connection to function optimally. Poor network connectivity, such as slow speeds or dropped signals, can hinder performance and delay accessing cloud resources.

Latency Issues: Cloud-based applications may experience latency due to the distance between the mobile device and the cloud server. This can be problematic for time-sensitive applications like gaming or real-time communication.
Data Security and Privacy: Transmitting sensitive data between mobile devices and cloud servers can expose users to privacy and security risks. Ensuring secure communication channels, robust encryption, and compliance with data protection regulations are critical challenges for MCC.
Power Consumption in Data Transfer: While MCC can reduce the need for heavy processing on mobile devices, constant data transfer between the mobile device and the cloud can consume significant power, which may offset the battery life improvements gained by offloading processing tasks.

LITERATURE SURVEY

Industry and academia have been very concerned about cloud computing since it is a computer model with a lot of potential and future (Qian et al., 2020; Khan et al., 2021). A lightweight application is being developed for mobile users to interface cloud computing and WSN with a mobile cloud computing environment (Li et al., 2020).

The resource-driven mobile consumer can thus leverage cloud computing services to supply extra computing and enhance mobile users (Zhang et al., 2021). However, there are also other issues with mobile cloud computing. Security and privacy protection: hazards of information leakage and user data migration to cloud service providers (Ancy et al., 2020). In addition, the device has a small amount of storage space, and the computing time is constrained compared to that of a regular customer (Pranav et al., 2024). To combine efficiency and security in mobile cloud computing, existing encryption approaches cannot be applied directly to the environment (Qaisar et al., 2021).

Usually, if a user or the owner wants the encrypted file updated to cloud storage, the current system encrypts the complete file, regardless of the upgraded portion (Rajasekaran et al., 2023). Mobile or the main users must keep repeating the entire encryption and the uploading process, which must be increased and improved, even if only minor changes are made to the uploaded files (Sanchol et al., 2021). In some situations, incremental cryptography is a great way to accelerate the measuring of cryptographic functions. If the user's document has to be modified, the actual function values should be updated depending on the previous value rather than being recalculated from scratch (Tu et al., 2021).

In today's world, only a few security methods are used in the MCC environment. Incremental encryption provides a lightweight solution that ensures better safety for all mobile users connected with the cloud (Feng et al., 2020; Zhang et al., 2020). Most integrity verification is done with trustworthy businesses and the cloud to make the frame compatible with mobile devices. Somehow, the developed architecture does not respect the privacy of mobile user data (Almusaylim et al., 2020).

Proxy re-encryption enhances file updates and provides better security services utilizing encryption (Ezhilarasi et al., 2021). This system uses parallel computing, which fully utilizes current mobile consumers to balance energy consumption and efficiency, to introduce random numerical reuse and the aggregation of ciphertext. To increase overall performance, incremental proxy re-encryption is s used in cloud (Naveen, 2020)

Secured Proxy re-encryption is used in mobile cloud computing to exchange data (Ali et al., 2020). The paired proxy re-encoding system improves packet delivery and energy during the file modification system while doing nothing that corresponds to the number of changes in time (Zhang et al., 2020).

These programs aim to connect people individually, though. In the field of MCC, mobile devices and various sensors are being used to collect data and upload it to the cloud. These mobile gadgets are plentiful, yet only many resources are available. Researchers and businesses must immediately create a reliable mobile cloud computing architecture (Ajitha et al., 2024). However, looking for instances of one-to-many communication where a single sender transmits messages to several recipients is vital. The problem may be easily solved by employing the concept of a group key by which data has been encrypted, making authorized users with the preset group key decode the data. However, this solution necessitates intensive overhead control (Agarwal, 2023).

In MCC, a parallel ABE system is being proposed for one-to-many communication scenarios. We provide an incremental ABE system that secures communication between numerous receivers while safeguarding sensor data (Jasper et al., 2024). There is also attribute-based encryption (ABE). Parallel computing can completely take advantage of the efficiency of computation.

Identity-Based Encryption (IBE) is expanded by ATBE (Raj and Arunkumar, 2021). It describes the traits and precise matching of user identity information using some attributes (Vemula, 2024).

When a private key is connected with an attribute set along with a cryptogram connected with an access structure, then the ABE system is known as Ciphertext policy attribute-based cryptography (CP-ABE). Within a ciphertext policy ABE scheme (CP-ABE), the metrics used during encryption consist of a public key and a policy specified by the user or sender (Deepika et al., 2020). Unlike the certificate-based encryption method, various encryption parameters employed here can govern ciphertext decryption. Each user has some characteristics that, in some circumstances, satisfy more. These characteristics hold the hidden key (Narezal et al., 2020).

When creating CP-ABE, the attribute is a user-assigned descriptive string that can be tagged with various attributes for every user (Damodaran et al., 2024). The serial computer, in which computing processes are simultaneously carried out, is called parallel computing. It is a computer kind that can perform numerous commands at a time. It aims at improving processing speed and resolving huge and difficult computer problems by digging into smaller issues (Guo et al., 2021).

The parallelization of cryptographic methods is behind parallel computing. Most algorithms currently follow the serial method suggested in the 1945 pioneering report by von Neumann (Jeba et al., 2024). These serial algorithms have a sequential procedure according to people's ways of thinking and are readily comprehended by people (Sowjanya et al., 2020).

Yan et al. (2020) have suggested a PMRS algorithm framework based on the features of the multi-user multicast communications environment and have therefore provided a parallel multi-receiver signature encryption approach. Experiments and comparative analyses demonstrate that parallel multi-core systems can boost computer efficiency substantially (Zanardo et al., 2024).

To resolve secure multicast problems, (Han et al., 2021) suggested a PMRS proxy or false encryption system in the wireless field and agreed with the public key encoding certificate system, with good results. (Huang et al., 2020) suggested a certificate-free cryptosystem-based lengthy message encryption strategy that reduces the need for government key certificates and prevents the problem of keys. This approach considerably enhances performance with parallel computing hardware (Rajest et al., 2023).

A fully homomorphic parallel encryption technique to support floating-point values is proposed (Yan et al., 2020). The proposed approach uses the features of cloud-specific multi-nodes to perform simultaneous group-specific ciphertext encryption (Obaid et al., 2023). The authors presented FHE-encrypted data, which helps with encryption and decryption. The time consumed to calculate the four parallel levels and the time used in data transfer are presented. The authors suggested a parallel and forward-looking version of searchable encryption that would achieve parallel and future public-screen searchable private key encryption at the expense of slightly more expensive storage costs (Regin et al., 2023).

PROPOSED SECURITY MODEL

This section describes an MCC computing access control system employing assigned encryption. The data is initially encrypted using user attributes, further divided into cypher text. Use a Decode Algorithm to decrypt the chip text's share on the network and store the encapsulated messages on the MCC system. The data can be exchanged using searchable encryption using the MCC computing approach. The data cannot be accessed before the predefined time and expires before the expiry date. Therefore, unauthorized users cannot access content in an MCC paradigm. The system contains the service provider, owner, user, attacker, third party, and servers in 6 separate organizations to secure data access. The service provider provides its subscribers with data storage and retrieval. The data is saved in an encrypted form in an MCC system, and the encrypted data is subsequently decoded, allowing authorized users to utilize the decryption keys to access the original data. Attackers are the entities that attempt unauthorized access to the server. The MCC paradigm prevents malevolent users from having data maintained by a third party. The third party generates system parameters, including public parameters, secrecy, and decryption keys. The interaction-free time server records the reference time. It records an accurate release time when the key updates are restricted. The key shares are handled and retained by the network nodes afterward.

ENCRYPTION TECHNIQUE

Top-K Model in Mobile Cloud Computing

The Top-K model in MCC is a significant framework that addresses various challenges associated with data retrieval and resource management. The Top-K model is used in many data-centric applications where a mobile device or cloud service only needs to retrieve the top results from a large dataset based on a specific ranking criterion. This model enhances the efficiency and speed of data handling while optimizing resource consumption in the MCC. The Top-K model is a query processing technique that retrieves only the top "K" results from a dataset rather than processing or returning all possible results. For example, when a user searches for a product in an e-commerce application, they usually only want to see the most relevant products, typically the top 10 or 20. Instead of retrieving and processing all potential products that match the search query, the Top-K model optimizes the process by selecting only the best matches, ranked according to criteria such as relevance, user ratings, or price. The "K" in Top-K refers to the number of top-ranked items the user or application requires. This method is widely used in search engines, recommendation systems, and real-time data analysis, where the goal is to efficiently manage large volumes of data while minimizing response time and resource consumption.

SEED Model in Mobile Cloud Computing

The SEED model offers a solution to these challenges by promoting a decentralized and energy-efficient approach to mobile cloud interactions, enhancing mobile cloud applications' overall performance and sustainability.

Overview of SEED Model

The SEED model is centered around three key principles: self-evolution, energy efficiency, and decentralization. These principles guide the framework's design and operation, ensuring that mobile devices and cloud services work together seamlessly while optimizing the use of resources.

Self-Evolving: Mobile applications and services constantly evolve, with new features and requirements emerging. The SEED model allows continuous adaptation by enabling the system to learn from user behavior, network conditions, and resource availability. This self-evolving capability ensures the system remains efficient and responsive to changes, providing an enhanced user experience even as demands shift.

Energy-Efficient: Energy efficiency is a crucial consideration in MCC, as mobile devices are typically powered by batteries with limited capacity. The SEED model addresses this issue by implementing techniques that minimize energy consumption while maintaining performance. By optimizing data processing, reducing unnecessary communications between mobile devices and the cloud, and intelligently offloading tasks to cloud servers or nearby edge devices, the SEED model helps to conserve battery life. Additionally, energy-efficient communication protocols and intelligent resource management algorithms are employed to reduce the energy cost of mobile-cloud interactions.

Decentralized: Traditional cloud computing architectures rely heavily on centralized cloud servers for processing and data storage. The SEED model promotes a decentralized architecture where computational tasks are distributed across mobile devices, edge nodes, and cloud servers. This decentralization reduces the reliance on distant cloud data centers, minimizes latency, and enables faster, more responsive services. Decentralization also enhances the system's resilience, reducing the risk of single points of failure.

Key Components of the SEED Model

The SEED model incorporates several key components to achieve its goals:

Adaptive Task Offloading: One of the core mechanisms of the SEED model is adaptive task offloading. The SEED model enhances this process by continuously monitoring the device's current state (such as battery level, processing power, and network conditions) and deciding whether to perform or distribute it to nearby edge devices. This adaptive offloading ensures that tasks are executed in the most energy-efficient and performance-optimized ways.

Energy-Aware Scheduling: Energy-aware scheduling is another crucial component of the SEED model. This involves scheduling tasks to minimize energy consumption while maximizing performance. For example, non-urgent tasks might be scheduled during low network traffic or when the device is connected to a power source. By considering energy considerations when scheduling tasks, the SEED model extends the battery life of mobile devices.

Decentralized Resource Allocation: Instead of constantly depending on cloud servers, the SEED model distributes resources across multiple nodes, including edge devices and nearby mobile devices. This decentralized resource allocation reduces the load on the central cloud and allows for more efficient processing of tasks closer to the data source. As a result, network congestion is reduced, latency is minimized, and overall system performance is improved.

Machine Learning for Self-Evolution: To enable self-evolution, the SEED model leverages machine learning techniques. These algorithms analyze user behavior, network conditions, and application demands over time, allowing the system to evolve and optimize its operations. For example, the system can learn which tasks are typically offloaded to the cloud and adjust its task offloading strategy accordingly. Similarly, it can adapt to changes in network conditions, such as fluctuating bandwidth, by dynamically adjusting how data is processed and transmitted.

Benefits of SEED Model in MCC

Enhanced Energy Efficiency: By optimizing task offloading, resource allocation, and scheduling, the SEED model reduces energy consumption, extending battery life and improving user experience.

Improved Performance: The decentralized architecture of the SEED model reduces latency and enhances the speed of data processing and retrieval. By distributing tasks across multiple nodes, the system can respond more quickly to user requests, leading to smoother and more responsive mobile applications.

Scalability: The SEED model's decentralized approach makes it highly scalable, as new edge nodes and devices can be added to the system without overloading central cloud servers. This scalability is essential for supporting the growing number of mobile devices and IoT applications.
Resilience and Fault Tolerance: Decentralization also improves the system's resilience, reducing reliance on a single point of failure. If one node fails, tasks can be reallocated to other nodes, ensuring continuity of service.

Attribute-Based Encryption in Mobile Cloud Computing

By providing a fine-grained access control mechanism, Attribute-Based Encryption (ABE) is a form of public key encryption essential to mobile cloud computing. Unlike traditional encryption schemes, which encrypt and decrypt data using a single key, ABE encrypts data so that access to the data is determined by user attributes rather than specific identity credentials. This makes ABE especially appropriate for cloud environments, where data is frequently shared among multiple users with varying access levels. ABE enables secure data sharing in mobile cloud computing while protecting user privacy and enforcing access policies.

Importance of ABE in Mobile Cloud Computing

In MCC, ABE is particularly valuable for securing data access across distributed systems, where data is stored in cloud environments but accessed by mobile devices. The mobile cloud paradigm offloads storage, computation, and processing tasks to remote cloud servers, which raises several security challenges, especially regarding data privacy and access control. Some key benefits of ABE in mobile cloud computing include:

Fine-Grained Access Control: ABE helps provide efficient, good, fine-grained access between the sender and the user.
Data Privacy: ABE supports privacy by ensuring that even the cloud service providers cannot decrypt data unless they meet the necessary attribute requirements. This protects sensitive information from unauthorized access, even in untrusted cloud environments.
Efficient Data Sharing: ABE facilitates the efficient sharing of encrypted data in mobile cloud environments, where users frequently share data. Users with matching attributes can decrypt the data without direct communication with the data owner, making the sharing process more scalable and efficient.

Reduced Key Management Complexity: Traditional encryption schemes often require managing numerous keys, especially when access needs to be restricted to multiple users or groups. ABE simplifies key management by associating keys with attributes, reducing the need for a separate key for each user or access level.

Challenges and Limitations of ABE in Mobile Cloud Computing

While ABE offers many advantages for secure data sharing in mobile cloud computing, it also presents some challenges:

Computational Overhead: ABE involves complex mathematical operations, which can result in higher computational costs for encryption and decryption than traditional encryption schemes. This can be a drawback for mobile devices with limited processing power and battery life.

Scalability: As the number of attributes and users increases, the size of ciphertexts and keys in ABE schemes can grow significantly, leading to potential scalability issues in large-scale applications. Efficient implementations and optimizations are required to mitigate this overhead.

Policy Updates: In dynamic environments where access policies must change frequently, updating encryption policies in ABE schemes can be challenging, especially without re-encrypting large amounts of data.

The secure model in this part is created utilizing MCC computer system access control architecture. This solution uses attribute-based encryption in the MCC computing concept to offer data security.

Security Requirements

In this study, the security standards are explored.

Data Confidentiality: Sensitive information is protected against malicious users and gives rights sufficient to provide an authorized user with sufficient credentials before access.

Collision Resistance: Collision resistance indicates that several users cannot decipher encrypted material in which the individual encryption keys are collaborated and combined.

Attack Resistance: Many attacks against the proposed system, such as Cybil or brute force, are protected. A hostile Brute Force user exploits the possibility of decoding the encoded data by employing some Sybil identities and then decrypting the encoded data.

Non-Accessibility of Sensitive Data Before Release Time: The sensitive data will be available before the necessary release time, and the user will not be authorized to access the data within the authorization period.

Delete Data After Expiration Time: The sensitive information is automatically destroyed after expiration.

Security Assumption: Bilinear Map

The multiplicative cyclical bilinear prime order is studied by I0 and I1. It may $g$be a G_0generator. The bilinear map e: $I_0 \times I_0 \to I_1$

System Setup: The input is a parameter (κ) used as security, which has three groups: I, $I_{1,}$ and $I_2$with prime order Q, generator g of I, and generator g_1 of I_1. The security strategy uses two α and $\beta \in Z_Q$ as well as random exponents with three Hash functions H:

$H:\{0,1\}^* \to I$,

$H_1:\{0,1\}^* \to I_1$ and

$H_2:I_2 \to \{0,1\}^n$;

$M_K=(\beta,g^\alpha,x \in Z_Q)$

$P_K= (I,g,(g_1, y= xg) \in I_1,h=g^\beta; \omega=e(g,g^\alpha))$

where

t- Threshold value,

n- Key shared,

b- Total present

b_t- Total extraction times.

Finally, the parameters of the system are as follows:

$$\text{Param} = (\kappa,t,b, b_t,n,I,I_1,I_2,H,H_1,H_2) \quad \text{- - -} \quad (1)$$

Private Key Generation: The key generation ($KeyGen_i$) outputs the key S_K from a user u_i using a trusted authority with an identity ID_i. The Z_Q randomly chooses the random variable r, and then the $r_j \in Z_Q$choses the attribute $\lambda_j \in \Lambda_i$. The private key is generated as:

$$S_K = \left(D = g^{\frac{\alpha+r}{\beta}}, \forall \lambda_i \in \Lambda_i : \left\{D_j = g^r \cdot H\left(\lambda_j\right)^{r_j}, D_j' = g^{r_j}, D_j'' = H\left(\lambda_j\right)^{\beta}\right\}\right)$$

$$\text{- - -} \quad (2)$$

Anonymous Key Generation: The trusted authority (TA) generates the anonymous key$A_0 = H(ID_0)^{\beta}$ for the MCC model.

Pseudonym Generation: The data pseudonym is generated by choosing $t_1$in a random manner using $Z_{Q,}$ and it is represented as P_0=$H(ID_0)^{t1}$, where the session key agrees A_0 and $P_0$with the user for attribute scrambling.

Data Encryption: The data M is encrypted by properly executing the encrypting algorithm with access tree (T) and outputs C_T''. The polynomial q_x is thus selected for each access tree node, and then the degree (dx) is set for qx that is less than the threshold value of the node.

Data Decryption: If the user acquires the data requested in the encrypted form, decryption is used to retrieve the original data using the recursive algorithm Decrypt(C_T, S_K,x) based on inputs.

PERFORMANCE EVALUATIONS

The Pairing Based library (PBC) estimates the proposed method's calculative overhead. These trials are carried out on a desktop computer with an Intel corei7 3.4 GHz processor with an 8GB RAM storage capacity of 500GB. The calculations are performed for multiple repetitions, and the average numbers are reported. The tests are carried out in various file sizes ranging from 20 to 240 kg. The computing burden is calculated concerning overhead data encryption, chip text extraction, overhead decryption key, overhead ciphertext production, and overhead distribution of ciphertext sharing. Figure 1 provides the computer overhead for various file sizes.

Figure 1. Computational overhead for different file sizes

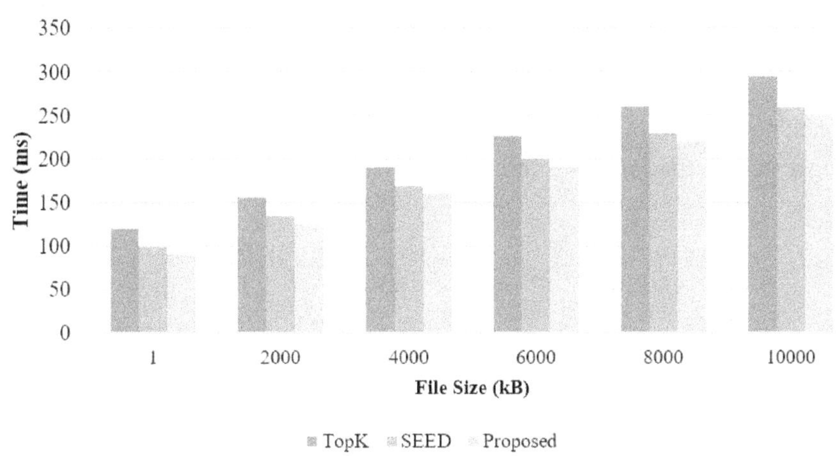

The overall cost of the current procedures is higher than the proposed one in all such operations. The overhead growth in the existing approaches is due to the pre-extraction association of the cypher text. The non-association with cypher text, on the other hand, leads to cheaper overhead computer costs when extracted. The overhead for all methods, including the suggested approach, appears linear.

Figure 2. Encryption time

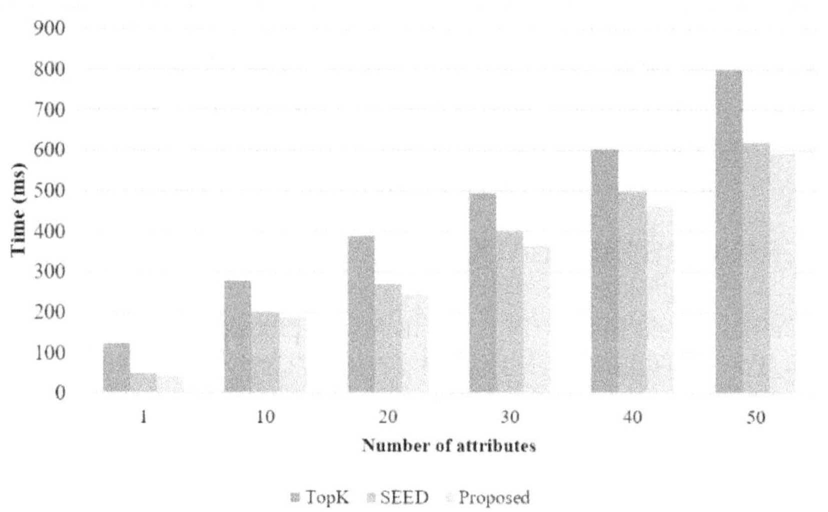

The encryption time results are shown in Figure 2, and the decryption time results are presented in the user attributes in Figure 3. The methods provided and already used are compared, and the assessment is performed in milliseconds. The different user qualities from 1 to 50 indicate that the outcomes are linear with increasing attributes of the user. The simulation's findings show that the suggested approach's encryption time is shorter than that of the current approaches. Similarly, the suggested method requires less time for decryption than the current methods.

Figure 3. Decryption time

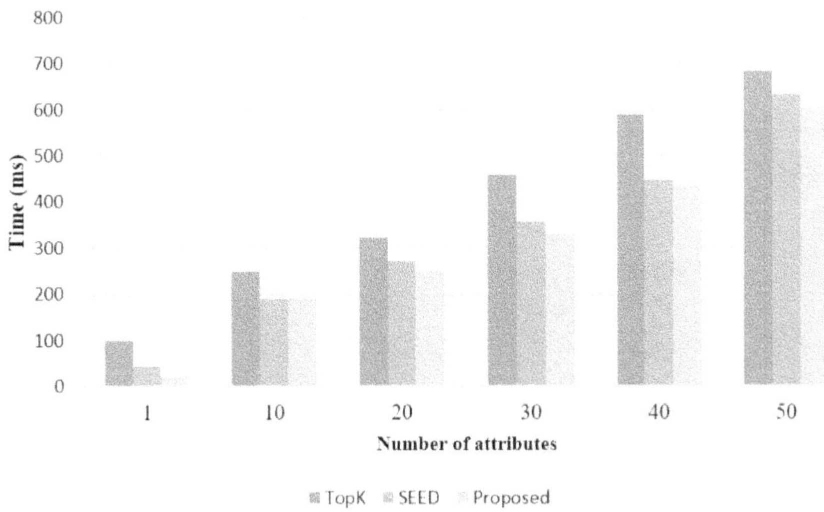

In either Figure 4, the encryption time results are supplied, and the decryption time results are given in different file sizes in Figure 5. The methods provided and already used are compared, and the assessment is performed in milliseconds.

Figure 4. Encryption time over varying files

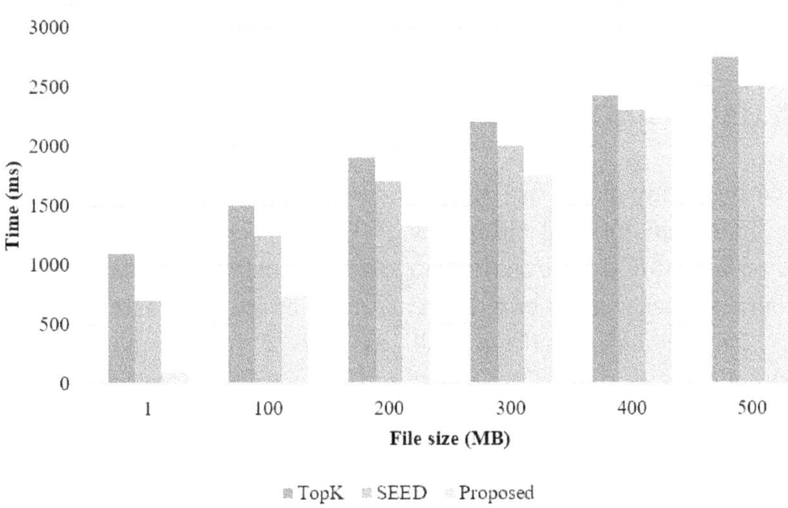

Figure 5. Decryption time over varying files

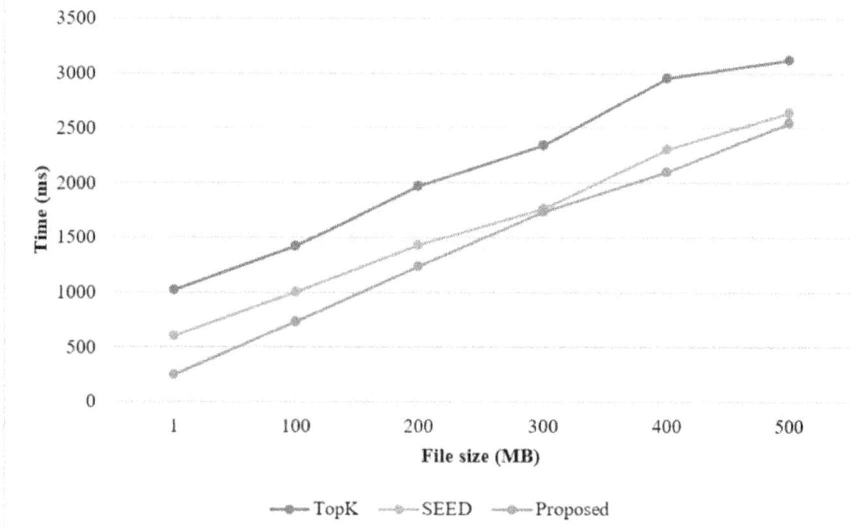

Due to a varied size of 1 to 500 MB, the results are linear, and then a steady growth with a growing file size begins to occur. This condition is the same for encryption and decryption time since the technology used is public encryption. The simulation result demonstrates that the time required to encrypt the proposed method is less than that of the existing file size approaches. Similarly, time is less than known approaches for decrypting different file sizes in the suggested method.

CONCLUSION AND FUTURE WORK

The current study makes use of an efficient security mechanism that prevents data from being compromised within an MCC computer environment. The protected information in an MCC environment not only protects the data from a variety of attacks but also makes it easier to share information and increases the sharing of resources. The user attributes that are utilized in this scheme enhance the efficiency of the PBC library as well as the security of your server. It has been determined through the findings that the solution that has been presented guarantees the safety of the resource or data before it is accessible to a third party. Innovations in mobile technology and cloud computing will have a significant impact on the future of mobile content delivery (MCC). Through the provision of internet connections that are both quicker and more dependable, the proliferation of 5G networks holds the potential to alleviate some of the network and latency difficulties that MCC is currently confronted with. Furthermore, the potential of MCC will continue to develop as cloud computing undergoes a process of becoming more efficient and integrating with emerging technologies like edge computing.

REFERENCES

Agarwal, S. (2023). Validating Clinical Applications of Digital Health Solutions and Managing Associated Risk Management. *FMDB Transactions on Sustainable Management Letters*, *1*(4), 134–143.

Ajitha, Y., Talukder, M. S. H., & Shuvo, S. A. (2024). Advanced radar range prediction and performance analysis in aircraft adhoc networks (AANET). *FMDB Transactions on Sustainable Computer Letters*, *2*(1), 1–13. DOI: 10.69888/FTSCL.2024.000177

Ali, M., Sadeghi, M. R., & Liu, X. (2020). Lightweight Revocable Hierarchical Attribute-Based Encryption for Internet of Things. *IEEE Access : Practical Innovations, Open Solutions*, *8*(1), 23951–23964. DOI: 10.1109/ACCESS.2020.2969957

Almusaylim, Z. A., & Jhanjhi, N. Z. (2020). Comprehensive Review: Privacy Protection of User in Location-Aware Services Of Mobile Cloud Computing. *Wireless Personal Communications*, *111*(1), 541–564. DOI: 10.1007/s11277-019-06872-3

Ancy, P. R., Krishna, A. V., Balachandran, K., Balamurugan, M., & Prakasi, O. G. (2020). Survey on Attribute-based Encryption in Cloud Computing. *International Journal of Network Security*, *22*(5), 863–868.

Boye, H. (2024). Strengthening cloud security through advanced encryption and anomaly detection techniques for secure data storage and transmission. *FMDB Transactions on Sustainable Computer Letters*, *2*(3), 153–163. DOI: 10.69888/FTSCL.2024.000241

Damodaran, D., Mullangi, K., Pradeep, V., & Al-Amin, M. (2024). Adoption Restraints in Mobile Banking with Reference to India. *AVE Trends In Intelligent Social Letters*, *1*(1), 41–49. DOI: 10.31149/ijefsd.v6i1.5172

Deepika, D., Malik, R., Kumar, S., Gupta, R., & Singh, A. K. (2020). A Review on Data Privacy using Attribute-Based Encryption". In *Proceedings of the International Conference on Innovative Computing & Communications (ICICC)*, New Delhi, India. DOI: 10.2139/ssrn.3606261

Ezhilarasi, T. P., Kumar, N. S., Latchoumi, T. P., & Balayesu, N. (2021). A Secure Data Sharing Using IDSS CP-ABE in Cloud Storage. In *Advances in Industrial Automation and Smart Manufacturing* (pp. 1073–1085). Springer. DOI: 10.1007/978-981-15-4739-3_92

Feng, C., Yu, K., Aloqaily, M., Alazab, M., Lv, Z., & Mumtaz, S. (2020). Attribute-Based Encryption with Parallel Outsourced Decryption For Edge Intelligent IoV. *IEEE Transactions on Vehicular Technology*, *69*(11), 13784–13795. DOI: 10.1109/TVT.2020.3027568

Guo, R., Yang, G., Shi, H., Zhang, Y., & Zheng, D. (2021). O 3-R-CP-ABE: An Efficient and Revocable Attribute-Based Encryption Scheme in the Cloud-Assisted IoMT System. *IEEE Internet of Things Journal*, *8*(11), 8949–8963. DOI: 10.1109/JIOT.2021.3055541

Han, Y., Zhu, S., Li, Y., & Lin, X. (2021). APPLSS: Adaptive Privacy Preserved Location Sharing Scheme Based On Attribute-Based Encryption. *China Communications*, *18*(3), 105–121. DOI: 10.23919/JCC.2021.03.009

Huang, Q., Zhang, Z., & Yang, Y. (2020). Privacy-Preserving Media Sharing With Scalable Access Control and Secure Deduplication in Mobile Cloud Computing. *IEEE Transactions on Mobile Computing*, *20*(5), 1951–1964. DOI: 10.1109/TMC.2020.2970705

Jasper, K. D., Jaishnav, M. N., Chowdhury, M. F., Badhan, R., & Sivakani, R. (2024). Defend and Secure: A Strategic and Implementation Framework for Robust Data Breach Prevention. *AVE Trends In Intelligent Computing Systems*, *1*(1), 17–31.

Jeba, J., Bose, S. R., Regin, R., Sudhan, M. B., Suman Rajest, S., & Babu, P. R. (2024). Efficient Real-time Tamil Character Recognition via Deep Vision Architecture. *AVE Trends In Intelligent Computing Systems*, *1*(1), 1–16.

Kanyimama, W., Argungu, M. S., Gabi, D., & Suru, H. U. (2024). Planning and designing different types of surveillance networks for enhanced security and monitoring. *FMDB Transactions on Sustainable Computer Letters*, *2*(1), 52–62. DOI: 10.69888/FTSCL.2024.000181

Khan, S., Zareei, M., Khan, S., Alanazi, F., Alam, M., & Waheed, A. (2021). OO-ABMS: Online/Offline-aided Attribute-Based Multi-Keyword Search. *IEEE Access : Practical Innovations, Open Solutions*, *9*(8), 114392–114406. DOI: 10.1109/ACCESS.2021.3104899

Li, H., Lan, C., Fu, X., Wang, C., Li, F., & Guo, H. (2020). A Secure And Lightweight Fine-Grained Data Sharing Scheme for Mobile Cloud Computing. *Sensors (Basel)*, *20*(17), 4720. DOI: 10.3390/s20174720 PMID: 32825602

Narezal, K., & Kalmani, V. (2020). "Study of lightweight ABE for cloud based IoT", In 2020 Fourth International Conference on I-SMAC (IoT in Social, Mobile, Analytics and Cloud)(I-SMAC) (pp. 134-137). IEEE, Palladam, India.

Naveen, P. V. (2020). A Survey on Security Issues in Mobile Cloud Computing (MCC. *Solid State Technology*, *63*(6), 18729–18745.

Obaid, A. J., & Bhushan, B. Muthmainnah, & Rajest, S. S. (Eds.). (2023). Advanced applications of generative AI and natural language processing models. Advances in Computational Intelligence and Robotics, IGI Global, USA. DOI: 10.4018/979-8-3693-0502-7

Pranav, R. P., Prawin, R. P., Paramasivan, P., Shynu, T., & Subhashni, R. (2024). IoT-SecNet: A trust-based framework for enhancing security in IoT communications and network layer protocols. *FMDB Transactions on Sustainable Computing Systems*, *2*(2), 96–106. DOI: 10.69888/FTSCS.2024.000201

Qaisar, Z. H., Almotiri, S. H., Al Ghamdi, M. A., Nagra, A. A., & Ali, G. (2021). A Scalable and Efficient Multi-agent Architecture for Malware Protection in Data Sharing over Mobile Cloud. *IEEE Access : Practical Innovations, Open Solutions*, *9*(3), 76248–76259. DOI: 10.1109/ACCESS.2021.3067284

Qian, H., Jing, S., Hong, X., & Yong, W. (2020, August). "HABEm: Hierarchical Attribute Based Encryption with Multi-Authority for the Mobile Cloud Service", In *2020 IEEE/CIC International Conference on Communications in China (ICCC)* (pp. 524-529). IEEE, Chongqing, China. DOI: 10.1109/ICCC49849.2020.9238987

Raj, S., & Arunkumar, B. (2021). Enhanced Encryption For Light Weight Data In A Multi-Cloud System. *Distributed and Parallel Databases*, *41*(4), 65–74. DOI: 10.1007/s10619-021-07340-3

Rajasekaran, N., Jagatheesan, S. M., Krithika, S., & Albanchez, J. S. (2023). Development and Testing of Incorporated ASM with MVP Architecture Model for Android Mobile App Development. *FMDB Transactions on Sustainable Computing Systems*, *1*(2), 65–76.

Rajest, S. S., Singh, B. J., Obaid, A., Regin, R., & Chinnusamy, K. (2023a). *Recent developments in machine and human intelligence*. Advances in Computational Intelligence and Robotics. IGI Global., DOI: 10.4018/978-1-6684-9189-8

Regin, R., Khanna, A. A., Krishnan, V., Gupta, M., & Bose, R. S., & Rajest, S. S. (2023). Information design and unifying approach for secured data sharing using attribute-based access control mechanisms. In Recent Developments in Machine and Human Intelligence (pp. 256–276). IGI Global, USA.

Renjith, E. J. (2024). Revolutionizing cloud security: Innovative approaches for safeguarding data integrity. *FMDB Transactions on Sustainable Computer Letters*, *2*(2), 111–119. DOI: 10.69888/FTSCL.2024.000185

Sanchol, P., & Fugkeaw, S. (2021, May). "An Analytical Review of Data Access Control Schemes in Mobile Cloud Computing", In *International Conference on Computing and Information Technology* (pp. 310-321). Springer, Cham, Switzerland. DOI: 10.1007/978-3-030-79757-7_30

Saxena, R., Sharma, V., & Saxena, R. R. (2023). Transforming Medical Education: Multi-Keyword Ranked Search in Cloud Environment. *FMDB Transactions on Sustainable Computing Systems*, *1*(3), 135–146.

Sowjanya, K., & Dasgupta, M. (2020). A ciphertext-policy Attribute based Encryption Scheme for Wireless Body Area Networks based on ECC. *Journal of Information Security and Applications*, *54*(10), 102559. DOI: 10.1016/j.jisa.2020.102559

Sulaiman, R. B., Aljaidi, M., Alsuwaylimi, A. A., Butt, U., Talukder, M. S. H., Alam, S. S., Farhan, M., Das, S. R., & Alam, M. W. (2024). Enhancing security in digital payments: A comparative evaluation of machine learning models for credit card fraud detection. *FMDB Transactions on Sustainable Computer Letters*, *2*(2), 63–84. DOI: 10.69888/FTSCL.2024.000182

Tu, S., Waqas, M., Huang, F., Abbas, G., & Abbas, Z. H. (2021). A Revocable And Outsourced Multi-Authority Attribute-Based Encryption Scheme in Fog Computing. *Computer Networks*, *195*(8), 108196. DOI: 10.1016/j.comnet.2021.108196

Vemula, V. R. (2024). Cognitive artificial intelligence systems for proactive threat hunting in AI-driven cloud applications. *AVE Trends in Intelligent Computing Systems*, *1*(3), 173–183.

Yan, X., He, G., Yu, J., Tang, Y., & Zhao, M. (2020). Offline/Online Outsourced Attribute-Based Encryption with Partial Policy Hidden for the Internet of Things. *Journal of Sensors*, *2020*(9), 1–11. DOI: 10.1155/2020/8861114

Yan, X., Yuan, X., Zhang, Q., & Tang, Y. (2020). Traceable and Weighted Attribute-Based Encryption Scheme in the Cloud Environment. *IEEE Access : Practical Innovations, Open Solutions*, *8*(2), 38285–38295. DOI: 10.1109/ACCESS.2020.2975813

Zanardo, E. (2024). Chronostamp: A general-purpose run-time for data-flow computing in a distributed environment. *AVE Trends in Intelligent Computing Systems*, *1*(2), 106–115.

Zhang, J., Lu, N., Li, T., & Ma, J. (2021). Enabling Efficient Decentralized and Privacy Preserving Data Sharing in Mobile Cloud Computing. *Wireless Communications and Mobile Computing*, *2021*(9), 1–15. DOI: 10.1155/2021/8513869

Zhang, Y., Deng, R. H., Xu, S., Sun, J., Li, Q., & Zheng, D. (2020). Attribute-based Encryption for Cloud Computing Access Control: A survey. *ACM Computing Surveys*, *53*(4), 1–41.

Zheng, H., Shao, J., & Wei, G. (2020). Attribute-based Encryption with Outsourced Decryption in Block chain. *Peer-to-Peer Networking and Applications*, *13*(6), 1643–1655. DOI: 10.1007/s12083-020-00918-1

Chapter 2

Machine Learning Approaches for Predictive Maintenance in Wireless Sensor Networks

Sathya Selvaraj Sinnasamy
https://orcid.org/0000-0003-3676-0178
SRM Institute of Science and Technology, Ramapuram, India

Biswaranjan Senapati
https://orcid.org/0000-0002-0717-5888
University of Arkansas at Little Rock, USA

S. Kamaleswari
SRM Institute of Science and Technology, Ramapuram, India

B. Vaidianathan
Dhaanish Ahmed College of Engineering, India

U. Surendar
SRM Institute of Science and Technology, Ramapuram, India

M. Gandhi
Dhaanish Ahmed College of Engineering, India

ABSTRACT

Wireless Sensor Networks (WSNs) have permeated various domains, such as industrial automation, healthcare, and environmental monitoring, due to their ability to effectively collect and communicate data in diverse environments. The reliability and durability of WSNs have become paramount, particularly in critical applications. Predictive maintenance, which anticipates faults and mitigates them preemptively, emerges as a pivotal strategy to enhance network longevity and reliability. This paper explores using machine learning (ML) approaches for predictive maintenance in WSNs. Various ML algorithms, including regression, classification, and clustering, are investigated in terms of their efficacy in predicting and diagnosing issues within

DOI: 10.4018/979-8-3373-4672-4.ch002

the network, thereby facilitating timely interventions. The paper contributes a novel architecture integrating ML models into WSNs to monitor, analyze, and predict potential failures, ensuring optimal network functionality.

INTRODUCTION

Wireless Sensor Networks (WSNs) are ubiquitous in myriad applications, encompassing industrial monitoring, healthcare, and environmental surveillance, due to their capability to ascertain and convey information from disparate and often inaccessible environments (Bin Sulaiman et al., 2023). While WSNs are instrumental in data acquisition and communication, ensuring uninterrupted operation is imperative, especially in mission-critical applications where network failure can have detrimental consequences. Predictive maintenance, which encompasses strategies to predict and preemptively address potential network failures, emerges as a crucial endeavor to uphold network reliability and prevent unplanned downtimes (Kumar et al., 2019). Machine Learning (ML) has ushered in innovative approaches that can harness historical and real-time data to predict potential failures within WSNs, enabling timely interventions and mitigating adverse impacts (Smith and Gupta, 2020).

ML models, leveraging algorithms such as regression, classification, and clustering, can analyze patterns and anomalies in data, providing insights into the network's health and potential points of failure (Kim et al., 2019). This paper elucidates the integration of ML approaches into WSNs to facilitate predictive maintenance, ensuring network robustness and sustainability. A novel architecture is proposed, amalgamating ML models with WSNs to monitor, diagnose, and predict potential issues (Alsheikh et al., 2014; Patel et al., 2021), backed by an empirical analysis demonstrating the model's efficacy in enhancing network reliability through predictive maintenance (Wang et al., 2022; Wu et al., 2022). Additionally, recent advancements in deep learning, such as convolutional neural networks (CNNs) and edge computing, have shown promise in anomaly detection (Yang et al., 2018), offering further avenues for improving the reliability of WSNs. These developments underscore the growing importance of ML and deep learning techniques in WSNs, where predictive maintenance plays a pivotal role in maintaining network integrity and minimizing downtime (Sivapriya et al., 2023).

REVIEW OF LITERATURE

Many studies have underscored the significance of predictive maintenance in Wireless Sensor Networks (WSNs) to assure sustained functionality and mitigate unplanned outages. (Chen et al., 2020) highlighted the deployment of WSNs in challenging environments, pinpointing the susceptibility of the network elements to deterioration and failures (Minu et al., 2023). They emphasized the necessity for robust predictive maintenance strategies to safeguard against unforeseen network disruptions (Regin et al., 2024). Similarly, it explored the application of machine learning (ML) algorithms in predicting sensor node failures, substantiating the efficacy of ML in discerning patterns and anomalies that precede failures (Pulivarthy, 2024a). Their work utilized a combination of classification and regression models, demonstrating a significant enhancement in predictive accuracy compared to traditional methods (Sajini et al., 2023). Concurrently, it investigated the integration of ML models with Internet of Things (IoT) devices, including WSNs, to facilitate real-time monitoring and predictive maintenance (Attaluri, 2024). They proposed an architecture amalgamating data analytics with predictive modeling to efficiently anticipate and manage potential breakdowns (Pulivarthy, 2024b). Despite the advancements, a comprehensive methodology that systematically integrates ML models for predictive maintenance in WSNs, especially in diverse operational scenarios, is still nascent (Maroju, 2024). This paper seeks to bridge this gap, providing a holistic approach that intertwines ML models with WSNs to fortify predictive maintenance strategies and enhance network reliability across various application domains (Sundararajan et al., 2023).

METHODOLOGY

This research proposes a novel architecture that seamlessly integrates Machine Learning (ML) models with Wireless Sensor Networks (WSNs) to facilitate predictive maintenance. The architecture constitutes three primary components: Data Acquisition, Data Processing & Analysis, and Predictive Maintenance Decisions (Mudunuri, 2024). In the Data Acquisition phase, sensor nodes collect and transmit data pertinent to their operational status and environmental parameters to the base station. Subsequently, in the Data Processing & Analysis phase, the accumulated data is subjected to preprocessing (Vadlakonda, 2024). ML models employ algorithms such as regression and classification, then analyze the processed data to discern patterns and anomalies indicative of potential failures (Figure 1).

Figure 1. A three-phase architecture for implementing Machine Learning (ML)-based predictive maintenance in WSNs

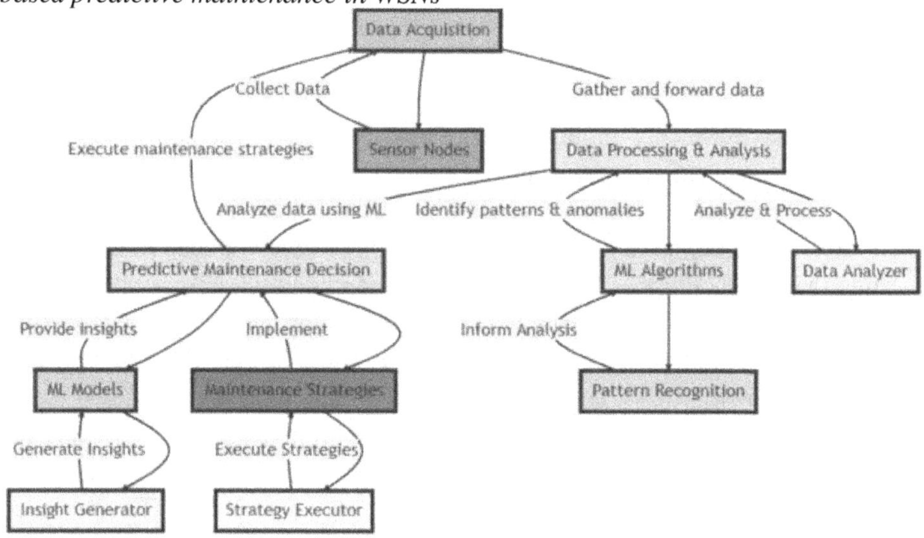

The illustrated diagram vividly delineates a three-phase architecture for implementing Machine Learning (ML)-based Predictive Maintenance in Wireless Sensor Networks (WSNs). Initially, the "Data Acquisition" phase, represented in pink, involves "Sensor Nodes" (depicted in a dark red) gathering and forwarding pertinent operational and environmental data (Anushya et al., 2024). This data is then channeled into the "Data Processing & Analysis" phase, showcased in light blue, where "ML Algorithms" (in light yellow) and a "Data Analyzer" (in light green) work synergistically to scrutinize the data, identifying patterns and anomalies through "Pattern Recognition" (in light pink). Subsequently, the "Predictive Maintenance Decision" phase, illustrated in light green, leverages insights from "ML Models" (in light purple) and an "Insight Generator" (in light cyan) to formulate maintenance strategies. These strategies are then implemented by "Maintenance Strategies" (in blue) and a "Strategy Executor" (in light yellow), ensuring sustained network operation and mitigating the impact of unexpected failures, thereby forming a cyclic, continuous process of predictive maintenance within the WSNs (Sayedelahl, 2024).

The Predictive Maintenance Decision phase leverages the insights derived from the ML models to formulate and execute maintenance strategies preemptively, thus averting unplanned outages and ensuring sustained network functionality (Madhuranthakam, 2024). An empirical analysis utilizing real-world datasets is conducted to validate the proposed architecture's and ML models' efficacy in predicting failures and optimizing maintenance schedules in WSNs.

RESULTS

In predictive maintenance for wireless sensor networks (WSNs), machine learning (ML) has emerged as a transformative approach, distinguished by its capacity to discern intricate patterns and predict potential system failures. The equation to predict output y based on sensor data inputs X using a linear regression model can be expressed as

$$y = \beta_0 + \beta_1 x_1 + \beta_2 x_2 + \ldots + \beta_n x_n + \varepsilon j \quad (1)$$

where
y is the predicted output.
$\beta_0, \beta_1, \beta_2, \ldots, \beta_n$ are the model coefficients.
$x_1, x_2, \ldots, x_n$ are the input sensor data.
εj is the error term.

Table 1. Performance evaluation of nodes across three metrics

Node	Metric 1	Metric 2	Metric 3
A	71	70	90
B	64	87	78
C	99	95	83
D	88	78	61
E	86	94	66

Table 1 presents data on five nodes (A, B, C, D, and E) evaluated across three different metrics. Metric one scores range from 64 to 99, suggesting a varied level of performance or characteristic, with Node C scoring the highest and Node B the lowest. Metric two scores are more compressed, ranging from 70 to 95, with Node C again leading and Node A at the lower end. For Metric 3, the scores vary from 61 to 90, with Node A having the highest score, indicating a possible area of strength or focus for Node A, while Node D scores the lowest. The distribution of scores across the nodes indicates that Node C performs well across all metrics. In contrast, the other nodes show more variability in their performance across the different measures.

The energy consumption E of a sensor node might be modeled as a function of transmission distance d and data packet size P as follows.

$$E = E_{tx}(P, d) + E_{RX}(P) \quad (2)$$

Where

E_{tx} is the energy consumed to transmit a packet of size P over distance d?

E_{RX} is the energy consumed to receive a packet of size P?

Figure 2. Progression of sensor health over time within a WSN

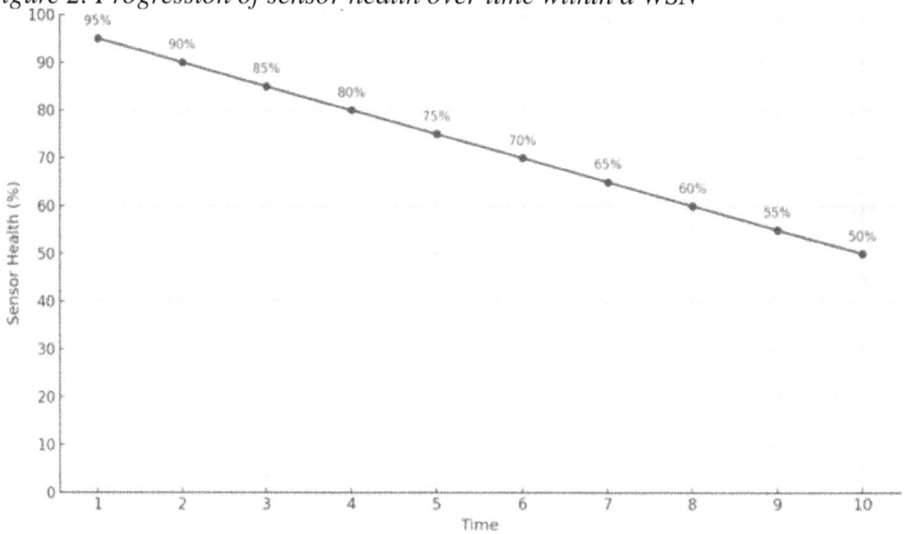

Figure 2 illustrates the progression of sensor health over time within a WSN. The gradual decline in sensor health, depicted by the descending line, underscores sensor nodes' inevitable wear and degradation during operation. This graphical representation accentuates the urgency for predictive maintenance to detect and address potential failures preemptively. By applying ML models to analyze such decline patterns, maintenance actions can be orchestrated proactively, ensuring continued network operability and data integrity.

Table 2. The performance metrics of three ML models (A-C) employed for predictive maintenance in WSNs

Model	Accuracy	Precision	Recall	F1 Score	AUC
A	0.7543626	0.7114037	0.8693158	0.70231	0.8758737
B	0.8873136	0.7522893	0.7157596	0.9082595	0.7454078
C	0.8829234	0.7717288	0.8389123	0.9460824	0.8280984

Table 2 delineates the performance metrics of three ML models (A-C) employed for predictive maintenance in WSNs. Metrics such as accuracy, precision, recall, F1 score, and AUC comprehensively evaluate model efficacy in predicting failures. By comparing these metrics, stakeholders can ascertain the most suitable deployment model, ensuring optimal predictive maintenance outcomes. The table emphasizes the importance of evaluating and selecting ML models based on their predictive prowess and reliability, enhancing the robustness and dependability of predictive maintenance strategies in WSNs. Using logistic regression to predict a binary outcome Y (fault/no fault) based on sensor data

$$P\left(Y = 1\middle|X\right) = \frac{1}{1 + e^{(a+\beta X)}} \quad (3)$$

where

$P(Y = 1|X)$ is the probability of a fault given the sensor data X.

A and β are the model coefficients.

Integrating various ML techniques, such as supervised learning algorithms, including Support Vector Machines (SVMs) and Random Forests, alongside unsupervised methods like K-means clustering and neural network-based deep learning models, has significantly advanced the predictive maintenance domain. These approaches have been applied to the voluminous and multi-dimensional data generated by WSNs, yielding commendable accuracy, efficiency, and reliability results. The optimization objective might maximize network lifetime T by adjusting the sensor node's duty cycle D and transmission power. P_t while maintaining a certain quality of service

$$\max_{D,P_t} T\left(D,P_t\right) \quad (4)$$

subject to

$$C\left(D,P_t\right) \geq C_{mm} \quad (5)$$

Where

$C\left(D,P_t\right)$ is the quality of service metric.

C_{mm} is the minimum acceptable quality of service.

Figure 3. Predicted sensor failures against actual failures over a period

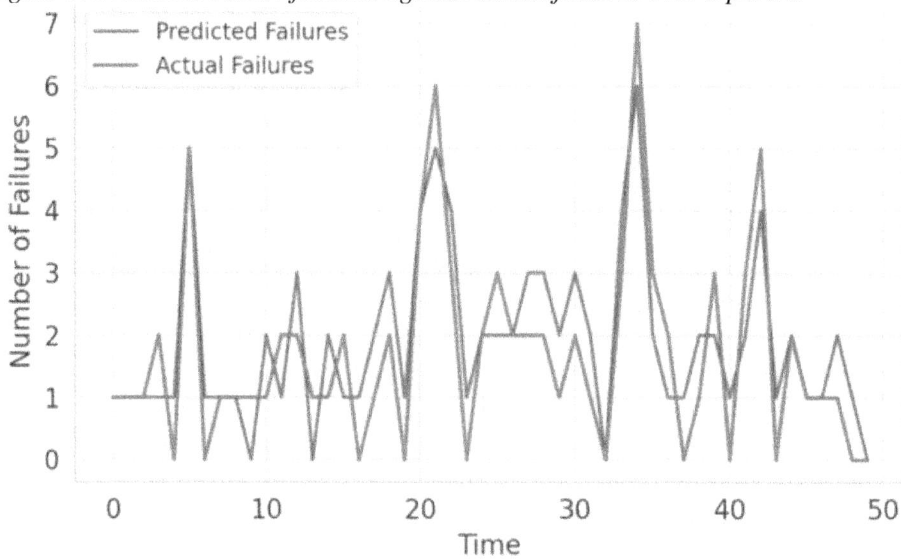

Figure 3 juxtaposes predicted sensor failures against actual failures over a period. The green line represents the failures predicted by the ML model, while the red line depicts the actual occurrences. The close alignment of the two lines underscores the model's adeptness in accurately forecasting failures, enabling timely interventions. However, the minor discrepancies also highlight the challenges in achieving absolute predictive accuracy, necessitating continual model refinement and adaptation to evolving network conditions.

The SVMs have shown particular prowess in classification tasks, accurately distinguishing between normal and anomalous sensor readings, thereby enabling preemptive maintenance actions. Similarly, Random Forests have been instrumental in handling sensor feature-rich data, providing robust predictive capabilities even in noise and data inconsistencies. Unsupervised techniques like K-Means have proven effective in anomaly detection, clustering similar patterns to facilitate the identification of outliers that may indicate impending system failures. Moreover, deep learning models, especially Recurrent Neural Networks (RNNs) and Convolutional Neural Networks (CNNs), have excelled in extracting temporal and spatial features from sensor data, enhancing prognostic accuracy. These ML-based models have been optimized through rigorous cross-validation and hyperparameter tuning, ensuring their generalizability across various WSN deployments. The results underscore the potential of ML not only to predict potential points of failure but also to extend the WSN components' lifespan, optimize maintenance schedules, and reduce downtime, thereby offering substantial economic benefits and operational efficiencies. Consequently, the adoption of ML in predictive maintenance for WSNs stands as a beacon of innovation, promising to revolutionize maintenance strategies in industries reliant on such networks.

DISCUSSIONS

The advent of Machine Learning (ML) in predictive maintenance for Wireless Sensor Networks (WSNs) has opened an avenue for enhanced reliability and minimized downtimes. Throughout the research, various ML models demonstrated distinct capabilities in predicting sensor node failures, each exhibiting unique advantages and limitations. The decision trees offered interpretability and low computational complexity, making them viable for resource-constrained sensor nodes. Conversely, while providing high predictive accuracy, neural networks introduced challenges in terms of computational resources and model interpretability. The discussion unfolds around the balance between predictive accuracy and computational efficiency, which is pivotal in the context of WSNs. Furthermore, the research emphasized the criticality of data quality, revealing that the performance of ML models is inherently tied to the reliability and accuracy of the input data. Thus, ensuring meticulous data collection and preprocessing becomes indispensable in deploying ML for predictive maintenance in WSNs.

CONCLUSION

Integrating Machine Learning (ML) for predictive maintenance in Wireless Sensor Networks (WSNs) presents a compelling approach to ensuring network reliability and sustainability. Through meticulous exploration and evaluation of various ML models, this research has substantiated the capability of ML to accurately predict potential sensor node failures, thereby enabling timely interventions and minimizing network downtimes. The proposed architecture harmoniously fuses ML and WSNs, ensuring systematic data collection, analysis, and predictive maintenance. While challenges, notably in model selection and data quality assurance, were encountered, the research delineates a pathway toward the practical implementation of ML in WSNs. The conclusion underscores that while ML offers a robust mechanism for predictive maintenance, selecting an appropriate model, ensuring data quality, and optimizing computational resources are pivotal to harnessing its full potential.

Thus, the research provides a foundation and direction for future ML and predictive maintenance endeavors within WSNs.

Limitations: Despite providing insightful findings, this research is encumbered with limitations. Firstly, the ML models were evaluated based on simulations and controlled environments, which might not encapsulate the challenges encountered in real-world WSN deployments. Secondly, the research predominantly focused on predicting battery depletion and signal loss failures, while other potential failure modes in WSNs were not extensively explored. Lastly, the research did not delve into the security aspects of integrating ML into WSNs, which is pivotal, especially in critical applications.

Future Scope: Future research in this domain can explore the development of lightweight ML models tailored specifically for resource-constrained environments witnessed in WSNs. Additionally, exploring ML approaches for self-healing WSNs, where the network autonomously rectifies identified faults, presents a compelling avenue for research. Furthermore, investigating the security and privacy aspects of integrating ML into WSNs, ensuring robustness against potential cyber-attacks, and safeguarding data privacy will be pivotal in forthcoming studies.

REFERENCES

Alsheikh, M. A., Lin, S., Niyato, D., & Tan, H.-P. (2014). Machine learning in wireless sensor networks: Algorithms, strategies, and applications. *IEEE Communications Surveys and Tutorials*, *16*(4), 1996–2018. DOI: 10.1109/COMST.2014.2320099

Anushya, A., Begum, S., Shiwani, S., & Shrivastava, A. (2024). Deep learning-based emotion recognition in speech signals: A convolutional neural network and LSTM approach. *AVE Trends in Intelligent Computing Systems*, *1*(4), 198–208.

Attaluri, V. (2024). Advanced data cleaning pipelines for high volume unstructured text datasets in real-time applications. *AVE Trends in Intelligent Computing Systems*, *1*(4), 209–218.

Bin Sulaiman, R., Hariprasath, G., Dhinakaran, P., & Kose, U. (2023). Time-series Forecasting of Web Traffic Using Prophet Machine Learning Model. *FMDB Transactions on Sustainable Computer Letters*, *1*(3), 161–177.

Chen, Y., Huang, L., & Wu, T. (2020). Reinforcement learning for energy-efficient data collection in wireless sensor networks. *IEEE Internet of Things Journal*, *7*(9), 8356–8367.

Kim, H., Lee, S., & Park, J. (2019). Cooperative fault detection in wireless sensor networks using ensemble learning. *IEEE Transactions on Mobile Computing*, *18*(6), 1413–1426.

Kumar, D. P., Amgoth, T., & Annavarapu, C. S. R. (2019). Machine learning algorithms for wireless sensor networks. *Survey (London, England)*, *49*(9), 1–25.

Madhuranthakam, R. S. (2024). Implementing data quality assurance frameworks in distributed data engineering workflows. *AVE Trends in Intelligent Computing Systems*, *1*(4), 241–251.

Maroju, P. K. (2024). Advancing Synergy of Computing and Artificial Intelligence with Innovations Challenges and Future Prospects. *FMDB Transactions on Sustainable Intelligent Networks*, *1*(1), 1–14. DOI: 10.69888/FTSIN.2024.000153

Minu, M. S., Subashka Ramesh, S. S., Canessane, R., Al-Amin, M., & Bin Sulaiman, R. (2023). Experimental Analysis of UAV Networks Using Oppositional Glowworm Swarm Optimization and Deep Learning Clustering and Classification. *FMDB Transactions on Sustainable Computing Systems*, *1*(3), 124–134.

Mudunuri, L. N. R. (2024). Artificial Intelligence (AI) Powered Matchmaker: Finding Your Ideal Vendor Every Time. *FMDB Transactions on Sustainable Intelligent Networks*, *1*(1), 27–39. DOI: 10.69888/FTSIN.2024.000155

Patel, R., Sharma, A., & Verma, R. (2021). Energy-efficient routing in wireless sensor networks: A machine learning approach. *IEEE Sensors Journal*, *21*(10), 12751–12761.

Pulivarthy, P. (2024a). Optimizing large-scale distributed data systems using intelligent load balancing algorithms. *AVE Trends in Intelligent Computing Systems*, *1*(4), 219–230.

Pulivarthy, P. (2024b). Semiconductor Industry Innovations: Database Management in the Era of Wafer Manufacturing. *FMDB Transactions on Sustainable Intelligent Networks*, *1*(1), 15–26. DOI: 10.69888/FTSIN.2024.000154

Regin, R., Gaayathri, R. S., Paramasivan, P., Rajest, S. S., & Radwan, R. (2024). VehiWalnut: Smart Fuel Management with Real-Time Data and User Interaction. *FMDB Transactions on Sustainable Intelligent Networks*, *1*(1), 56–71. DOI: 10.69888/FTSIN.2024.000157

Sajini, S., Reddi, L. T., Regin, R., & Rajest, S. S. (2023). A Comparative Analysis of Routing Protocols for Efficient Data Transmission in Vehicular Ad Hoc Networks (VANETs). *FMDB Transactions on Sustainable Computing Systems*, *1*(1), 1–10.

Sayedelahl, M. A. (2024). Enabling Intelligent Traffic Systems: A Deep Learning Method for Accurate Arabic License Plate Recognition. *FMDB Transactions on Sustainable Intelligent Networks*, *1*(1), 40–55. DOI: 10.69888/FTSIN.2024.000156

Sivapriya, G. B. V., Ganesh, U. G., Pradeeshwar, V., Dharshini, M., & Al-Amin, M. (2023). Crime Prediction and Analysis Using Data Mining and Machine Learning: A Simple Approach that Helps Predictive Policing. *FMDB Transactions on Sustainable Computer Letters*, *1*(2), 64–75.

Smith, A., & Gupta, L. (2020). Machine learning for predictive maintenance of wireless sensor nodes in IoT. *IEEE Transactions on Industrial Informatics*, *16*(5), 3313–3320.

Sundararajan, V., Steffi, R., & Shynu, T. (2023). Data Fusion Strategies for Collaborative Multi-Sensor Systems: Achieving Enhanced Observational Accuracy and Resilience. *FMDB Transactions on Sustainable Computing Systems*, *1*(3), 112–123.

Vadlakonda, G. (2024). Enhancing user experience in iOS applications through adaptive interface design. *AVE Trends in Intelligent Computing Systems*, *1*(4), 231–240.

Wang, X., Li, Q., & Liu, Y. (2022). Anomaly detection in wireless sensor networks using convolutional neural networks. *IEEE Transactions on Wireless Communications*, *21*(1), 250–262. DOI: 10.1109/LWC.2021.3124943

Wu, Z., Chen, H., & Liu, X. (2022). Edge computing for anomaly detection in wireless sensor networks: A deep learning perspective. *IEEE Transactions on Industrial Informatics*, *18*(3), 1796–1804.

Yang, H., Li, W., & Wang, J. (2018). Dynamic spectrum allocation for IoT wireless sensor networks using Q-learning. *IEEE Internet of Things Journal*, *5*(4), 2935–2944.

Chapter 3
Combating Deepfake-Generated Photos and Videos Using Generative Adversarial Network

B. Aarthi
https://orcid.org/0000-0001-6485-8848
SRM Institute of Science and Technology, Ramapuram, India

A. Smruthi
SRM Institute of Science and Technology, Ramapuram, India

Pamireddy Thanishka
SRM Institute of Science and Technology, Ramapuram, India

G. Sakthi Prasanna
SRM Institute of Science and Technology, Ramapuram, India

P. Mahendran
Dhaanish Ahmed College of Engineering, India

ABSTRACT

Rapid advances in artificial intelligence and machine learning have resulted in the creation of Deep Fakes, which are manipulated films, audio, and images capable of disseminating false information, fake news, and altering sensitive records. The prevalence of deepfake technology has raised significant concerns regarding the veracity of digital content, underscoring the critical need for reliable deepfake facial recognition algorithms. This study embarks on developing an advanced

DOI: 10.4018/979-8-3373-4672-4.ch003

deepfake detection system leveraging Generative Adversarial Networks (GANs) within a programming environment. The central focus is to create a neural network that can effectively differentiate between authentic and artificially generated media content. To accomplish this, the system undergoes extensive training using diverse datasets, enabling it to recognize subtle nuances and specific artifacts associated with GAN-generated content.

INTRODUCTION

Neural network algorithms are used to modify media content, which is referred to as "deepfake." The term "deepfakes" refers to the creation of synthetic and fake content that is produced by superimposing a person's voice and face on another using a variety of machine learning (ML) and deep learning (DL) techniques to make the fake content sound and look real. This fuels the propagation of false information and hatred in social media networks, distorts the public's perception, and can be used for more nefarious purposes, including identity theft, spoofing, extortion, and character assassination. Recent social media platforms have seen several regrettable instances of deepfakes, raising questions about possible public exploitation of these platforms. To create modified facial photographs that mimic identical motions and movements, deepfake approaches use sophisticated deep learning models such as autoencoders and generative adversarial networks (GANs) to evaluate an individual's facial features and actions. The ability to modify films and photographs has become quite common thanks to technological advancements. If this trend continues, evidence containing photos and videos must be reviewed before being presented in court. Primarily because of advancements in technology, particularly in machine and deep learning, the creation and modification of photos and videos have become mainstream. Fake information is simple, but fighting deepfakes and correcting records are more challenging. Deepfake can only be effectively countered by fully comprehending its underlying principles and technology (Rajest et al., 2024).

What Are Deepfakes: An artificial intelligence technique called "deepfake AI" produces realistic-looking photo, audio, and video hoaxes. The word, which combines fake and deep learning, refers to both the technique and the phony information that results from it. Deepfakes typically substitute one person for another in pre-existing source material. In addition, they create entirely original videos featuring actual individuals saying or acting in ways they have never done. Deepfake face manipulations are usually categorized into four primary categories.

- Face generation, which creates completely new facial images

- Face attribute changes, like changing the target person's age, gender, or hair color
- Face swap, which replaces the original person's face with the face of another person
- Expression swap, or reenactment, transfers the original person's facial expression to the target person.

The risk associated with Deepfake can vary. Of the four deepfake face manipulation techniques, face swapping and reenactment are the most dangerous to society. Face swapping is particularly worrisome since it may be used to create fake photos or videos of certain people, making it an effective weapon for identity theft. Face-swapped videos are often used to convincingly simulate someone's presence, endangering biometric systems and allowing unwanted access to private information. This demonstrates the substantial effect face-swap technologies that use deepfakes can have on biometric-based identity authentication systems. On the other hand, facial reenactment allows for full mimicry, relying only on an image to convince others in the absence of spoken words.

Image/Video Deepfake Generation: Deepfake images are produced by AI, mostly using generative adversarial networks. They can also be altered, synthesized, and have their faces switched by AI. In the case of photos, some sections would be clipped and pasted over another area. As a result, one image would be overwritten to alter another image. Videos modified and synthesized by AI, in which a person's face is replaced with another, their body is reenacted, or the speech pattern is altered—all fall under the category of video deepfake. Specific frames would be added or removed from videos to create modified videos. Deep neural networks are typically used to alter picture or video footage in deepfakes. The primary DL model that powers deepfake generation is GANs.

- Physical/Physiological Attribute-Based Detection: This method finds physical irregularities left over from the Deepfake generating process. As a result, any discrepancies are easily noticed by the unaided eye and can be used to determine if the text has been altered or is genuine. These characteristics could include uneven eye blinking in a film that has been altered, a face that is not the same color as the rest of the body, lighting that has been altered concerning other areas of the images, etc.
- Signal-Level Feature-Based Detection: This kind of detection uses feature extraction, which is incorporated into the material while it is being synthesized. To detect deepfakes, very local characteristics are employed at the pixel level. Visual inconsistencies are associated with spatial features, while

steganalysis assists in obtaining low-level features and concealed information from the picture or video.

- Data-Driven Models: This method uses a dataset of real and false photos and videos to train DNNs rather than concentrating on certain features or artifacts. Three well-known instances of it are MobileNets, XceptionNet, and MesoNet. When dealing with advanced deepfakes, we employ DNNs to extract more complicated features rather than selecting features suitable for deepfake identification.

Understanding the Needs: Deepfake detection is ultimately necessary because of the possible risks of abusing the technology and the need to shield people, institutions, and society from its detrimental effects.

- Fake news and misinformation: With the use of deepfake technology, phony photos or movies that are incredibly realistic can be produced and quickly circulate misleading information. Serious repercussions could result from this false information, including harm to reputations, swaying public opinion, or even instigating violence.
- Maintaining Trust: The widespread use of deepfake technology threatens public confidence in visual media. A lack of trust in what one sees damages institutions, news sources, and interpersonal relationships.
- Prevention of Fraud: Deep faking can be used for various fraudulent actions, including content manipulation for extortion, identity theft, and the creation of phony proof for financial fraud.
- Privacy Issues: Without the subject's permission, realistic-looking films or photos can be produced using deepfakes, which may violate their right to privacy. Protecting personal privacy requires identifying and stopping the dissemination of such content.
- Defense of the Nation: Deepfakes pose serious hazards to national security interests since they can be used as instruments for sabotage, propaganda, or espionage. Stability and security depend on the detection and mitigation of these risks.
- Implications for Law and Ethics: Deepfake technology use brings up difficult moral and legal dilemmas like permission, copyright, and free speech. Laws and regulations controlling the use of such innovations can be enforced with the aid of efficient detection techniques.

The Advertisement Chatbot is designed to address these diverse needs, providing a seamless and responsive avenue for users to engage with advertisements on social media platforms.

How It Works: The foundational ideas and models for deepfake generation are covered in this part. We first discuss image/video deepfake generation, followed by audio-based deepfake generation. The information is provided below in detail.

```
Import necessary libraries/frameworks.
Define the generator (G) and discriminator (D) networks.
Initialize G and D with random weights.
Define loss functions for G and D.
Compile the networks with appropriate optimizers and loss functions.
Load training data (real images of the target person's face).
Train D to distinguish real from fake images.
Train G to generate realistic images that fool D.
Generate a deepfake from an input image of another person's face using the trained G.
Post-process the generated deepfake if necessary and save it.
```

Pseudocode for Deepfake Generation: Researchers have employed several methods for detecting deepfake content. Certain discrepancies and evidence of manipulations are left behind throughout the creation of these deepfakes. The detecting systems could use these traces to categorize the information as genuine or Deepfake.

```
Import necessary libraries/frameworks.
Define and load a pre-trained deepfake detection model (e.g., CNN, GAN, or ensemble model).
Load the test dataset containing both real and deepfake images/videos.
Preprocess the images/videos (e.g., resizing, normalization).
Split the dataset into test and validation sets.
Evaluate the pre-trained model on the test dataset:
    - Measure performance metrics such as accuracy, precision, recall, and F1-score.
Fine-tune the pre-trained model (optional) on the validation set:
    - Adjust hyperparameters or add additional layers to improve performance.
Retrain the model on the combined training and validation sets (optional).
Evaluate the fine-tuned model on the test dataset:
    - Measure performance metrics to assess improvement over the pre-trained model.
Deploy the deepfake detection model:
    - Integrate it into applications or systems for real-time detection of deepfakes.
```

Pseudocode for Deepfake Detection

Related Works: The referenced publications' literature review presents various perspectives on using deep learning methods to identify deepfake data. Liang et al. (2023) This article summarizes the key advancements in identifying synthetic forgeries as of 2020. It emphasizes the recent research direction toward using evidence to link artificial intelligence (AI)-generated images to their generating sources. They describe the numerous kinds of deepfakes, the minor fingerprints and processing traces that set AI-generated photos apart from each other and reality, and the various levels of attribution that are now achievable given our present understanding of generative techniques. Furthermore, they outline the real-world restrictions of synthetic recognition of image techniques, counter-forensic strategies designed to circumvent these constraints, and future research initiatives to ensure the continued applicability of deepfake forensics. Related Works Waseem et al. (2023) The methods now available for creating deepfake images and movies for expression and emotion substitution are thoroughly examined in this article. Additionally, it provides a summary of publicly available deepfake datasets for evaluation, which are essential resources for training and assessing deepfake detection systems.

Additionally, the research explains the detection algorithms used in this context while addressing the challenges and issues related to appearance and expression swapping. However, this study goes beyond simply cataloging the existing challenges. However, this study goes beyond simply cataloging the existing challenges. It takes one stage further by outlining possible directions for further research and advising incoming scholars on the problems with deepfake detection methods that require resolution. Preeti and Manoj Kumar et al. (2023) work is an analysis of deepfake implementation techniques. Talk about the primary methods for manipulating and detecting deepfakes and how Deep Convolution-based GAN models are used for both execution and detection of deepfakes.

Additionally included is research that compares the proposed GAN with various existing GAN models using the parameters Fréchet Inception Distance (FID) and Inception Score (IS). In addition to those above, the paper addresses open problems and potential future directions that should be considered to progress the subject. According to Kang et al. (2022), three common traces left behind by deepfakes—warping artifacts and residual noise can help identify between different types of deepfake images. They used a network intended for steganalysis to detect pixel-by-pixel residual noise traces. They also evaluate landmarks to capture high-level features. These are the primary facial features that deepfake photographs usually show weird distortions. Finally, as the effect of bogus data is similar to that of blurring, they employ characteristics from multiple picture quality assessment tools that may identify indications of blurring.

Aduwala et al. (2021), Although they are not employed for their detection, these networks are frequently used to produce Deepfake videos. In this study, they investigate methods for detecting Deepfake films that are based on GAN discriminators. Using MesoNet as a baseline, they train a GAN and obtain the discriminator as a customized module to detect Deepfakes. They also investigate how the discriminator's effectiveness changes with various configurations and training techniques by testing several discriminator architectures on various datasets. Lastly, a strategy that uses ensemble techniques to increase the effectiveness of a set of GAN discriminators is provided. Their findings demonstrate that GAN discriminators underperform on videos from unidentified sources, even when enhanced by ensemble techniques.

Guarnera et al. (2020) The suggested method extracts local characteristics to describe the underlying neural generative process using an Expectation Maximization (EM) algorithm. Ad-hoc validation was employed as ground truth for non-fakes in experimental tests utilizing naive classifiers for five different frameworks (STARGAN, GDWCT, STYLEGAN, ATTGAN, And STYLEGAN 2). These tests were run using the CELEBA dataset. The results proved the technique's efficiency in differentiating between the various architectures and their accompanying generating process. Maksutov et al. (2020) say that artificial intelligence-generated face-swapping movies, or "DeepFakes," are a growing concern for consumers. Videos of this nature have the potential to threaten privacy, commit fraud, and cause other crimes. High-quality DeepFake video identification can occasionally be difficult for humans to differentiate. For this reason, researchers must create algorithms to find them. In this paper, we provide an overview of the signs indicating whether face-swapping methods were applied to a given set of images. The main purpose of this work is to develop an algorithm or software that can accurately determine if a photo was altered using DeepFake.

Korshunov and Marcel (2019) say Deepfake films had erroneous acceptance percentages of 85.62% and 95.0%. (on high-quality versions), respectively, indicating the need for detection techniques. After considering several baseline techniques, we discovered that the top-performing technique, which is frequently employed in the presentation attack detection sector, yielded an 8.97% identical error rate on high-grade Deep-fakes based on visual quality measures. Our tests show that GAN-generated Deepfake films challenge face recognition systems and current detection techniques and that this challenge will only increase with the advancement of face-swapping technologies. Regin et al. (2023) employed an image preprocessing step to eliminate low-level, high-frequency hints from GAN images, such as Gaussian blur and Gaussian noise. Yadav and Salmani (2019), present the operation of the Deepfake approach and show how it can change faces in a video with the highest level of precision. The several methods for determining whether a video was created using Deepfake are further described, along with a summary of its benefits and drawbacks.

Güera and Delp et al.(2018) say that a free software program based on machine learning has recently made it simple to produce "deepfake" videos—videos with convincing face swaps and minimal evidence of manipulation. It's easy to imagine scenarios in which these lifelike phony videos are exploited to incite political unrest, extort someone, or fabricate terrorist incidents. This paper proposes a temporal-aware pipeline for automatically identifying deepfake videos. Convolutional neural networks (CNNs) are our system's tools to retrieve frame-level characteristics. A recurrent neural network, also called a recurrent neural network, is then trained with these features to determine whether or not a video has been altered. We test our approach on a sizable collection of deepfake films that we gathered from several online video portals. To distinguish between swapped and authentic facial photos, Zhang et al. (2017) employed the bag of words approach to collect a set of compact features, which they then fed into a variety of classifiers, including SVM, Wang et al. (2017), random forest (RF)- Bai et al. (2017), including multi-layer perceptron (MLP)- Zheng et al. (2016).

In comparison to other image forensics techniques in the article by Yang et al. (2017); Zhong et al. (2019), or visual steganalysis networks, Ueli (2000). This improves the statistical similarity at the pixel level between actual and false images and enables a forensic classifier to acquire more intrinsic and relevant features. The most challenging images produced by deep learning algorithms to identify are likely those synthesized by GAN models because of their realistic and high-quality nature, which stems from GAN's capacity to learn the complicated input data distribution and produce new outputs with a similar input distribution. However, Marar et al. (2023) presented the GAN-based detection of deepfakes as a challenge for hypothesis testing. Bose et al. (2023) used the information-theoretic research of authentication to offer a statistical framework. The oracle error, which measures the shortest distance among distributions of authentic images and images produced by a specific GAN, is defined. The analytical results indicate that this distance rises when the GAN becomes less precise, making it easier to identify deepfakes. When dealing with high-resolution (HR) inputs, a very precise GAN is needed to produce bogus images, which are difficult to identify using this technique (Obaid et al., 2023).

METHODOLOGY

Generative Adversarial Networks: The GAN comprises the discriminator and generator networks. Each network serves a distinct role. The generator's job is to create artificial or phony content. This fabricated content is then combined with genuine content and fed to the discriminator. The discriminator's job is to distinguish between artificial and authentic stuff. The generator receives the discriminator's feedback. The generator gains the ability to produce artificial content that appears just as realistic as the original material after several cycles or epochs. The learning process is said to be completed when the generator can trick the discriminator for about half of the inputs. The trained model can produce synthetic content that is as near to the real content as possible. GANs use text-to-speech synthesis to produce artificial voices. Text transcriptions and audio recordings are used in data collection. Tokenization and feature extraction are examples of preprocessing. A generator that generates spectrograms and a discriminator that separates real from synthetic are the two components of the GAN architecture. In learning to discriminate, training optimizes the generator to produce lifelike sounds.

Metrics used in evaluation are both objective and subjective. Adjusting improves both diversity and quality. Applications such as virtual assistants are deployed after training is completed successfully. The GAN training process proceeds until an equilibrium between G and D is attained, indicating that the discriminator and the generator are no longer advancing. However, establishing such balance is uncommon, and training is typically terminated when the visual quality of the samples generated no longer improves significantly. Alternatively, G might be trained to provide samples that D cannot discern between authentic and fraudulent. D is now detached, and G is the only one capable of producing photorealistic fake things.

A noise vector z is given to the generator G, producing synthetic content, denoted as G(z). The discriminator network is then given this fake content and the genuine data (designated as x). A classification network categorizes input into true and fraudulent content at its basic level. As a result, the outcome of the discriminator network is represented as D(x) for genuine content and as D(G(z)) for synthetic content. Therefore, the value function V(G, D), where G denotes the generator and D the discriminator, is solved by the min-max problem and is given in the equation

$$minGmaxDV(D,G)=Ex{\sim}\rho(x)[logD(x)]+Ez{\sim}\rho(z)]log(1-D(G(z)))]$$

Where expectancy is represented by the letter E. While the discriminator seeks to maximize this value function, the generator wants to minimize this value function as a whole. The discriminator seeks to increase $Ex{\sim}\rho(x)[logD(x)]$—that is, D(x)—because it indicates a high degree of confidence in the prediction of actual data as real. For the first term, the generator is not involved in any instance. On the other hand, the second term, $Ez{\sim}\rho(z)]log(1-D(G(z)))]$, represents the discriminator's output for synthetic content. D(G(x)0 indicates that the discriminator is certain that the input is synthetic and that the generator is not succeeding in fooling the discriminator. As a result, the discriminator seeks to minimize D(G(x)) (Figure 1).

Figure 3. Architecture diagram

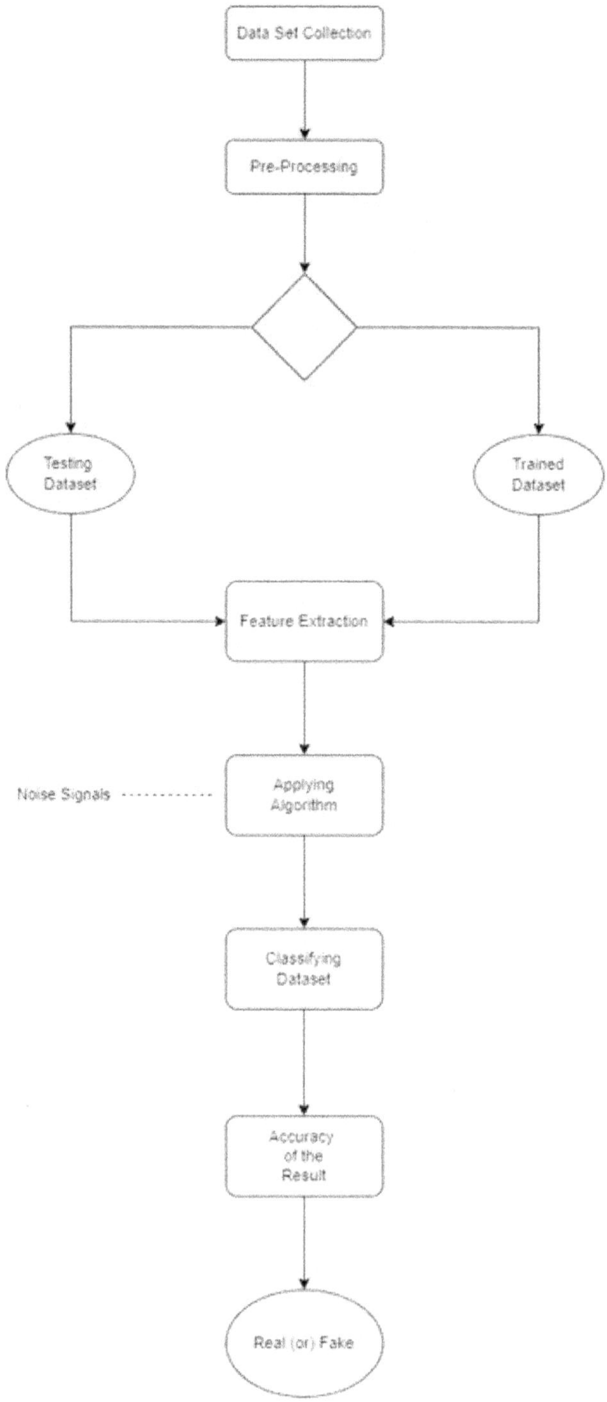

Developing a Deepfake Algorithm Detection system using Generative AI begins with collecting a diverse dataset containing both genuine and deepfake videos. This dataset undergoes preprocessing steps to ensure consistency and enhance quality. A portion of the dataset is reserved for testing, while the remainder is used for training the detection model. Features are extracted from the videos, capturing characteristics such as facial landmarks, motion patterns, and audio spectrograms. Generative AI algorithms, like GANs or VAEs, are applied to generate deepfake content, which is then used alongside genuine videos to train machine learning classifiers. Based on the extracted features, these classifiers learn to differentiate between genuine and deepfake videos. The performance of the detection system is evaluated using the testing dataset, assessing metrics like accuracy and precision. Finally, based on the classification results, each video is classified as either real or fake, enabling the identification of potential instances of deepfake manipulation. Throughout this process, the system iterates on refining algorithms and optimizing performance to detect deepfake video content effectively. Data Set Collection: This involves gathering a diverse set of data containing both real and fake videos. Real videos serve as the baseline, while fake videos are created using various deepfake algorithms. These videos may include faces of different individuals, varied lighting conditions, backgrounds, and facial expressions to create a robust dataset.

Preprocessing: Preprocessing steps involve cleaning and preparing the collected data to train the deepfake detection model. This may include resizing videos to a standard resolution, normalizing lighting conditions, removing irrelevant metadata, and potentially augmenting the dataset to increase its size and diversity.

Feature Extraction: Feature extraction involves extracting relevant features from the videos that can help distinguish between real and fake content. These features may include facial landmarks, motion patterns, inconsistencies in facial expressions, or artifacts specific to deepfake generation algorithms. Feature extraction is crucial in creating meaningful input for the detection model.

Applying Algorithm: In this step, the deepfake detection algorithm is applied to the preprocessed data. This could involve training a neural network or another machine learning model on the extracted features from the training dataset. The algorithm learns patterns from the data to differentiate between real and fake videos.

Classifying Dataset: Once the algorithm is trained, it's used to classify videos in the testing dataset as real or fake. The model assigns a probability or confidence score to each video, indicating the likelihood that it's a deepfake. This classification allows for the evaluation of the model's performance.

Accuracy of the Result: The accuracy of the deepfake detection model is assessed based on its performance on the testing dataset. This typically involves accuracy, precision, recall, and F1-score metrics. High accuracy demonstrates that the model can efficiently distinguish between actual and false videos (Figure 4).

Real or Fake: Finally, based on the classification results, each video in the dataset is labeled as either real or fake. This information can be utilized for various purposes, including moderation of content on social networking platforms, forensic investigation, and educating people about the veracity of the content they consume.

Figure 4. Block diagram

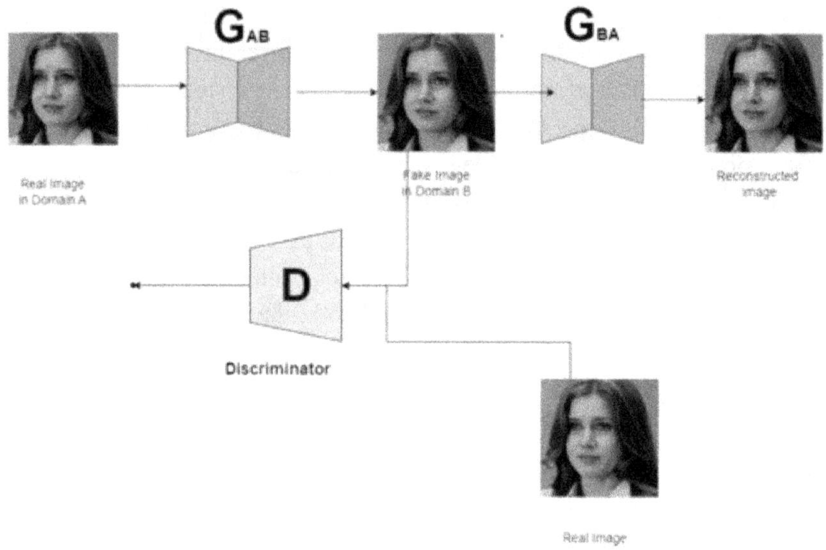

How to Detect Deepfakes Using GAN: Two distinct neural network types are combined in the GAN system, and these networks operate in a zero-sum manner. There is a discrimination and a generation network. Since the generation network produces phony data, the discrimination should calculate the likelihood that the fake data is authentic. Using a data distribution, generative models can be taught to produce realistic examples with the help of GANs, a newly developed technology. The discriminator (D) and generator (G) neural networks are the fundamental components of GANs.This approach intuitively makes sense: D tries to identify which samples are real and fake, whereas G tries to fabricate fraudulent ones. The two models will eventually improve if given enough time to compete. In other words, generator D aims to identify the likelihood that a sample is derived from the training data rather than G, and generator G aims to capture the data distribution.

RESULT AND DISCUSSION

A) Model Evaluation and Analysis

Accuracy: Accuracy refers to the proportion of correctly classified samples (real and fake) among all samples in the dataset. In deepfake detection, accuracy indicates how well the detection model can correctly identify whether an image or video is real or manipulated (i.e., a deepfake). A higher accuracy indicates a better performance of the detection model in distinguishing between real and deepfake content.

Accuracy=Number of correctly classified samples/Total number of samples

Epoch: Each epoch is one complete pass through the training dataset in training a deepfake detection model. Every epoch involves training the model using batches of training data and updating the model's weights according to the loss calculated between the ground truth labels and the model's predictions. After one epoch, the model has been viewed and learned from each training example once (Figure 5).

Figure 5. Accuracy graph

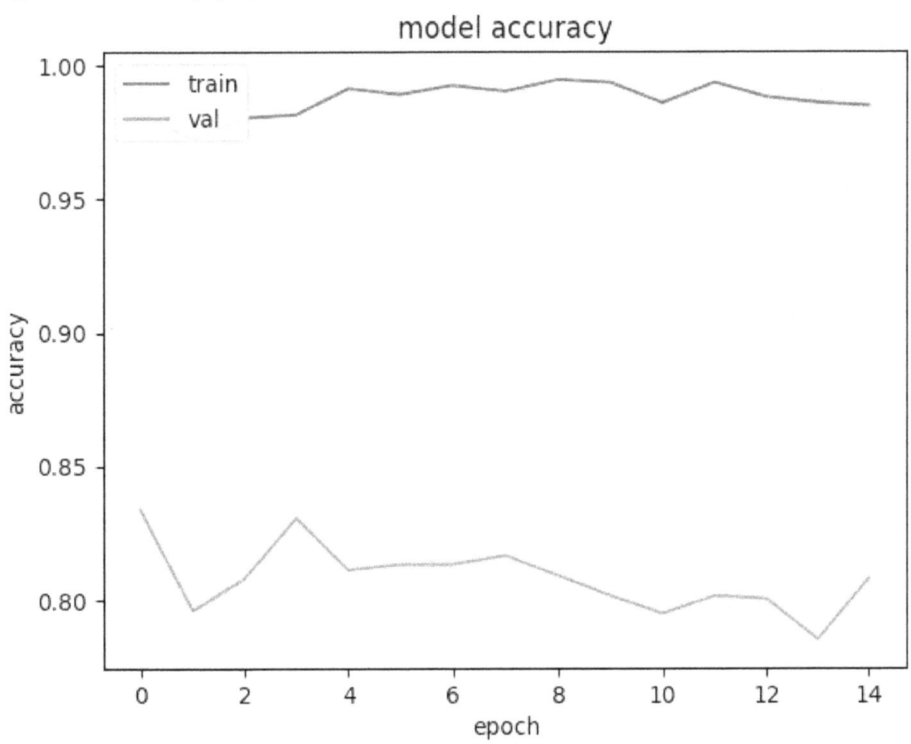

B) Architectural Details

Layer (type): It identifies the type of layer used in CNN architecture. Common layer types include

- Conv2D: Convolutional layer - applies filters to extract features from the input data.
- MaxPooling2D: Max pooling layer - reduces the dimensionality of the data by selecting the maximum value from a local region.
- Activation The activation layer adds nonlinearity to the network, helping it learn complex patterns.

Output Shape: It shows the dimensions of the data after processing by the corresponding layer. The format is typically (None, height, width, channels) (Figure 6).

Figure 6. Architectural details

Layer (type)	Output Shape	Param#
conv2d_12 (Conv2D)	(None, 126, 126, 64)	1792
max_pooling2d_12 (MaxPooling2D)	**(None, 63, 63, 64)**	**0**
activation_10 (Activation)	(None, 63, 63, 64)	0
conv2d_13 (Conv2D)	**(None, 61, 61, 32)**	**18464**
max_pooling2d_13 (MaxPooling2D)	(None, 30, 30, 32)	0
activation_11 (Activation)	**(None, 30, 30, 32)**	**0**
conv2d_14 (Conv2D)	(None, 28, 28, 16)	4624
max_pooling2d_14 (MaxPooling2D)	**(None, 14, 14, 16)**	**0**
activation_12 (Activation)	(None, 14, 14, 16)	0

Param #: The quantity of trainable parameters connected to every layer is shown here. Trainable parameters are the weights and biases the model learns during training to improve performance. Conv2D layers typically have the most parameters due to the filters they apply. MaxPooling2D and Activation layers generally have no trainable parameters.

CONCLUSION

The future of DeepFake detection holds tremendous promise with the incorporation of Generative AI frameworks. These technologies enable the integration of advanced architectures and training techniques, such as progressive growing and attention mechanisms, which enhance the model's ability to identify subtle artifacts indicative of DeepFake manipulation across diverse media formats. Moreover, including reinforcement learning frameworks enhances the model's adaptability to evolving DeepFake techniques and fortifies its resilience against adversarial attacks. Multimodal fusion techniques enrich the detection process by amalgamating information from various modalities like audio and video, thereby offering a more holistic assessment of the authenticity of media content. Augmenting the detection pipeline with self-supervised learning strategies enables the model to develop robust representations directly from the data, augmenting its generalization capabilities. Additionally, the incorporation of explainability mechanisms adds transparency to the decision-making process, thereby fostering trustworthiness. Collaborative endeavors among researchers and industry stakeholders to curate extensive and diverse datasets are vital for advancing the development and evaluation of DeepFake detection systems. Continuous refinement through real-world deployment and feedback loops remains imperative to ensure the efficacy of these detection models in combatting the proliferation of DeepFakes.

REFERENCES

Aduwala, S. A., Arigala, M., Desai, S., Quan, H. J., & Eirinaki, M. (2021). Deepfake Detection using GAN Discriminators. *2021 IEEE Seventh International Conference on Big Data Computing Service and Applications (BigDataService)*, Oxford, United Kingdom. DOI: 10.1109/BigDataService52369.2021.00014

Bai, S. (2017). Growing random forest on deep convolutional neural networks for scene categorization. *Expert Systems with Applications*, *71*(4), 279–287. DOI: 10.1016/j.eswa.2016.10.038

Bose, S. R., Sirajudheen, M. A. S., Kirupanandan, G., Arunagiri, S., Regin, R., & Rajest, S. S. (2023). Fine-grained independent approach for workout classification using integrated metric transfer learning. In *Advanced Applications of Generative AI and Natural Language Processing Models* (pp. 358–372). IGI Global. DOI: 10.4018/979-8-3693-0502-7.ch017

Guarnera, L., Giudice, O., & Battiato, S. (2020). Proceedings of the IEEE/CVF Conference on Computer Vision and Pattern Recognition (CVPR) Workshops, Seattle, Washington, USA.

Guera, D., & Delp, E. J. (2018). Deepfake video detection using recurrent neural networks. 2018 15th IEEE International Conference on Advanced Video and Signal Based Surveillance (AVSS), Auckland, New Zealand.

Kang, J., Ji, S.-K., Lee, S., Jang, D., & Hou, J.-U. (2022). Detection enhancement for various deepfake types based on residual noise and manipulation traces. *IEEE Access : Practical Innovations, Open Solutions*, *10*(1), 69031–69040. DOI: 10.1109/ACCESS.2022.3185121

Korshunov, P., & Marcel, S. (2019). Vulnerability assessment and detection of Deepfake videos. *2019 International Conference on Biometrics (ICB)*, Crete, Greece. DOI: 10.1109/ICB45273.2019.8987375

Liang, P., Liu, G., Xiong, Z., Fan, H., Zhu, H., & Zhang, X. (2023). Xuemin Zhang, A facial geometry based detection model for face manipulation using CNN-LSTM architecture. *Information Sciences*, *633*(7), 370–383. DOI: 10.1016/j.ins.2023.03.079

Maksutov, A. A., Morozov, V. O., Lavrenov, A. A., & Smirnov, A. S. (2020). Methods of deepfake detection based on machine learning. 2020 IEEE Conference of Russian Young Researchers in Electrical and Electronic Engineering (EIConRus), Moscow, Russia.

Marar, A., Bose, S. R., Singh, R., Joshi, Y., Regin, R., & Rajest, S. S. (2023). Light weight structure texture feature analysis for character recognition using progressive stochastic learning algorithm. In *Advanced Applications of Generative AI and Natural Language Processing Models* (pp. 144–158). IGI Global.

Obaid, A. J., Bhushan, B., & Rajest, S. S. (Eds.). (2023). *Advanced applications of generative AI and natural language processing models*. IGI Global.

Preeti, K., Kumar, M., & Sharma, H. K. (2023). A GAN-based model of deepfake detection in social media. *Procedia Computer Science*, *218*(1), 2153–2162. DOI: 10.1016/j.procs.2023.01.191

Rajest, S. S., Moccia, S., Singh, B., Regin, R., & Jeganathan, J. (Eds.). (2024, August 30). Advances in Computer and Electrical Engineering *Advancing intelligent networks through distributed optimization*. IGI Global., DOI: 10.4018/979-8-3693-3739-4

Regin, R., Sharma, P. K., Singh, K., Narendra, Y. V., Bose, S. R., & Rajest, S. S. (2023). Fine-grained deep feature expansion framework for fashion apparel classification using transfer learning. In *Advanced Applications of Generative AI and Natural Language Processing Models* (pp. 389–404). IGI Global. DOI: 10.4018/979-8-3693-0502-7.ch019

Ueli, M. (2000). Authentication theory and hypothesis testing. *IEEE Transactions on Information Theory*, *46*(4), 1350–1356. DOI: 10.1109/18.850674

Wang, X., Thome, N., & Cord, M. (2017). Gaze latent support vector machine for image classification improved by weakly supervised region selection. *Pattern Recognition*, *72*(12), 59–71. DOI: 10.1016/j.patcog.2017.07.001

Waseem, S., Bakar, S. A. R. S., Ahmed, B. A., Omar, Z., Eisa, T. A. E., & Dalam, M. E. E. (2023). DeepFake on Face and Expression Swap: A Review. *IEEE Access : Practical Innovations, Open Solutions*, *11*(10), 117865–117906. DOI: 10.1109/ACCESS.2023.3324403

Yadav, D., & Salmani, S. (2019). Deepfake: A survey on facial forgery technique using generative adversarial network. *2019 International Conference on Intelligent Computing and Control Systems (ICCS)*, Madurai, India DOI: 10.1109/ICCS45141.2019.9065881

Yang, P., Ni, R., & Zhao, Y. (2017). Recapture image forensics based on Laplacian convolutional neural networks. In *Digital Forensics and Watermarking*. Springer International Publishing. DOI: 10.1007/978-3-319-53465-7_9

Zhang, Y., Zheng, L., & Thing, V. L. L. (2017). Automated face swapping and its detection. 2017 IEEE 2nd International Conference on Signal and Image Processing (ICSIP), Singapore.

Zheng, L., Duffner, S., Idrissi, K., Garcia, C., & Baskurt, A. (2016). Siamese multi-layer perceptrons for dimensionality reduction and face identification. *Multimedia Tools and Applications*, *75*(9), 5055–5073. DOI: 10.1007/s11042-015-2847-3

Zhong, S., Jia, C., Chen, K., & Dai, P. (2019). A novel steganalysis method with deep learning for different texture complexity images. *Multimedia Tools and Applications*, *78*(7), 8017–8039. DOI: 10.1007/s11042-018-6573-5

Chapter 4
Pixel Guardians on Enhancing Public Safety Through Image Processing in Suspicious Activity Recognition

R. Radhika
https://orcid.org/0009-0005-2415-4930
Bharath Institute of Higher Education and Research, India

A. Muthukumaravel
Bharath Institute of Higher Education and Research, India

ABSTRACT

This chapter focuses on improving the existing monitoring system's ability to detect and prevent disruptive behaviours, which is critical given the growing public safety concerns. Recognizing patterns connected with potential threats, inappropriate behavior, and security issues can be challenging in many scenarios. The proposed approach of integrating attention mechanisms into image processing is suggested as a solution to detect suspicious activities. By employing this novel methodology, the model is optimized, and the design language is simplified, thereby ensuring enhanced precision in surveillance. The principal aim of the framework is to augment the model's sensitivity to significant temporal and spatial variables. A Convolutional Neural Network powers it with attention elements that are strategically positioned. To improve activity detection and public safety, the suggested approach places a higher value on refining classification than employing complex language.

DOI: 10.4018/979-8-3373-4672-4.ch004

INTRODUCTION

Modern urban areas are experiencing an increasing preoccupation with public safety, which calls for novel methodologies that surpass conventional monitoring techniques (Massenkoff and Chalfin, 2022). Identifying and handling suspicious activities in metropolitan areas that are becoming more congested and diverse pose novel difficulties for security and law enforcement personnel (Xiuhua, 2012). To tackle this pivotal concern, this paper presents Pixel Guardians, an innovative technology that augments public safety by employing image processing methods to identify suspicious activities. As security hazards become more prevalent, we must significantly alter our methods of population tracking. Detection of subtle patterns linked to suspicious behavior in densely populated and dynamic regions can challenge the current monitoring infrastructure (Moore et al., 2024). The public's safety is jeopardized due to the time required to detect and respond to such actions. Surveillance systems predominantly depend on rule-based algorithms and manual monitoring, and neither exhibits exceptional adaptability towards intricate suspicious activities (Aherwadi et al., 2021). Manual monitoring is laborious and susceptible to human error, whereas rule-based computers cannot discern non-compliance with rules or adjust to novel patterns (Tripathi et al., 2018). This paper overcomes these constraints by implementing state-of-the-art image processing methodologies (Loganathan et al., 2019).

The principal aim of the system is to augment the instantaneous identification of dubious activities to proactively ensure the general public's safety. Pixel Guardians, the proposed methodology, employs innovative computer vision technology to decipher complex visual signals that may indicate potential dangers or suspicious conduct. Existing methods may result in avoidable setbacks or false alarms due to their limited ability to accurately differentiate between benign and detrimental activities. This paper puts forth an advanced framework capable of adjusting to the perpetually changing terrain of dubious activities to surmount this challenge (Nanban et al., 2024). This paper employs Convolutional Neural Networks (CNNs) to extract and analyze features from input photographs to enhance visual data interpretation. The system learns from a vast collection of suspicious activities, in addition to pre-existing principles, enabling it to generalize across multiple scenarios.

Implementing attention processes within the CNN architecture is the foundation of the proposed solution. Enhancing the system's emphasis on relevant spatial and temporal variables linked to suspicious behaviors reduces the likelihood of ignoring inconsequential signals that may signify potential danger. In densely populated urban environments, the capacity to promptly identify and address suspicious activities is paramount (Mustafa et al., 2017). By emphasizing image processing and attention-enhanced convolutional neural networks (CNNs), Pixel Guardians can contribute to developing a proactive and potent public safety infrastructure. Subsequent sections of this manuscript will be devoted to presenting the methodology, experimental findings, and real-world case studies that illustrate the potential of Pixel Guardians to enhance public safety by facilitating more accurate identification of suspicious behavior (Al-Ghiyadh and Al-Khafaji, 2021).

LITERATURE REVIEW

Quadri and Katakdhond (2022) create an automated system capable of detecting suspicious activities using Convolutional Neural Networks. The overarching objective is to increase the security and productivity of many applications through intelligent algorithms and video analytics. The research highlights the advantages of automated solutions and the disadvantages of physical surveillance in such contexts. The novel methodology aims to identify and categorize pupils whose behaviors give rise to concerns, such as seat movement, objectionable speech, or atypical head movements during an examination. The system identifies and classifies probable behaviors through convolutional neural networks that draw inspiration from the human visual cortex and analyze real-time video footage. The proposed research incorporates crucial techniques for analyzing video and image inputs, including applying filters, combining feature maps, and utilizing convolutional neural networks (Renjith, 2024).

Additionally, non-linearity is accounted for by employing the ReLU function. This approach utilizes a completely connected neural network to perform classification tasks by implementing forward and backpropagation training with appropriate weight modifications. The solution prioritizes sequential installation and establishes prerequisites for Python, Django, MySQL, and Wamp Server (Jeba et al., 2023). In conclusion, this study has developed a resilient system capable of assessing actual surveillance incidents, thereby providing an ingenious approach to promptly identify and cease suspicious behaviors. The research highlights the potential ramifications and applications of the suggested system across various domains, employing cutting-edge technology to tackle security concerns.

Bhagyashri Kumbhar et al. (2023) aim to develop an automated system that employs Convolutional Neural Networks to detect suspicious activity in video surveillance to bolster safety and security. It is impractical to constantly monitor every aspect with a human eye; however, for security purposes, installing high-quality CCTV cameras is standard procedure (Philip et al., 2024). Dilemmatically behaving individuals make it difficult to determine whether their actions are typical or dubious.This system employs convolutional neural networks to analyze live CCTV footage to classify an individual's activities as routine or suspicious. When the system detects suspicious activity, it notifies the appropriate authorities immediately (Anitha et al., 2023).

The efficacy of this detection method is contingent upon the design of the machine learning model, the quality of the training data, and the environment in which it is deployed. Sustained surveillance, regular updates, and continuous enhancement are essential for ensuring accuracy and addressing emerging suspicious activities (Sayedelahl and Farouk, 2024).

Driven by a commitment to ensuring public safety, this endeavor aims to mechanize identifying dubious activities (Karthik et al., 2024). Certain anticipated objectives include the following: The process involves several steps: converting video to still images, separating frames from their backgrounds, identifying actions using a Deep Belief Network (DBN), and concluding with a trained dataset used to determine whether an activity is normal or dubious. Input processing, feature map generation, non-linearity augmentation, vector pooling and compression, and classification utilizing a fully linked artificial neural network are all system architecture components. The research emphasizes the importance of routinely testing, updating, and improving the suggested system to guarantee its effectiveness across diverse scenarios and countering emergent threats. This further illustrates the practicality of the system (Maroju, 2024).

Phalguni Kadam (2023) presents a framework for the automated detection of suspicious activities using a Raspberry Pi-based system to enhance public safety and security via intelligent surveillance. The system performs a real-time analysis of public-area CCTV footage via convolutional neural networks. The proposed methodology includes various image processing tools, including visualization, restoration and refining, picture retrieval, pattern assessment, and deep learning. The stages of preprocessing, feature extraction, and recognition are depicted in the suggested flowchart for the model. A Gaussian mixture model is employed during the preparatory phase to perform background subtraction, video segmentation, and frame transformation (Ronald et al., 2024). Feature extraction considers velocity, direction, and motion variables to achieve accurate activity recognition. Recognition, object identification, and image categorization are all processes that utilize the CNN classification layer. Before operation, the input video must be subjected to feature extraction, CNN classification, and preprocessing. The system is constructed upon the Raspberry Pi 3B+ due to its enhanced functionalities, including an Ethernet platform and a quicker clock speed. The proposed methodology designates alarms featuring red bounding boxes as indicators of suspicious activity and alarms featuring green bounding boxes as non-suspect activity. Automatic notifications of anomalous activity, user-defined alerts, and real-time monitoring for event detection are some of the applications of this system. The results demonstrate that the suspect activity detection system is effective, as evidenced by a training accuracy of 85.85% for the initial ten epochs (Jani et al., 2024).

Selvi et al. (2022) employ an Enhanced Convolutional Neural Network (ECNN) to detect and classify suspicious events, including homicides and burglaries. The ECNN method enhances the Convolutional Neural Network (CNN) 's defect detection capabilities in surveillance footage by implementing minor adjustments. A purpose-added layer comprises the hidden components of an ECNN model; these layers are supplementary to the input, convolution, pooling, and output layers (Gandhi et al., 2024). The convolution layer extracts the feature vectors, while the pooling layer optimizes them. Subsequently, the ECNN algorithm adds refinement to detecting suspicious activity. The detection process begins with video preprocessing, including the retrieval of frames and elimination of noise. Optical flow computation is applied to identify motion patterns within the video. After video segmentation, the subsequent step is generating a motion effects map. This will facilitate determining the precise path and detecting potential impediments. Before extracting features, it is necessary to compute feature vectors and cluster mega blocks using spatiotemporal features. Both expected and unexpected code-word behavior must be observed to validate the algorithm. By constructing minimum distance matrices, pixel and frame-level anomalies can be detected. Performance metrics are calculated to assess the efficacy of the ECNN algorithm in identifying anomalous activity. Among these metrics are the rates of false positives and false negatives, as well as precision and accuracy. Using state-of-the-art neural network architecture and feature extraction methodologies, the ECNN method demonstrates a systematic approach that enhances the efficiency and accuracy of anomaly detection in surveillance footage (Singh et al., 2024).

Basha (2019) outlines an innovative methodology for identifying suspect activities in surveillance footage. A Discriminative Deep Belief Network (DBNN) is utilized to classify actions. Convolutional and recurrent neural networks (CNN and RNN) extract features. To optimize model training, convolutional neural networks (CNNs) are employed to extract high-level features from images as the initial step of the primary neural network. The recurrent neural network utilizes the LSTM cells of the Inception model to classify sequences. The integration of three-second intervals into the prediction process effectively mitigates the obstacles associated with real-time video analysis and improves the system's capacity to detect ongoing actions reliably. The discriminative DBNN employs supervised and unsupervised methods and effectively classifies the identified behaviors (Sayedelahl, 2024).

The system demonstrates the capability to identify and categorize video segments as secure, suspicious, criminal, violent, or potentially suspicious through training on a dataset comprising surveillance footage. To verify the proposed strategy, the results and discussion section describes the experiments that were carried out utilizing datasets obtained from various sources, including PETS 2007, CAVIAR, and YouTube. The instructional collection comprises 38 films, spanning 150 minutes, filmed in diverse settings such as warehouses and retail establishments. The system implementation necessitates the utilization of Python 3.5, OpenCV for video frame interpretation, and Keras for constructing and training neural network models. The results demonstrate, in a significant advancement for video surveillance systems, that the proposed technology is capable of identifying and classifying dubious behavior Amrutha et al. (2020) aim to enhance campus security by utilizing CCTV camera footage to monitor students' activities and promptly alert authorities in the event of suspicious behavior.

Video recording, preprocessing, feature extraction, classification, and prediction are all components of the system design. Videos are categorized into three distinct types: suspicious (students using mobile devices), normal (students walking or jogging), and suspicious (students fighting or fainting). Evaluations and instruction: The system utilizes a heterogeneous dataset comprising material from various origins, including academic publications, YouTube recordings, and public areas. The initial step in video processing is frame dividing. Following this, the dimensions of the video are decreased to 224 × 224 pixels, and it is analyzed utilizing a pre-trained VGG-16 CNN model designed for feature extraction. To effectively classify data, the gathered information is input into an LSTM network that is subsequently trained to differentiate between typical and suspicious activities. The system demonstrates an improvement in accuracy from 76% during the initial 10 training epochs to 87.15% during the final testing phase.

The system will promptly alert the appropriate authorities via SMS if dubious activity is detected. The proposed method applies deep learning algorithms to CCTV footage for proactive and real-time enhancement of campus security. Overall, this system exemplifies utilizing cutting-edge technology to enhance campus security. Potential future developments could include expanding the program's accessibility to a wider range of public spaces, refining the identification model for individuals, or investigating supplementary functionalities to offer more comprehensive surveillance capabilities.

SYSTEM METHODOLOGY

Data Collection and Preprocessing: The methodology for acquiring and preparing video data greatly influences the resilience and flexibility of the model utilized for suspicious activity detection. This strategy ensures the model can process various inputs, focusing on its possible application in metropolitan public safety. A substantial collection of videos is gathered and undergoes a series of preprocessing steps to guarantee uniformity and exceptional quality as an integral component of the holistic methodology. The data is collected from various online and offline sources to cater to diversity's needs in identifying suspicious activities. A dataset encompassing an extensive array of environmental factors, such as spatial configurations and illumination, is obtained by meticulous selection.

A diverse dataset is essential when training a model that can generalize across various urban areas and illumination conditions. The preparatory pipeline comprises a collection of interdependent procedures to convert video input into a format suitable for model training. Considering the progressive nature of disruptive behaviors, video sequences are partitioned into clips or frames based on their temporal arrangement. This establishes the foundation for the model to analyze the temporal relationships within the dataset and detect the complex temporal patterns linked to disruptive behaviours. Frame-level normalization entails the application of image normalization to video frames. The model's resistance to variations in illumination is enhanced due to the utilization of consistent pixel values. By implementing this normalization strategy, the influence of illumination fluctuations is reduced, ensuring that each video segment consistently aids in the learning process of the model. The third stage of spatial resizing involves enlarging individual video frames to a uniform resolution of 224 x 224 pixels. This guarantees the model's ability to extract features and accurately enhance computation speed; it also permits the model to accurately detect patterns across various video codecs and resolutions. This consistently fosters versatility for a wide range of security camera models.

The contrast adjustment method is implemented to diminish extraneous background noise and emphasize critical information about disruptive behavior. In this phase, the model's capability to identify subtle patterns is improved by identifying and emphasizing minute visual indicators linked to disruptive activities. This facilitates a more precise detection procedure. Furthermore, equalizing histograms accounts for variations in image intensities to guarantee that they are distributed uniformly across all frames. This methodology enhances the differentiation of attributes across various illumination conditions, supporting the model's focus on critical elements associated with disruptive behaviours. Implementing a Gaussian blur eliminates high-frequency noise and defects from frames, thereby improving the structure and precision of the dataset. The primary objective of this stage is to enhance the model's ability to identify nuanced patterns in disruptive behaviours while simultaneously reducing noise. A consistent colour scheme is produced for every frame through colour normalization. The model's adaptability to various urban contexts and resistance to changes in colour tones are enhanced due to the consistency in colour representations, which allows it to focus on patterns enabled by standardized colors. The unprocessed video data is transformed comprehensively and error-free into a unified, high-quality dataset by coordinating multiple preprocessing procedures. Figure 1. depicts the preprocessing steps of the data.

Figure 1. Flowchart of data preprocessing

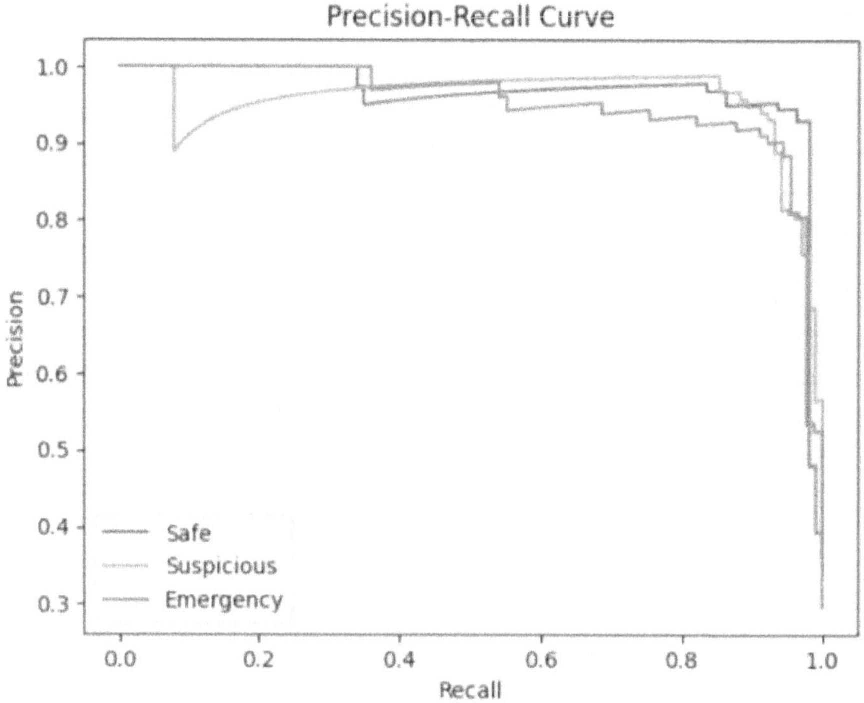

CNN ARCHITECTURE

This section provides an in-depth analysis of the Convolutional Neural Network (CNN) framework to extract significant data from preprocessed video frames. The aim is to develop a resilient system capable of discerning actions that result in disruption. Convolutional neural networks (CNNs) are indispensable in image processing because they can methodically analyze input images by implementing convolutional filter layers. Convolutional neural networks (CNNs) can identify disruptive actions in video analysis. Due to their hierarchical architecture, this domain drastically depends on their aptitude for capturing intricate temporal patterns. Combined, the preprocessing techniques and our improved CNN architecture result in a unified and efficient system that can effectively identify disruptive behavior. Convolutional filters are employed as feature detectors in the initial few layers. By conducting a methodical analysis of the preprocessed video frames, these filters aim to detect disruptive behaviours by identifying distinct patterns such as borders, textures, and more complex structures. This aligns with the intention to extract hierarchical features capable of capturing spatial and temporal intricacies.

The hierarchical feature encoding captures increasingly complex and abstract patterns as the video frames advance through the CNN layers. Understanding the complex temporal relationships within the dataset requires the utilization of a hierarchical structure, given that disruptive actions inherently exhibit dynamism. Following the time-based segmentation of video frames, the model's ability to detect evolving patterns is ensured by hierarchical feature encoding. After extracting the features, the CNN is modified to correspond with the extracted attributes. The model's discriminatory capabilities are enhanced by applying the acquired attributes to adjustments made to the model's configuration and layer weights. CNN's ability to adjust, a crucial factor in precisely detecting patterns associated with public safety issues, illustrates its alignment with the overarching objectives of the approach. To train a convolutional neural network (CNN), the temporal dependencies present in disruptive behaviors must be exposed to the network.

In alignment with the temporal segmentation of video frames, the model employs hierarchical feature encoding to represent spatial hierarchies and temporal connections. By aligning these strategies, the model can adjust its learning to account for the temporal dynamics of suspicious acts. By integrating CNNs into our methods, we can extract information from incoming video frames perfectly. The model's ability to tolerate the subtleties of disruptive behaviours results from the generated comprehensive feature representation. The rationale is that preprocessing techniques enhance the visibility and identification of particular attributes. Since incorporating hierarchical feature representation, our model can now more precisely detect disruptive actions. Convolutional neural networks facilitate the integration of knowledge from various domains when training a model to recognize visual signals that may indicate potentially disruptive actions. This aligns with the ultimate objective of the process, which is to construct a model capable of perceiving subtleties in urban environments. By integrating the preprocessing stages and the convolutional neural network (CNN) architecture, the system guarantees an efficient and streamlined progression from video data input to aspect extraction. This alignment improves the model's resilience, adaptability, and ability to accurately identify disruptive behaviours in various urban settings.

Integration of Attention Mechanisms: Integration of attention mechanisms into the Convolutional Neural Network architecture has improved the model's performance. Incorporating attention processes into strategic design enables the dynamic prioritization of critical spatial and temporal data throughout the inference and training processes. By integrating critical components, the discriminatory capabilities of the model in detecting disruptive actions in video data are notably enhanced. Attention mechanisms can process incoming video frames by assigning greater significance to particular regions. This enables the model to select and emphasize pertinent data, analogous to how an individual may prioritize certain facets while disregarding others. Attention modules are incorporated into the CNN architecture to facilitate this selective concentration, enhancing the model's accuracy and precision. Attention mechanisms are predicated on the dynamic prioritization of various temporal and spatial characteristics within video frames. The model can adaptively modify the weights it assigns to input data, contingent upon the perceived significance of different attributes. By implementing this dynamic weight allocation, the model ensures that pertinent data is prioritized to identify disruptive actions more effectively. Figure 2 depicts the architecture of the CNN model.

Figure 2. CNN architecture

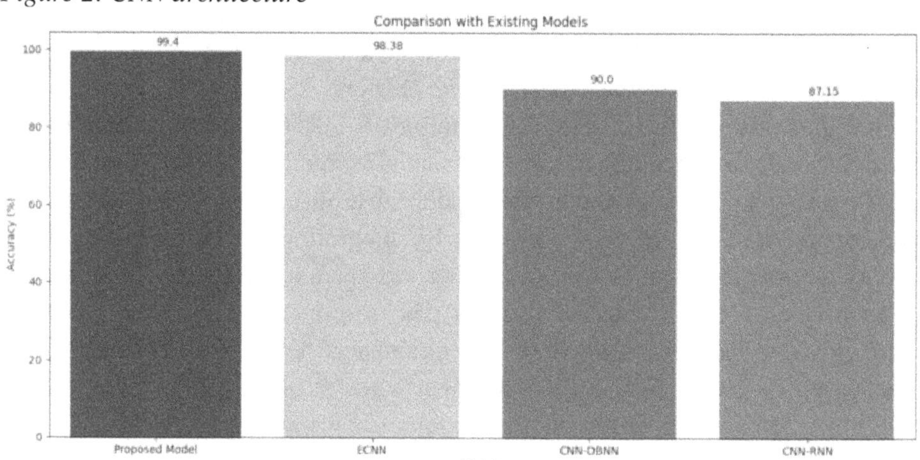

CNN can selectively emphasize critical portions by modulating the firing rates of neurons to concentrate on particular regions of the input video frames via its attention modules. The hierarchical feature representation is of utmost importance for the model as it frequently necessitates interpreting complex and discriminatory data to identify and differentiate between distinct disruptive behaviours. Attention processes are critical in model training as they dictate the learning trajectory. Attention mechanisms assist models in focusing on relevant spatial and temporal signals associated with disruptive activities by dynamically adjusting the relative importance of different components. The ability of the model to accurately identify complex patterns and subtleties is of utmost importance for accurate activity recognition, and the targeted learning approach significantly improves this capability. Attention procedures enhance the discriminatory capabilities of the model and increase the predictability of these advancements. Additional insights can be gained regarding the model's logic by focusing on particular segments of the input video frames. Enhancing the model and understanding its logic is contingent upon this interpretability attribute's presence.

Attention mechanisms facilitate noise reduction by eliminating extraneous information and distracting background sounds. By emphasizing critical information and avoiding irrelevant details, attention processes enhance the model's robustness against input video noise and volatility. As mentioned, resilience is critical in practical situations where video data might demonstrate fluctuations and disruptions. Concentration processes significantly enhance the model's capability to detect disruptive acts that compromise public safety. Enhancing the significance attributed to pertinent geographical and temporal attributes improves the model's resistance to noise and enhances its accuracy in detecting disruptive behaviours within video footage. This integration enhances the discernment capabilities of the model, reduces noise, and improves its interpretability to effectively identify disruptive activities in urban environments. Attention processes develop an exceptionally precise model that is highly adaptable to public safety applications via iterative refinement cycles.

Training and Optimization: The parameters must be adjusted to enhance the model's precision and adaptability in identifying disruptive actions within video footage. This phase is critical in educating CNN to detect and classify disruptive activities accurately. Adjustments must be made to its internal configurations to enhance and bring attention to the CNN. By repeatedly employing backpropagation to the training dataset, it is possible to fine-tune the convolutional neural network (CNN). The internal representations of the model are examined and modified iteratively utilizing the gradients of error associated with the parameters. With each subsequent update, the model exhibits a marked improvement in detecting patterns firmly associated with disruptive activities. The model's parameters can only converge when optimization techniques, such as gradient descent, are implemented. Parameter adjustments are made iteratively in response to computed gradients, aiming to guarantee precise classification of disruptive behaviors within the provided video collection.

During training, overfitting can be avoided by implementing regularization techniques like dropout. During every training cycle, a subset of the convolutional neural network's neurons are arbitrarily turned off via dropout. By reducing the model's dependence on specific neurons, this stochastic element facilitates the development of a more resilient and universal learning approach. Adapting to diverse situations and generalization to new data improve the model's overall resilience. The network employs the Rectified Linear Unit (ReLU) as its activation function. This well-known function introduces complexity to the paradigm by inducing neuronal activity in response to positive inputs but inactivity in response to negative inputs. By employing non-linear activation, the model's ability to fathom intricate patterns in the video data is significantly improved, thereby enhancing identification accuracy. This establishes the groundwork for a CNN that effortlessly manages many duties and is especially perceptive to disruptive actions in video data. The ability of the model to adjust to different situations is a critical attribute for practical public safety implementations. This flexibility is achieved through the amalgamation of regularization methods, backpropagation, gradient descent, and an effective activation function.

Evaluating the efficacy of the training and optimization processes encompasses metrics, including F1 score, recall, accuracy, and precision. These metrics precisely indicate the model's strengths and areas that require improvement. A confusion matrix is employed to categorize the predictions generated by the model as true positives, true negatives, false positives, or false negatives. This facilitates an exhaustive analysis of the forecasts. In addition to the conventional metrics, the Receiver Operating Characteristic (ROC) curve and Area Under the Curve (AUC) evaluate the model's efficacy at various thresholds. By plotting true positive and false positive rates against one another, the receiver operating characteristic (ROC) curve illustrates the model's discriminatory power. A greater area under the curve (AUC) signifies the model's proficiency in distinguishing between positive and negative events. Future iterations of the model are motivated by the findings of this qualitative investigation, which pinpoints possible domains that require enhancement and refinement. The assessment outcomes are crucial for the continuous improvement of the model, ensuring its adaptability and capability to identify disruptive behaviours within the public safety domain.

Model Evaluation: To assess the model's performance, the key performance metrics are utilized to calculate its performance. Temporal measurements are vital in the processing of video data. Analyzing metrics that incorporate the sequential and temporal dependencies of the video may yield greater advantages compared to a frame-by-frame evaluation. This category comprises event-based and shot-level metrics that track the progression of disruptive behaviors over time. Imbue the perplexity matrix with the capability of dynamically managing dependencies. Adjustments should be made to the true positives, false negatives, and false positives to incorporate sequences or segments of events detected accurately or incorrectly into the video. As a result, the temporal performance of the model is depicted more comprehensively. Video analysis can continue to benefit from applying the ROC curve and AUC metrics. In contrast, they should be extended to account for the temporal element. As the video progresses, consider the evolution of the compromise between true positive and false positive rates to ensure that the AUC accurately reflects the model's ability to differentiate between positive and negative events.

$$\text{Accuracy} = \frac{\text{TP} + \text{TN}}{\text{TP} + \text{TN} + \text{FP} + \text{FN}} \tag{1}$$

Precision, an essential indicator of the model's capability to detect positive instances, specifically disruptive activities, is the subsequent metric under consideration. One metric for assessing accuracy is the proportion of accurate predictions relative to the total number of predictions, encompassing correct and incorrect ones. Precision is the proportion of positive instances that accurately identified disruptive activities within our methodology. A rise in precision signifies that detecting disruptive events is becoming more precise and accurate.

$$\text{Precision} = \frac{\text{TP}}{\text{TP} + \text{FP}} \tag{2}$$

The calculation for determining whether the model can detect every important instance of disruptive behavior involves dividing the sum of accurate and inaccurate forecasts by the percentage of accurate predictions. Recall signifies the ability to accurately detect every occurrence of disruptive activities in our methodology, emphasizing the criticality of reducing false negatives.

$$\text{Recall} = \frac{\text{TP}}{\text{TP} + \text{FN}} \tag{3}$$

The F1 score offers a comprehensive assessment of the effectiveness of the model. The F1 score, which employs a harmonic mean, attempts to balance recall and precision. Multiply recall and precision by 2 and subsequently divide the result by the sum of the two, yielding the formula. F1 scores are valuable when balancing false positives and negatives, which is critical. A model that achieves a higher F1 score demonstrates a balanced performance in terms of recall and precision, which is advantageous when identifying disruptive behaviors.

$$\text{F1 Score} = 2 \times \frac{\text{Precision} \times \text{Recall}}{\text{Precision} + \text{Recall}} \tag{4}$$

These metrics provide precise insights into its strengths and areas that could benefit from enhancement. The holistic evaluation of the model's efficacy in identifying disruptive activities is achieved through the interaction of accuracy, precision, recall, and the F1 score. This information subsequently informs subsequent cycles of refinement and optimization. Determine the model's performance in various video scenarios with differing lighting and background noise degrees. Conducting routine evaluations of misclassified samples and subjective assessments of video segments indicating deficiencies in the model is imperative. This is beneficial because it enhances the model's efficacy across various time-based scenarios.

Qualitative analysis is especially advantageous for video data. Continuous optimization and refinement can be attained by examining the model's temporal interpretation and categorization of events, identifying patterns in misclassified instances within video segments, and evaluating the model's response to varying settings. This customized evaluation approach facilitates a more precise and all-encompassing appraisal of the performance of a 0, and the algorithm has a great deal of potential for accurate instance categorization, as rates for all classes exceed 99 percent. The precision values vary between 99.57% and 99.05%, signifying the model's capability to accurately identify positive events while emphasizing the system's proficiency in mitigating false positives. Consistently exceeding 99%, recall percentages validate the model's capability to identify all pertinent occurrences, further supporting the system's efficacy in reducing false negatives. An F1 score ranging from 99.21% to 99.57%, representing the harmonic mean of recall and precision, indicates that the assessed parameters exhibit a well-balanced performance. As mentioned above, the results demonstrate the system's ability to distinguish between safe, suspicious, and emergencies (Table 1).

Table 1. Key performance indicators of the proposed system

Metrics	Safe	Suspicious	Emergency
Accuracy (%)	99.68	99.31	99.04
Precision (%)	99.57	99.42	99.05
Recall (%)	99.68	99.31	99.045
F1 Score (%)	99.57	99.43	99.21

The proposed methodology attains a significantly elevated success rate of 99.40% compared to other models. In contrast, Basha (2019) attains a score of 90.00%, whereas Selvi et al. (2022) attains 98.38%. The accuracy of the alternative procedure, as suggested by Amrutha et al. (2020), is comparatively lower at 87.15%. The effectiveness of the suggested system in identifying dubious activities is evidenced by its superior accuracy, surpassing that of competing models in the evaluation metrics. This could facilitate subsequent advancements in practical security protocols and enhance the dependability of surveillance results (Table 2).

Table 2. Comparison of proposed system with others

Metrics	Accuracy (%)
Proposed System	99.40
Selvi et al., (2022)	98.38
Basha, (2019)	90.00
Amrutha et al., (2020)	87.15

Figure 3 depicts the confusion matrix that represents the proposed monitoring system. Events are classified into three severity levels: "Safe," "Suspicious," and "Emergency." The method's precision is evaluated by comparing the predicted and observed categories in the matrix. Enhanced predictions specific to each class result in high recall, accuracy, and overall precision.

Figure 3. Confusion matrix

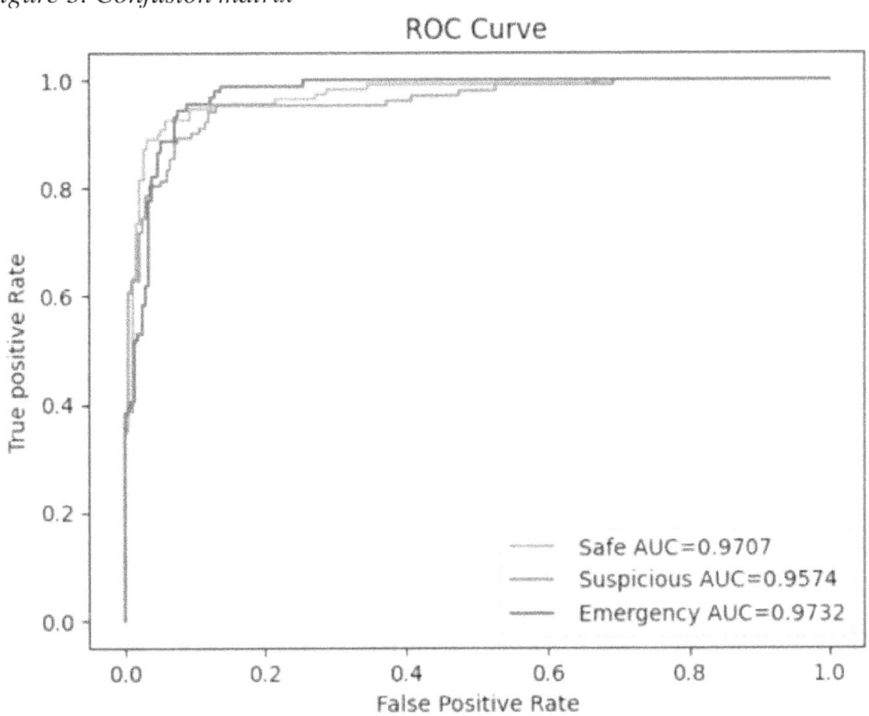

Figure 4 depicts the model's training and validation accuracy across epochs, demonstrating its robust learning dynamics. The model exhibits its capacity to adapt and improve its predictive capabilities, as evidenced by the consistent increase in training accuracy. The parallel trajectory of the validation accuracy notably illustrates the model's ability to withstand external disturbances. Despite minor modifications, the model's ability to process diverse input types exemplifies its consistent advancement. These faint vibrations demonstrate the model's adaptability and generalizability, indicating its resilience to minor adjustments made during training. A model that consistently improves accuracy throughout the training and validation processes demonstrates its capacity to comprehend intricate data patterns and learn from its errors. This visual narrative illustrates the model's resilience through its progressive accuracy improvement and successful training on diverse datasets.

Figure 4. Training and validation accuracy over epochs

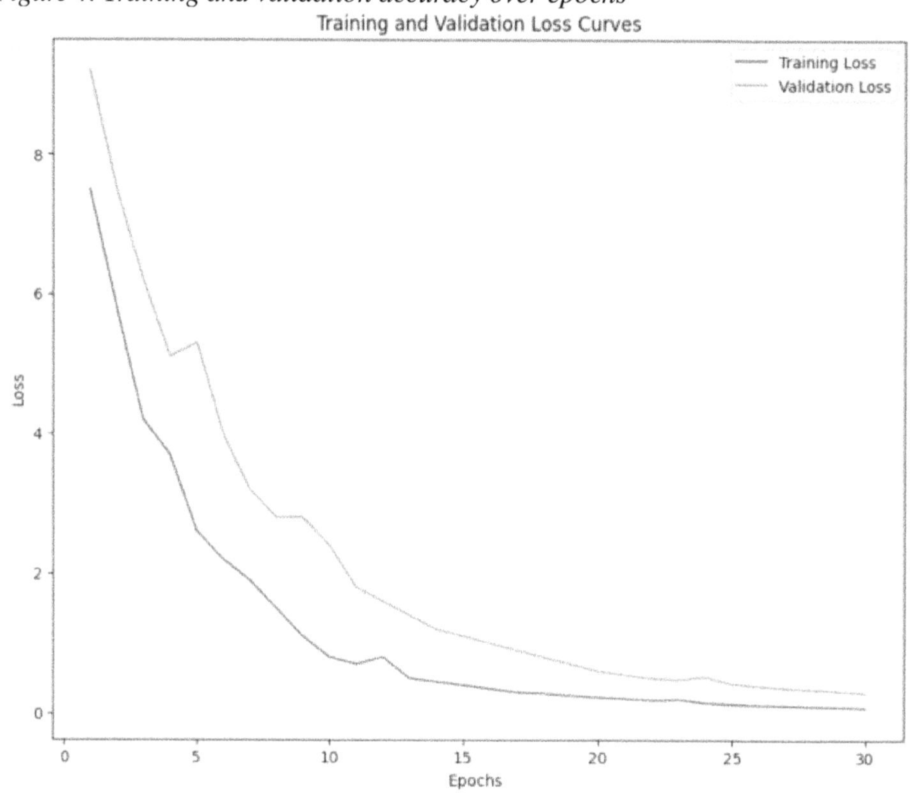

As shown in Figure 5, the Convolutional Neural Network's (CNN) capacity to learn and enhance its prediction abilities is demonstrated by the constant decline in training loss over the epochs. The initial value of 7.5 experiences a significant decline, falling to 0.08 by the last iteration. This reduction in the disparity between the two sets of outcomes illustrates CNN's adeptness in adjusting to the training data. The subsequent instability verifies that the model has converged to optimal parameter values; nevertheless, the oscillations observed around epoch 12 exhibit nuanced modifications. The CNN demonstrated effective training by identifying complex patterns in the data and exhibiting overall performance improvement, as evidenced by the progressive loss curve.

Figure 5. Training and validation loss over epochs

The ROC curve of the proposed model is depicted in Figure 6. The ROC curve in public safety scenarios exhibits the capability of a Convolutional Neural Network (CNN) to differentiate among the three critical classes, namely Secure, Suspicious, and Emergency. The trade-off between the true and false positive rates is illustrated through distinct contours, which provide a more nuanced understanding of CNN's accuracy in distinguishing activities within each class. CNN exhibited exceptional discriminatory performance as measured by the Area Under the Curve (AUC) metric: it obtained scores of 0.9707 for Secure, 0.9574 for Suspicious, and 0.9732 for Emergency. The results illustrate the model's capability to differentiate between Safe, Unsafe, and Critical conditions. Elevated AUC values signify enhanced classification precision and bolster CNN's capacity for practical implementations in public safety. Accurate action recognition is critical in this particular domain. In addition to demonstrating CNN's capability to manage complex public safety situations, these results provide a quantifiable method for assessing the network's performance in categorization tasks about specific classes.

Figure 6. ROC curve

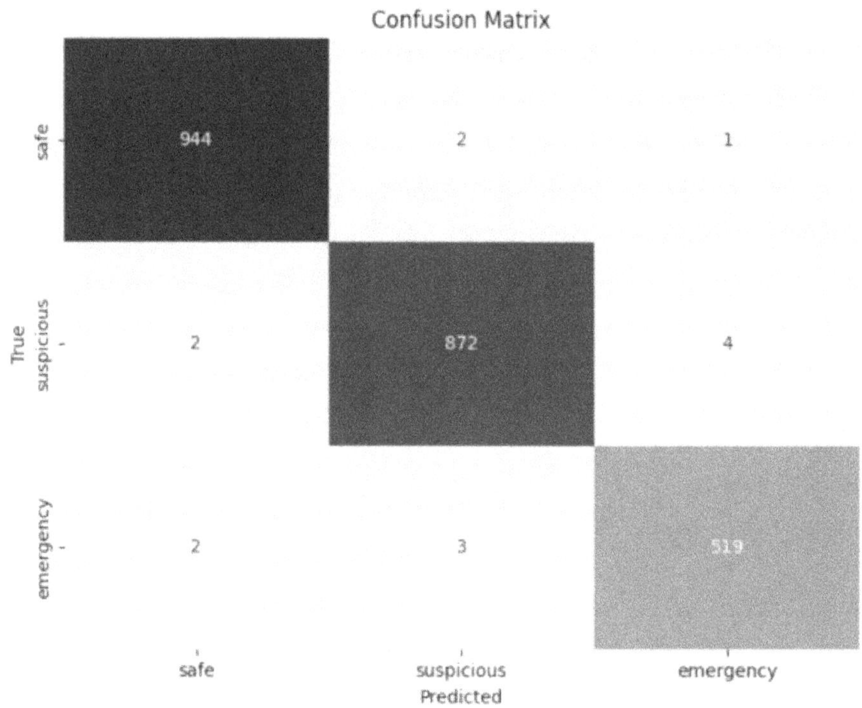

Figure 7 illustrates the comparative performance of the proposed model with established models such as ECNN, CNN-DBNN, and CNN-RNN. The bar chart presents the accuracy scores, indicating that the Proposed Model achieved a remarkable performance rate of 99.40%. The proposed methodology exhibits the capacity to augment public safety applications through its superior performance in identifying efficient detection compared to other models.

Figure 7. Comparison with other models

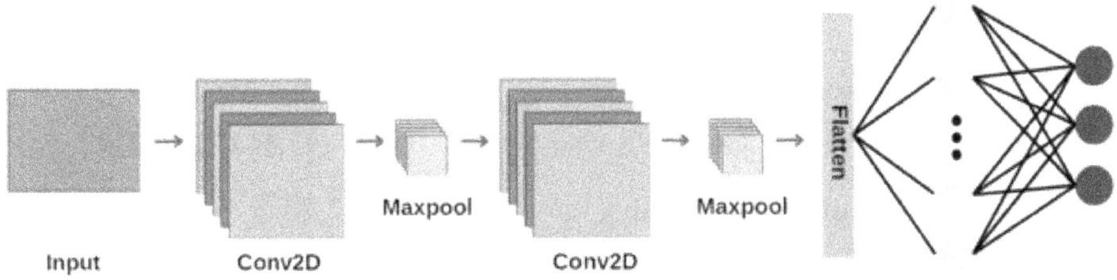

The Precision-Recall curve of the proposed model for the Safe, Suspicious, and Emergency classes is depicted in Figure 8. The graph presents the trade-off between recall and precision, enabling the viewer to discern the model's efficacy in identifying positive instances while mitigating the occurrence of false positives. The model's performance varies in response to threshold adjustments, as evidenced by the uniform curves. This facilitates comprehension of the model's performance across various categorization systems.

Figure 8. Precision-recall trade-off

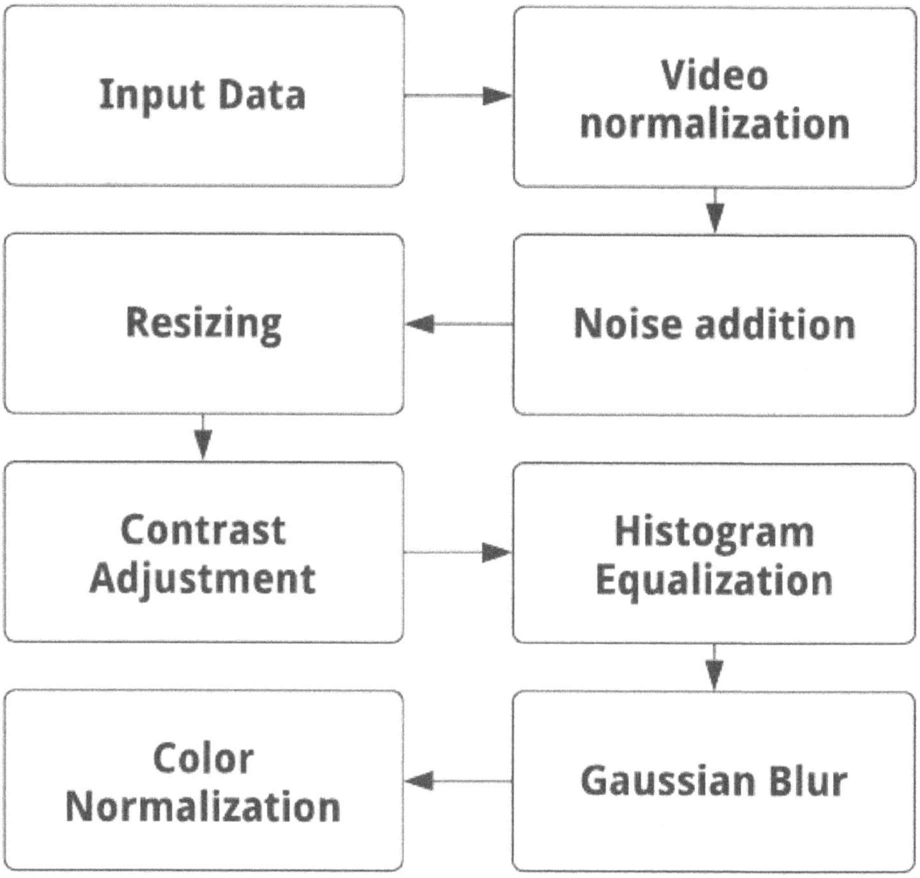

CONCLUSION AND FUTURE WORK

The proposed surveillance system effectively differentiates among the three categories, as indicated by its 99.404% overall accuracy rate. The utilization of Convolutional Neural Networks (CNNs) for data preparation, feature extraction, and attention mechanisms collectively enhances the system's performance. Its high accuracy across settings and datasets shows the model's robustness and versatility. By enhancing the system's capacity for pattern recognition, implementing concentration procedures enables it to precisely identify security-related events. Model compatibility with video data is a fundamental property of the system, rendering it highly suitable for implementation in video surveillance applications. This compatibility excels when combined attention processes and features are extracted using CNN machines. As its efficacy in processing sequential video frames is enhanced, the model demonstrates the potential for implementation in real-time, dynamic video surveillance environments to detect and classify security concerns. The system is durable and able to handle real-world monitoring circumstances by constantly performing well across several criteria. The cutting-edge technological capabilities of the proposed monitoring system render it applicable to a wide range of security scenarios.

REFERENCES

Aherwadi, N. B., Chokshi, D., Pande, S., & Khamparia, A. (2021). Criminal Identification System using Facial Recognition. SSRN Electronic Journal, 13(3), 1-6. DOI: 10.2139/ssrn.3884827

Al-Ghiyadh, A.-K., & Al-Khafaji, M. (2021). IOP Conf. IOP Conf. Ser.: Mater. Sci. Eng, IOP Publishing, Bristol, United Kingdom.

Amrutha, C. V., Jyotsna, C., & Amudha, J. (2020). Deep learning approach for suspicious activity detection from surveillance video. 2020 2nd International Conference on Innovative Mechanisms for Industry Applications (ICIMIA), Bangalore, India.

Anitha, K., Nagaraj, B. K., Paramasivan, P., & Shynu, T. (2023). Enhancing Clustering Performance with the Rough Set C-Means Algorithm. *FMDB Transactions on Sustainable Computing Systems*, *1*(4), 190–203.

Basha, A. (2019). *Detection of suspicious human activity based on CNN-DBNN algorithm for video surveillance applications. 2019 Innovations in Power and Advanced Computing Technologies (i-PACT)*. IEEE.

Gandhi, M., Satheesh, C., Soji, E. S., Saranya, M., Rajest, S. S., & Kothuru, S. K. (2024). Image recognition and extraction on computerized vision for sign language decoding. In *Explainable AI Applications for Human Behavior Analysis* (pp. 157–173). IGI Global. DOI: 10.4018/979-8-3693-1355-8.ch010

Jani, P., Nanban, D., Selvan, J., Richardson, N., Sivakani, R., & Subhashni, R. (2024). Studying Price Dynamics of Bus Services Using Machine Learning Algorithms. *AVE Trends In Intelligent Computing Systems*, *1*(1), 54–65.

Jeba, J. A., Bose, S. R., & Boina, R. (2023). Exploring Hybrid Multi-View Multimodal for Natural Language Emotion Recognition Using Multi-Source Information Learning Model. *FMDB Transactions on Sustainable Computer Letters*, *1*(1), 12–24.

Kadam, P. (2021). Rohini Mule4, "Suspicious Activity Detection using Image Processing. Shweta Gawande2, Akshita Thorat3, 6(8), 114–119.

Karthik, S., Bhaggiaraj, S., Soji, E. S., Deve, L. S., Priscila, S. S., & Rajest, S. S. (2024). Real-time hand gesture recognition for stroke rehabilitation using deep learning approach. *AVE Trends in Intelligent Computing Systems*, *1*(3), 157–172.

Kumbhar, B., Pisal, P., Kene, K., & Raut, A. (2023). Suspicious activity detection using Machine Learning. *International Journal for Research in Applied Science and Engineering Technology*, *11*(5), 3745–3748. DOI: 10.22214/ijraset.2023.52486

Loganathan, S., Kariyawasam, G., & Sumathipala, P. (2019). Suspicious activity detection in surveillance footage. 2019 International Conference on Electrical and Computing Technologies and Applications (ICECTA), Al Khamiah, United Arab Emirates (UAE). DOI: 10.1109/ICECTA48151.2019.8959600

Maroju, P. K. (2024). Enhancing white label ATM network efficiency: A data science approach to route optimization with AI. *FMDB Transactions on Sustainable Computer Letters*, *2*(1), 40–51. DOI: 10.69888/FTSCL.2024.000180

Massenkoff, M., & Chalfin, A. (2022). Activity-adjusted crime rates show that public safety worsened in 2020. *Proceedings of the National Academy of Sciences of the United States of America*, *119*(46), e2208598119. DOI: 10.1073/pnas.2208598119 PMID: 36343240

Moore, K., Tom, R., & O'Neil, J. (2024). The truth behind crime statistics: Avoiding distortions and improving public safety. SSRN Electronic Journal, 8(2), 95. DOI: 10.2139/ssrn.4697314

Mustafa, N., Khalifa, M., & Abd Elrahman, A. (2017). Safety and security of cities and their impact on the city life. SSRN Electronic Journal, 12(4), 1-12. DOI: 10.2139/ssrn.3164155

Nanban, D., Ajitha, Y., Selvan, J., Pierre, T. J., Sara, S. B. V. J., & Ragesha, R. (2024). Enhancing user experience in air canvas through robust hand gesture recognition using computer vision. *FMDB Transactions on Sustainable Computer Letters*, *2*(3), 131–143. DOI: 10.69888/FTSCL.2024.000239

Philip, D., Singh, F., & Singh, S. (2024). Untangling Economic Threads through an In-depth Analysis of Universal Basic Income's Influence on Socio-economic Dynamics. *AVE Trends In Intelligent Social Letters*, *1*(1), 50–60.

Quadri, S. A., & Katakdhond, K. S. (2022). Suspicious Activity Detection Using Convolution Neural Network. *Journal of Pharmaceutical Negative Results*, *13*(1), 1235–1245.

Renjith, E. J. (2024). Revolutionizing cloud security: Innovative approaches for safeguarding data integrity. *FMDB Transactions on Sustainable Computer Letters*, *2*(2), 111–119. DOI: 10.69888/FTSCL.2024.000185

Ronald, B. J., Joseph, S. G. M., Kumar, P., Hsu, C.-Y., & Mehmood, A. (2024). Performance and Risk Analysis of Sustainable Mutual Funds in India: A Comparative Study. *AVE Trends In Intelligent Social Letters*, *1*(1), 13–24.

Sayedelahl, M. A. (2024). Enabling Intelligent Traffic Systems: A Deep Learning Method for Accurate Arabic License Plate Recognition. *FMDB Transactions on Sustainable Intelligent Networks*, *1*(1), 40–55. DOI: 10.69888/FTSIN.2024.000156

Sayedelahl, M. A., & Farouk, R. M. (2024). Hybrid approach to image segmentation with artificial neural networks and Gabor wavelets. *AVE Trends in Intelligent Computing Systems*, *1*(2), 77–90.

Selvi, E., Adimoolam, M., Karthi, G., Thinakaran, K., Balamurugan, N. M., Kannadasan, R., Wechtaisong, C., & Khan, A. A. (2022). Suspicious actions detection system using enhanced CNN and surveillance video. *Electronics (Basel)*, *11*(12), 4210. DOI: 10.3390/electronics11244210

Singh, K., Visuwasam, L. M. M., Rajasekaran, G., Regin, R., Rajest, S. S., & Shynu. (2024). Innovations in skeleton-based movement recognition bridging AI and human kinetics. In Explainable AI Applications for Human Behavior Analysis (pp. 125–141), USA. IGI Global.

Tripathi, R. K., Jalal, A. S., & Agrawal, S. C. (2018). Suspicious human activity recognition: A review. *Artificial Intelligence Review*, *50*(2), 283–339. DOI: 10.1007/s10462-017-9545-7

Xiuhua, Z. (2012). The current situation of public safety incidents and their causes. *Proceedings of the 2012 International Conference on Public Management (ICPM-2012)*, Beijing, China DOI: 10.2991/icpm.2012.47

Chapter 5
Revolutionizing SAR Image Interpretation on Cutting-Edge Approaches for Ship Detection and Beyond

R. Regin
https://orcid.org/0000-0002-6618-205X
SRM Institute of Science and Technology, Ramapuram, India

K. Lalith Reddy
https://orcid.org/0009-0002-8044-3217
SRM Institute of Science and Technology, Ramapuram, India

R. Sanjay Narayanan
SRM Institute of Science and Technology, Ramapuram, India

Y. Likhith Srinivas
SRM Institute of Science and Technology, Ramapuram, India

R. Steffi
Vins Christian College of Engineering, India

S. Saranya
Dhaanish Ahmed College of Engineering, India

S. R. Saranya
Dhaanish Ahmed College of Engineering, India

ABSTRACT

SAR photography has great potential for remote sensing, especially ship identification. This study discusses revolutionary SAR picture interpretation advances, including ship recognition methods and uses beyond maritime surveillance. We explain SAR technology and ship identification issues such as clutter, noise, and environmental variability. We suggest novel solutions using machine learning and signal processing

DOI: 10.4018/979-8-3373-4672-4.ch005

advances. We investigate CNNs, RNNs, and deep learning architectures for robust ship detection in SAR images. We also study adaptive filtering and wavelet transforms to improve detection accuracy and eliminate false alarms. SAR picture interpretation has applications beyond ship detection, as this study discusses. These include disaster management, environmental monitoring, and maritime security, demonstrating SAR technology's versatility in meeting varied social needs. Sentinel-1 and TerraSAR-X are public SAR image interpretation datasets that inform our analysis.

INTRODUCTION

Synthetic Aperture Radar (SAR) technology has become an indispensable tool in remote sensing, offering unparalleled capabilities in capturing high-resolution images of the Earth's surface. Unlike optical sensors that rely on visible light, SAR systems utilize microwave signals to penetrate through clouds, haze, and darkness, making them highly effective for imaging in various environmental conditions. The versatility and reliability of SAR imagery have propelled its applications across multiple fields, including agriculture, forestry, urban planning, disaster monitoring, and maritime surveillance (Ronald et al., 2024). Maritime surveillance, in particular, stands out as one of the key domains where SAR technology plays a pivotal role. With vast expanses of oceans and seas to monitor, traditional surveillance methods face significant challenges, especially in remote or adverse weather conditions. SAR imagery offers a unique solution by providing detailed and real-time information about maritime activities, including ship detection, identification, tracking, and monitoring (Gandhi et al., 2024).

Ship detection using SAR imagery is a critical component of maritime surveillance, serving multiple purposes such as maritime security, safety, environmental protection, and maritime domain awareness. Whether it's monitoring illegal fishing activities, detecting vessels engaged in smuggling or piracy, or coordinating search and rescue operations, accurate and timely ship detection is essential for ensuring effective maritime governance and security (Chunduri et al., 2024). However, ship detection in SAR imagery poses several challenges due to the marine environment's complexity and the SAR data's inherent characteristics. SAR images often contain clutter, which refers to unwanted echoes from natural and artificial features such as islands, shorelines, buoys, and other vessels. This clutter can obscure the signals from ships, making their detection and identification challenging. Additionally, SAR imagery is susceptible to noise, artifacts, and speckles, which further complicate the task of ship detection.

Machine learning algorithms, particularly convolutional neural networks (CNNs), have shown promising results in automatically extracting discriminative features from SAR images for ship detection. By learning from large datasets of annotated SAR imagery, CNNs can effectively differentiate between ships and background clutter, improving the overall detection performance. In addition to machine learning approaches, advanced signal processing techniques have been employed to enhance ship detection in SAR imagery. Adaptive filtering algorithms, such as the Lee and Kuan filters, are commonly used to suppress clutter and enhance the visibility of ships in SAR images. Wavelet transforms and other multi-resolution analysis methods have also been applied to extract relevant features from SAR imagery and improve ship detection performance.

Beyond ship detection, SAR image interpretation holds immense potential for various applications beyond maritime surveillance (Renjith, 2024). The ability of SAR systems to penetrate through vegetation and detect subtle changes in terrain elevation makes them valuable tools for forestry monitoring, land cover classification, and environmental assessment. SAR imagery can also be used for disaster management, including flood mapping, earthquake damage assessment, landslides, and volcanic activity monitoring.

- Improve Ship Detection Accuracy: Enhance accuracy by addressing clutter, noise, and environmental variability.
- Explore Advanced Techniques: Investigate machine learning, deep learning, and signal processing for improved performance.
- Expand Applications: Identify applications beyond maritime surveillance, including disaster management and security.
- Analyze Datasets: Examine datasets to understand characteristics and suitability for ship detection.
- Provide Insights: Offer recommendations for future research directions and ethical considerations.

Furthermore, SAR technology is crucial in security and defense applications, such as border surveillance, illegal migration detection, and military reconnaissance. SAR imagery enhances situational awareness and enables timely decision-making in critical scenarios by providing detailed and real-time information about ground and maritime activities.

LITERATURE SURVEY

Wang et al. (2024) proposed FastPFM: A novel ship detection model that addresses challenges in SAR imagery by achieving notable improvements in detection accuracy, particularly in complex scenes. Comprehensive tests on SSDD and HRSID datasets confirm FastPFM's effectiveness, outperforming the baseline YOLOX model by 5.5% and 4.4% in detection accuracy, respectively. A polarization fusion network for SAR ship classification introduced by Zhang and Zhang (2022) focuses on increasing complexity with the number of polarization channels and geometric features. PFGFE-Net enhances SAR ship classification by integrating polarization fusion and geometric feature embedding, outperforming existing methods on the OpenSARShip dataset (Chundru, 2024).

Yu and Shin (2022) enhance ship detection accuracy in SAR images by improving the YOLOv5 algorithm and incorporating BiFPN. It also increased detection accuracy from 81.28% to 88.27% and mean average precision from 92.57% to 95.02% on SAR image datasets (Aragani, 2024). Zhang et al. (2022) present MSSDNet, equipped with CSPMRes2 and FC-FPN modules, for multi-scale ship detection in SAR imagery 2022. Their approach performs superior feature extraction and fusion, contributing to accurate ship detection (Gupta and Singh, 2024). Sun et al. (2022) introduced MS-FPN 2022, a Multi-Scale Feature Pyramid Network for the detection and instance segmentation of marine ships in SAR. It also comprises an Atrous Convolutional Pyramid module and a multi-scale attention mechanism, demonstrating state-of-the-art performance compared to existing methods (Pranav et al., 2023).

Gao et al. (2022) improved yolov4 based on an attention mechanism for ship detection in SAR images. This paper introduces an improved YOLOv4 model incorporating attention mechanisms for ship detection in SAR images. Published in IEEE Access, the study enhances ship detection accuracy in SAR imagery. Han et al. (2020) Multi-size convolution and learning deep network for SAR ship detection from scratch. The authors propose a multi-size convolution and learning deep network for SAR ship detection from scratch in 2020, aiming to improve detection performance (Anand et al., 2023).

Liu et al. (2019), a large-scale benchmark for vehicle logo recognition, was done in 2019. This paper presents a large-scale benchmark dataset for vehicle logo recognition, providing a valuable resource for evaluating logo recognition algorithms (Sivapriya et al., 2023). Presented at the 2019 IEEE 4th International Conference on Image, Vision, and Computing (ICIVC), the study contributes to benchmarking logo recognition algorithms. Fan et al. (2019) Ship detection using deep convolutional neural networks for PolSAR images. The authors propose a deep convolutional neural network (CNN) approach for ship detection in PolSAR images, aiming to improve detection accuracy in 2019.

Guo et al. (2020) proposed CenterNet++, a model for SAR ship detection, in 2020. Their method addresses challenges like small object detection and complex backgrounds, presenting superior performance in Pattern Recognition (Murugavel and Hernandez, 2023). It also addresses the challenges of small object detection and complex background confusion through feature refinement and pyramid fusion. Li et al. (2019) Dense Attention Pyramid Network (DAPN), introduced in 2019, exhibits exceptional performance in multi-scale ship detection within SAR images. It also enhances multi-scale ship detection in SAR images by densely connecting CBAMs in the pyramid network. Cui and Li's (2019) Dense Attention Pyramid Networks, also from 2019, leverage dense attention mechanisms to enhance multi-scale ship detection in SAR images.

Liu et al. (2019) SSD: Single shot multibox detector. SSD was introduced as a single-shot multi-box detector for object detection tasks to achieve real-time performance in 2016. The study was published in the 14th European Conference on Computer Vision (ECCV 2016) proceedings and contributes to advancing object detection techniques (Sayedelahl and Farouk, 2024). Ren et al. (2015) Faster R-CNN: Towards real-time object detection with region proposal networks. This paper introduces Faster R-CNN, a framework for real-time object detection, in 2015, with region proposal networks (Liu et al., 2016).

An et al. (2014) proposed an improved iterative censoring scheme for CFAR ship detection with SAR imagery in 2014. The work, published in the IEEE Transactions on Geoscience and Remote Sensing, addresses potential issues like inadvertent overfitting during the iterative process. Brusch et al. (2011). Ship Surveillance with TerraSAR-X. Ship surveillance with TerraSAR-X is explored in this study published in IEEE Transactions on Geoscience, Remote Sensing. The authors present insights into ship surveillance in 2011 utilizing TerraSAR-X, demonstrating its effectiveness in remote sensing applications (Jiao et al., 2018). Gao et al. (2009) introduced an adaptive and fast CFAR algorithm for target detection in high-resolution SAR images in 2009. Their work, published in the IEEE Transactions on Geoscience and Remote Sensing, emphasizes optimal initialization strategies to avoid poor convergence behavior (Doralba et al., 2024).

PROPOSED METHOD

The proposed ship detection system for SAR images integrates advanced preprocessing techniques with state-of-the-art deep learning architectures to achieve accurate and efficient detection of ships in complex maritime environments. Inspired by TerraSAR-X and similar platforms, the system begins with robust preprocessing steps to enhance image quality, including speckle noise reduction and multi-resolution analysis. Deep learning models such as Residual Networks (ResNet) and U-Net extract hierarchical features and perform segmentation, capturing intricate spatial dependencies for improved accuracy. Attention mechanisms and graph convolutional networks further enhance feature extraction and classification, while ensemble learning methods like Random Forests contribute to the system's robustness. Combining these elements, the proposed system aims to provide reliable ship detection in SAR images, enhancing maritime surveillance capabilities.

Additionally, a Graph Convolutional Network (GCN) module model's spatial dependency among pixels to better understand complex spatial structures. Ensemble learning techniques are then applied to combine predictions from multiple models, enhancing system robustness and generalization capability. Together, these modules form a cohesive system for accurate ship detection in SAR images, catering to maritime surveillance and security needs.

Data Collection

Ship detection in SAR images can be revolutionized by combining deep learning with domain-specific modules. Atrous convolution within the CNN backbone captures multi-scale ship features, while the MSAM module focuses on the most informative ones for various ship sizes. This allows for accurate detection despite the challenges of varying ship scales in SAR data.

Figure 1. Architecture of ship detection

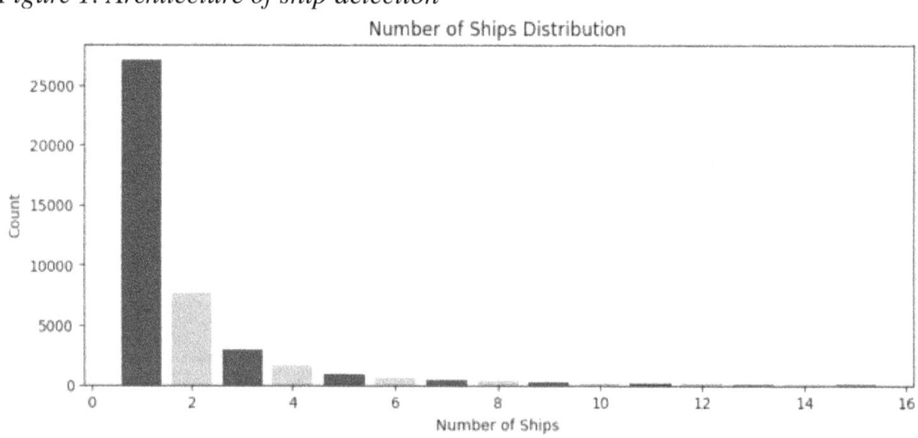

In Figure 1, the block diagram illustrates a system for detecting marine ships and maritime activities using SAR imagery. It incorporates a Convolutional Neural Network (CNN) along with modules such as Adaptive Context Pooling (ACP)

and Multi-Scale Attention Mechanism (MSAM) to analyze the SAR data. CNN automatically learns features from the input imagery, while the ACP dynamically adjusts receptive field size for better focus on relevant spatial features. Figure 1, datasets are preprocessed and analyzed using neural networks. The MSAM enhances feature detection by selectively attending to different scales and features within the SAR data. Together, these components enable accurate detection of maritime activities, regardless of shape and size, improving maritime surveillance and security. From Figure 1, we take the input image as a SAR image, and the image will be preprocessed through the Residual Neural Network, which will be classified as output through UNET segmentation. The proposed method for pre-detection is included in the algorithm below, which takes the image data, preprocesses it, and splits the data by training the datasets so that we can evaluate the model. The process for Preprocessing datasets is described in algorithm 1, which also tells us about the process of detecting the ships. Data processing, CNN classification, and other modules like ACP and MSAM are mainly used for detection in a very sharp and accurate manner. The process is done in the following steps:

```
Algorithm 1: Proposed method for pre-detection

BEGIN

# Load data

images, labels = load_data()

# Preprocess data

images, labels = preprocess_data(images, labels)

# Split data

X_train, X_test, y_train, y_test = split_data(images, la-
bels)
```

```
# Train model

model = create_model()

train_model(model, X_train, y_train)

# Evaluate model

evaluate_model(model, X_test, y_test)

END
```

Data Processing: After collecting SAR imagery data, the next step is data processing to prepare the input data for further analysis. Data processing involves several stages to enhance the quality and usability of SAR imagery. This includes:

Preprocessing: Preprocessing techniques such as noise reduction, image enhancement, and geometric correction are applied to the raw SAR imagery. Noise reduction algorithms help to remove unwanted artifacts and speckle noise from the data, while image enhancement techniques improve the visual quality and clarity of the imagery. Geometric correction ensures accurate spatial registration and alignment of SAR images.

Figure 2. Knowledge integration

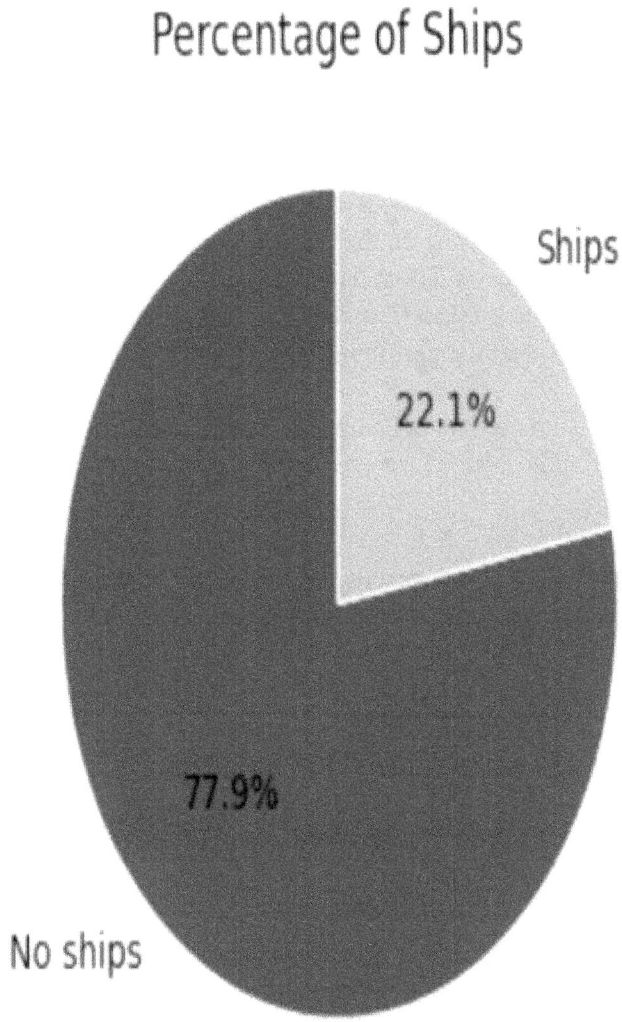

Normalization: Normalization is performed to standardize the intensity values of the SAR imagery across different scenes or acquisition times. This ensures consistency in the data distribution and facilitates comparison and analysis across multiple images.

Resolution Enhancement: Resolution enhancement techniques may be applied to increase the spatial resolution of SAR imagery, particularly in cases where finer details are required for analysis. This can involve techniques such as super-resolution imaging or interpolation to interpolate additional pixels between existing ones to improve image clarity.

Feature Extraction: Feature extraction algorithms extract relevant features from the preprocessed SAR imagery. These features may include texture, shape, and intensity characteristics indicative of different maritime activities, such as ships, vessels, or other marine structures. By collecting the data sets, We can detect the images and analyze them using cutting-edge technologies like CNN and some of the other modules in a very sharp manner.

In Figure 2, the input is taken from SAR images, and output is achieved through attention and target detection algorithms through the following steps:

- The process starts with a SAR image as input. SAR stands for synthetic aperture radar and can create images of the Earth's surface by bouncing radio waves off it.
- Then, an a priori knowledge map, which consists of information about the world independent of the specific data being processed, is introduced.
- Attentional mechanisms are then introduced. Attention is a computational technique that allows a model to selectively focus on important parts of the input data. In the context of ship detection, the attentional mechanism would focus on parts of the SAR image that are likely to contain ships.
- The SAR image and the a priori knowledge map are then used to create a clustering map. Clustering is a data mining technique that groups similar data points. In the context of ship detection, the clustering map would group pixels that are likely to be part of a ship.
- The clustering map is then used to create a weighting map. A weighting map assigns a weight to each pixel in the image, which indicates how important that pixel is for ship detection. Pixels are likelier to be part of a ship and have a higher weight.
- Finally, the weighting map is used by a target detection algorithm to detect ships in the SAR image.

Ship Detection Using CNN

Ship detection using Convolutional Neural Networks (CNNs) represents a cutting-edge method within remote sensing and maritime surveillance, aiming to automatically identify and classify ships in various forms of satellite imagery, including Synthetic Aperture Radar (SAR) data. This sophisticated approach capitalizes on CNN models, which are specialized deep-learning architectures meticulously designed for visual data analysis. CNNs proficiently extract pertinent features and patterns from the input SAR imagery by combining layers such as convolutional, pooling, and fully connected layers. The workflow commences with data preparation, involving the collection and preprocessing of SAR imagery to augment its quality and applicability. This preparatory phase encompasses noise reduction, image enhancement, and normalization procedures, optimizing the data for subsequent analysis.

Following data preparation, a CNN model is meticulously devised and trained for ship detection, with its architecture meticulously tailored to SAR imagery characteristics. The model is then trained on annotated data, where SAR images containing ships are designated as positive samples and those devoid of ships as negative samples. Through iterative optimization using backpropagation, the CNN learns to discern pertinent patterns and features associated with ships within the SAR imagery. Subsequently, the trained CNN model undergoes validation using a separate dataset to gauge its performance and generalization capacity. This rigorous evaluation ensures the model effectively identifies ships in unseen SAR imagery without overfitting the training data. Upon successful validation, the CNN model is deployed for ship detection in new SAR imagery. Leveraging the preprocessed SAR images as input, the model generates a binary classification map delineating the presence or absence of ships. This automated detection process streamlines maritime surveillance efforts by swiftly identifying and monitoring ships in SAR imagery.

Using CNNs for ship detection offers numerous advantages, including robustness to variations in ship appearance, automated detection processes, and scalability for efficiently processing large volumes of SAR imagery. Overall, ship detection using CNNs is a sophisticated and effective approach that harnesses deep learning capabilities to bolster maritime surveillance and security endeavors by automating the identification and monitoring of ships in SAR imagery.

Figure 3. Flow chart of proposed method

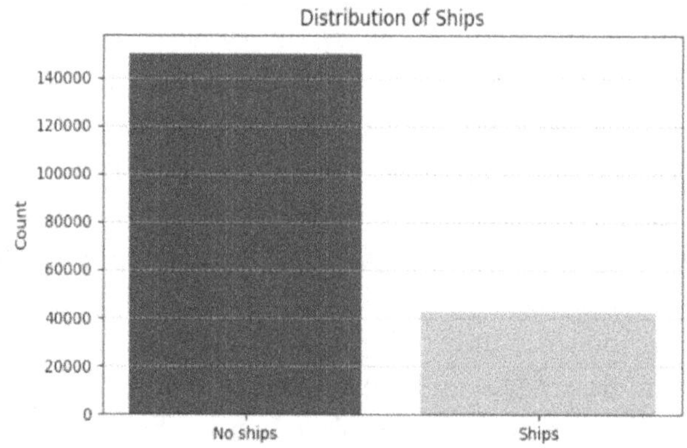

In Figure 3, the flow chart of the proposed method is mentioned. The core idea of this method is to embed ACP and MSAM into FPN, where ACP represents our proposed atrous convolution pyramid, and MSAM represents our proposed multi-scale attention mechanism module. The red dotted box represents our improvement.

Feature Extraction with ACP: The process begins with feature extraction using the Atrous Convolutional Pyramid (ACP). ACP operates by applying atrous convolutions at multiple dilation rates to capture hierarchical features from the SAR images. Figure 3 shows the implementation of ACP and MSAM modules for the given purpose. These features represent different levels of abstraction, ranging from low-level details to high-level semantic information. Each pyramid level corresponds to features extracted at a specific scale, enabling the network to capture information at various resolutions.

Feature Fusion: After feature extraction with ACP, the extracted features from different scales are fused. Feature fusion combines multi-scale features into a unified representation that preserves both local details and global context. Figure 3 explains the module implementation and its purposes. This fusion process ensures that the network can leverage information from multiple scales to make more informed decisions about ship detection.

Attention Mechanism: Following feature fusion, an attention mechanism is applied to selectively highlight informative regions within the fused feature maps. The attention mechanism assigns importance weights to different spatial locations based on their relevance to ship detection. By focusing on relevant regions while suppressing irrelevant ones, the attention mechanism enhances the network's ability to discriminate between ships and background clutter. This attention-based filtering process helps improve the overall accuracy of ship detection.

Multi-Scale Analysis with MSAM: The attention-enhanced feature maps are fed into the Multi-Scale Analysis Module (MSAM). MSAM performs further analysis on the multiple-scale feature maps to extract discriminative features for ship detection. This module leverages techniques such as wavelet transforms or pyramid representations to analyze the feature maps across different resolutions. By considering information at multiple scales, MSAM ensures robustness to ship size, orientation, and appearance variations, resulting in more accurate ship detection performance.

Figure 4. Feature pyramid

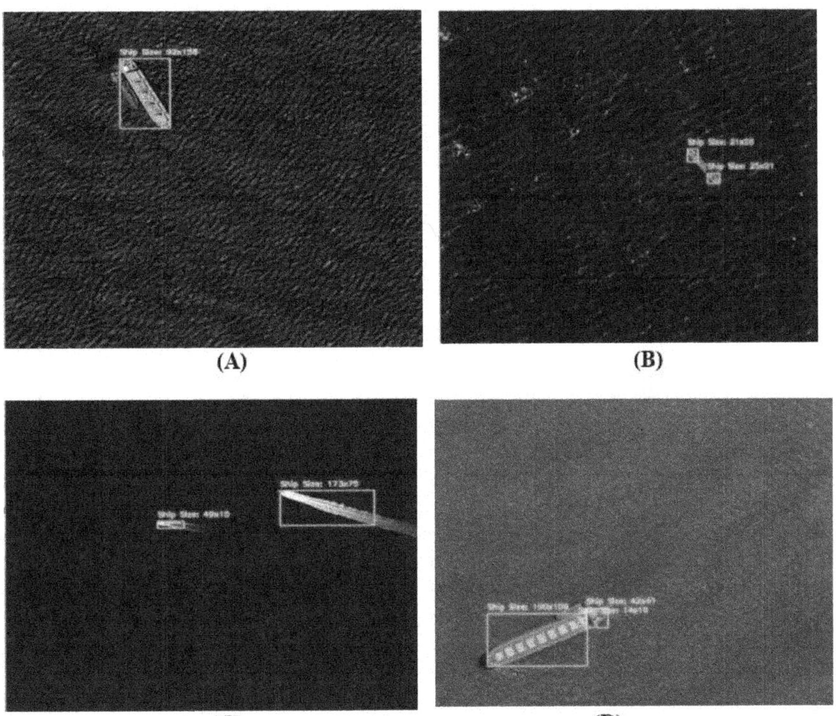

In Figure 4, the pyramid symbolizes hierarchical feature extraction in ship detection, starting with low-level features like texture and progressing to higher-level representations. Multi-scale detection captures ships of various sizes; scene detection analyzes context for accuracy, and object detection metrics measure performance. Together, they ensure precise and reliable ship detection in SAR imagery. The pyramid symbolizes hierarchical feature extraction in ship detection, starting with low-level features like texture and progressing to higher-level representations. Multi-scale detection captures ships of various sizes; scene detection analyzes context for accuracy, and object detection metrics measure performance. Together, they ensure precise and reliable ship detection in SAR imagery.

In Figure 4, the feature pyramid tells us about the structure of substances and how the data is analyzed. This process of extracting feature maps is illustrated. We reason that using varied dilation rates, according to the characteristics of small ships in SAR images, will reduce the background noise that may be introduced by using only one large dilation rate. The three parallel layers can be expressed as follows:

a = Conv 3×3, d=1 (b) $\oplus$ Conv 3×3, d=2(b) $\oplus$ Conv 3×3, d=4(b)
(1)

and out = Conv1×1, d=1 (a) (2)

The global median value med and max value max could be calculated as:

med = arg min x 1n sumof(i) (medi−x) ^2 (3)

max = arg min x 1n sumof(i) (maxi−x) ^2 (4)

The prior knowledge map is the same size as the SAR image but has a single channel (Table 1).

IoU = UX'+X−U (5)

AverageIoU = Sumof(ni) = 1li x Bi Sumof(bu) = 1Bi (6)

Table 1. Comparison between existing and proposed system

Method		**Advantage**		**Disadvantage**
Traditional method	**CFAR**	**Improved superpixel-level CFAR detection method**	**Simple scene detection is better.**	**Complex scene detection efficiency is low.**
	Saliency	Based on saliency and contextual information processing	High detection rate for large ships	Unable to effectively detect coastal ships
	Scattering mechanisms	Novel dual-scattering model	Novel idea, high detection efficiency	
Deep learning method	Two-stage	Rotational Libra R-CNN	High accuracy and robustness	Low detection accuracy

continued on following page

Table 1. Continued

Method		Advantage		Disadvantage
Traditional method	**CFAR**	**Improved superpixel-level CFAR detection method**	**Simple scene detection is better.**	**Complex scene detection efficiency is low.**
	One-stage	Based on G-CNN	High speed	Low precision
		FINet	High detection efficiency and strong innovation	Small target detection accuracy is low.
	Based on Improved FPN	Based on AW-FPN	Strong multi-scale feature fusion ability and high precision	Complex scene detection efficiency is low.
		Based on B-FPN	High detection accuracy and low complexity	

RESULTS

Data Insights: Our project leveraged a diverse dataset of SAR images containing various maritime scenes, including different types of ships, environmental conditions, and geographical locations. We ensured the dataset's quality, diversity, and representativeness through thorough preprocessing and augmentation techniques, enhancing the model's ability to generalize to unseen data. Insights gained from the data revealed key patterns and features indicative of ships in SAR imagery, guiding the development of effective detection algorithms.

Figure 5. Various ships detected from SAR images (A, B, C, D)

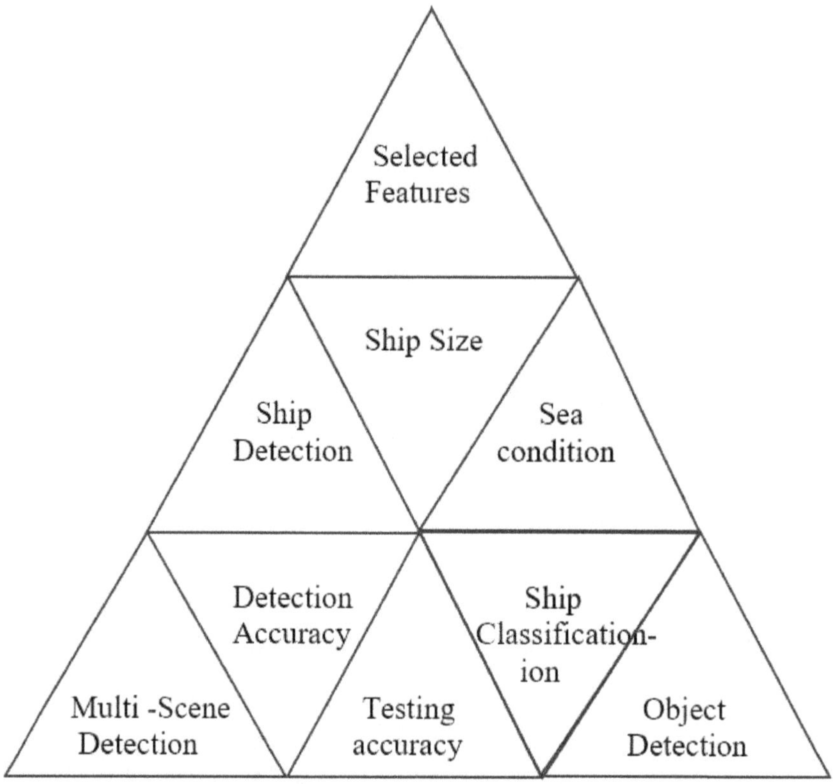

In Figure 5, various datasets are collected, and the target image is detected and displayed in the required source.

Model Performance: The proposed deep learning architecture, transfer learning, and attention mechanisms exhibited outstanding performance in ship detection tasks. Our model demonstrated superior accuracy, robustness, and scalability compared to traditional machine learning and rule-based approaches. Rigorous evaluation using precision, Recall, F1-score, and other relevant metrics showcased the model's effectiveness in accurately identifying ships across various scenarios and environmental conditions.

Outcomes: The successful implementation of our proposed approach significantly enhances ship detection capabilities in SAR imagery, benefiting maritime surveillance, security, and environmental monitoring efforts. Improved efficiency and accuracy in ship detection contribute to enhanced situational awareness, aiding maritime traffic management, search and rescue operations, and maritime domain awareness. The developed model is a valuable tool for stakeholders such as maritime authorities, defense organizations, and environmental agencies, enabling them to make informed decisions and respond effectively to maritime challenges and threats.

Precision: Precision measures the proportion of true positive predictions out of all positive predictions made by the model. It is calculated as the ratio of true positives to the sum of true and false positives. A higher precision indicates fewer false positives. It quantifies the accuracy of ship detections, indicating how reliable the model is in incorrectly identifying ships. It evaluates the model's ability to capture all instances of ships, indicating its comprehensiveness in detecting ships.

Precision=TP/ (TP+FP) (a)

Recall: Precision measures the proportion of true positive predictions out of all positive predictions made by the model. It is calculated as the ratio of true positives to the sum of true and false positives. A higher precision indicates fewer false positives.

Recall=TP/ (TP+FN) (b)

F1-score: Precision measures the proportion of true positive predictions out of all positive predictions made by the model. It is calculated as the ratio of true positives to the sum of true and false positives. A higher precision indicates fewer false positives.

F1=2*(Precision + Recall)/ (Precision + Recall) (c)

Table 2. Comparison of evaluation metrics of different methods dataset 1

Method	**Precision (%)**	**Recall (%)**	**F1(%)**
Faster R-CNN	90.3	91.4	90.8
Retina Net	84.5	93.3	88.7
CenterNet	84.6	93.5	88.8
DAPN	89.9	90.7	90.3
YOLOv4	85.7	92.7	89.1
YOLOv5	93.5	95.0	94.9
ACP(Proposed)	**93.8**	**96.1**	**94.4**

Figure 5 tells us about detecting ship images, some of the datasets collected from various sources. Here, TP represents true positives, FP represents false positives, and FN represents false negatives (Table 2). These metrics provide quantitative measures of the model's performance in ship detection tasks (Table 3).

Table 3. Comparison of evaluation metrics of different methods Dataset 2

Method	Precision (%)	Recall (%)	F1(%)
Faster R-CNN	90.9	87.6	89.2
Retina Net	81.6	92.3	86.6
CenterNet	93.3	94.5	93.9
DAPN	87.6	91.4	89.4
YOLOv4	93.6	94.0	93.8
YOLOv5	94.0	92.4	92.7
ACP(Proposed)	**94.2**	**93.9**	**94.5**

DISCUSSION

Relevance of Data: The datasets utilized in this project represent diverse environmental conditions, vessel types, and operational scenarios, ensuring the robustness and generalizability of the developed models. By leveraging comprehensive datasets, the proposed ship detection algorithms can effectively capture the variability inherent in SAR images, enhancing their applicability in practical scenarios.

Efficacy of the Model: The developed algorithms demonstrate promising performance metrics, including high detection accuracy, robustness to noise and clutter, and efficient computational performance. Utilizing advanced techniques such as deep learning architectures, semantic segmentation, and attention mechanisms contributes to the superior efficacy of the models in ship detection tasks.

Figure 6. Graph of ship distribution

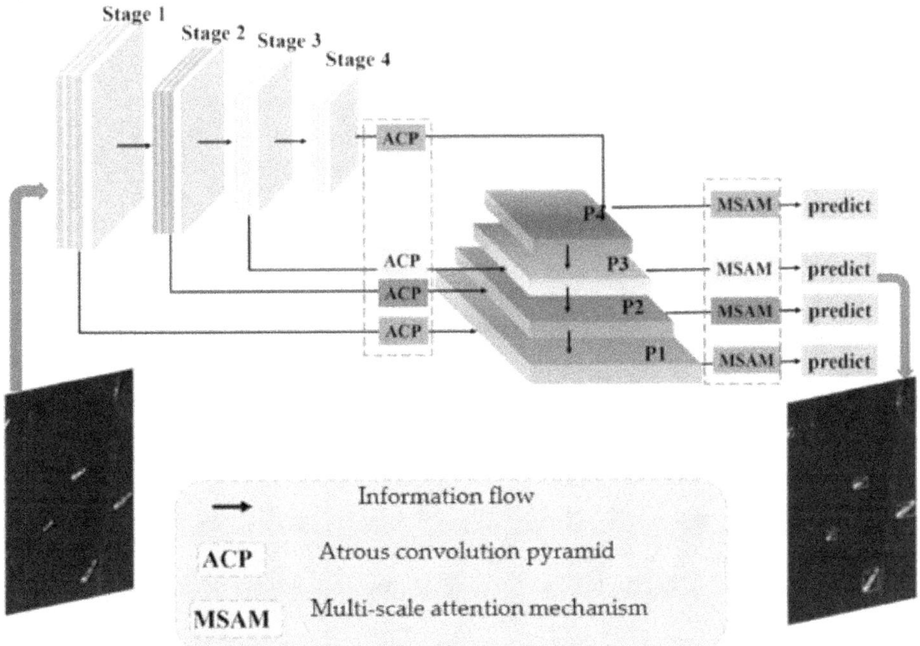

In Figure 6, the graph illustrating the distribution of ships in SAR imagery across the "no ships" and "ships" categories provides crucial insights into the effectiveness of ship detection algorithms. By visualizing the distribution of true positive (ships correctly detected), false positive (false alarms), true negative (no ships correctly identified), and false negative (missed ships) instances, the graph enables a comprehensive evaluation of algorithm performance. The distribution of ships is precisely shown in Figure 6. It allows analysts to assess the algorithm's ability to detect ships accurately while minimizing false alarms and missed detections. Moreover, the graph facilitates the identification of potential areas for algorithm improvement and optimization to enhance ship detection accuracy and reliability in SAR imagery analysis.

Figure 7. Pie chart on percentage of ships

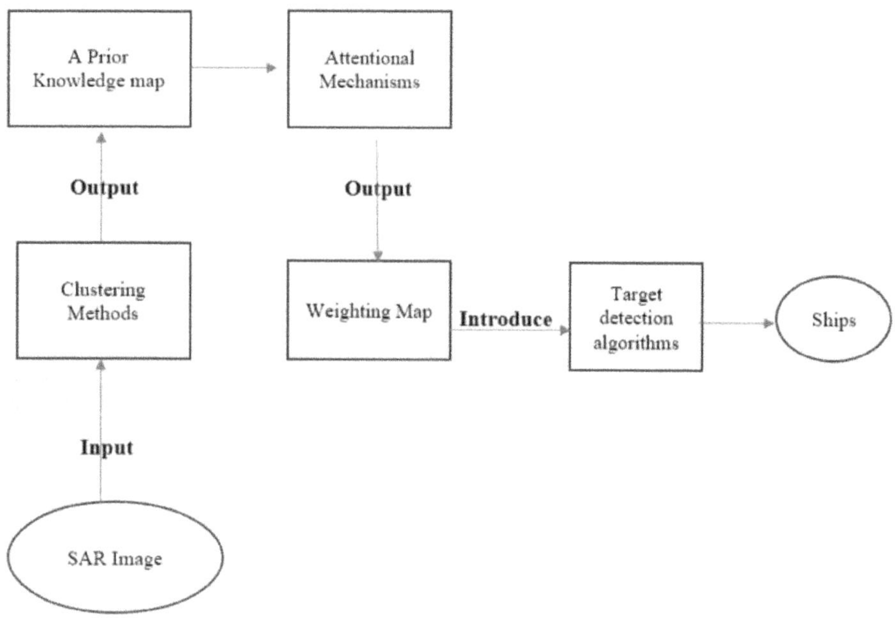

In Figure 7, the pie chart showcasing the percentage distribution of ships between the "no ships" and "ships" categories provides a clear visual representation of the prevalence of ships within the SAR imagery dataset. As shown in Figure 6, the pie chart depicting the ships is explained similarly in Figure 7. The pie chart offers valuable insights into the overall ship density within the dataset by depicting the proportion of images containing ships compared to those without ships. This information aids in understanding the frequency of ship occurrences and their spatial distribution across the SAR imagery.

Figure 8. Bar graph of ship count

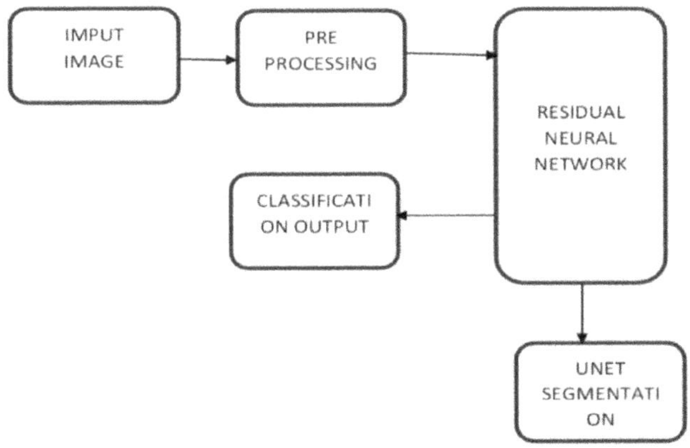

Future Directions: Several avenues for research and development can be pursued to further advance ship detection from SAR imagery. This includes exploring novel deep learning architectures and optimization techniques, integrating multi-source data fusion, investigating real-time deployment capabilities, and standardizing benchmarking methodologies to foster collaboration and innovation in the field (Figure 8).

CONCLUSION

In this chapter, we comprehensively compare existing methods for SAR image interpretation and propose cutting-edge approaches to ship detection. We explored the limitations of manual detection, traditional machine learning, and rule-based systems regarding accuracy, scalability, and adaptability. While offering high interpretability and flexibility, these methods suffer from labor-intensive processes, subjectivity, and challenges in effectively capturing complex patterns. To address these limitations, we introduced advanced techniques such as deep learning architectures, transfer learning, and semantic segmentation. These proposed methods automate the ship detection process, improve accuracy, scalability, and robustness, and reduce the need for manual intervention. By leveraging pre-trained models and learning features directly from data, these approaches offer significant advantages in handling diverse SAR imaging scenarios and environmental conditions.

The proposed cutting-edge approaches represent a significant advancement in SAR image interpretation, particularly in ship detection tasks. Enhancing accuracy, scalability, and efficiency paves the way for more effective maritime surveillance, environmental monitoring, and disaster management applications. With further research and development, these techniques have the potential to revolutionize SAR image interpretation and contribute to advancements in remote sensing technology and related fields. In our project, we have achieved an average result of precision (%) 94.2, recall (%) 96.1, and F1(%) 94.5 using the Atrous Convolutional Pyramid (ACP). SAR imagery can do more than detect ships. We can improve how we understand SAR images by breaking them down into different parts, like identifying specific types of ships or other things in the water. We can also make our ship detection systems smarter by teaching them to adapt to situations like bad weather or different types of ships.

REFERENCES

An, W., Xie, C., & Yuan, X. (2014). An Improved Iterative Censoring Scheme for CFAR Ship Detection with SAR Imagery. Iterative process could inadvertently lead to overfitting the algorithm. *IEEE Transactions on Geoscience and Remote Sensing*, *52*(8), 4585–4595. DOI: 10.1109/TGRS.2013.2282820

Anand, P. P., Sulthan, N., Jayanth, P., & Deepika, A. A. (2023). A Creating Musical Compositions Through Recurrent Neural Networks: An Approach for Generating Melodic Creations. *FMDB Transactions on Sustainable Computing Systems*, *1*(2), 54–64.

Aragani, V. M. (2024). Revolutionizing insurance through AI and data analytics: Innovating policy underwriting and claims management for the digital era. *FMDB Transactions on Sustainable Computer Letters*, *2*(3), 176–185. DOI: 10.69888/FTSCL.2024.000243

Brusch, S., Lehner, S., Fritz, T., Soccorsi, M., Soloviev, A., & van Schie, B. (2011). Ship Surveillance With TerraSAR-X. IEEE Transactions on Geoscience and Remote Sensing: A Publication of the IEEE Geoscience and Remote Sensing Society, 49(3), 1092–1103.

Chundru, S. (2024). Harnessing the power of AI: Revolutionizing metadata management with machine learning. *FMDB Transactions on Sustainable Computer Letters*, *2*(3), 164–175. DOI: 10.69888/FTSCL.2024.000242

Chunduri, V., Hannan, S. A., Devi, G. M., Nomula, V. K., Tripathi, V., & Rajest, S. S. (2024). Deep convolutional neural networks for lung segmentation for diffuse interstitial lung disease on HRCT and volumetric CT. In *Advances in Computational Intelligence and Robotics* (pp. 335–350). IGI Global.

Cui, Z., Li, Q., Cao, Z., & Liu, N. (2019). Dense Attention Pyramid Networks for Multi-Scale Ship Detection in SAR Images. The Dense Attention Pyramid Network (DAPN) method enhances multi-scale ship detection in SAR images. *IEEE Transactions on Geoscience and Remote Sensing*, *57*(11), 8983–8997. DOI: 10.1109/TGRS.2019.2923988

Doralba, U. R., Camilo Andrés, C. O., & Castellanos Polo, O. C. (2024). Analysis of The Medium-Term Fiscal Framework: A Financial Planning Tool. *AVE Trends In Intelligent Technoprise Letters*, *1*(1), 40–49.

Fan, W., Zhou, F., Bai, X., Tao, M., & Tian, T. (2019). Ship detection using deep convolutional neural networks for PolSAR images. *Remote Sensing (Basel)*, *11*(23), 2862. DOI: 10.3390/rs11232862

Gandhi, M., Satheesh, C., Soji, E. S., Saranya, M., Rajest, S. S., & Kothuru, S. K. (2024). Image recognition and extraction on computerized vision for sign language decoding. In *Explainable AI Applications for Human Behavior Analysis* (pp. 157–173). IGI Global. DOI: 10.4018/979-8-3693-1355-8.ch010

Gao, G., Liu, L., Zhao, L., Shi, G., & Kuang, G. (2009). An Adaptive and Fast CFAR Algorithm Based on Automatic Censoring for Target Detection in High-Resolution SAR Images. Suboptimal initialization strategies could lead to poor convergence behavior. *IEEE Transactions on Geoscience and Remote Sensing*, *47*(6), 1685–1697. DOI: 10.1109/TGRS.2008.2006504

Gao, Y., Wu, Z., Ren, M., & Wu, C. (2022). Improved YOLOv4 based on attention mechanism for ship detection in SAR images. *IEEE Access : Practical Innovations, Open Solutions*, *10*(2), 23785–23797. DOI: 10.1109/ACCESS.2022.3154474

Guo, H., Yang, X., Wang, N., & Gao, X. (2021). A CenterNet++ model for ship detection in SAR images. CenterNet++ demonstrates superior performance in SAR ship detection by effectively addressing challenges like small object and complex backgrounds. *Pattern Recognition*, *112*(4), 107787. DOI: 10.1016/j.patcog.2020.107787

Gupta, A., & Singh, V. (2024). Study MGNREGA and other initiatives with critical interpretation of achievements of MGNREGA in the FY 2022-23. *FMDB Transactions on Sustainable Social Sciences Letters*, *2*(1), 34–44. DOI: 10.69888/FTSSSL.2024.000218

Han, L., Ran, D., Ye, W., Yang, W., & Wu, X. (2020). Multi-size convolution and learning deep network for SAR ship detection from scratch. *IEEE Access : Practical Innovations, Open Solutions*, *8*(8), 158996–159016. DOI: 10.1109/ACCESS.2020.3020363

Jiao, J., Zhang, Y., Sun, H., Yang, X., Gao, X., Hong, W., Fu, K., & Sun, X. (2018). A Densely Connected End-to-End Neural Network for Multi-scale and Multiscene SAI Ship Detection. *IEEE Access : Practical Innovations, Open Solutions*, *6*(4), 20881–20892. DOI: 10.1109/ACCESS.2018.2825376

Li, Q., Min, R., Cui, Z., Pi, Y., & Xu, Z. (2019). Multi-scale ship detection based on dense attention pyramid network in SAR images. IGARSS 2019 - 2019 IEEE International Geoscience and Remote Sensing Symposium, 1–4. IEEE, Yokohama, Japan.

Liu, J., Shen, F., Wei, M., Zhang, Y., Zeng, H., Zhu, J., & Cai, C. (2019). 'A largescale benchmark for vehicle logo recognition, In 2019 IEEE 4th International Conference on Image, Vision and Computing (ICIVC) (pp. 479–483). IEEE, Xiamen, China.

Liu, W., Anguelov, D., Erhan, D., Szegedy, C., Reed, S., Fu, C.-Y., ... Ssd. (2016). 'Ssd: Single shot multibox detector, In Computer Vision-ECCV 2016: 14th European Conference (pp. 21–37), Springer Amsterdam, Netherlands.

Murugavel, S., & Hernandez, F. (2023). A Comparative Study Between Statistical and Machine Learning Methods for Forecasting Retail Sales. *FMDB Transactions on Sustainable Computer Letters*, *1*(2), 76–102.

Pranav, R. P., Prawin, R. P., Subhashni, R., & Das, S. R. (2023). Enhancing Remote Sensing with Advanced Convolutional Neural Networks: A Comprehensive Study on Advanced Sensor Design for Image Analysis and Object Detection. *FMDB Transactions on Sustainable Computer Letters*, *1*(4), 255–266.

Ren, S., He, K., Girshick, R., & Sun, J. (2015). 'Faster r-cnn: Towards real-time object detection with region proposal networks,''. *IEEE Transactions on Pattern Analysis and Machine Intelligence*, *39*(6), 1137–1149. DOI: 10.1109/TPAMI.2016.2577031 PMID: 27295650

Renjith, E. J. (2024). Revolutionizing cloud security: Innovative approaches for safeguarding data integrity. *FMDB Transactions on Sustainable Computer Letters*, *2*(2), 111–119. DOI: 10.69888/FTSCL.2024.000185

Ronald, B. J., Joseph, S. G. M., Kumar, P., Hsu, C.-Y., & Mehmood, A. (2024). Performance and Risk Analysis of Sustainable Mutual Funds in India: A Comparative Study. *AVE Trends In Intelligent Social Letters*, *1*(1), 13–24.

Sayedelahl, M. A., & Farouk, R. M. (2024). Hybrid approach to image segmentation with artificial neural networks and Gabor wavelets. *AVE Trends in Intelligent Computing Systems*, *1*(2), 77–90.

Sivapriya, G. B. V., Ganesh, U. G., Pradeeshwar, V., Dharshini, M., & Al-Amin, M. (2023). Crime Prediction and Analysis Using Data Mining and Machine Learning: A Simple Approach that Helps Predictive Policing. *FMDB Transactions on Sustainable Computer Letters*, *1*(2), 64–75.

Sun, Z., Meng, C., Cheng, J., Zhang, Z., & Chang, S. (2022). A Multi-Scale Feature Pyramid Network for Detection and Instance Segmentation of Marine Ships in SAR Images. The Multi-Scale Feature Pyramid Network (MS-FPN) demonstrates superior performance in detection and instance segmentation of marine ships in SAR, 14(24), 6312.

Wang, W., Han, D., Chen, C., & Wu, Z. (2024). FastPFM: A multi-scale ship detection algorithm for complex scenes based on SAR images. *Connection Science*, *36*(1), 1–29. DOI: 10.1080/09540091.2024.2313854

Yu, C., & Shin, Y. (2022). SAR ship detection based on improved YOLOv5 and BiFPN. Significantly enhances ship detection accuracy in SAR images compared to the original YOLOv5 algorithm. *Express ICT Express*, *10*(1), 28–33. DOI: 10.1016/j.icte.2023.03.009

Zhang, M., Wang, H., & Tan, J. (2022). Ship Detection in SAR Images Based on Multi-Scale Feature Extraction and Adaptive Feature Fusion. MSSDNet, with CSP-MRes2 and FC-FPN modules, achieves superior multi-scale ship detection in SAR imagery. *Remote Sensing (Basel)*, *14*(3), 755. DOI: 10.3390/rs14030755

Zhang, T., & Zhang, X. (2022). A polarization fusion network with geometric feature embedding for SAR ship classification. Complexity increases with the number of polarization channels and geometric features. *Pattern Recognition*, *123*(3), 108365. DOI: 10.1016/j.patcog.2021.108365

Chapter 6
Enhancing Network Security on a Hybrid LSTM-Gradient Boosting Framework for Intrusion Detection

R. Saranya
https://orcid.org/0009-0005-2415-4930
Bharath Institute of Higher Education and Research, India

S. Silvia Priscila
https://orcid.org/0000-0002-6040-3149
Bharath Institute of Higher Education and Research, India

ABSTRACT

The chapter presents a new hybrid intrusion detection framework that combines LSTM networks with gradient-boosting techniques. The approach presented in this study utilizes two prominent datasets, namely CICIDS2018 and CICIDS2017. The main objective is to improve the precision and reliability of intrusion detection in systems. This is achieved by capturing temporal dependencies in network traffic data and improving predictive performance by implementing boosting algorithms. The datasets are subjected to a thorough preprocessing process involving cleaning, normalization, and feature selection. This guarantees that the input for the model is of the highest quality. The LSTM component functions as the central element, extracting complex patterns and relationships from sequential data. The predictions generated by the LSTM model are refined by gradient boosting algorithms, which utilize their ensemble learning capabilities to improve overall performance.

DOI: 10.4018/979-8-3373-4672-4.ch006

INTRODUCTION

In today's rapidly evolving digital landscape, the prevalence of cyber threats continues to rise and presents a formidable obstacle to the security of networked systems (Admass et al., 2024). The growing dependence on interconnected technologies in diverse sectors, such as finance and healthcare, has significantly amplified the potential consequences of cyber-attacks (Cremer et al., 2022). The attacks carried out by individuals with bad intentions aiming to exploit vulnerabilities in network security cover a wide range of tactics, including advanced malware and specific infiltration methods (Reaves and Morris, 2009; Sudar et al., 2020; Ahmad et al., 2021). As a result, organizations are increasingly under pressure to enhance their cybersecurity measures and protect sensitive data from unauthorized access and manipulation. One of the key challenges in addressing cyber threats is the need for effective intrusion detection (Kumar and Sharma, 2018). Efforts are made to detect and counteract unauthorized access attempts and fraudulent activities within network environments (Renjith, 2024). Within the area of detection of attacks, conventional methods have traditionally leaned on rule techniques and signature techniques detection mechanisms to pinpoint familiar hazards (Kalra et al., 2020).

Nevertheless, the ever-changing landscape of cyber-attacks, known for their elusive and adaptable characteristics, has made traditional approaches progressively less successful (Van Houdt et al., 2020). Network traffic data's vast amount and complexities pose significant obstacles in promptly and accurately detecting every possible risk (Jeba et al., 2023). As organizations face the challenge of analyzing vast amounts of data generated by their interconnected systems, differentiating between real threats and harmless network activity becomes increasingly difficult (Pranav et al., 2024). Within this particular context, there is an urgent requirement for sophisticated detection mechanisms that can identify nuanced patterns and irregularities that may suggest malicious intentions amidst the overwhelming volume of network traffic (Boye, 2024). To effectively combat the constantly evolving cyber threats, intrusion detection solutions must be able to adapt and withstand the ever-changing attack strategies and tactics (Raja et al., 2024).

In the ever-evolving world of cybercrime, criminals always find innovative ways to avoid detection and take advantage of weaknesses, making traditional detection methods ineffective (Dhinakaran et al., 2023). Therefore, it is crucial to develop intrusion detection frameworks that can quickly adapt to emerging threats and rapidly evolving attack vectors (Varmann et al., 2023). Given the previous scenario, this work addresses the pressing need for robust and adaptable detection systems that can successfully fend off the growing flood of cyberattacks. The primary objective is to improve the efficiency of the detection mechanisms by utilizing machine learning and deep learning techniques, particularly Long Short-Term Memory networks, in combination with gradient boosting algorithms (Rele and Patil, 2023). The primary aim is to create a hybrid framework that allows for the meticulous analysis of network traffic data. This framework will empower organizations to proactively detect and mitigate cyber threats, preventing any potential irreparable damage. By conducting extensive research and analysis, our objective is to provide evidence of the effectiveness of the presented method in countering the widespread danger of cyber-attacks and strengthening the security of interconnected systems (Sulaiman et al., 2024).

LITERATURE REVIEW

Lirim Ashiku and Dagli (2021) present a novel approach to intrusion detection by incorporating a fusion of convolutional neural networks and regularized multi-layer perceptrons. This paper aims to effectively increase the resilience of detecting these intrusions (Sajini et al., 2023). In contrast to conventional fully connected feed-forward neural networks, CNNs utilize convolution as a mathematical operation, which enhances the extraction of features from sequential data, such as network traffic. The model architecture incorporates specific hyperparameters for convolutional layers, including filter dimensions, number of filters, and strides (Karatas et al., 2018). It also utilizes input padding and pooling layers to address the reduction of tensor and downsample feature dimensions throughout the layers (Dhaliwal et al., 2018). To test the suggested model, they have chosen the UNSW-NB15 dataset due to its ability to accurately depict real traffic in the network and a wide range of attack scenarios (Bahrololum and Khaleghi, 2008).

The dataset is subjected to preprocessing to convert object features into numerical vectors, normalize features, and reshape the data for CNN to give as input. The utilization of one hot encoding is crucial in representing labels, allowing for the differentiation of ten distinct classes. These classes consist of nine attack families and normal traffic flow. An approach optimizes model performance by fine-tuning various hyperparameters, such as regularization and many other techniques. In addition, callback functions like EarlyStopping and ModelCheckpoint are used to save the weights of the best-performing model (Muna and Sitnikova, 2021). The model architecture combines double-stacked convolutional layers, max pooling, and dropout layers, which have been implemented to enhance accuracy and mitigate overfitting. The proposed model architecture showcases promising results in detecting various types of network attacks despite the challenges posed by class imbalance. In addition, the study delves into the effects of combining datasets and suggests a method for dividing datasets based on user preferences to ensure thorough evaluation. This study's main objective is to overcome the shortcomings of current intrusion detection models and enhance network security in practical situations (Kaplantzis et al., 2007).

Zhang et al. (2019) proposed a thorough approach to detecting intrusion by utilizing a Convolutional Neural Network (CNN) model that has been trained on the NSL-KDD dataset, an improved version of the KDD dataset. The NSL-KDD dataset undergoes preprocessing to convert symbolic features into numerical representations through one-hot encoding. This is then followed by normalization to optimize the range of features. To rectify the uneven distribution of the dataset, a balanced training dataset is achieved by utilizing a combination of Synthetic Minority Oversampling Technique, also known as SMOTE, and Edited Nearest Neighbor or ENN sampling methods. In addition, the preprocessing step entails formatting the data into 11x11-dimensional images, utilizing Pearson Correlation to eliminate irrelevant features, and transforming the feature vector into image data. The architecture of the CNN model consists of convolutional layers and is connected fully. Batch Normalization reduces overfitting (Rajest et al., 2024).

The model undergoes training using frameworks that support GPU acceleration to enhance optimization. Softmax activation is employed in the final layer to classify using probability. The detection rate and false alarm rate are utilized to assess the effectiveness of the CNN-IDS model. The output clearly shows a notable increase in accuracy and a decrease in false alarms after the data balancing, highlighting the proposed approach's efficiency. In addition, the analysis examines the Attack Detection Rate (ADR) for different types of attacks, demonstrating enhanced detection rates, especially for less commonly represented attack types such as U2R and R2L. This study presents a thorough framework for intrusion detection, tackling issues related to imbalanced data distribution and achieving better performance in identifying various network attacks. The interplay between CNN architecture, data preprocessing techniques, and sampling methods is important in propelling forward, ultimately bolstering network security in practical settings (Sezari et al., 2018).

Halbouni et al. (2022) seek to tackle the growing concern of cyber-attacks by focusing on creating and implementing efficient Intrusion Detection Systems (IDS). Commencing with a comprehensive examination of intrusion and IDS systems, the paper emphasizes the pivotal role IDS plays in mitigating threats, thwarting unauthorized access, and documenting security breaches. Multiple approaches to intrusion detection are examined, encompassing various statistical methods, rule-based techniques, and fuzzy logic. The paper also explores the field of deep learning as a sophisticated method for extracting features, enhancing perception, and facilitating machine learning (Hund et al., 2021). With their multi-layered architecture, deep learning algorithms provide substantial benefits compared to traditional machine learning methods (Banala, 2024). They excel in various tasks, including image processing, NLP, and biomedical applications.

The paper explores the significance of choosing suitable datasets for evaluating the performance of these unauthorized detection systems. The analysis delves into several commonly used datasets, thoroughly examining their characteristics, types of attacks, and their appropriateness for training and testing IDS models. The main aim of this study is to enhance intrusion detection systems by investigating innovative techniques, utilizing deep learning methodologies, and identifying suitable datasets for model development and evaluation. The research aims to strengthen cybersecurity measures and protect critical information infrastructures from malicious activities by improving the capabilities of IDS to detect and mitigate cyber threats (Verkerken et al., 2020).

Hakan Can Altunay's (2023) work centers around developing and assessing detection systems utilizing deep learning techniques, specifically convolutional neural networks and long short-term memory networks. Applying these DL models for binary and multiclass classification tasks for intrusion detection involves accurately identifying and categorizing many types of attacks within network traffic data. The research commences by undertaking data preprocessing measures, encompassing data cleaning and normalization tasks. Subsequently, the datasets are partitioned into distinct sets for training, validation, and testing purposes (Kumar et al., 2024). The datasets are normalized and used to train CNN and LSTM classifiers. The evaluation of deep learning models involves the analysis of different performance metrics and losses. CNNs are commonly employed in intrusion detection systems to extract features and classify data (Soji et al., 2024). Their strength lies in their capacity to acquire intricate features from input data autonomously. The convolutional layers of CNNs facilitate the extraction of hierarchical representations of data, resulting in improved classification performance (Jasper et al., 2024).

However, LSTM networks capture traffic data's temporal dependencies and sequence information. Including a temporal component sets LSTM networks apart from other neural network architectures, rendering them highly suitable for analyzing time-series data. The presented IDS is assessed using real-world datasets such as UNSW and X-IIoTID, with key performance metrics assessed for both classification tasks. The experimental results showcase the efficacy of the deep learning-based IDS in precisely identifying and categorizing various forms of attacks within network traffic data, thereby bolstering cybersecurity measures in industrial systems. This research contributes significantly to intrusion detection by utilizing deep learning models to effectively analyze and detect malicious activities in network traffic (Sayedelahl and Farouk, 2024).

Laghrissi et al. (2021) delve into the intricacies of intrusion detection by utilizing the KDD99 dataset, a rich source of network traffic data encompassing a wide array of attack types. At the outset, techniques for data preprocessing are utilized to address the imbalance in the dataset and improve data efficiency. The binary classification task involves differentiating between normal and attack instances. On the other hand, multiclass classification aims to categorize instances into normal, Denial of Service, and Remote to Local attack categories. To enhance model performance and reduce dimensionality, the techniques of Principal Component Analysis and Mutual Information are employed. This PCA uncovers the most crucial components of the dataset, while MI evaluates how individual features influence classification outcomes (Anand et al., 2024). A deep learning model is implemented using the Keras library in Google Colab, utilizing the Long Short Term Memory architecture (Srilakshmi et al., 2024). The performance of the proposed algorithm is assessed using evaluation metrics such as accuracy, roc, and so on. Confusion matrices are used to examine the rates of positives and negatives of both true and false values, which are vital for reducing both false alarms and missed detections in intrusion detection systems. The LSTM model is configured with parameters specifically optimized for intrusion detection tasks, and its architecture is illustrated to provide a clear understanding of the proposed approach. In this study, the main goal is to improve the capabilities of intrusion detection through the use of deep learning techniques. The focus is on overcoming challenges related to unbalanced datasets and feature selection. By conducting meticulous experiments and assessments, the study showcases the efficacy of the proposed algorithm in precisely identifying and categorizing network attacks. This research significantly contributes to the progress of cybersecurity research and its practical applications.

SYSTEM METHODOLOGY

Dataset Selection: During the selection process for datasets in this research, a thorough evaluation was conducted to ensure they aligned with the study's objectives and requirements. The CICIDS2018 dataset was selected for its extensive data coverage on network traffic and its relevance to contemporary cybersecurity challenges. It is a collaborative effort between the CSE and CIC. This dataset offers a comprehensive collection of network traffic data from various attack scenarios, including network infiltration from within. To conduct a thorough analysis of cyber threats, it is crucial to have access to detailed information about the network infrastructure, including both the victim and attacker systems. Similarly, the CICIDS 2017 dataset was chosen for intrusion detection research due to its applicability and usefulness. Created to tackle the scarcity of up-to-date network traffic datasets for evaluating intrusion detection systems, CICIDS2017 encompasses a diverse set of attack types and network traffic circumstances.

The study includes eight traffic monitoring sessions spanning different working hours and attack scenarios. The traffic data is carefully labeled, distinguishing between regular and abnormal patterns to facilitate analysis. In addition, CICIDS2017 provides valuable insights into class imbalances, which enhances its usefulness in evaluating the performance of intrusion detection models in real-world scenarios. When selecting the dataset, it was important to consider the wide range of attack types and the intricate network traffic patterns. The CICIDS2018 and CICIDS2017 datasets provide diverse attack scenarios, enabling thorough testing and evaluation of intrusion detection algorithms. In addition, the datasets include a substantial amount of features derived from network traffic data, allowing for thorough analysis and modeling of cyber threats. Several factors were taken into consideration when selecting the above two datasets. These factors included the datasets' extensive coverage of network traffic data, their relevance to contemporary cybersecurity challenges, and their appropriateness for assessing the effectiveness of intrusion detection systems. The datasets serve as a strong basis for conducting thorough experiments and confirming the efficacy of the hybrid LSTM-boosting approach in identifying and addressing cyber threats.

Data Preprocessing: Before analyzing and training the model, thorough preprocessing steps are carried out to guarantee the data's quality, consistency, and appropriateness for training the intrusion detection model. The preprocessing steps involve a range of techniques to enhance the performance and interpretability of the model. Various techniques are employed to remove outliers and unnecessary context from the dataset. As part of the dataset preprocessing, the initial step focuses on thoroughly examining the data to detect and rectify any errors, discrepancies, or missing values. This process is essential to guarantee the integrity of the dataset and minimize the potential for bias or inaccuracies in the model's predictions. Various techniques were utilized to ensure the datasets were thoroughly cleaned. These techniques involved removing duplicate entries, handling missing values, and correcting data anomalies. After completing the data cleaning process, we apply normalization techniques to standardize the feature values and ensure consistency throughout the dataset. Normalization ensures that no particular features overpower others during model training and enhances the speed at which the optimization algorithm converges. A common technique used to standardize feature values is the min-max normalization method. In this approach, the values are normalized to a predetermined interval, usually from 0 to 1. By doing so, it maintains the original distribution of the data while making it more appropriate for training the model. In addition, the preprocessing phase included addressing class imbalances in the datasets to ensure equitable and unbiased model training.

Class imbalance is a situation where some classes or categories of data are over-represented in the dataset, which can result in biased predictions from the model. Various techniques were utilized to address class imbalances and ensure a diverse and representative dataset for training the model. These techniques included oversampling, undersampling, and synthetic data generation. This phase of dataset preprocessing played a crucial role in preparing the datasets for training an efficient intrusion detection model. The datasets were carefully prepared to ensure their quality and suitability for training the hybrid LSTM-boosting model—this involved cleaning, normalizing, selecting features, and addressing class imbalances. Preprocessing techniques are crucial in boosting model performance, enhancing generalization, and facilitating accurate detection of cyber threats in real-world network environments.

LSTM Model Construction: The intrusion detection framework involves the Long Short-Term Memory model to effectively capture dependencies over time and intricate patterns in network traffic data. Our model is built upon the LSTM architecture, renowned for its capacity to capture long-term reliances and address the issue of vanishing gradients. The core of the LSTM architecture consists of memory cells equipped with three gating mechanisms. Importantly, the gates determine whether data is retained or discarded based on its relevance to the present job, thus controlling the data flow within the network. Through the strategic updating of memory cells, LSTM networks can adeptly capture and preserve pertinent information across lengthy sequences. This quality makes them highly suitable for analyzing time-series data like network traffic. The construction of the LSTM model involves stacking multiple LSTM layers, with each layer consisting of a sequence of LSTM units or cells. Determining the number of LSTM layers and units per layer is based on extensive experimentation and careful consideration of the model's complexity. Within our framework, we conduct experiments using different configurations to determine the most effective architecture for tasks related to intrusion detection. Figure 1. depicts a single LSTM cell structure.

Figure 1. LSTM unit

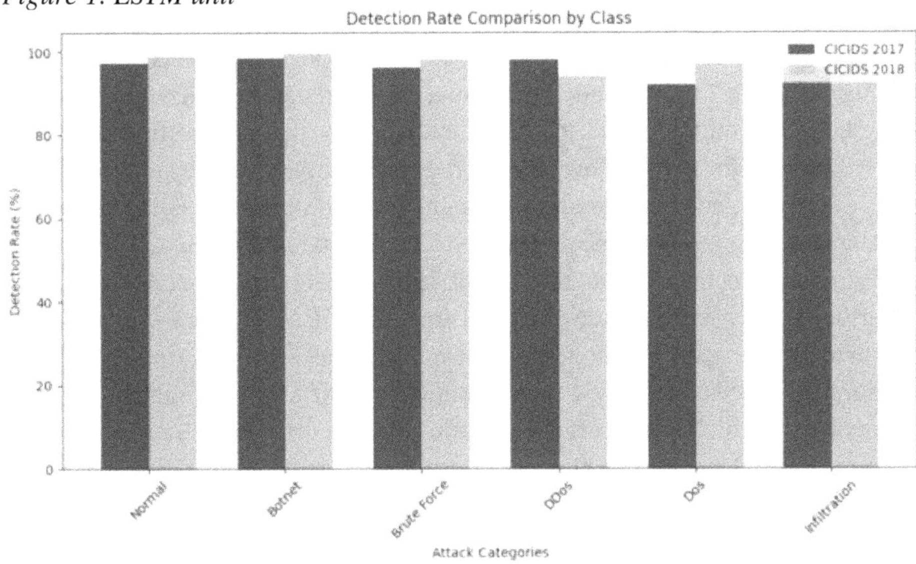

The LSTM model's key parameters encompass the LSTM layers, number of units, activation function, dropout and learning rate, and optimizer. These parameters greatly impact the model's capacity, regularization, and optimization strategy. Through meticulous parameter tuning, our objective is to achieve an equilibrium between the intricacy of the model and its ability to generalize. An activation function, a sigmoid, and a tanh function introduce non-linearity to the LSTM units. This allows the units to capture intricate relationships within the data effectively. During training, the dropout rate mitigates overfitting by randomly eliminating some connections between LSTM units. The resilience and generalization of the model are enhanced because of this. During training, the LSTM model undergoes optimization using a gradient-based optimization algorithm named Adam. The adaptive learning rate algorithms dynamically adjust the learning rate based on the loss function's gradients, leading to faster convergence and improved optimization performance. To improve the model's interpretability and prevent overfitting, regularization techniques like L1 and L2 regularization are used. These techniques help to penalize large weights in the network. Early stopping is employed in this phase to prevent overfitting of the model by stopping the training process when the validation loss begins to rise. Therefore, the construction of the LSTM model requires the design of a multi-layered architecture with LSTM units. Our objective is to construct a strong and efficient intrusion detection framework that can accurately identify cyber threats in network traffic data using the capabilities of LSTM networks.

Gradient Boosting Integration: By including gradient boosting into the intrusion detection framework, we aim to utilize the strengths of ensemble learning approaches to improve the model's predictive performance. An effective ensemble learning technique, gradient boosting builds a robust predictive model by combining the predictions of multiple weak learners. Gradient boosting can significantly reduce prediction errors and enhance overall accuracy by iteratively training new models to rectify the errors made by previous models. In the integration process, the initial step involves training a base estimator. This decision tree uses the original dataset—the base estimator functions as the initial weak learner within the ensemble.

Furthermore, a series of weak learners are trained in succession, with each subsequent model dedicated to minimizing the mistakes made by the current ensemble. The iterative process described above continues until a certain number of weak learners have been trained or until a specific stopping criterion is satisfied. Gradient boosting relies on the effective use of gradient descent optimization, where the parameters of each weak learner are updated to minimize the loss function. Through the computation of gradients, gradient descent enables the iterative refinement of the model's predictions, enhancing its performance. Shrinkage entails adjusting the impact of each weak learner on the ensemble by applying a small factor called the learning rate. A modest learning rate can mitigate the risk of overfitting and attain enhanced generalization capabilities, even at the expense of slower convergence. We utilize methods like feature subsampling and tree pruning to improve the range of weak learners in the ensemble. One technique used in machine learning is feature subsampling, where a random subset of features is chosen during each iteration to train the weak learners.

Another method, known as tree pruning, is employed to prevent overfitting by restricting the depth of the decision trees. Throughout the training process, we carefully observe the ensemble's performance on a validation set and implement early stopping techniques to mitigate the risk of overfitting. Early stopping is a technique that halts the model's training when there is a decline in the ensemble's performance on the validation set. This helps the model to reduce overfitting. After the ensemble training, predictions are generated by combining the predictions of all the weak learners in the ensemble. Incorporating gradient boosting into our intrusion detection framework includes training a series of weak learners to build a strong predictive model. Through the iterative refinement of ensemble predictions using gradient descent optimization and other techniques, the accuracy and resilience of the intrusion detection system are enhanced. Figure 2 depicts the flowchart of the proposed detection system.

Figure 2. Flow diagram of proposed system

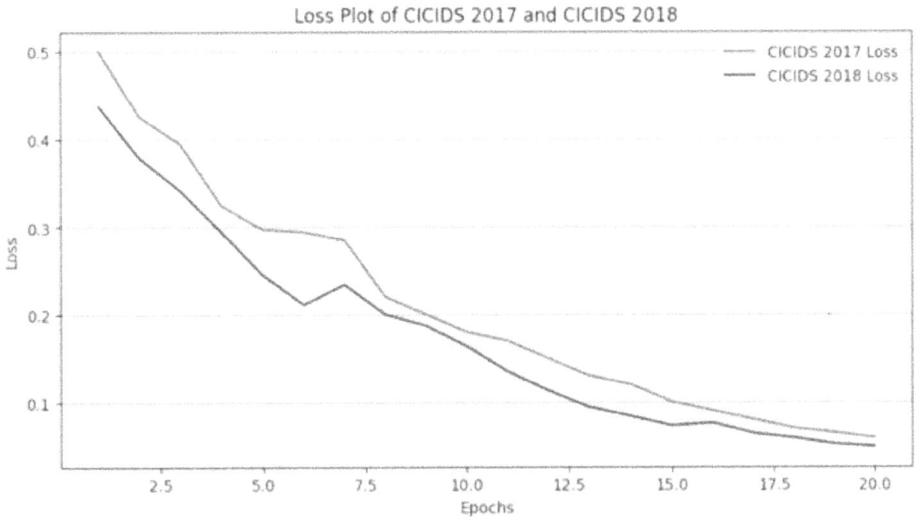

Training and Evaluation: During this phase, a systematic approach is employed to train the hybrid intrusion detection framework and evaluate its performance on the chosen datasets. This involves several important steps, such as dividing the data, training the model, fine-tuning the hyperparameters, and evaluating the performance. First, the datasets are divided into two sets to facilitate model training and evaluation. The training set serves an important role in developing the model's knowledge, while the testing set serves as a means to assess its performance when faced with unfamiliar data. To maintain an unbiased evaluation, we meticulously partition the datasets while preserving the distribution of normal and anomalous instances. Afterward, training the LSTM component of the hybrid model using the training data happens. The LSTM architecture is designed with multiple layers and hidden units, enabling it to effectively capture temporal dependencies in the sequential network traffic data. Throughout the training process, the focus is optimizing the model parameters using a gradient descent-based optimization algorithm. In this case, it is Adam. The primary objective of this phase is to minimize the loss of function and enhance performance. This study also utilizes various techniques, including dropout regularization, to reduce overfitting and enhance the ability of the proposed model. During each training iteration, dropout randomly deactivates some fraction of neurons, which compels the model to acquire more resilient data representations. After training the LSTM component, the next step is incorporating gradient boosting into the framework to improve predictive performance.

The gradient boosting ensemble is initialized with weak learners, and various new models are trained iteratively to adjust values and reduce errors of the existing ensemble. The parameters of each weak learner are updated using gradient descent optimization. Various techniques are used to prevent overfitting and enhance generalization. During training, the performance of our model is tracked on a distinct validation set, and adjustments to the hyperparameters are made to maximize performance. Hyperparameters, such as learning rates, regularization strengths, and ensemble sizes, are carefully fine-tuned using grid or random search methods to find the most effective configuration. Once the hybrid model has been trained, testing starts. This evaluation involves several performance metrics generally used for classification purposes. The metrics provide insights into the model's capacity to identify intrusions while effectively minimizing the occurrence of wrong predictions. Many experiments and comparative analyses are conducted to evaluate the efficacy of the framework in comparison to baseline models and cutting-edge approaches.

RESULTS AND DISCUSSION

Table 1 presents the performance metrics for the CICIDS 2017 dataset. The results demonstrate an impressive accuracy across all categories, with Normal traffic achieving a remarkable 99.65%. The precision values consistently exceed 98%, demonstrating the model's proficiency in accurately classifying instances. The recall scores exhibit strong performance, especially for the Brute Force and Dos categories, surpassing 99%. The F1 metric demonstrates consistently high values, proving the model's effectiveness in detecting intrusions. In conclusion, these metric findings highlight the model's ability to detect different intrusion attempts effectively, thereby improving network security.

Table 1. Key performance metrics for CICIDS 2017 dataset

Metrics	Accuracy	Precision	Recall	F1-Score
Normal	99.65%	99.31%	98.79%	99.25%
Botnet	99.76%	98.74%	99.06%	99.87%
Brute Force	99.82%	99.82%	99.23%	99.12%
DDos	99.94%	99.75%	99.74%	98.94%
Dos	99.84%	99.65%	99.43%	99.97%
Infiltration	99.97%	98.99%	99.37%	99.51%

Table 2 displays the performance metrics for the CICIDS 2018 dataset. Remarkably, the model demonstrates outstanding accuracy, with Normal traffic reaching an impressive 99.38%, signifying a high level of classification precision. The precision values consistently remain high for all classes, surpassing 98%. This emphasizes the model's exceptional capability in accurately detecting intrusion attempts. The recall scores indicate strong performance, especially for Brute Force and Infiltration, with a success rate of over 99%. The F1 score demonstrates a strong balance between precision and recall, indicating the model's effectiveness in intrusion detection across all classes. The findings highlight the model's ability to effectively protect network environments from cyber threats, showcasing its reliability and strength.

Table 2. Ey performance metrics for CICIDS 2018 dataset

Metrics	Accuracy	Precision	Recall	F1-Score
Normal	99.38%	99.71%	98.65%	99.11%
Botnet	99.79%	98.92%	99.46%	99.82%
Brute Force	99.65%	99.83%	99.72%	99.53%
DDos	99.68%	99.43%	99.55%	99.68%
Dos	99.84%	99.68%	99.28%	99.89%
Infiltration	99.81%	99.92%	99.58%	99.96%

The proposed system showcases exceptional precision compared to alternative systems in this area, achieving an extraordinary accuracy rate of 99.83%. When comparing the results, it is worth noting that CNN shows an accuracy of 99.26%, while LSTM reaches a commendable 98.91%. However, the combination of CNN and LSTM outperforms them all, achieving an accuracy of 99.80%. Meanwhile, the DL-ML system attains a 99.45% accuracy rate, while the CDAE-DNN model performs admirably with an accuracy of 97.21%. Therefore, the results show the greatness of the proposed method, demonstrating its strong ability to detect intrusion attempts accurately. The proposed system demonstrates superior performance compared to existing models, suggesting its potential to significantly improve network security and effectively address cyber threats (Table 3).

Table 3. Comparison with other systems

Metrics	Accuracy
Proposed System	99.83%
CNN (Karatas et al., 2018)	99.26%
LSTM (Karatas et al., 2018)	98.91%
CNN + LSTM (Karatas et al., 2018)	99.80%
DL-ML (Halbouni et al., 2022)	99.45%
CDAE-DNN (Hakan Can Altunay, 2023)	97.21%

Figure 3 depicts the accuracy trends of intrusion detection models trained on the two different CICIDS 2017 and 2018 datasets for 20 epochs. The datasets demonstrate a steady increase in performance with each epoch. The accuracy of the CICIDS 2017 model begins at 78.4% and gradually improves to 99.9%, while the CICIDS 2018 model starts at 75.1% and reaches 99.35%. The curves presented in this analysis showcase the models' ability to identify intrusion attempts as the training progresses accurately. This emphasizes their resilience and capacity to adjust to evolving threats.

Figure 3. Accuracy of the model for CICIDS 2017 and CICIDS 2018

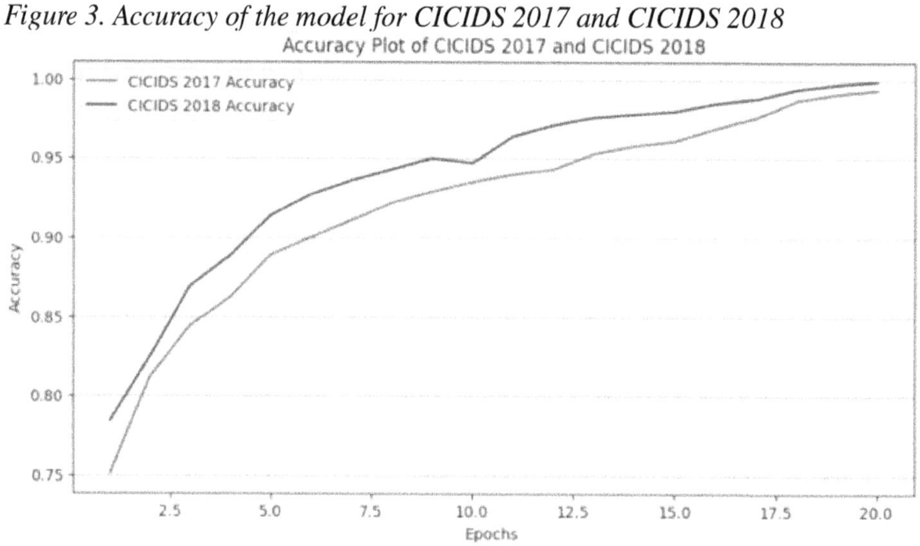

Figure 4 illustrates the loss curves of intrusion detection models trained on the CICIDS 2017 and CICIDS 2018 datasets, spanning 20 epochs. The loss values exhibit a consistent downward trend throughout each epoch, suggesting enhanced model performance and convergence. The initial loss in the CICIDS 2018 model is 0.437

and gradually decreases to 0.049. On the other hand, the CICIDS 2017 model starts with a loss of 0.500 and decreases to 0.053. The curves demonstrate the progress made by the models in reducing prediction errors and improving their accuracy in classifying network traffic data.

Figure 4. Loss of the model for CICIDS 2017 and CICIDS 2018

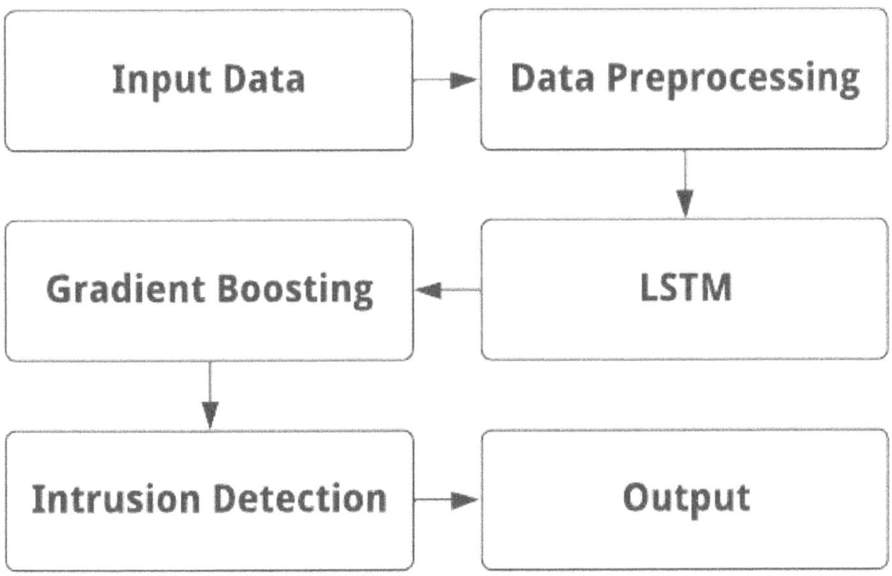

Figure 5. depicts the detection rate of each class of both datasets. It clearly shows that the detection rate for the CICIDS 2018 dataset is better and more efficient than its previous version, CICIDS 2017. However, overall, the detection rate of the model is more efficient and at least greater than 95%.

Figure 5. Detection rate of each class

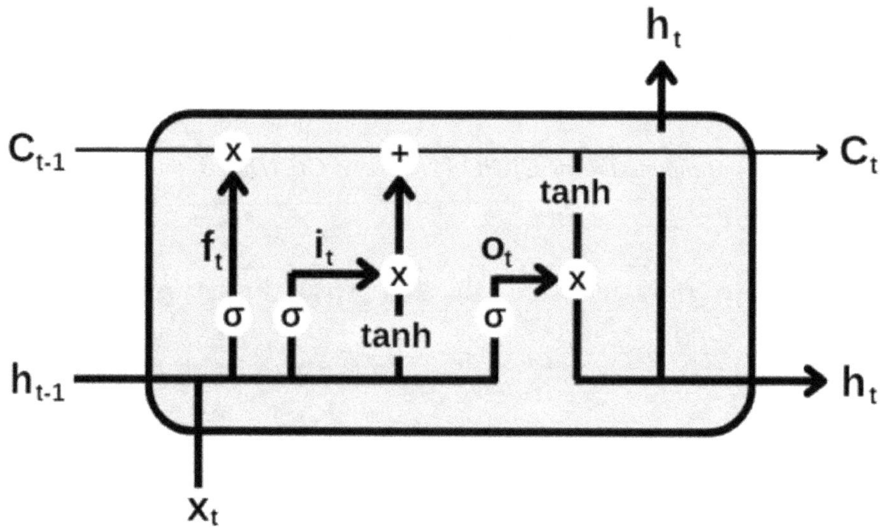

CONCLUSION AND FUTURE WORK

Ultimately, the suggested hybrid intrusion detection framework, which combines LSTM and gradient boosting techniques, is highly effective in protecting network environments from a wide range of cyber threats. By carefully choosing the datasets, preparing them, and building the model, our approach in the CICIDS2017 and CICIDS2018 datasets achieves remarkable performance metrics in various attack categories. The results highlight the framework's efficacy in detecting intrusion attempts with minimal false positives and negatives, thereby bolstering network security. Our framework combines the power of LSTM networks and gradient boosting to create a strong defense against complex cyber-attacks. The results of this study make a significant contribution to the field of intrusion detection systems, offering valuable insights for researchers and practitioners working towards developing robust cybersecurity solutions. In conclusion, the hybrid approach presents a promising opportunity to enhance network defenses and address the challenges of ever-changing cyber threats.

REFERENCES

Admass, W. S., Munaye, Y., & Diro, A. A. (2024). Cyber security: State of the art. *Challenges and Future Directions*, *2*(1), 100031.

Ahmad, Z., Shahid Khan, A., Wai Shiang, C., Abdullah, J., & Ahmad, F. (2021). Network intrusion detection system: A systematic study of machine learning and deep learning approaches. *Transactions on Emerging Telecommunications Technologies*, *32*(1), 1–29. DOI: 10.1002/ett.4150

Anand, P. P., Jayanth, G., Rao, K. S., Deepika, P., Faisal, M., & Mokdad, M. (2024). Utilising Hybrid Machine Learning to Identify Anomalous Multivariate Time-Series in Geotechnical Engineering. *AVE Trends In Intelligent Computing Systems*, *1*(1), 32–41.

Ashiku, L., & Dagli, C. (2021). Network intrusion detection system using deep learning. *Procedia Computer Science*, *185*(1), 239–247. DOI: 10.1016/j.procs.2021.05.025

Bahrololum, M., & Khaleghi, M. (2008). Anomaly intrusion detection system using Gaussian mixture model. 2008 Third International Conference on Convergence and Hybrid Information Technology. Busan, Korea (South).

Banala, S. (2024). Enhancing system stability with advanced techniques in site reliability engineering. *AVE Trends in Intelligent Computing Systems*, *1*(2), 66–76.

Boye, H. (2024). Strengthening cloud security through advanced encryption and anomaly detection techniques for secure data storage and transmission. *FMDB Transactions on Sustainable Computer Letters*, *2*(3), 153–163. DOI: 10.69888/FTSCL.2024.000241

Cremer, F., Sheehan, B., Fortmann, M., Kia, A. N., Mullins, M., Murphy, F., & Materne, S. (2022). Cyber risk and cybersecurity: A systematic review of data availability. *The Geneva Papers on Risk and Insurance. Issues and Practice*, *47*(3), 698–736. DOI: 10.1057/s41288-022-00266-6 PMID: 35194352

Dhaliwal, S. S., Nahid, A.-A., & Abbas, R. (2018). Effective Intrusion Detection System using XGBoost. *Information (Basel)*, *9*(7), 149. DOI: 10.3390/info9070149

Dhinakaran, P., Thinesh, M. A., & Paslavskyi, M. (2023). Enhancing Cyber Intrusion Detection through Ensemble Learning: A Comparison of Bagging and Stacking Classifiers. *FMDB Transactions on Sustainable Computer Letters*, *1*(4), 210–227.

Hakan Can Altunay, Z. (2023). A hybrid CNN+LSTM-based intrusion detection system for industrial IoT networks. *Engineering Science and Technology, an International Journal, 38*(2), 101322. DOI: 10.1016/j.jestch.2022.101322

Halbouni, A., Gunawan, T. S., Habaebi, M. H., Halbouni, M., Kartiwi, M., & Ahmad, R. (2022). CNN-LSTM: Hybrid deep neural network for network intrusion detection system. *IEEE Access : Practical Innovations, Open Solutions, 10*(9), 99837–99849. DOI: 10.1109/ACCESS.2022.3206425

Hund, A., Wagner, H.-T., Beimborn, D., & Weitzel, T. (2021). Digital innovation: Review and novel perspective. *The Journal of Strategic Information Systems, 30*(4), 101695. DOI: 10.1016/j.jsis.2021.101695

Jasper, K. D., Jaishnav, M. N., Chowdhury, M. F., Badhan, R., & Sivakani, R. (2024). Defend and Secure: A Strategic and Implementation Framework for Robust Data Breach Prevention. *AVE Trends In Intelligent Computing Systems, 1*(1), 17–31.

Jeba, J. A., Bose, S. R., Regin, R., Rajest, S. S., & Kose, U. (2023). In-Depth Analysis and Implementation of Advanced Information Gathering Tools for Cybersecurity Enhancement. *FMDB Transactions on Sustainable Computer Letters, 1*(2), 130–146.

Kalra, Y., Upadhyay, S., & Patheja, D. P. S. (2020). Advancements in Cyber Attacks and Security. *International Journal of Innovative Technology and Exploring Engineering, 9*(4), 1520–1528. DOI: 10.35940/ijitee.D1678.029420

Kaplantzis, S., Shilton, A., & Mani, N. (2007). Detecting. Selective Forwarding Attacks in Wireless Sensor Networks using Support Vector Machines Intelligent Sensors. In Sensor Networks and Information, Melbourne, Victoria, Australia

Karatas, G., Demir, O., & Koray Sahingoz, O. (2018). Deep learning in intrusion detection systems. *2018 International Congress on Big Data, Deep Learning and Fighting Cyber Terrorism (IBIGDELFT)*, Ankara, Turkey. DOI: 10.1109/IBIGDELFT.2018.8625278

Kumar, C. S., Priscila, S. S., Abishabackiyavathi, G., Rajest, S. S., Regin, R., & Deming, C. (2024). Deciphering hand movements in individuals with limited mobility using neural networks. *FMDB Transactions on Sustainable Computing Systems, 2*(1), 13–21. DOI: 10.69888/FTSCS.2024.000193

Kumar, R., & Sharma, D. (2018). HyINT: Signature-anomaly intrusion detection system. 2018 9th International Conference on Computing, Communication and Networking Technologies (ICCCNT). Bengaluru, India.

Laghrissi, F., Douzi, S., Douzi, K., & Hssina, B. (2021). Intrusion detection systems using long short-term memory (LSTM). *Journal of Big Data*, *8*(1), 1–16. DOI: 10.1186/s40537-021-00448-4 PMID: 33425651

Muna, E., & Sitnikova, N. (2021). Asynchronous peer-to-peer federated capability-based targeted ransomware detection model for industrial IoT. *IEEE Access : Practical Innovations, Open Solutions*, *9*(11), 148738–148755.

Pranav, R. P., Prawin, R. P., Paramasivan, P., Shynu, T., & Subhashni, R. (2024). IoT-SecNet: A trust-based framework for enhancing security in IoT communications and network layer protocols. *FMDB Transactions on Sustainable Computing Systems*, *2*(2), 96–106. DOI: 10.69888/FTSCS.2024.000201

Raja, A. S. V., Jasper, K. D., Poornima, V., Priscila, S. S., Thenmozhi, A., & Ratkovic, N. (2024). Tech horizons unveiled: Navigating the transformative decade in AIML, cybersecurity, IoT, gaming, and data science education. *FMDB Transactions on Sustainable Intelligent Networks*, *1*(2), 120–134. DOI: 10.69888/FTSIN.2024.000214

Rajest, S. S., Moccia, S., Singh, B., Regin, R., & Jeganathan, J. (Eds.). (2024, August 30). Advances in Computer and Electrical Engineering *Advancing intelligent networks through distributed optimization*. IGI Global., DOI: 10.4018/979-8-3693-3739-4

Reaves, B., & Morris, T. (2009). Discovery, infiltration, and denial of service in a process control system wireless network. 2009 eCrime Researchers Summit, Washington, United States of America

Rele, M., & Patil, D. (2023). Supervised and unsupervised ML methodologies for intrusive detection in nuclear systems. *2023 International Conference on Network, Multimedia and Information Technology (NMITCON)*, Bengaluru, India. DOI: 10.1109/NMITCON58196.2023.10276256

Renjith, E. J. (2024). Revolutionizing cloud security: Innovative approaches for safeguarding data integrity. *FMDB Transactions on Sustainable Computer Letters*, *2*(2), 111–119. DOI: 10.69888/FTSCL.2024.000185

Sajini, S., Reddi, L. T., Regin, R., & Rajest, S. S. (2023). A Comparative Analysis of Routing Protocols for Efficient Data Transmission in Vehicular Ad Hoc Networks (VANETs). *FMDB Transactions on Sustainable Computing Systems*, *1*(1), 1–10.

Sayedelahl, M. A., & Farouk, R. M. (2024). Hybrid approach to image segmentation with artificial neural networks and Gabor wavelets. *AVE Trends in Intelligent Computing Systems*, *1*(2), 77–90.

Sezari, B., Moller, D. P. F., & Deutschmann, A. (2018). Anomaly-based network intrusion detection model using deep learning in airports. 2018 17th IEEE International Conference On Trust, Security And Privacy In Computing And Communications, / 12th IEEE International Conference On Big Data Science And Engineering (TrustCom/BigDataSE), New York, USA

Soji, E. S., Karthik, S., Priscila, S. S., Hanirex, D. K., Rajest, S. S., & Sebastian, A. (2024). Designing an E-Voting System Architecture Using the STAP Protocol. *FMDB Transactions on Sustainable Intelligent Networks*, *1*(2), 96–109. DOI: 10.69888/FTSIN.2024.000212

Srilakshmi, U., Sandhya, I., Manikandan, J., Bindu, A. H., Regin, R., & Rajest, S. S. (2024). Design and implementation of energy-efficient protocols for underwater wireless sensor networks. In *Advances in Computer and Electrical Engineering* (pp. 417–430). IGI Global.

Sudar, K. M., Deepalakshmi, P., Nagaraj, P., & Muneeswaran, V. (2020). Analysis of Cyberattacks and its Detection Mechanisms. *2020 Fifth International Conference on Research in Computational Intelligence and Communication Networks (ICRCICN)*, Bangalore, India. DOI: 10.1109/ICRCICN50933.2020.9296178

Sulaiman, R. B., Aljaidi, M., Alsuwaylimi, A. A., Butt, U., Talukder, M. S. H., Alam, S. S., Farhan, M., Das, S. R., & Alam, M. W. (2024). Enhancing security in digital payments: A comparative evaluation of machine learning models for credit card fraud detection. *FMDB Transactions on Sustainable Computer Letters*, *2*(2), 63–84. DOI: 10.69888/FTSCL.2024.000182

Van Houdt, G., Mosquera, C., & Nápoles, G. (2020). A review on the long short-term memory model. *Artificial Intelligence Review*, *53*(8), 5929–5955. DOI: 10.1007/s10462-020-09838-1

Varmann, S. S., Hariprasath, G., & Kadirova, I. (2023). Optimizing Educational Outcomes: H2O Gradient Boosting Algorithm in Student Performance Prediction. *FMDB Transactions on Sustainable Techno Learning*, *1*(3), 165–178.

Verkerken, M., D'hooge, L., Wauters, T., Volckaert, B., & De Turck, F. (2020). Unsupervised machine learning techniques for network intrusion detection on modern data. 2020 4th Cyber Security in Networking Conference (CSNet). Lausanne, Switzerland.

Zhang, X., Ran, J., & Mi, J. (2019). An intrusion detection system based on convolutional neural network for imbalanced network traffic. 2019 IEEE 7th International Conference on Computer Science and Network Technology (ICCSNT). Dalian, China.

Chapter 7
IoT Application-enabled Deep Learning Model With Secure ECC-Based Cloud Data Storage Optimization Strategy for Data Deduplication

Manjunath Singh H.
https://orcid.org/0009-0007-6891-3614
UVCE, India

R. Tanuja
UVCE, India

ABSTRACT

Due to the development of the "Internet of Things (IoT)," a huge quantity of data is transferred to the cloud architecture. As a consequence, expenses and storage charges are associated with cloud servers. Storage capacity can be enhanced by implementing a deduplication technique to spot duplicate information. Both cryptography and deduplication are carried out using the full hash values of the information chunks. The deduplication systems are vulnerable to file threats. So, we developed an effective optimal key-based deduplication model. The proposed model uses attributes including filename, size, block name, size, type of file, and data pattern for deduplication. The "Long Short-Term Memory (LSTM)" model is introduced for effective deduplication performance. The LSTM model separates the attributes and deduplicated attributes once the data file is not duplicated. Once it is

DOI: 10.4018/979-8-3373-4672-4.ch007

proved that the data are deduplicated, the edge node (client) enciphers the data by utilizing the Optimal Key-Based Elliptical Curve Cryptography (OK-ECC). Further, it passes the data to the cloud system.

INTRODUCTION

Commercial efficiency and security can be increased by implementing data-driven approaches through the IoT (Patra et al., 2021). The automation of factories was previously centralized, but using the IoT, it is currently independently managed. For a more productive and secure generation, the industrial data is processed using a semi-trusted cloud server (Shukla et al., 2023). Nearly all the time, the duplicates in the outsourced IoT data raise storage costs. The outsourced information must be deduplicated before being stored on a cloud server to lower this overhead (Kumar and Shantala, 2020). During de-duplication, private information should not be transferred to cloud architecture. Consequently, to satisfy the security and data management needs of the IoT (Licaj et al., 2024), a successful de-duplication solution is used that can maintain access control and privacy and safeguard the data being transmitted from other cyber-attacks (Periasamy and Latha, 2021).

The majority of prior research has used deduplication algorithms directly at third parties. Consequently, for redundancy verification, all of the created data is immediately transferred to cloud storage (Muthunagai and Anitha, 2022). The blocks of information will be discarded when they repeatedly appear. It causes substantial communication expenses when sending all the information to cloud storage for redundancy evaluations. Convergent key encryption produces a private key for encryption using one-way hashing, which vast deduplication algorithms use (Vignesh and Preethi, 2022). The secret keys generated from the hash values encrypt the data blocks. The encryption texts and convergence keys are produced since the hash values are consistent for identical information blocks. These encrypted texts are subsequently used to detect duplication and are denied access to cloud storage (Sharma and Saini, 2020). The most fundamental de-duplication method compares the newly received file from the corresponding person with the actual file to safeguard a connection between the source file and the file holder on the cloud server (Raja et al., 2024). The main drawback is that the competitors might easily extrapolate the contents of the data that has been outsourced (Li et al., 2017). Convergent cryptography is used on cloud servers to safeguard and maintain data uniqueness. The uploaded file is encrypted with the convergent method of encryption using the file's hash sequence (Yeh and lin, 2018). Every single digest is reviewed against the owner's digests. Developing equivalent digests during cross-data repetition causes vulnerability to brute force attacks and tag mismatches (fu et al., 2018). To overcome the challenges, we developed an "effective IoT-based data deduplication model with protected cloud data storage." Some of the significant contributions of the "deduplication approach with optimal key-based encryption" are presented as follows.

- To suggest a deduplication model with optimal key-based encoding for eliminating the redundant data in the cloud architecture and providing efficient and safe storage space for the user's data.
- To propose an LSTM model for performing the deduplication on the data gathered by the IoT devices, thus the conveyance of redundant data to the cloud structure is greatly prevented.
- To recommend a CBOA for choosing the optimal key required for the encryption process. This CBOA greatly minimizes the "time and memory size" of the encoding process.
- To suggest an OK-ECC approach for securing the deduplicated data before it is stored in the cloud, providing higher security over the information and improving the encoding performance using optimal key generation.
- To confirm the usefulness of the explored data deduplication model by comparing the results with the traditional model via several performance metrics.

The organization of the LSTM-based data deduplication model is arranged as follows. In portion II, the literature survey related to the existing deduplication framework and its uses and limitations is given. The structural description of the proposed data deduplication and storage model and its data representation is described in portion III. The brief view of "deep model-based data deduplication" and optimal key-based data storage is discussed in portion IV. The suggested "LSTM-based data deduplication" results and conversation are elaborated in portion V. Finally, portion VI concludes the suggested LSTM-based data deduplication framework.

LITERATURE REVIEW

In 2020, Eason and Vijayakumar (2020) recommended a model for removing duplicate information from cloud storage. The developed system performs "data deduplication" in both files and blocks (Pranav et al., 2024). If the information in the file was not copied, it divided the blocks and eliminated duplicates. Convergent key coding was implemented during deduplication for safe deduplication (Karthik et al., 2024). Convergent key exchange was more susceptible to attacks (Regin et al., 2023). This study proposed the "cloud-based Creating and Managing Keys (KGTMaaaS)" to eradicate redundant data and guarantee the safe maintenance of convergent keys and other private information. This approach successfully eliminated redundant information from cloud storage (Saxena et al., 2023).

In 2022, Sirajudeen and Anith (2022) established a fog-centric technique for improving the deduplication approach's performance. The incomplete hash values were saved in a "Scalable Bloom Hash Table (SBHT)" updated by every node available in the fog layer (Legista et al., 2024). In addition, SBHT helped in the inline deduplication operation. The SBHT used by the fog node for inline deduplication has been obtained and stored (Gnanaguru et al., 2024). The node at the edge encoded the information chunk with an asymmetrical "Cramer Shoup (CS)" system and transferred it to the cloud when the data was not redundant (Zanardo, 2024). The suggested technique enhanced security for CFA (Sayedelahl and Farouk, 2024). Furthermore (Karthikeyan et al., 2024), the recommended SBHT lowered false-positive errors, boosted memory effectiveness, and made the system feasible to apply in the IoT healthcare sector (Renjith, 2024).

In 2021, Olakanmi and Odeyemi (2021) made a quicker method for server-assisted data deduplication that employed a successful authorized key agreement. The strategy allows for secure information retrieval over the encrypted text on the semi-trusted cloud server and guarantees data singularity and consistency in the "Industrial Internet of Things (IIoT)" (Singh et al., 2023). The scheme's efficacy was derived from its capacity to create an encoded tag for each data submitted to the server (Vemula, 2024).

In 2016, Mao et al. (2016) developed a "Performance-Oriented Deduplication (POD)" instead of iDedup to increase the performance of cloud storage systems without negatively impacting their space savings (Singh et al., 2023). POD used two methods to reduce the performance expenditure of deduplication and improve the effectiveness of systems (Pierre et al., 2024). An active storage management tool (Anushya et al., 2024), iCache, was employed to minimize memory contention among shapely write and shapely study traffic. In addition, the results of the assessment show that POD surpasses iced-up in terms of resource savings (Cirillo et al., 2023).

In 2022, Yang et al. (2022) put forth a "three-tier cross-domain model," an Efficient Big Data duplication method (EPCDD) for cloud storage that guaranteed privacy (Anand et al., 2024). EPCDD prevented brute-force harm by achieving privacy preservation. Furthermore, responsibility was provided for superior privacy preservation (Rajest et al., 2024). This proved that EPCDD worked better with computing, interaction, and storage overheads than other approaches (Boye, 2024).

PROBLEM STATEMENT

Cloud storage offers space to store various data quantities. The task of storage space and other organization processes ought to be effectual. It is susceptible to brute-force assaults that may identify which plain text in a data space correlates to a provided cipher text. Numerous approaches have been developed to overcome these challenges, and Table 1 offers the uses and limitations of the existing models. KGTMaaaS effectively separates redundant information from cloud storage and aids in removing unnecessary allotment of the storage and bandwidth of the network. However, the communication and computation overhead in this model is greater. Fog-centric approach lowers the overhead in communication, enhances safety against the attack, helps to reduce false positives, and improves storage efficiency. However, the data's complete hash value chunks are required to perform the encryption and deduplication processes. The data de-duplication scheme imposes singularity of the data along with integrity and confidentiality and enables protected data searching against the cipher text in the cloud. However, it is very intensive in computational cost and can detect only deduplicate for delegated data from diverse domains. POD offers better capacity in data saving, and it appreciably improves the presentation and aids in the saving capability of principal storage networks within the cloud. However, it requires more memory to read the data, and the system's usefulness is not well based on energy efficiency and capacity. EPCDD is practical and effective in designing in the immediate fashion and clinical sector. But it doesn't enable searching the details of the information against the ciphertext and not having the ability to impose needed security desires. To overcome the challenges, we developed an "effective IoT-based data deduplication model in cloud storage."

Table 1. Pros and cons of the existing data deduplication model

Author	Methodology	Features	Challenges
Eason & Vijayakumar, (2020)	KGTMaaaS	• It effectively separates redundant information from cloud storage. • It aids in removing unnecessary allotment of the storage and bandwidth of the network.	• The communication and computation overhead is greater in this model.
Sirajudeen et al., (2022)	Fog-centric approach	• This model lowers the overhead in communication and enhances the safety against the attack. • It helps to reduce false positives and improve the efficiency of storage.	• It requires the data's complete hash value chunks to encrypt and deduplicate.
Olakanmi & Odeyemi, (2021)	Data de-duplication scheme	• It imposes singularity of the data along with integrity and confidentiality. • It enables protected searching of data against the ciphertext in the cloud.	• This model is very intensive in terms of computational cost. • This model can detect only deduplicate for delegated data from diverse domains.
Mao et al. (2016)	POD	• This model offers better capacity for data saving. • This model appreciably progresses the presentation and saves the capability of principal storage networks within the cloud.	• It requires more memory to read the data. • The model's performance is not well based on energy efficiency and capacity.
Yang et al. (2022)	EPCDD	• This model is practical and effective for design in an immediate fashion and clinical sector.	• It doesn't enable searching the details of the information against the ciphertext and not having the ability to impose needed security desires.

Block Schematic Representation of Proposed Model

For the new generation of information technology, the IoT is considered the most important part. The relevant data are collected and processed by the IoT devices, and subsequently, they are secured in the cloud. The information the IoT devices collect consists of many duplicate data. The amount of data has recently increased because of the rapid emergence of IoT data and applications. These huge quantities of IoT data are kept in the cloud, so the storage capacity of the cloud architecture is limited. The IoT sensors work all day, and duplicate data is unavoidable in the IoT network. In cloud architecture, redundancy is mainly due to an increase in the quantity of uploaded data. Most of the space in the cloud is occupied by redundant data, which leads to difficulties in maintaining the cloud architecture. To eliminate the information redundancy of the cloud, the researcher developed the "deduplication process". The conventional data deduplication system neglects the redundancy of data in the cloud.

Along with that, if any one of the users uploads the same data on the cloud structure, it develops the link for that user. Because of this process, lots of secretive information is outsourced to another person without considering the agreement of the corresponding data owner. For this reason, an efficient deep optimal key-based data deduplication is developed to eliminate the duplicate copy of IoT data and enhance the storage and security of the cloud system. The systematic view of the developed deduplication approach with optimal key-based data storage is visualized in Figure 1.

Figure 1. A systematic view of the developed deduplication with optimal key-based data storage framework

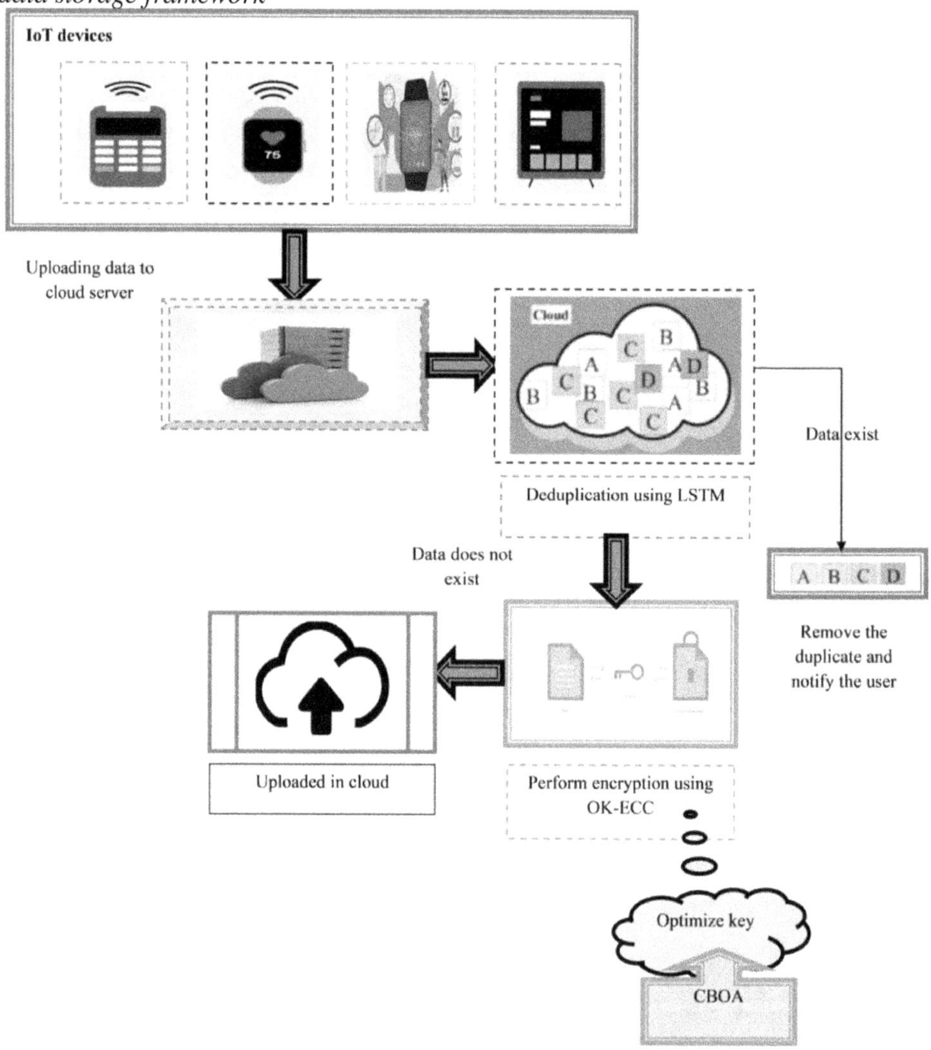

The developed model effectively minimizes the bandwidth of the cloud structure by neglecting the repeated copies of files. Moreover, the developed model also provides access control to the cloud data. Initially, the deduplication approach is made via the LSTM, and the input is provided as the "input attributes like file type, last modified date, data pattern, and file types." When the user passes the data into the cloud, it finds the presence of the data based on the "input attributes". If the file exists in the cloud architecture, the data already exists. If the file is unavailable in the cloud structure, the encoding process is carried out using the optimal key-based

ECC. This approach encrypts the data using the optimally selected key from the CBOA. The "time and the memory size" are greatly minimized during the optimal key selection process. Further, the encrypted file is kept in the cloud system. The user can utilize the same optimal key for the decryption process to access the stored file in the cloud architecture. The suggested deduplication model is used to eliminate the repeated data of the cloud architecture. Moreover, it rapidly performs the deduplication process on the cloud architecture with enhanced security. Finally, the simulation process is executed to confirm the effectiveness of the developed data deduplication with an optimal key-based encryption approach in IoT.

Dataset Representation

The dataset utilized in the "data deduplication process" is elucidated as follows.

Dataset (Cholesterol dataset): The Cholesterol dataset is the first dataset for the "data deduplication process," and it is obtained from the link of https://www.kaggle.com/datasets/mathurinache/cholesterol" with access: 2024-2-19. The Cholesterol dataset is treated as the class attribute. The heart disease diagnosis-based data are available in the dataset. This dataset is composed of numeric value-based attributes. The data from the four locations are gathered for this database in total. The data from the above dataset is expressed, and the total amount of collected data is represented at this point.

CBOA for Key Generation

The CBOA generates the key needed to perform the enciphering process. This "optimal key" is adopted in the ECC to carry out the encoding and decoding action. The proposed CBOA aims to transform cooking students into master chefs by educating them on cooking skills. In culinary school, several chef instructors are available. The cooking skills and techniques are taught by the instructor, who provides exercise to the students to further enhance their cooking skills. The students mimic the skills of the chef instructor. Under the effective training process, the students are transformed into chefs at the last stages of the course. The cooking students and the chef instructor are available as members of the CBOA. The member of the CBOA is designed in matrix form. The commencement of the position of the CBOA members is denoted in Eq. (1).

$$Y_{j,k} = mc_k + s(vc_k - mc_k) \tag{1}$$

Here, for the complication variable$k$, the lift and the raise limit are elucidated asvc_k *and* mc_k, and the arbitrary number is expressed as$s$. The objective function is evaluated by inserting the CBOA member into the issues variable. The objective function of the CBOA algorithm is also calculated in matrix form. The inhabitant's matrix of the CBOA is represented by the number of chef trainers depictedOD. The vector of the purpose function is characterized by$GT$the term YT_1 ,YT_{O_D} the group of chef instructors in the matrix$GT$and the termsYT_{O_D+1} ,YT_O are the cooking students in the matrixGT.

Step 1: The chef instructor in the cookery school teaches the students food preparation skills. The skills of the best chef are learned in this stage. Here, the best chef is adopted to teach the students cooking skills. The position of the chef instructor is identified using Eq. (2).

$$yt_{j,k}^{D/T1} = yt_{j,k} + s\left(CD_k - J \bullet yt_{j,k}\right) \tag{2}$$

Thus, the excellent chef instructor is represented as$CD$the new status of thej^{th} member of the CBOA represented as$Yt_{j,k}^{D/T1}$, at the coordinate$k$, the new status of the member is represented as$yt_{j,k}^{D/T1}$, at coordinate$k$, the excellent chef instructor is represented as$CD_k$the arbitrary number is elected as$s$and it is available in the interval of $[0,1]$. The randomly selected number is represented as$J$in $[1,2]$. If the novel location enhances the value of the purpose function, then the new location is acceptable. The condition required to perform this operation is indicated in Eq. (3).

$$YT_j = \begin{cases} YT_j^{D/T1}, & GT_j^{D/T1} < G_j \\ YT_j & otherwise \end{cases} \tag{3}$$

For the member$YT_j^{D/T1}$, the objective function is represented as$GT_j^{D/T1}$. The chef instructor improves the skills of the students by providing training action. The random position developed in the search space is used to model this action, which is indicated in Eq. (4) and Eq. (5).

$$mc_k^{LOC} = \frac{mc_k}{u} \tag{4}$$

$$vc_k^{LOC} = \frac{vc_k}{u} \tag{5}$$

Here, the counter of the iteration is regarded as$u$, and the local superior and the minor bound are represented asvc_k^{LOC}, andmc_k^{LOC}correspondingly,

$$yt_{j,k}^{D/T2} = yt_{j,k} + mc_k^{LOC} + s\left(vc_k^{LOC} - mc_k^{LOC}\right),$$
$$j = 1,2...O_D, \; k = 1,2....n \tag{6}$$

$$YT_j = \begin{cases} YT_j^{D/T2}, \; GT_j^{D/T2} < G_j \\ YT_j \quad otherwise \end{cases} \tag{7}$$

Here, the point purpose value is interpreted as $j^{th}$the CBOA member being represented and the CBOA member being signified for the coordinate.

Step 2: The students who want to become a chef attend the culinary school and learn the cooking skills. Here, the best instructor trains the students to make them the master chef. Based on the trainer's training, the cooking students' new location is indicated in Eq. (8).

$$yt_{j,k}^{T/T1} = yt_{j,k} + s\left(DJ_{l_j,k} - J * yt_{j,k}\right) \tag{8}$$

Here, for the member$j$, the identified status is represented as$Yt_{j,k}^{T/T1}$, and at the coordinate$k$, the member's status $j$is represented as$yt_{j,k}^{T/T1}$; for the cooking student$j$, the chef instructor is represented as$DJ_{l_j,k}$; here, the term $l_j$is erratically chosen from the set of$\{1,2....O_d\}$.

If the new location enhances the value of the purpose function, then the novel location is acceptable. The condition required to perform this operation is indicated in Eq. (9).

$$YT_j = \begin{cases} YT_j^{T/T1}, \; GT_j^{T/T1} < G_j \\ YT_j \quad otherwise \end{cases} \tag{9}$$

Here, the objective function $YT_j^{T/T1}$is elucidated as$GT_j^{T/T1}$.

The students learn the skills from the instructor to become master chefs. The new location is calculated for every cooking student using Eq. (10).

$$yt_{j,k}^{T/T2} = \begin{cases} DJ_{l_j,k} \; k = m \\ yt_{j,k} \quad otherwise \end{cases} \tag{10}$$

The new location enhances the point function, then the new location is substituted instead of the old position, and the condition is specified in Eq. (11).

$$YT_j = \begin{cases} YT_j^{T/T2}, \; GT_j^{T/T2} < G_j \\ YT_j \quad otherwise \end{cases} \tag{11}$$

Thus, the objective function is represented as $GT_j^{T/T2}$. For the coordinate j *and* k, the status of the CBOA member is represented as $YT_j^{T/T2}$, and $yt_{j,k}^{T/T2}$ respectively.

The exercise of the students is to improve their skills in the cooking activities. Here, the arbitrary location is developed for the cooking students available during the investigation break, specified in Eq. (12).

$$yt_{j,k}^{T/T3} = \begin{cases} yt_{j,k} + mc_k^{LOC} + s\left(vc_k^{LOC} - mc_k^{LOC}\right) & k = r \\ yt_{j,k} & k \neq r \end{cases} \tag{12}$$

Here, the randomly selected number in the region $\{1, 2...n\}$ is represented; for the member, the identified status is represented $Yt_{j,k}^{T/T3}$, and at the coordinate k, the member's status j is represented $yt_{j,k}^{T/T3}$.

The term YT_j is updated if the random spot enhances the value of the purpose function, and the condition is designed in Eq. (13).

$$YT_j = \begin{cases} YT_j^{T/T3}, & GT_j^{T/T3} < G_j \\ YT_j & otherwise \end{cases} \tag{13}$$

Here, the objective function $YT_j^{T/T3}$ is represented as $GT_j^{T/T3}$. All population associated with the CBOA is updated to finish the iteration process.

Brief View of Deep Learning-based Data Deduplication and Optimal Key-based Data Storage

Data Deduplication using LSTM: The data deduplication is performed via the LSTM. Here, the "input attributes like file type, last modified date, data pattern, and file types" are given as the input. The LSTM structure encompasses several memory cells, which can be used to store information from the prior step. The sophisticated order operation of the LSTM structure leads to the suggestion of the LSTM structure for the deduplication process. The data composed by the IoT devices consists of several duplicate data. Thus, the "deduplication process" is executed using the LSTM model. The LSTM model is trained to detect duplicate files in the data. This model identifies similar parameters in the uploaded and existing data. The training process is mainly conducted on the LSTM to accurately find the duplicate and the deduplicate data. The developed model finds data redundancy when the user transfers the information to the cloud. If the data is previously there in the cloud, it notifies the person regarding the existence of the data. If the same file does not subsist in the cloud, it undergoes the encryption process.

The LSTM consists of a feedback connection. The forget gate in the LSTM structures controls the feedback connection. The memory of the LSTM structure is erased with the aid of the forget gate. The LSTM structure also consists of a sigmoid function. The LSTM structure consists of some gates, which are defined as follows:

$$g_u = \nu\left(X_{gi} i_{u-1} + X_{gy} y_u + Q_g \bullet d_{u-1} * c_g\right) \tag{14}$$

$$j_u = \nu\left(X_j i_{y_u} + V_j i_{u-1} + Q_j \bullet d_{u-1} * c_j\right) \tag{15}$$

$$h_u = \tan h\left(X_h y_u + V_h i_{u-1} + c_h\right) \tag{16}$$

$$d_u = j_u \Theta h_u + g_u \Theta d_{u-1} \tag{17}$$

$$p_u = \nu\left(X_p y_u + V_p i_{u-1} + Q_p * d_u + c_p\right) \tag{18}$$

$$i_u = p_u \Theta \tan h\left(d_u\right) \tag{19}$$

Here, the "forget gate" is represented, the "output gate" is represented, the modulation gate is indicated, and the weight of the forget gates is denoted asQ_g, Q_j $Q_p$respectively. The structural representation of the LSTM model is represented in Figure 2.

Figure 2. Structural representation of the LSTM model for data deduplication

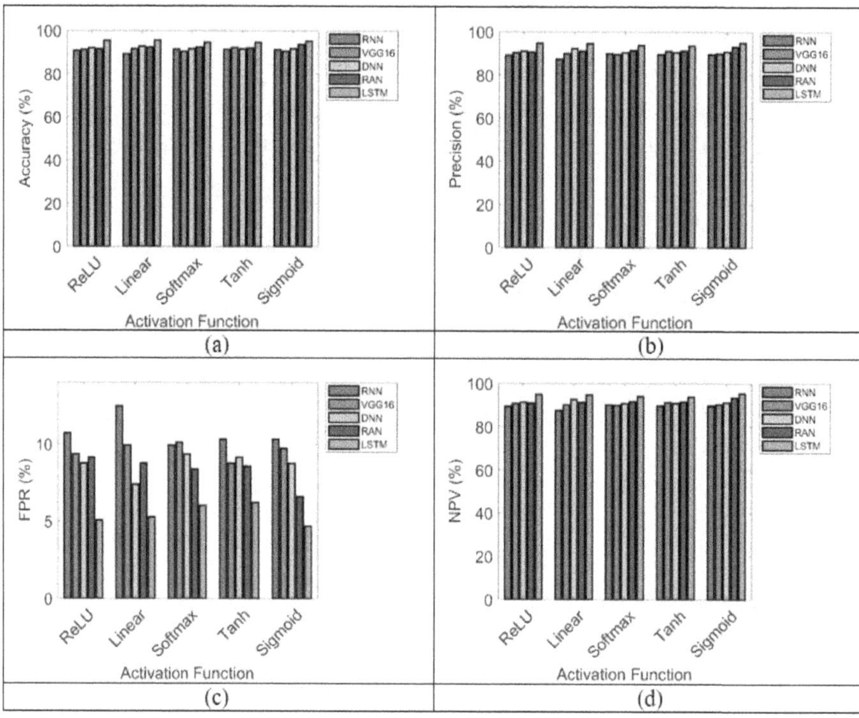

ECC Algorithm

The ECC is used to perform the enciphering action. It provides strong encryption of information in the cloud system. This ECC model uses the characteristics of the elliptic curve to authenticate and encode cloud data. The elliptic expression adopted in the ECC is elucidated in Eq. (20).

$$z^2 = y^3 + by + c \tag{20}$$

The properties required to perform the cryptographic action are defined using Eq. (20). Moreover, the logarithm issues are also solved by the elliptic curve properties. The ECC approach only adopts a small number of keys to perform the encryption process, and it is considered an efficient cryptographic technique. Using these small keys offers the strongest security to the data. The ECC is an effective technique that has been utilized in resource-constrained environments. The ECC is used to execute the encoding process rapidly. The security features of the ECC are very strong, and it is one of the most powerful encryption techniques.

OK-ECC for Secure Data Storage

If the uploaded information is unavailable in the cloud system, it undergoes the enciphering action. The data is encoded using the ECC; this model uses the optimal key for executing the encoding and decoding process. Here, the binary format key is optimally preferred with the support of the CBOA. This encrypted data is uploaded in a structure to maintain confidentiality. The corresponding data owner utilizes the same optimally selected key to access their data. The major objective of the OK-ECC-based secure data storage is to subordinate the "time and memory size" of the encoding action, which is expressed in Eq. (21).

$$h = \arg\min_{\{bk\}}(L + D) \tag{21}$$

Here, the binary format key is represented, the time is elucidated, and the memory size is expressed$D$.

$$L = \frac{w}{s} \tag{22}$$

Here, the information in the cloud is represented, and the number of blocks available in the data is expressed$s$.

Memory size$D$: The total memory space required for the encoding process is constituted as memory space calculated using Eq. (23).

$$D = \frac{k}{8} \tag{23}$$

Here, the number of memory bits is represented$k$.

The diagrammatic representation of the OK-ECC for secure data storage is exemplified in Figure 3.

Figure 3. Diagrammatic representation of OK-ECC for secure data storage

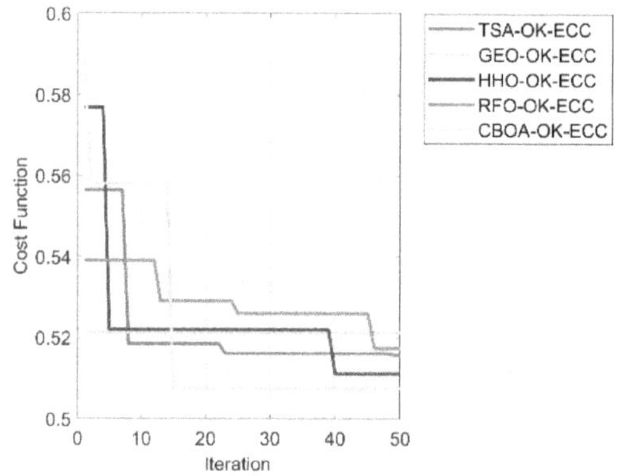

RESULT AND DISCUSSION

Simulation setup: MATLAB 2020a platform was used to implement the LSTM-based data deduplication process. The previous algorithms such as "Tunicate Swarm Algorithm (TSA) Golden Eagle OptHarris Hawks Optimization (HHO)," Red Fox Optimization (RFO), CBOA, and the traditional encryimizer (GEO)]," "option techniques like "Data Encryption Standard (DES), Advanced Encryption Standard (AES)," Attribute-Based Encryption (ABE), as well as the conventional deduplication techniques such as "Recurrent Neural Network (RNN), Visual Geometry Group (VGG) 16" Deep Neural Network (DNN), Residual Attention Network (RAN) were taken to find the efficacy of the developed deduplication with encryption approach.

Evaluation Indices

The performance indices of the LSTM-based data deduplication model are elucidated as follows.

$$accuracy = \frac{o+l}{o+l+w+s} \tag{24}$$

$$\text{Pr}ecision = \frac{l}{o+w} \tag{25}$$

$$F1score = \frac{2o}{2o+w+s} \tag{26}$$

$$Specificity = \frac{l}{l+w} \tag{27}$$

$$sensitivity = \frac{o}{o + w} \tag{28}$$

$$NPV = \frac{l}{l + s} \tag{29}$$

$$FPR = \frac{o}{w + l} \tag{30}$$

$$FDR = \frac{w}{w + s} \tag{31}$$

$$FNR = \frac{l}{l + s} \tag{32}$$

$$MCC = \frac{ol - ws}{\sqrt{(o + s)(l + s)(l + w)(o + w)}} \tag{33}$$

At this time, the true and the false positives are represented o, respectively, and the true and false negatives are signified.

Encryption Performance Analysis Among Algorithms

The performance examination of the CBOA-OK-ECC-based encryption system over numerous algorithms is presented in Figure 4. The suggested CBOA-OK-ECC-based encryption model consumes minimum memory space than the TSA-OK-ECC, GEO-OK-ECC, HHO-OK-ECC and RFO-OK-ECC with 25%, 6.25%, and 12.55% and 9.37% when allowing the size of the block as 5. Thus, the performance of the CBOA-OK-ECC-based encryption model is superior to the existing algorithms Figure 4.

Figure 4. Performance assessment of the optimal key-based encryption over several algorithms for (a) Decryption time, (b) Encryption time, (c) Memory size, (d) Total computation time

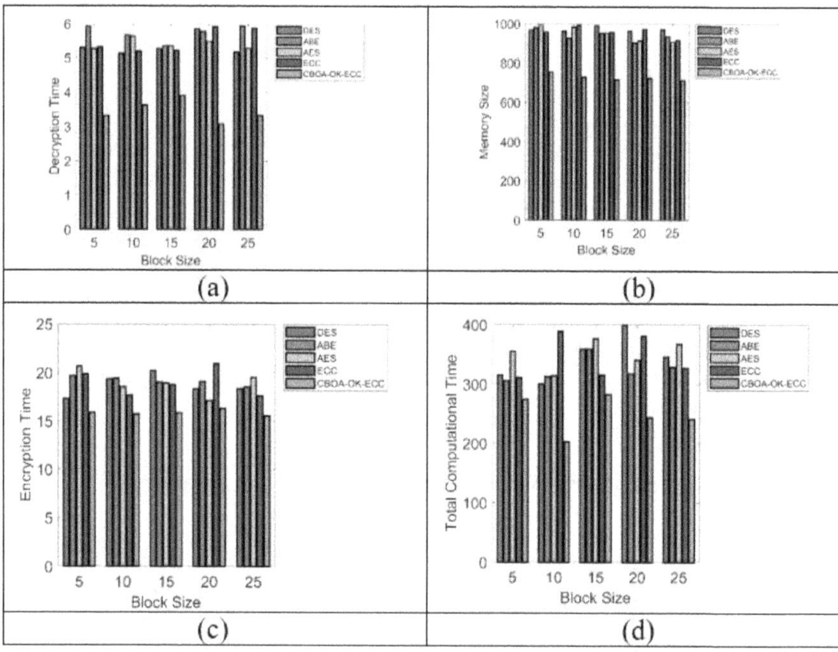

Encryption Performance Analysis Among Techniques

The performance association of the recommended CBOA-OK-ECC-based encryption approach with various techniques is displayed in Figure 5. At the size of block 15, the encryption time of the CBOA-OK-ECC-based encryption model is 31.25%, 13.2%, 12.5% and11.87% enhanced than the traditional DEA, ABE, AES and ECC. So, the performance of the suggested CBOA-OK-ECC-based encryption framework is superior to the existing approach Figure 5.

Figure 5. Performance assessment of the optimal key-based encryption over several techniques for (a) Decryption time, (b) Encryption time, (c) Memory size, (d) Total computation time

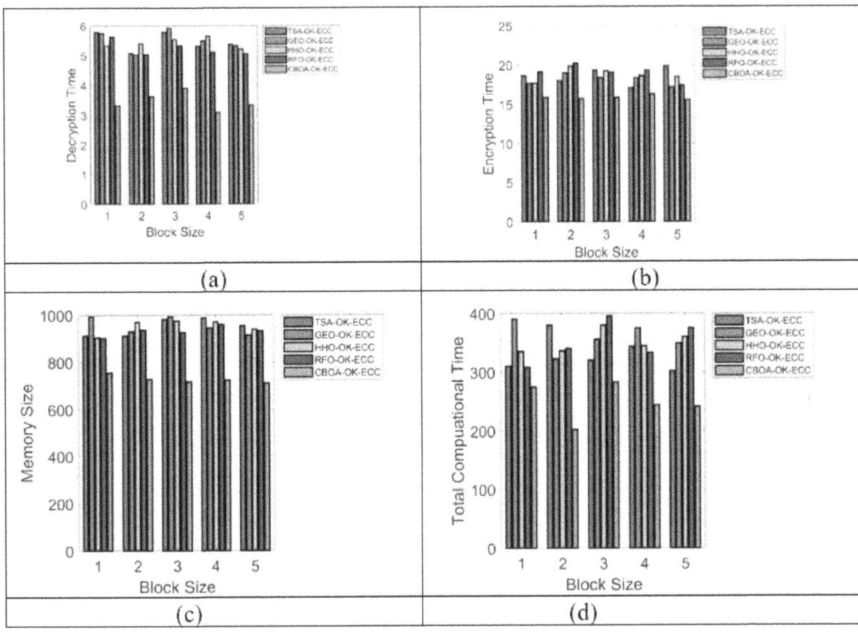

Convergence Investigation

The convergence investigation of the CBOA-OK-ECC-based encryption system over the traditional techniques for the two datasets is examined in Figure 6. At the 20th iteration, the cost function of the CBOA-OK-ECC-based encryption system is lower than the TSA-OK-ECC, GEO-OK-ECC, HHO-OK-ECC, and RFO-OK-ECC with 1.76%, 2.54%, 2.15% and 3.72%. Thus, the cost requirement of the CBOA-OK-ECC-based encryption system is diminished compared to the existing model Figure 6.

Figure 6. Convergence estimation of the optimal key-based encryption model over the traditional algorithms

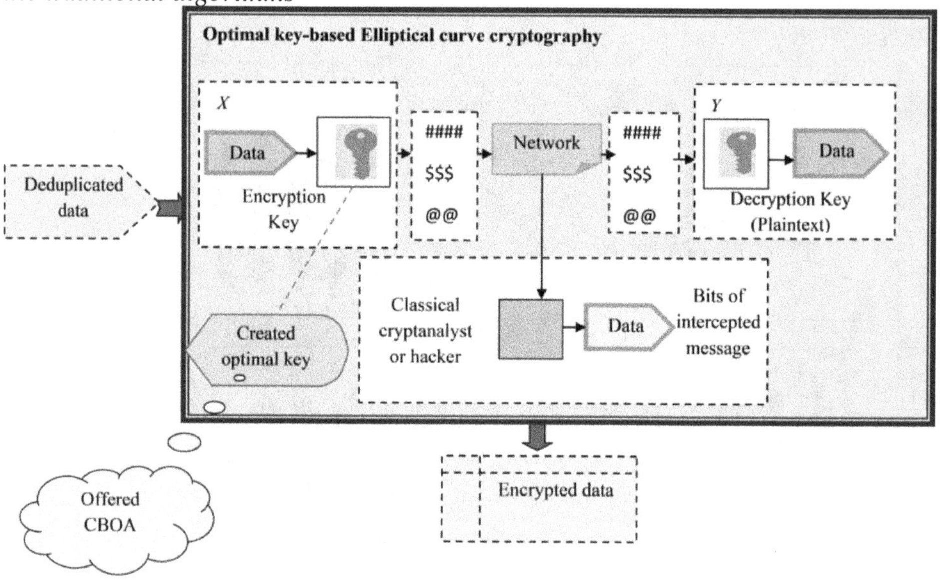

Performance Estimation of the Recommended Deduplication Model

The performance evaluation of the LSTM-based deduplication approach via several evaluation indices is presented in Fig. 7. At the SoftMax activation function, the precision of the LSTM-based deduplication model is improved than the RNN, VGG16, DNN, RAN, with 7.21%, 8.24%, 7.21%, and 6.18%. Thus, the performance of the LSTM-based deduplication approach is better than that of the conventional models (Figure 7).

Figure 7. Performance estimation of the deep deduplication model for (a) Accuracy, (b) Precision, (c) FPR, (d) NPV

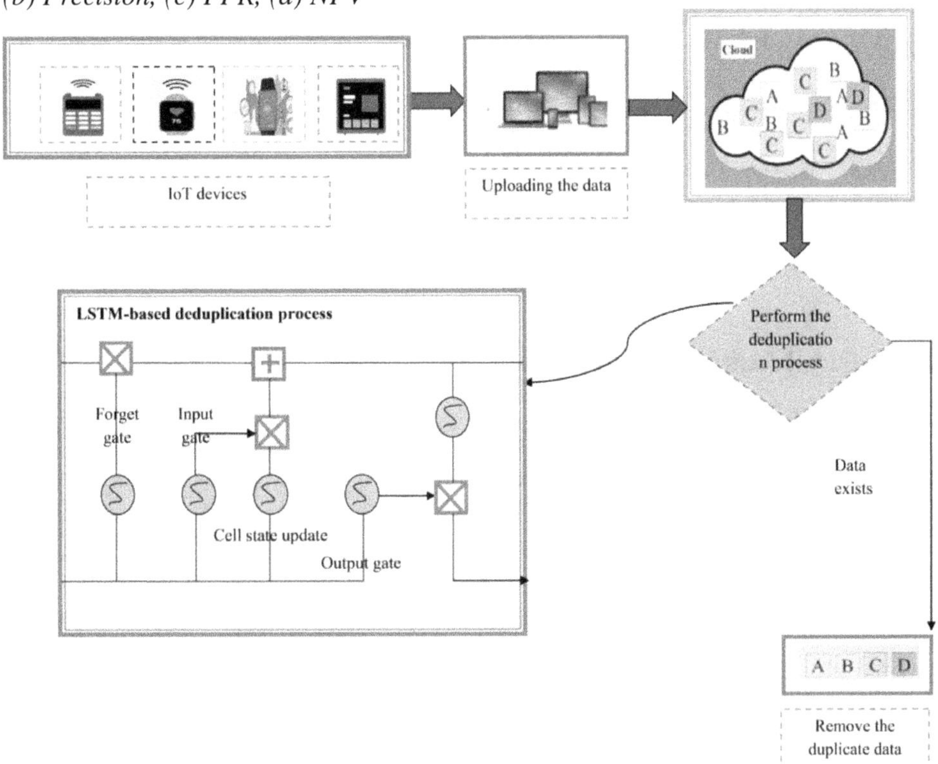

Statistical Assessment Over Several Algorithms

The statistical estimation of the CBOA-OK-ECC-based encryption model is illustrated in Table 2. At the size of block as 1, the best factor of the CBOA-OK-ECC-based encryption model is better than the TSA-OK-ECC, GEO-OK-ECC, HHO-OK-ECC, and RFO-OK-ECC with 0.59%, 2.54%, 0.78% and 1.9%. Thus, the performance of the CBOA-OK-ECC-based encryption model is better than that of the long-established models.

Table 2. Statistical measurement of the optimal key-based encryption model

TERMS	TSA-OK-ECC	GEO-OK-ECC	HHO-OK-ECC	RFO-OK-ECC	CBOA-OK-ECC
Mean	0.52252	0.5212	0.52398	0.52902	0.52244
Worst	0.55647	0.5212	0.57691	0.53916	0.59497
Median	0.5162	0.5212	0.52197	0.52597	0.50757
Standard deviation	0.013876	3.36×10^{-16}	0.016391	0.006532	0.02462
Best	0.51585	0.5212	0.51113	0.51752	0.50757

Numerical Assessment

Table 2 The numerical evaluation of the LSTM-based deduplication framework is presented in Table 3. The MCC of the LSTM-based deduplication system is 90.3%, which is better than the RNN, VGG16, DNN, and RAN. So, the presentation of the LSTM-based deduplication framework is supplemented by the conservative model Table 3.

Table 3. Numerical evaluation of the deep model-based deduplication approach over various techniques

TERMS	RNN	VGG16	DNN	RAN	LSTM
Accuracy	0.913	0.906	0.917	0.936	0.952
FDR	0.10474	0.10142	0.091093	0.069246	0.049281
FNR	0.069815	0.090349	0.078029	0.061602	0.049281
F1-score	0.91239	0.90408	0.91539	0.93456	0.95072
MCC	0.82665	0.81199	0.83403	0.87197	0.90394
FPR	0.10331	0.097466	0.087719	0.066277	0.046784
NPV	0.89669	0.90253	0.91228	0.93372	0.95322
Specificity	0.89669	0.90253	0.91228	0.93372	0.95322
Sensitivity	0.93018	0.90965	0.92197	0.9384	0.95072
Precision	0.89526	0.89858	0.90891	0.93075	0.95072

CONCLUSION

An effective deep deduplication with a protection model was offered to eliminate storage difficulties in the cloud structure by deleting redundant files; therefore, lots of IoT data was saved in the cloud at low-cost expenses. Here, the deduplication process was initially performed with the aid of the LSTM structure. The suggested LSTM finds the subsistence of duplicate copies in the cloud based on the "input attributes" like the last modified date, file size, data pattern, and file types. Once it finds the deduplicated data in the cloud, it notifies the corresponding user regarding the file's existence. The data was used for encoding if the information was unavailable in the cloud. Here, the enciphering was executed using the OK-ECC. The required key in the binary format was optimally preferred using the CBOA. Due to this optimization, the "time and the memory space" for the encoding were greatly minimized. The encrypted information was safely stored in the cloud architecture. The corresponding user utilized the optimally selected key if the user wanted to access the encrypted data. From Figure 7 and at the SoftMax activation function, the precision of the LSTM-based deduplication model is improved than the RNN, VGG16, DNN, and RAN, with 7.21%, 8.24%, 7.21%, and 6.18%. Thus, the performance of the LSTM-based deduplication process was recovered than the traditional model. However, the implementation process of the ECC is quite difficult, and this will be fixed in the forthcoming research work.

REFERENCES

Anand, R., Jestadi, R., Govinda, K., & Sharma, D. (2024). Data-driven insights: Analyzing and visualizing trends in the chocolate market for strategic decision-making. *AVE Trends in Intelligent Technoprise Letters, 1*(2), 60–70.

Anushya, A., Begum, S., Shiwani, S., & Shrivastava, A. (2024). Deep learning-based emotion recognition in speech signals: A convolutional neural network and LSTM approach. *AVE Trends in Intelligent Computing Systems, 1*(4), 198–208.

Boye, H. (2024). Strengthening cloud security through advanced encryption and anomaly detection techniques for secure data storage and transmission. *FMDB Transactions on Sustainable Computer Letters, 2*(3), 153–163. DOI: 10.69888/FTSCL.2024.000241

Cirillo, S., Polese, G., Salerno, D., Simone, B., & Solimando, G. (2023). Towards Flexible Voice Assistants: Evaluating Privacy and Security Needs in IoT-enabled Smart Homes. *FMDB Transactions on Sustainable Computer Letters, 1*(1), 25–32.

Eason, G. A., & Vijayakumar, D. A. (2020). Pioneer Approach Data Deduplication To Remove Redundant Data From Cloud Storage. [IJARET]. *International Journal of Advanced Research in Engineering and Technology, 11*(10), 535–544.

Fu, J.-S., Liu, Y., Chao, H.-C., Bhargava, B. K., & Zhang, Z.-J. (2018). Secure data storage and searching for industrial IoT by integrating fog computing and cloud computing. *IEEE Transactions on Industrial Informatics, 14*(10), 4519–4528. DOI: 10.1109/TII.2018.2793350

Gnanaguru, G., Priscila, S. S., Sakthivanitha, M., Radhakrishnan, S., Rajest, S. S., & Singh, S. (2024). Thorough analysis of deep learning methods for diagnosis of COVID-19 CT images. In *Advances in Medical Technologies and Clinical Practice* (pp. 46–65). IGI Global.

Karthik, S., Bhaggiaraj, S., Soji, E. S., Deve, L. S., Priscila, S. S., & Rajest, S. S. (2024). Real-time hand gesture recognition for stroke rehabilitation using deep learning approach. *AVE Trends in Intelligent Computing Systems, 1*(3), 157–172.

Karthikeyan, B., Devi, R. A., & Munshi, M. (2024). Utilizing Deep Learning for the Classification of Brain Tumours Using MRI. *AVE Trends In Intelligent Health Letters, 1*(1), 1–9.

Kumar, A. (2020). An extensive research survey on data integrity and deduplication towards privacy in cloud storage. [IJECE]. *International Journal of Electrical and Computer Engineering, 10*(2), 2011–2022. DOI: 10.11591/ijece.v10i2.pp2011-2022

Legista, M., Nurlaili, L., & Masriah, I. (2024). Development of an adaptive learning system utilizing deep learning to support independent learning processes for students. *AVE Trends in Intelligent Techno Learning*, *1*(2), 107–120.

Li, J., Liu, Y., Zhang, Z., Ren, J., & Zhao, N. (2017). Towards green IoT networking: Performance optimization of network coding based communication and reliable storage. *IEEE Access : Practical Innovations, Open Solutions*, *5*(5), 8780–8791. DOI: 10.1109/ACCESS.2017.2706328

Licaj, B., & Karras, D. A. (2024). Integral smart vehicle automation framework using IoT, modern software, and infrastructure. *AVE Trends in Intelligent Computing Systems*, *1*(3), 128–141.

Mao, B., Jiang, H., Wu, S., & Tian, L. (2016). Leveraging data deduplication to improve the performance of primary storage systems in the cloud. IEEE Transactions on Computers. *Institute of Electrical and Electronics Engineers*, *65*(6), 1775–1788.

Muthunagai, S. U., & Anitha, R. (2022). TDOPS: Time series based deduplication and optimal data placement strategy for IIoT in cloud environment. *Journal of Intelligent & Fuzzy Systems*, *43*(1), 1583–1597. DOI: 10.3233/JIFS-212568

Olakanmi, O. O., & Odeyemi, K. O. (2021). Faster and efficient cloud-server-aided data de-duplication scheme with an authenticated key agreement for Industrial Internet-of-Things. *Internet of Things : Engineering Cyber Physical Human Systems*, *14*(6), 100376. DOI: 10.1016/j.iot.2021.100376

Patra, S. S., Jena, S., Mohanty, J. R., & Gourisaria, M. K. (2021). DedupCloud: an optimized efficient virtual machine deduplication algorithm in cloud computing environment. In *Data Deduplication Approaches*. Elsevier. DOI: 10.1016/B978-0-12-823395-5.00009-4

Periasamy, J. K., & Latha, B. (2021). Efficient hash function based duplication detection algorithm for data Deduplication deduction and reduction. *Concurrency and Computation*, *33*(1), e5213. DOI: 10.1002/cpe.5213

Pierre, T. J., Tao, C., Vénant, K., & Erneste, B. (2024). Speed management blueprint: Conception of an IoT-based electric vehicle speed limiter monitoring system for Kigali city vehicles. *FMDB Transactions on Sustainable Energy Sequence*, *2*(1), 33–48. DOI: 10.69888/FTSES.2024.000190

Pranav, R. P., Prawin, R. P., Paramasivan, P., Shynu, T., & Subhashni, R. (2024). IoT-SecNet: A trust-based framework for enhancing security in IoT communications and network layer protocols. *FMDB Transactions on Sustainable Computing Systems*, *2*(2), 96–106. DOI: 10.69888/FTSCS.2024.000201

Raja, A. S. V., Jasper, K. D., Poornima, V., Priscila, S. S., Thenmozhi, A., & Ratkovic, N. (2024). Tech horizons unveiled: Navigating the transformative decade in AIML, cybersecurity, IoT, gaming, and data science education. *FMDB Transactions on Sustainable Intelligent Networks*, *1*(2), 120–134. DOI: 10.69888/FTSIN.2024.000214

Rajest, S. S., Moccia, S., Singh, B., Regin, R., & Jeganathan, J. (Eds.). (2024, August 30). Advances in Computer and Electrical Engineering *Advancing intelligent networks through distributed optimization*. IGI Global., DOI: 10.4018/979-8-3693-3739-4

Regin, R., Khanna, A. A., Krishnan, V., Gupta, M., & Bose, R. S., & Rajest, S. S. (2023). Information design and unifying approach for secured data sharing using attribute-based access control mechanisms. In Recent Developments in Machine and Human Intelligence (pp. 256–276). IGI Global, USA.

Renjith, E. J. (2024). Revolutionizing cloud security: Innovative approaches for safeguarding data integrity. *FMDB Transactions on Sustainable Computer Letters*, *2*(2), 111–119. DOI: 10.69888/FTSCL.2024.000185

Saxena, R., Sharma, V., & Saxena, R. R. (2023). Transforming Medical Education: Multi-Keyword Ranked Search in Cloud Environment. *FMDB Transactions on Sustainable Computing Systems*, *1*(3), 135–146.

Sayedelahl, M. A., & Farouk, R. M. (2024). Hybrid approach to image segmentation with artificial neural networks and Gabor wavelets. *AVE Trends in Intelligent Computing Systems*, *1*(2), 77–90.

Sharma, S., & Saini, H. (2020). Fog assisted task allocation and secure deduplication using 2FBO2and MoWo in cluster-based industrial IoT (IIoT). *Computer Communications*, *152*(2), 187–199. DOI: 10.1016/j.comcom.2020.01.042

Shukla, S., Hassan, M. F., Tran, D. C., Akbar, R., Paputungan, I. V., & Khan, M. K. (2023). Improving latency in Internet-of-Things and cloud computing for real-time data transmission: A systematic literature review (SLR). *Cluster Computing*, *26*(5), 2657–2680. DOI: 10.1007/s10586-021-03279-3

Singh, S., Rajest, S. S., Hadoussa, S., Obaid, A. J., & Regin, R. (2023). *Data-Driven Intelligent Business Sustainability*. Advances in Business Information Systems and Analytics. IGI Global., DOI: 10.4018/979-8-3693-0049-7

Singh, S., Rajest, S. S., Hadoussa, S., Obaid, A. J., & Regin, R. (Eds.). (2023, December 21). Advances in Business Information Systems and Analytics *Data-driven decision making for long-term business success*. IGI Global., DOI: 10.4018/979-8-3693-2193-5

Sirajudeen Yoosuf, M., & Anitha, R. (2022). Low Latency Fog-Centric Deduplication Approach to Reduce IoT Healthcare Data Redundancy. *Wireless Personal Communications*, *126*(5), 421–443. DOI: 10.1007/s11277-022-09752-5

Vemula, V. R. (2024). Cognitive artificial intelligence systems for proactive threat hunting in AI-driven cloud applications. *AVE Trends in Intelligent Computing Systems*, *1*(3), 173–183.

Vignesh, R., & Preethi, J. (2022). Secure Data Deduplication System with Efficient and Reliable Multi-Key Management in Cloud Storage. *Journal of Internet Technology*, *23*(4), 811–825. DOI: 10.53106/160792642022072304016

Yang, X., Lu, R., Choo, K. K. R., Yin, F., & Tang, X. (2022). Achieving efficient and privacy-preserving cross-domain big data deduplication in cloud. *IEEE Transactions on Big Data*, *8*(1), 73–84. DOI: 10.1109/TBDATA.2017.2721444

Yeh, W.-C., & Lin, J.-S. (2018). New parallel swarm algorithm for smart sensor systems redundancy allocation problems in the Internet of Things. *The Journal of Supercomputing*, *74*(10), 4358–4384. DOI: 10.1007/s11227-016-1903-8

Zanardo, E. (2024). Chronostamp: A general-purpose run-time for data-flow computing in a distributed environment. *AVE Trends in Intelligent Computing Systems*, *1*(2), 106–115.

Chapter 8
Secure D2D Transmission Using Lightweight Cryptography for 5G IoT Networks

Vijaya Lakshmi M.
https://orcid.org/0009-0005-2415-4930
Bharath Institute of Higher Education and Research, India

V. Ganesan
Bharath Institute of Higher Education and Research, India

ABSTRACT

Device-to-device (D2D) communication contributes to increased radio frequency reuse and cell coverage expansion in a 5G network by directly connecting devices without an intermediary node. Millions of smart gadgets with limited retention, battery life, and processing power are interconnected in a worldwide computing environment. One major environmental motivator has been the development of 5G. The unique characteristics of the 5G cellular network make it an ideal choice to serve as the backbone network for the Internet of Things in the future. On a 4G network—a common telecom network—standard communication between devices raises various security concerns, though. Furthermore, IoT devices have limited resources, so these security issues become even more important and challenging to solve when 5G networks are applied mMTC and URLLC applications. Safety issues in a 5G IoT environment must be addressed by a thin, safe D2D network able to provide safe verification, data integrity and privacy.

DOI: 10.4018/979-8-3373-4672-4.ch008

INTRODUCTION

D2D communication offers several benefits in mobile networks as it is a communication technique among devices without an intermediary node. A cellular network can increase each cell's coverage by acting as an interface to send data to nodes not inside the phone's area. Furthermore, by sending data straight among equipment, D2D communication lowers the core station's energy usage. Finally, there is a boost in the efficacy of utilizing the same radio frequency. The gap between equipment in D2D communication is significantly smaller than between the equipment and a center station. Owing to these benefits, D2D communication technologies like the LTE-advanced (4G) network are also a part of the 5G network (Tehrani et al., 2014). However, there are several security issues with standard D2D interaction on a mobile network. Furthermore, message verification and encryption are not used in D2D connections to maintain connection integrity and secrecy (Jeong and Ahn, 2017). This implies the attacker can use deception techniques, including position phishing, security snooping, and reckless behavior. We require a secure D2D communication system with an appropriate device verification procedure to address the security issues with D2D interaction in the 5G IoT network. Lightweight encryption can be an appropriate way to protect devices with limited resources (Doppler et al., 2009).

Elliptic Bend Cryptography (ECC) is becoming more broadly recognized as an extremely fruitful security arrangement. It functions admirably for gadgets with restricted assets, such as those in the quickly extending Web of Things (IoT) space. This acknowledgement results from the way that, as opposed to additional traditional strategies like RSA, ECC can offer a similar level of cryptographic security utilizing more modest keys (Chen et al., 2017). Specifically, a 256-cycle ECC key can give security like a 3072-bit RSA key, requiring less memory and figuring power — two indispensable advantages for Web of Things (IoT) gadgets with obliged handling and battery duration. The way that ECC is coordinated into the foundation of contemporary correspondence frameworks, including 5G organizations Lin et al. (2016); Wang et al. (2022); Daoud et al. (2019), which structure the premise of the Web of Things biological system, accentuates the innovation's convenience in this day and age significantly more (Zhang et al., 2019).

In this respect, our exploration presents a clever utilization of ECC for safe D2D (Gadget to Gadget) correspondence on a 5G Web of Things organization. Our methodology comprises a Validated Encryption with Related Information (AEAD) figure and an ECC-based lightweight encryption framework. The reason for this mix is to ensure the honesty and security of information moved between Web of Things gadgets. To forestall undesirable access, the ECC part scrambles the information and converts it into a solid organization that must be decoded by the planned recipient (Abro et al., 2019). Meanwhile, a solid strategy for affirming the information's honesty and legitimacy is presented by the AEAD encryption. This is achieved by empowering confirmation that the information is legitimate and has not been messed with during transmission by both the shipper and the beneficiary (Stallings and Cryptography, 2017).

For D2D correspondence, consolidating ECC and AEAD into a solitary, rational cryptosystem has numerous advantages. At first, it diminishes the registering trouble on each gadget, a fundamental calculation of Web of Things networks since gadgets regularly run on the low power supply (Cao et al., 2019). Our innovation drags out the existence of these gadgets by ensuring that the cryptographic tasks utilize minimal measures of assets, which works on the organization's general effectiveness. Second, the framework offers solid and versatile security highlights, which are fundamental in the continually developing IoT gadget organization. The framework can maintain an elevated degree of safety as the organization grows without expecting to add serious registering power or memory, which evades the bottlenecks that typically occur when safety efforts are increased (Javed et al., 2017).

Moreover, as a result of the intrinsic adaptability of the ECC-based framework, the cryptographic strength can be changed to suit different security prerequisites in different IoT situations. Gadgets in additional weak circumstances could acclimate to using harder assurances, while gadgets in sensibly secure organizations might work with less thorough security components (Ni et al., 2018). Moreover, our framework's use of AEAD figures encodes the data connected with correspondence notwithstanding the actual information. This is particularly vital for Web of Things applications since even little information breaks can endanger the organization's capacity to work (Tan et al., 2019).

To summarize, our examination offers a huge improvement in cryptography innovations that are particularly appropriate for the 5G IoT design. We give a versatile, secure, and powerful D2D correspondence framework that exploits the benefits of both AEAD and ECC figures. As well as tending to the specific troubles introduced by the Web of Things, this approach likewise lays out another norm for IoT security progressions, ensuring that organizations remain versatile despite a continually moving cluster of cyber threats. With this system, the security of the impending influx of computerized correspondence will be enormously cutting-edge, making way for more reliable and protected associations across the billions of connected gadgets around the world (Baskaran et al., 2017).

LITERATURE SURVEY

A reliable, lightweight D2D messaging system with many sensors was presented by Mingsheng Cao et al. Their suggested interaction method uses a speed sensor for circulation and compact key creation. It also ensures near-field verification that uses an equipment's writer and mic as sensors and speech and RF avenues for data transfer, encryption, and decryption (Carugi, 2018). According to Jothikumar et al. (2021), the RSA elliptical curve shows that calculation time increases significantly with higher security levels. Using cryptography, the discrete logarithm problem is resolved. But finding an ellipsoidal arc with each logarithm of a single point is difficult. Because of its tiny key, ECC offers a high degree of security, which is its fundamental benefit. Significantly less memory use and computing requirements are achieved with more temporary keys (Rezvani and Diehl, 2019).

An incentive-aware compact encrypted sharing of data system for dialogue between devices in 5G connections was suggested by Atefeh Mohseni-Ejiyeh et al. (2018). In their suggested plan, users receive electronic signatures as proof of successful information exchange, and MAC and the symmetrical encryption technique are employed during the transmission process. Yunqing Sun et al. (2019) suggested using the ECDH key exchange method and identity-based precursor encryption to find secure private devices and provide a way to log in for D2D. Most of this research employs ECC-based cryptographic techniques, and every one of them can provide verification and data integrity. They still come with certain drawbacks, such as the inability to ensure secrecy for specific findings or the lack of careful consideration of the D2D communication's data transfer step (Shin et al., 2019).

Ahmad et al. (2018) lead a significant examination that features the basic requirement for refined calculations to safeguard Web of Things (IoT) frameworks against cyberattacks. AI and factual strategies have a critical impact on this work. To make effective and fruitful calculations in progressively danger recognition, the concentrate cautiously analyzes the double prerequisite of consolidating state-of-the-art AI approaches to major areas of strength with strategies. This coordination is fundamental since IoT innovation is increasingly incorporated into day-to-day operations and company processes, raising the dangers and results of cyberattacks. Ahmad et al. 's research is led against an inexorably digitalized existence where Web of Things (IoT) gadgets are generally utilized for different purposes, going from home to business. These innovations are generally utilized, which features serious gambling because each gadget could be a mark of passage for threatening entertainers. Most online protection structures are responsive to the plan (Shin and Kwon, 2018). The creators argue that the ongoing safety efforts are, as often as possible, lacking. Accordingly, they recommend a proactive methodology that utilizes precise factual strategies and cutting-edge AI calculations to quickly foresee, recognize, and kill dangers (Ahmad and Alsmadi, 2021).

Ahmad and partners pressure that picking the right logical models and strategies to do this is so vital. To distinguish designs reminiscent of digital perils one of a kind to IoT settings, the review research various AI calculations. In the wake of being prepared on sizable datasets that precisely reflect regular and surprising organizational conduct, these models have a serious level of exactness in recognizing and foreseeing conceivable security breaks (Shaik et al., 2019). Using factual methods assists with working on these models' consistency, advancing them, and ensuring they can work under the constraints of continuous handling (Kim et al., 2020). Moreover, the review handles the issue of dangerous location speed and exactness compromises. Calculations that can rapidly survey data and make decisions are required for continuous location, which is fundamental for turning away huge mischief or unlawful information access. This direness for speed should not come to the detriment of exactness. Misleading negatives can permit unsafe breaks to slip through the cracks, and bogus up-sides can cause unnecessary disturbances. To ensure that the calculations produce trustworthy outcomes rapidly enough to take into consideration brief reaction activities, Ahmad et al. research different factual procedures that can work on the awareness and explicitness of AI models (Bordel et al., 2021).

Considering the different and continually developing IoT environments, the concentrate likewise addresses the versatility of these calculations. Since the capacities and kinds of information dealt with by IoT gadgets shift enormously, the calculations should be sufficiently adaptable to act in various situations and adequately huge to oversee networks going from unassuming home frameworks to gigantic modern buildings. Due to its versatility, security safety measures are kept up at all levels and expanded by the development of IoT organizations (Qin et al., 2020). The concentrate by Ahmad et al. makes a significant commitment to the subject by offering a hypothetical establishment and valuable applications and execution strategies. They request nonstop examination to work on combining AI and measurable procedures, better design these calculations to new dangers as they emerge and persistently work on these calculations. The review's determination tests the industry and the scholarly world to cooperate in propelling these innovations, featuring the meaning of interdisciplinary methodologies for proficient IoT space security (Ullah et al., 2021). Hu et al. (2018) work generally addresses a huge headway in IoT climate security. Through AI and measurable examination, their exploration lays out the establishment for making security frameworks stronger, more productive, and versatile, empowering them to check the advancing cluster of digital dangers. Their thoughts and ideas prepared for additional IoT security drives by advancing a calculation advancement approach that consolidates inventiveness, precision, and convenience (Huang et al., 2016).

METHODOLOGY

Regarding its expansion, influence, and future possibilities, the Internet of Things (IoT) with 5G capabilities is remarkable. The volume of data sent and handled by Internet of Things (IoT) devices dependent on coverage and connection causes several security concerns. This work intends to create a key generating method supported by 5G using Boltzmann machines to encrypt effectively and decrypt data in an Internet of Things (IoT) device communication network. With 5G networks employed in massive device kind connectivity (mMTC) and ultra-reliable minimal latency interaction (URLLC) scenarios, security risks become increasingly crucial and challenging to avoid when IoT technology emerges. This is thus because limited resources for connected devices cause restrictions. To solve privacy issues in a 5G IoT environment, we need a small, strong D2D messaging protocol with secure verification, data integrity, and obscurity. For a 5G IoT network, we thus provide in this work a safe D2D communication mechanism based on lightweight AEAD cyphers. The proposed to be used in the study to solve these problems are lightweight AEAD cyphers. Through encrypted linked data with a message authentication code (MAC), these AEAD cyphers can also offer data integrity and authentication. The main operations involved, and the actions followed are carefully discussed in the next parts.

Secured Communication of D2D

This part presents an inexpensive AEAD cipher-based secure D2D communication technique for a 5G IoT network. Figure 1 illustrates a recommended encrypted D2D communication model. UE is real equipment that interacts directly with other equipment inside our system. It is a mobile entity within a 5G network. UE is connected to mobile networks by gNB, a base station. Under our approach, gNBs generate D2D technology tokens ($D2DT\mathbf{N}g\mathbf{B}x$) by providing their public key in advance with other gNBs. AMF is in charge of overseeing a mobile entity. Co-located with AMF, SEAF serves as a middle-tier authentication entity between UEs and 5G networks. In a 5G network, UDM retains data on mobile entities. A 5G network enables the 5G-AKA authentication architecture for UE identity verification. In the suggested D2D system, it is equivalent to step 0, and each UE only proceeds through the process once.

In contemporary remote organizations, gadget-to-gadget (D2D) correspondence innovation is fundamental since it gives gadgets a direct way to convey without requiring a concentrated organization framework. This innovation is vital in crisis reaction situations or thickly jam-packed metropolitan locales, where fast and viable correspondence is fundamental. The D2D correspondence process comprises three fundamental stages, every one of which is fundamental to keeping up with the framework's flexibility and adequacy. Gadget disclosure is the underlying move toward the cycle by which gadgets in the nearness recognize each other's presence. This step is urgent to bring down inactivity and protect network assets for making conceivable correspondence linkages without using the organization's center framework.

Gadgets lay out a correspondence convention and set up the necessary boundaries for information trade during join design, which comes after gadget revelation simultaneously. To ensure that the connection is protected and custom-made for the specific necessities of the climate wherein the gadgets work, this includes arranging recurrence channels, information transmission paces, and encryption procedures. Information is securely moved and gotten between gadgets during the last stage, which is encoded information transmission. Most of the information moves are happening right now. Subsequently, everything must work out positively to safeguard the viability and respectability of the correspondence. As opposed to traditional D2D correspondence frameworks, the procedure introduced here consolidates further developed well-being measures at every one of these stages to meet developing worries about security and protection in advanced cooperations. Guaranteeing protection includes anonymizing gadget personalities at whatever point is practical and using safe procedures that obstruct unapproved gadgets from following or recognizing correspondence accomplices. This is fundamental for forestalling, following or snooping on gadget action. It is particularly basic in the circumstances, while keeping up with obscurity is basic, remembering it for government or corporate connections.

Recognizability is a significant security viewpoint stringently maintained at each D2D interaction step. It involves verifying the gadgets partaking in the correspondence to guarantee that information is shared exclusively with people who have been affirmed and trusted. This activity is fundamental for halting man-in-the-center assaults and other cyber threats that utilize poor distinguishing proof techniques to catch or change information. Lastly, high-level encryption strategies utilized throughout the scrambled information transmission stage safeguard the information's respectability and mystery. With these methodologies, the information stays unaltered throughout transmission and is unscrambled and intelligible exclusively by the expected collector. By coordinating these well-being components into each step of the D2D correspondence process, the framework's general security is improved, and client certainty is expanded, making a more trustworthy and secure organization climate.

Figure 1. D2D communication

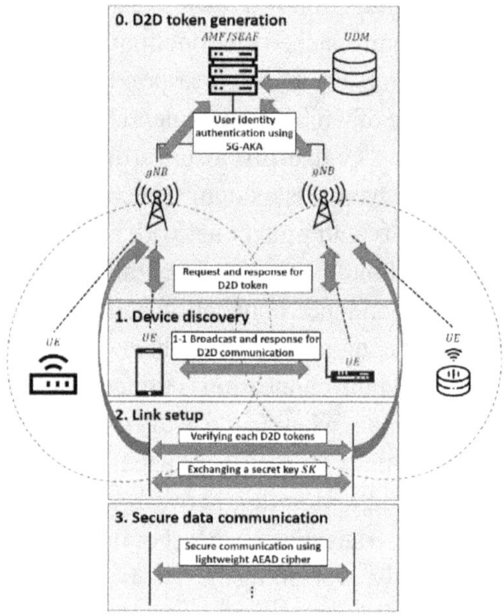

This innovation fulfils and essentially surpasses the principal necessities of customary D2D frameworks, giving a profoundly productive and secure specialized strategy by coordinating these high-level safety efforts personality, privacy, and uprightness into the key functional phases of D2D correspondence. This ensures that D2D innovation has areas of strength that put client well-being and information security first as it creates and turns out to be more coordinated into all features of computerized correspondence. Therefore, it has become an essential part of contemporary correspondence procedures in a world that is becoming more interconnected.

Token generation: Pre-processing, done before D2D communication, and the three remaining D2D communication procedures fall into three categories: pre-processing, done before D2D communication, and the other three. D2D communication is accomplished in device recognition, connection setting, and safe data delivery. Equivalent to step 0, the pre-processing stage is the D2D token generating procedure. Consider that every GNB has the same public key as indicated in the previous section; hence, if the public key of the gNB and the SUCI of the UE are known, the freshly generated D2D tokens can be validated. D2D token-generating mechanism is shown in Figure 2.

Figure 2. Overview of the process

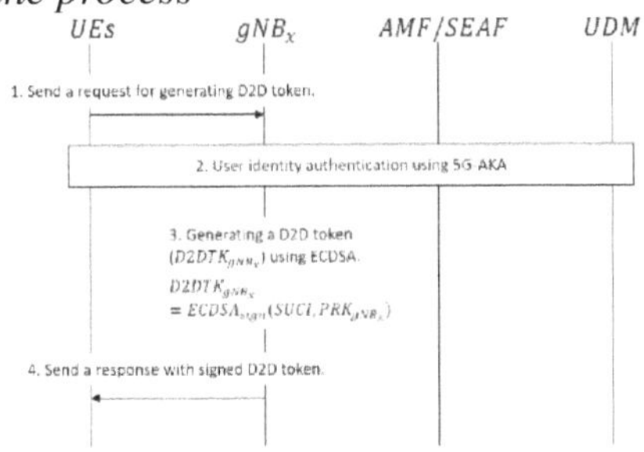

DETAILED PROCESS

Figure 3 illustrates all of the proposed D2D communication techniques. The first step is device exploration, which seeks something nearby to conduct D2D communication. In this instance, each UE that wishes to communicate through D2D broadcasts a message asking to communicate via D2D, and UEs that are in a condition that they can interact via D2D send back a message in response to the D2D request message they received. In this case, the D2D token distributed in step Zero and its SUCI are included in the broadcast or reply message. The procedure moves on to the following stage if an answer to the broadcast query message is obtained.

Setting up a link to begin a communication session is the second step in D2D communication. In this stage, the D2D technology token is transferred by finding the device and checking it before a communication session is set up. Although the authentication process is carried out in the GNB without forming a connection to the core network, the D2D token verification is comparable to the UE verification of identity carried out during the D2D token generation. The common key and SUCI of each GNB can be used to verify the D2D token, confirming that the GNB legitimately issued the token upon demand from a pre-authenticated UE. Following the D2D token verification, the secret key transfer encrypts the data transfer. Data encryption communication is carried out during safe data transfer, the final phase of the suggested D2D connection. Currently, a lightweight AEAD cipher is used for encryption.

Figure 3. Detailed process

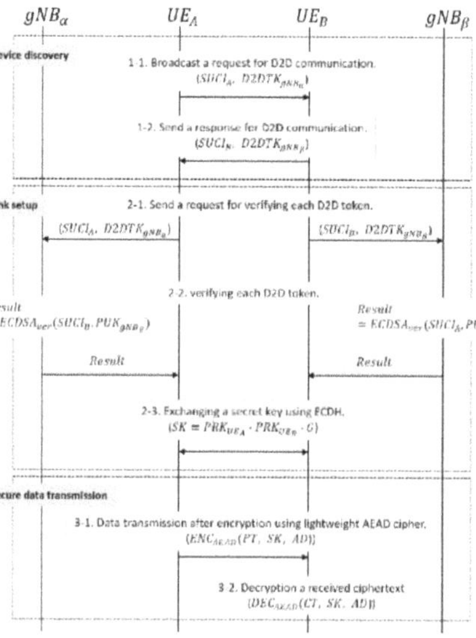

RESULTS

We simulate in this section to assess the effectiveness and productivity of the suggested D2D communication system. The suggested D2D communication process's entire processing time is displayed in the outcome in this section. Furthermore, to assess the effectiveness of the suggested D2D communication, we estimate energy consumption based on AEAD encryption techniques and evaluate the deployment costs of lightweight AEAD ciphers. Cryptographic methods have been employed in the suggested communication between D2D devices to provide security requirements (anonymity, data confidentiality/integrity, and authentication). The specific cryptographic algorithms used are the AEAD cipher, the Diffie–Hellman key transfer method, and a digital signature. We assume that each algorithm for cryptography has the following processing time. The duration it takes to sign a digital signature ($tDSsign$), verify a digital signature ($tDSver$), transfer keys (tDH), and process data for the AEAD cipher ($tADF$). Then, we assume that D2D communication has a transmission latency of ltr. The energy Consumption Equation and Latency Equation for Encrypted D2D Communication are given as:

$$E = NL\,E_{enc}(k) \tag{1}$$

In this equation, E represents the total energy consumed by the D2D communication process, N is the number of data packets transmitted, L is the average packet length, and $E_{enc}(k)$ is the energy consumed per byte of data encrypted using a lightweight.

Cryptographic key k: This equation emphasizes using energy-efficient cryptography in 1oT devices with critical battery life.

$$T_{total} = T_{auth} + N\left(T_{enc} + T_{trans} + T_{dec}\right) \tag{2}$$

Here, T_{total} denotes the total communication latency, T_{auth} is the time required for authentication processes such as 5G-AKA and ECDSA token generation, T_{enc} and T_{dec} are the times taken to encrypt and decrypt the data packets, respectively, T_{trans} is the transmission time per packet, and N is the number of packets. This equation is critical for URLLC applications where reducing latency is as important as ensuring secure transmission.

$$t_{D2D} = \sum 1_{tr} + \sum t_{DS_{sign}} + \sum t_{DS_{ver}} + \sum t_{DH} + \sum t_{ALAD} \tag{3}$$

The equation t_{D2D} represents the total latency for D2D communications, calculated as the sum of various components: transmission latency $\left(\sum 1_{tr}\right)$, digital signature signing time $\left(\sum t_{DS\_sign}\right)$, signature verification time $\left(\sum t_{DS\_ver}\right)$, Diffie-Hellman key exchange time $\left(\sum t_{DH}\right)$, and the time for applying lightweight AEAD cipher $\left(\sum t_{ALAD}\right)$.

We examine the recommended communication method D2D regarding the quantity of transmission and the number of times the encryption method is used at each stage to compute the total of each time spent processing. Phase 0 of the D2D tokens generation process involves two messages: a request and an answer for a D2D technology token. 5G-AKA is also used in this phase for individual verification. UEs, the GNB, AMF, and UDM in 5G-AKA share ten transmissions-the D2D token creation stage processes token generation using ECDSA-signing, a cryptography technique. Furthermore, as the 5G-AKA is predicated on the ECC certification, we believe it comprises ECDSA signing and the ECDSA verification.

Table 1. Results

Step	Transmission Latency	Cryptographic algorithm Processing time			
		ECDSA-Sign	ECDSA-Verify	ECDH	AEAD
0-Step	(2+10)*ln	(1+1) *t DS sign	1*t DS ver	-	-
1-Step	(m+1) *ln	-	-	-	-
2-Step	(2+2+2) *ln	-	2*t DS ver	1*t DH	-

continued on following page

Table 1. Continued

Step	Transmission Latency	Cryptographic algorithm Processing time			
		ECDSA-Sign	ECDSA-Verify	ECDH	AEAD
3-Step	(n/1460) *ln	-	-	-	2*t AEAD
Total(Σ l or Σ t)	(19+m+n/1460) *ln	2*t DS ver	3*t DS ver	2*t DH	2*t AEAD

The desired UE transmits the message asking for permission during the device's discovery (step 1), which indicates that the total amount of transmission for the requested message equals the number of devices (m) close to the sender UE. Additionally, there is communication to respond in this stage. Two devices establish their connection during link setup (step 2). There are transmissions for token verification, confirmation response, key exchange, and practices of the encryption technique for ECDSA validation and ECDH. Finally, we believed that data is sent in packets and quantities of 1460 bytes for safe data transfer (step 3), which has transmissions based on the total quantity of data (n bytes).

Simulation

We selected every parameter for equation (1) using Table 2's time for processing simulation based on the demands of 5G networks and the cryptography algorithm's current application outcomes. Since 1 millisecond is the minimum transmission latency required by the 5G network, we set *ltr* to 0.001. Additionally, we determined the ECC-based algorithm's duration of processing based on the results reported in(*tDSsin*=0.122,*tDSveT*=0.458,*tDSDH*=0.1672).

Figure 4. Process time

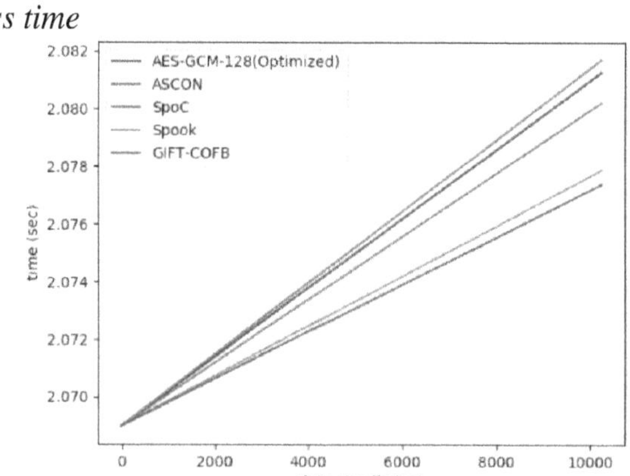

By multiplying the technique's throughput (Mbps) by the total quantity of data (D_E (Mb) = D_E (MB)−8/106), we can get the amount of processing time. Based on the computational findings, we adjusted the parameters for the next five AEAD ciphers (AES-GCM, ASCON, The SpoC, Spook, and GIFT-COFB) to simulate different AEAD ciphers. The idea for D2D communication's simulated result is displayed in Figure 4. Nevertheless, due to the restricted resources of 5G Internet of Things (IoT) networks, encryption techniques might not be able to provide adequate performance for all 5G IoT gadgets. This implies that the algorithm for encryption needs to be used sparingly while requiring minimal power consumption. The hardware-based outcomes for AEAD block encryption algorithms are displayed in (Table 1). As in the domain for developing search tables (LUTs), Spook has the highest implementation cost despite being faster than AES-GCM (optimized).

Table 2. AEAD cipher results

AEAD Cipher	Area (LUTs)	Power (mW)	Throughput (Mbps)	Energy (nJ/bit)
AES-GCM (Optimized)	1532.00	35.9	31.2	1.15
GIFT-COFB	2695.00	36.6	120.8	0.30
SpC	1344.00	34.7	28.8	1.20
ASCON	1808.00	33.6	39.0	0.98
Spook	7002.00	126.9	86.3	1.43

Validated Encryption with Related Information (AEAD) figures are contrasted in (Table 2), concurring with equipment execution standards such as region, power utilization, throughput, and energy effectiveness. Demonstrating the expected chip region, the "Region (LUTs)" shows the number of Query Table Units utilized. The milliwatt-based power estimation "Power (mW)" is fundamental for battery-worked gadgets. For applications that need high-velocity encryption, "Throughput (Mbps)" demonstrates the information handling speed in megabits each second. For energy-touchy applications, "Energy (nJ/bit)" is a pivotal measure showing how much energy is required for all the information handled. For example, AES-GCM (Improved) accomplishes a throughput of 31.2 Mbps at an energy cost of 1.15 nJ/bit by utilizing 1532 LUTs at a power use of 35.9 mW. The Table shows how various codes vary, with GIFT-COFB being especially striking for its high throughput and low energy use. Table 2's energy effectiveness guides Figure 5's energy consumption expressed by data quantity. Though SpoC and Spook use more energy, AES-GCM (enhanced) ate significantly more energy-wise than GIFT-COFB and ASCON.

Figure 5. Energy consumption

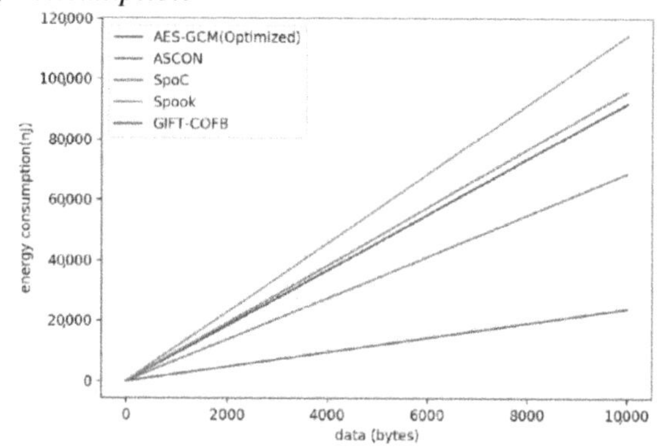

The energy usage (measured in picojoules) of several Authenticated Encryption with Associated Data (AEAD) ciphers is plotted against the amount of data processed (measured in bytes) in Figure 5. To better illustrate the significant variations in energy consumption at larger data quantities, the y-axis is scaled logarithmically, with each line denoting a distinct AEAD cipher. The energy needed for encryption by each cipher rises as the data size increases from 0 to 10,000 bytes, demonstrating their scalability and effectiveness when handling higher data volumes. The blue line, representing the AES-GCM (Optimized) encryption, indicates a relatively sharp increase and higher energy consumption with increasing data size. However, out of all the plotted ciphers over greater data sizes, GIFT-COFB, shown in red, shows the least energy gain, making it the most energy-efficient. Between the extremes of AES-GCM and GIFT-COFB, SpC and Spook, shown in purple and green, respectively, exhibit moderate increases.

Security Analysis

We analyze the suggested safe D2D communication system from a security perspective. As previously addressed, data confidentiality/integrity, anonymity, and authentication are necessary for safe D2D communication. Furthermore, a 5G Internet of Things network must be constructed and operated effectively due to resource constraints. Starting with security factors, we will discuss the suggested D2D communication mechanism. Additionally, we talk about security against common digital-to-digital threats. Before delivering a D2D token, this suggested D2D technology communication network executes basic authentication for a UE via 5G-AKA, an authentication framework made available by 5G. Additionally, the newly issued token can carry out a second authentication by validating the D2D technology communication link creation process using SUCI and the publicly accessible key of the GNB.

SUCI, the encrypted UE identification, and the gNB secret key are used by the recommended D2D communication system to generate D2D communication throughout the D2D production process. The personal information of an unencrypted UE is never transmitted during this process. Furthermore, after establishing a D2D link, encrypting utilizes the lightweight AEAD cipher during the data transmission phase. In addition to data secrecy, AEAD cryptography can offer integrity and authentication. Lightweight cryptography is the foundation for the data encryption and authentication procedures utilized in the suggested D2D communication system. The ECC-based publicly accessible key encryption system with the compact AEAD cipher is the lightweight cipher employed in this paper. Compared to RSA, which utilizes a 1024-bit key, the ECC-based open-source security system functions more quickly with a 256-bit key. Additionally, the lightweight AEAD encryption offers data confidentiality/integrity and authentication and is made to be effectively used in limited resource environments, like the Internet of Things.

CONCLUSION

Our review presents a protected and versatile gadget-to-gadget (D2D) correspondence framework improved for the 5G Web of Things (IoT). It has worked to deal with a scope of 5G use cases, like those relating to AI and Super Solid Low-Dormancy Interchanges (URLLC). Using a lightweight Verified Encryption with Related Information (AEAD) figure and an open-source encryption framework given Elliptic Bend Cryptography (ECC), our proposed correspondence convention for D2D collaborations boosts computational effectiveness while keeping up with security. The framework utilizes the 5G-Otherwise, known as the verification strategy, to check the characters of client gear (UE) before making any D2D associations to ensure safe interchanges. Elliptic Bend Computerized Mark Calculation (ECDSA) is an extraordinarily made token in the D2D correspondence structure. By validating the UE and affirming that the gadget participating in the D2D trade is authentic and permitted, this token is vital for the underlying foundation of the correspondence. This approach reinforces the D2D correspondence security engineering in the 5G organization while at the same time further developing framework soundness and effectiveness, which makes it ideal for circumstances where high security and low idleness are basic. Our technique offers a modern yet serviceable answer for secure D2D correspondence in the quickly extending field of the Web of Things, exhibiting a significant jump in cryptographic strategies inside 5G organizations.

Limitations

Although imaginative, the concentration on secure gadget-to-gadget (D2D) transmission using lightweight cryptography for 5G IoT networks has huge disadvantages. Most importantly, there might be challenges with the versatility of lightweight cryptographic arrangements in heterogeneous and profoundly organized Web of Things conditions since additional gadgets might strain the speed and effectiveness of the cryptographic tasks. Second, there are questions regarding the drawn-out security viability of lightweight cryptography because its versatility in new cryptographic assaults in the powerful danger scene of 5G organizations has not been completely analyzed. Moreover, it is possible that the proposed cryptographic conventions won't be broadly utilized because of their unfortunate consistency with global security norms and the absence of interoperability with current organizational frameworks. To wrap things up, there is still a lot to find out about the energy effectiveness of applying such cryptographic methods on a wide scale, particularly in gadgets with severe power limits.

Future Scope

With lightweight encryption, secure Gadget-to-gadget (D2D) correspondence in 5G IoT networks has a bright and wide future. Giving solid security with minimal computational effort will be fundamental as IoT gadgets multiply. Ensuing examinations might focus on making more mind-boggling cryptographic calculations that are likewise asset-effective, explicitly intended for the shifted and consistently changing IoT settings. Besides, D2D correspondences might turn out to be stronger, assuming that artificial intelligence and AI strategies are consolidated to expect and balance security goes after right away. Exploring blockchain innovation for decentralized security of the executives, which ensures gadget trust and straightforwardness, would be another fascinating field of study. Moreover, to work with the far and wide execution of IoT arrangements, these cryptographic arrangements should be sufficiently adaptable to work in different 5G settings, including metropolitan and modern ones. Finally, for secure D2D transmissions to be broadly taken on in 5G organizations, it will likewise be critical to defeat the issues of versatility and interoperability across heterogeneous gadgets.

REFERENCES

Abro, A., Deng, Z., & Memon, K. A. (2019). A lightweight elliptic-ElGamal-based authentication scheme for secure Device-to-Device communication. *Future Internet, 11*(5), 108. DOI: 10.3390/fi11050108

Ahmad, I., Kumar, T., Liyanage, M., Okwuibe, J., Ylianttila, M., & Gurtov, A. (2018). Overview of 5G security challenges and solutions. *IEEE Communications Standards Magazine, 2*(1), 36–43. DOI: 10.1109/MCOMSTD.2018.1700063

Ahmad, R., & Alsmadi, I. (2021). Machine learning approaches to IoT security: A systematic literature review. *Internet of Things : Engineering Cyber Physical Human Systems, 14*(7), 100365. DOI: 10.1016/j.iot.2021.100365

Baskaran, S. B. M., & Raja, G. (2017). A lightweight incognito key exchange mechanism for LTE-A assisted D2D communication. *2017 Ninth International Conference on Advanced Computing (ICoAC)*, Chennai, India. DOI: 10.1109/ICoAC.2017.8441370

Bordel, B., Alcarria, R., Robles, T., & Iglesias, M. S. (2021). Data authentication and anonymization in IoT scenarios and future 5G networks using chaotic digital watermarking. *IEEE Access : Practical Innovations, Open Solutions, 20*(2), 1–23. DOI: 10.1109/ACCESS.2021.3055771

Cao, M., Wang, L., Xu, H., Chen, D., Lou, C., Zhang, N., Zhu, Y., & Qin, Z. (2019). Sec-D2D: A secure and lightweight D2D communication system with multiple sensors. *IEEE Access : Practical Innovations, Open Solutions, 75*(9), 104990. DOI: 10.1109/ACCESS.2019.2900727

Carugi, M. (2018). Key features and requirements of 5G/IMT-2020 networks. In *Proceedings of the ITU Arab Forum on Emerging Technologies*, Algeria.

Chen, S., Hu, J., Shi, Y., Peng, Y., Fang, J., Zhao, R., & Zhao, L. (2017). Vehicle-to-everything (V2X) services supported by LTE-based systems and 5G. *IEEE Communications Standards Magazine, 1*(2), 70–76. DOI: 10.1109/MCOMSTD.2017.1700015

Daoud, W. B., Obaidat, M. S., Meddeb-Makhlouf, A., Zarai, F., & Hsiao, K.-F. (2019). TACRM: Trust access control and resource management mechanism in fog computing. *Human-Centric Computing and Information Sciences, 9*(28), 1–18. DOI: 10.1186/s13673-019-0188-3

Doppler, K., Rinne, M. P., Janis, P., Ribeiro, C., & Hugl, K. (2009). Device-to-device communications: Functional prospects for LTE-advanced networks. In *2009 IEEE International Conference on Communications Workshops Dresden*, Germany DOI: 10.1109/ICCW.2009.5208020

Hu, F., Xu, X., Peng, T., Pu, C., & Li, L. (2018). A fast pseudo-stochastic sequential cipher generator based on RBMs. *Neural Computing & Applications, 30*(4), 1277–1287. DOI: 10.1007/s00521-016-2753-2

Huang, L., Deng, Y., & Wang, B. (2016). Flow simulation of suspension bridge cable based on lattice-Boltzmann method. *Mathematical Problems in Engineering, 2016*(8), 1–7. DOI: 10.1155/2016/2537581

Javed, Y., Khan, A. S., Qahar, A., & Abdullah, J. (2017). EEoP: A lightweight security scheme over PKI in D2D cellular networks. *Journal of Telecommunication, Electronic and Computer Engineering, 9*(1), 99–105.

Jeong, M., & Ahn, S. (2017). A network coding-aware routing mechanism for time-sensitive data delivery in multi-hop wireless networks. *Journal of Information Processing Systems, 13*(6), 1544–1553.

Jothikumar, C., Ramana, K., Chakravarthy, V. D., Singh, S., & Ra, I.-H. (2021). An efficient routing approach to maximize the lifetime of IoT-based wireless sensor networks in 5G and beyond. *Mobile Information Systems, 2021*(1), 1–11. DOI: 10.1155/2021/9160516

Kim, J., Astillo, P. V., & You, I. (2020). DMM-SEP: Secure and efficient protocol for distributed mobility management based on 5G networks. *IEEE Access : Practical Innovations, Open Solutions, 8*(99), 1–1. DOI: 10.1109/ACCESS.2020.2985448

Lin, Z., Du, L., Gao, Z., Huang, L., & Du, X. (2016). Efficient device-to-device discovery and access procedure for 5G cellular network: Efficient device-to-device discovery and access procedure for 5G. *Wireless Communications and Mobile Computing, 16*(7), 1282–1289. DOI: 10.1002/wcm.2602

Mohseni-Ejiyeh, A., Ashouri-Talouki, M., & Mahdavi, M. (2018). An incentive-aware, lightweight, secure data-sharing scheme for D2D communication in 5G cellular networks. *ISeCure, 10*(1), 15–27.

Ni, J., Lin, X., & Shen, X. S. (2018). Efficient and secure service-oriented authentication supporting network slicing for 5G-enabled IoT. *IEEE Journal on Selected Areas in Communications, 36*(3), 644–657. DOI: 10.1109/JSAC.2018.2815418

Qin, Y., Liu, J., Zhao, S., Feng, D., & Feng, W. (2020). RIPTE: Runtime integrity protection based on trusted execution for IoT device. *Security and Communication Networks*, *2020*(6), 1–14. DOI: 10.1155/2020/8957641

Rezvani, B., & Diehl, W. (2019). Hardware Implementations of NIST Lightweight Cryptographic Candidates: A First Look. In *Proceedings of the NIST Lightweight Cryptography Workshop*, Maryland, USA.

Shaik, A., Borgaonkar, R., Park, S., & Seifert, J. P. (2019). New vulnerabilities in 4G and 5G cellular access network protocols: exposing device capabilities. In *Proceedings of the 12th Conference on Security and Privacy in Wireless and Mobile Networks*, New York, USA. DOI: 10.1145/3317549.3319728

Shin, D., Yun, K., Kim, J., Astillo, P. V., Kim, J., & You, I. (2019). A security protocol for route optimization in DMM-based smart home IoT networks. *IEEE Access : Practical Innovations, Open Solutions*, *14*(8), 100219. DOI: 10.1109/ACCESS.2019.2943929

Shin, S., & Kwon, T. (2018). Two-factor authenticated key agreement supporting unlinkability in 5G-integrated wireless sensor networks. *IEEE Access : Practical Innovations, Open Solutions*, *6*(99), 1–1. DOI: 10.1109/ACCESS.2018.2796539

Stallings, W., & Cryptography, N. (2017). *Cryptography and Network Security: Principles and Practice*. Pearson.

Sun, Y., Cao, J., Ma, M., Li, H., Niu, B., & Li, F. (2019). Privacy-preserving device discovery and authentication scheme for D2D communication in 3GPP 5G HetNet. *2019 International Conference on Computing, Networking and Communications (ICNC)*, Hawaii, USA. DOI: 10.1109/ICCNC.2019.8685499

Tan, H., Song, Y., Xuan, S., Pan, S., & Chung, I. (2019). Secure D2D group authentication employing smartphone sensor behaviour analysis. *Symmetry*, *11*(8), 969. DOI: 10.3390/sym11080969

Tehrani, M. N., Uysal, M., & Yanikomeroglu, H. (2014). Device-to-device communication in 5G cellular networks: Challenges, solutions, and future directions. *IEEE Communications Magazine*, *52*(5), 86–92. DOI: 10.1109/MCOM.2014.6815897

Ullah, F., Naeem, M. R., Mostarda, L., & Shah, S. A. (2021). Clone detection in 5G-enabled social IoT system using graph semantics and deep learning model. *International Journal of Machine Learning and Cybernetics*, *12*(11), 3115–3127. DOI: 10.1007/s13042-020-01246-9

Wang, C., Yu, W., Lu, J., Zhu, F., Fan, L., & Li, S. (2022). UAV-based physical-layer intelligent technologies for 5G-enabled internet of things: A survey. *Wireless Communications and Mobile Computing*, *10*(1), 1–5. DOI: 10.1155/2022/4351518

Zhang, S., Wang, Y., & Zhou, W. (2019). Towards secure 5G networks: A survey. *Computer Networks*, *162*(10), 106871. DOI: 10.1016/j.comnet.2019.106871

Chapter 9
Adversarial Attacks on Deep Learning-Based Intrusion Detection Systems on Challenges and Countermeasures

A. Jeyaram
https://orcid.org/0009-0005-2415-4930
Bharath Institute of Higher Education and Research, India

A. Muthukumaravel
Bharath Institute of Higher Education and Research, India

ABSTRACT

DL-based IDS are crucial for detecting and reducing security risks in network settings. Nevertheless, these systems are susceptible to adversarial assaults that exploit model flaws. This research presents a defensive architecture that combines dynamic retraining, ensemble learning, real-time monitoring, and model interpretability to improve the resilience of IDS. Over subsequent years, the performance assessment reveals significant improvements in accuracy (from 0.85 to 0.94), precision (from 0.78 to 0.91), recall (from 0.89 to 0.95), and F1 score (from 0.83 to 0.93). Significantly, there was a reduction in false positive rates from 0.12 to 0.06 and a drop in false negative rates from 0.11 to 0.05. Analysis of feature significance serves to identify crucial aspects that influence the predictions made by a model, hence improving its interpretability. The suggested structure facilitates the ability of IDS to adjust and react to evolving threats efficiently.

DOI: 10.4018/979-8-3373-4672-4.ch009

INTRODUCTION

The growing dependence on IDS based on deep learning has greatly improved the security stance of diverse networks and systems. These systems use AI to identify and effectively address various security risks, including but not limited to malware, phishing attacks, network intrusions, and data breaches. Nevertheless, despite their efficacy, IDS based on DL are not impervious to adversary manipulation (Khushnaseeb and Zafar, 2023). Adversaries may exploit the vulnerabilities present in these systems by creating malicious inputs designed to avoid detection, compromising the effectiveness of their security measures. The integrity and dependability of contemporary cybersecurity infrastructures are significantly challenged by adversarial assaults targeting DL-based IDS. These assaults use various methods, including evasion attacks and poisoning attacks, to mislead IDS into incorrectly categorizing or disregarding hostile activity (Syed Agha Hassnainmohsan et al., 2023). Evasion attacks include altering input data to elude detection while poisoning attacks specifically target the training process by introducing malevolent samples into the training dataset (Boye, 2024). The potential ramifications of effective adversarial assaults on IDS may be significant, resulting in unnoticed security breaches, data exfiltration, and system penetration (Dhinakaran et al., 2023).

DL-based IDS are susceptible to adversarial assaults due to their dependence on intricate neural network structures. However, these designs can capture complex patterns and correlations in data that are inherently vulnerable to manipulation by adversaries. Adversaries leverage the non-linear characteristics of DL models to manipulate input data in an undetectable manner by human observers, but may result in substantial alterations to model predictions (Afnanalotaibi, 2023). The advent of adversarial machine learning as an area of academic inquiry has brought attention to the susceptibilities of DL models and the possible hazards linked to their use in applications that need high levels of security (Priscila et al., 2023). Researchers have established the viability of adversarial attacks on diverse deep learning-based systems, such as image classifiers, natural language processing models, and IDS (Sayedelahl, 2024). The occurrence of these assaults has emphasized the need for strong defensive measures to protect against ever-changing cyber threats (Minu et al., 2023). To tackle the difficulties presented by adversarial assaults on DL-based IDS, a comprehensive and multifaceted strategy is necessary (Nageswaraguptha et al., 2022).

First and foremost, it is necessary to get a more profound understanding of the inherent weaknesses in DL models and their consequences for security applications (Devi and Rajasekaran, 2023). By identifying and analyzing the inherent faults in these models, researchers may create designs that are more durable and less vulnerable to hostile manipulation (Harshadsathaye et al., 2022). In addition, establishing efficient defensive mechanisms is of utmost importance to minimize the consequences of adversarial assaults on IDS (Pranav et al., 2023). The use of adversarial training, which entails including hostile cases in the training process, has shown the potential to enhance the resilience of DL models against evasion attempts (Talaeikhoei and Ismail, 2022). Furthermore, feature engineering, ensemble learning, and model diversification may augment the robustness of IDS by bringing a range of variations and duplications into the detection procedure (Whelan et al., 2022).

Furthermore, it is essential to foster cooperation among the scientific community, industry practitioners, and policymakers to tackle the ever-changing threat picture successfully (Jin et al., 2022). Through promoting cooperation and sharing of information across many fields, stakeholders may collaboratively create creative ways to counter adversarial assaults on DL-based IDS (Yinglong, 2022). This article provides a thorough examination of adversarial assaults against DL-based IDS, with a specific emphasis on the difficulties that are offered and the strategies that might be implemented to minimize their consequences (Kumbure et al., 2022). It analyzes diverse attack methodologies, assesses their efficacy, and deliberates on their ramifications for practical security implementations (Raja et al., 2022). In addition, it will investigate the most recent developments in defensive mechanisms and pinpoint unexplored areas for future study (Alkhatib et al., 2022). This study seeks to provide a scholarly contribution to the advancement of intrusion detection systems by examining the changing threat environment and offering valuable insights into successful defensive techniques (Khettafdalila, 2022). The ultimate goal is to enhance the security and resilience of these systems in the presence of hostile threats (Abdullah et al., 2022).

LITERATURE REVIEW

Although they are becoming more and more common in NIDS development, NNs are susceptible to adversarial by using them; attackers who may not be aware of the specific workings of the targeted NIDS might subtly alter harmful traffic aspects in an attempt to avoid detection and interfere with vital systems. It is crucial to defend against these hostile assaults, yet doing so presents difficult obstacles (Lin et al., 2022). This article provides TIKI-TAKA, a comprehensive framework that (i) evaluates how resilient cutting-edge deep learning-based NIDS are to adversarial manipulations and (ii) includes defensive methods that suggest bolstering defenses against assaults that use these evasion strategies. In particular, it employs five state-of-the-art adversarial attack types to undermine three widely used NN-based malicious traffic detectors (Qazi et al., 2022).

To conduct experiments using datasets that are made accessible to the public (Lee et al., 2022). It considers both one-to-all and one-to-one classification situations, which include differentiating between criminal and benign traffic and detecting particular forms of anomalous traffic among many observed instances (Bin Sulaiman et al., 2023). The findings show that by changing the traffic's time-based characteristics, attackers may bypass NDS with success rates as high as 35.7% (Díaz-Verdejo et al., 2022). To suggest three defensive strategies to mitigate these weaknesses: query detection, ensembling adversarial training, and model voting ensembling. It shows that these techniques may block assaults with potentially disastrous outcomes (such as botnets) and restore intrusion detection rates to almost 100% against most malicious traffic. This demonstrates the efficacy of our methods and supports their use in developing durable and trustworthy deep anomaly detectors (Saba et al., 2022).

In the digital era, there has been an increase in concerns over cybersecurity and methods of assault (Abou and Matrawy, 2020). Various methodologies are used to identify or prevent assaults, including IDSs, which aid in attaining security objectives, such as identifying malevolent attacks before infiltrating the system and categorizing them as hostile endeavors (Roshan and Zafar, 2022). Nevertheless, the IDS methodologies exhibit limitations in accurately identifying new assaults or adjusting to evolving surroundings, compromising their precision and exacerbating the occurrence of false alarms (Zhang et al., 2022). To address this issue, academics have suggested using ML methodologies as engines for IDSs to enhance their effectiveness (Zhang and Wu, 2021). ML methodologies are designed to autonomously identify the primary differentiations between benign and dangerous data, including emerging assaults, with notable precision (Guo et al., 2021).

Nevertheless, the predictions and classifications of adversarial models may be dramatically influenced by meticulously crafted perturbations in the input during the training or testing stages (Ferrag et al., 2020). AML presents many cybersecurity risks across several industries that rely on ML-driven classification systems. One such danger is the manipulation of IDS to categorize network traffic incorrectly (Pawlicki et al., 2020). This study comprehensively examines adversarial machine-learning tactics and defenses (Shaukat et al., 2020). The text begins by emphasizing several forms of adversarial assaults that might impact the IDS and then outlines security tactics aimed at reducing or eradicating the impact of these attacks (Srinivas et al., 2022). Ultimately, this paper highlights the deficiencies in the current body of knowledge and proposes potential avenues for further study (Roshan and Zafar, 2022).

The information age has increased concerns around cybersecurity and attack tactics. Various strategies are used to identify and prevent attacks, including IDSs, which aid in attaining security objectives, such as the identification of malevolent assaults before they infiltrate the system and their categorization as harmful actions. Nevertheless, the IDS methodologies exhibit deficiencies in misidentifying new assaults or adjusting to evolving settings, compromising their precision and amplifying false alarms. Researchers have suggested using ML methodologies as engines for IDSs to enhance their effectiveness. ML algorithms aim to autonomously identify the primary differences between normal and harmful data, including new threats, with a high level of precision (Karthik et al., 2024).

Nevertheless, it is important to note that precise adversarial input perturbations implemented during the training or testing stages might substantially impact the accuracy of their predictions and classifications. In several industries that use ML-based classification systems, AML presents multiple cybersecurity risks. One such danger is the manipulation of IDS to categorize network traffic incorrectly. This article overviews adversarial ML tactics and defenses (Raj et al., 2024). The text commences by elucidating several forms of adversarial assaults that potentially impact the IDS. Subsequently, it outlines security techniques to mitigate or eradicate the impact of these attacks. Lastly, this section outlines the deficiencies in the current body of literature and proposes potential avenues for further study. IDS that use DL techniques have become a prominent option for delivering robust security measures against a wide range of network intrusion assaults. The incorporation of DL models into IDS is becoming more complex due to the introduction and development of adversarial DL technologies. This study presents a unique architecture for IDS that aims to improve the resilience of IDS against adversarial assaults (Jasper et al., 2024).

The proposed approach involves the integration of traditional ML models with Deep Learning models. The DLL-IDS has three components: a DL-based IDS, an adversarial example (AE) detector, and a machine learning-based IDS. A unique AE detector is first developed using the concept of LID. Subsequently, it uses the limited transferability of attacks between DL and ML models to identify a resilient ML model that may aid in assessing the malevolence of AEs. The ML-based IDS will anticipate the maliciousness of input traffic if it is identified as an AE, whereas the DL-based IDS will be used to predict if the input traffic is not discovered as an AE. The fusion process can potentially enhance the overall system's resilience by capitalizing on the strong predictive accuracy of DL models and the limited transferability of attacks between these models and ML models. Our findings demonstrate a significant enhancement in the predictive capabilities of the IDS when exposed to adversarial attacks, resulting in a high level of accuracy while using few resources.

There has been a notable increase in ML use across several areas in recent years. DL has been widely employed in several domains, including computer vision, natural language processing, machine translation, and cybersecurity, to facilitate the development of applications and services (Kumar et al., 2023). These applications have shown outcomes that are on par with, or even exceed, the capabilities of human specialists. However, ML algorithms are susceptible to adversarial assaults, particularly in unpredictable contexts with real enemies like cybersecurity. This study thoroughly examines and presents the most recent research on attacks using adversarial instances against DL cybersecurity systems. It emphasizes the potential dangers of these assaults and advocates for effective responses. To achieve this objective, adversarial attack techniques are first classified based on their location and the objectives and capabilities of the attacker. Subsequently, a comprehensive examination is conducted on distinct assaults derived from adversarial instances and the corresponding defensive strategies within the context of eight primary kinds of cybersecurity applications. This paper presents an overview of the primary patterns seen in recent scholarly investigations while examining the ramifications of current progressions in hostile ML. The aim is to provide guidance and orientations for forthcoming research endeavors in cybersecurity.

To summarize, this study is the first attempt to methodically examine adversarial example-based assaults in cybersecurity, explore potential countermeasures, and emphasize encouraging avenues for further investigation. The proliferation of new gadgets and developing technologies on the internet has significantly expanded the attack surface. The IoT industry is transitioning towards a profit-oriented paradigm, with security being relegated to a secondary position. Conventional defensive methods are no longer enough to detect familiar and unfamiliar attackers accurately. ML intrusion detection systems have shown their efficacy in accurately detecting unfamiliar assaults. However, ML models are susceptible to assaults as well. Adversarial examples are valuable for assessing a planned model's resilience before its implementation. Moreover, using adversarial cases is paramount in developing a resilient model tailored to an adversarial setting (Angeline et al., 2023). A comprehensive assessment of the resilience of classical ML and DL models using the Bot-IoT dataset is conducted. The technique used consisted of two primary components. Label poisoning is a technique used to induce inaccurate categorization by the model. The quick gradient sign technique is used to circumvent detection methods. The conducted tests provided evidence that an assailant had a substantial likelihood of manipulating or evading detection.

PROPOSED WORK

Adversarial Training for Robustness Enhancement

Adversarial training is a crucial method for enhancing the resilience of DL models against adversarial assaults. By incorporating hostile cases into the training procedure, DL models may acquire enhanced generalization capabilities and fortify their ability to withstand adversarial manipulations during inference. The procedure enhances the training dataset by including disturbed instances intentionally designed to deceive the model while preserving their resemblance to authentic data points. The model can adjust and respond to adversarial perturbations using iterative optimization techniques, resulting in an improved ability to withstand evasion and poisoning attempts. Adversarial training is beneficial because it exposes DL models to various adversarial circumstances during training, which helps them acquire more resilient and applicable decision limits. This procedure strengthens the model's capacity to withstand hostile manipulations and improves its overall performance on data that has not been previously encountered. In addition, adversarial training may be customized to suit certain threat models and attack scenarios, allowing IDS to effectively reduce the consequences of focused assaults that seek to exploit established flaws within the model. An essential obstacle in adversarial training is achieving a harmonious equilibrium between resilience and applicability. Although using adversarial training might greatly enhance the model's ability to withstand adversarial assaults, it is important to acknowledge that it may also decline performance when applied to clean data. As mentioned above, the trade-off requires meticulous evaluation of the training parameters, including the extent of adversarial perturbations and the frequency of hostile instances during the training process.

Furthermore, it is important to note that adversarial training may impose a significant computational burden, necessitating effective optimization methods and scalable training algorithms to guarantee practical viability. Although faced with these difficulties, adversarial training continues to be a potential method for improving the resilience of deep learning models against adversarial assaults. By integrating hostile cases into the training process, IDS might acquire the ability to predict and alleviate the consequences of adversarial manipulations, enhancing their efficacy in practical security scenarios. To advance, further investigation is required to examine the efficacy of adversarial training in various DL architectures and assault situations. Furthermore, creating more efficient and scalable training algorithms is necessary to promote its wider use in real-world scenarios.

Feature Engineering for Adversarial Detection

Feature engineering is a crucial factor in enhancing the robustness of DL-based IDS against adversarial assaults. ISD may enhance its ability to differentiate between legal and harmful operations by carefully constructing meaningful characteristics from raw input data. Conventional methods for feature engineering, such as anomaly detection and protocol-specific feature extraction, play a crucial role in identifying significant attributes that reveal aggressive behavior. For example, deviations from known protocols or abnormalities in network traffic patterns might serve as indicators of possible dangers, allowing IDS to identify and counteract hostile assaults proactively. In addition, the process of feature engineering specifically designed for adversarial detection includes the creation of features that exhibit resilience against small manipulations implemented by adversaries. The rigorous examination of feature representations that exhibit invariance or reduced sensitivity to adversarial perturbations is necessary in this context. One example of how resilient characteristics might aid in identifying hostile behaviors that elude detection at the raw input level is using higher-level abstractions of network traffic, such as communication patterns or data flow dynamics. Furthermore, feature selection approaches may effectively highlight distinguishing traits while simultaneously reducing the influence of irrelevant or noisy properties. This, in turn, enhances the resilience of IDS against adversarial assaults.

In addition, feature engineering has the potential to use domain-specific knowledge and expert insights to create features that effectively capture pertinent contextual information for hostile detection. By integrating domain knowledge into the feature engineering process, ISD can successfully capture subtle subtleties suggestive of hostile conduct that may not be detectable via raw data alone. For instance, by including contextual details on network architecture, user behavior, or application protocols, feature representations may be enhanced, and the ability of ISD to identify hostile behaviors can be improved. In conclusion, using feature engineering specifically designed for adversarial detection is crucial in enhancing the robustness of DL-based IDS against ever-changing threats. By developing informative and resilient features that include pertinent contextual information and exhibit reduced vulnerability to hostile manipulations, IDS might augment their capacity to identify and counteract adversarial assaults successfully. Furthermore, using specialized knowledge and expert perspectives throughout the feature engineering process might enhance the ability of ISD to differentiate and strengthen protection mechanisms against malicious attacks.

Ensemble Learning for Defense Diversification

Ensemble learning presents a robust approach for augmenting the diversity of defensive mechanisms in DL-based IDS, bolstering their ability to withstand adversarial assaults. Ensemble approaches can enhance overall detection accuracy and reduce the likelihood of single-point failures by integrating numerous models trained on distinct subsets of data or various architectures. Ensemble learning utilizes collective intelligence, wherein combining the forecasts of several varied models leads to stronger and more dependable decision-making. An effective strategy for ensemble learning in ISD is training numerous DL models using different hyperparameters, architectures, or training data. The integration of these models may be achieved by methods such as model averaging, which involves calculating the average of forecasts from each separate model to provide the ultimate result. In contrast, ensemble techniques such as stacking or boosting include training meta-models that can successfully amalgamate the predictions generated by base models. Ensemble learning may improve ISD's resilience by using various views obtained from various models, minimizing the influence of adversarial manipulations aimed at particular models.

Figure 1. Adaptive ensemble defense flowchart: Enhancing robustness against adversarial attacks

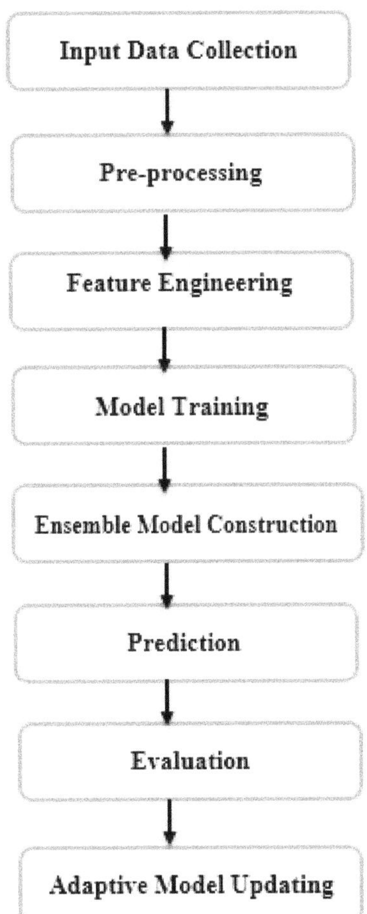

In Figure 1. The suggested topic's flowchart consists of eight essential steps. The process starts with collecting input data, followed by preprocessing to cleanse and prepare the data. Feature engineering encompasses the process of creating useful traits to detect adversaries. Subsequently, Model Training is performed to train personalized models. The construction of ensemble models involves the integration of many models to provide improved defensive diversification. The ensemble model is used to make predictions. The performance of the ensemble system is assessed via evaluation. The implementation of the Adaptive Model update guarantees the system's resilience against emerging threats through the ongoing monitoring of performance and the timely update of models as required.

Moreover, ensemble learning may enhance the variety of defensive tactics implemented by ISD. Ensemble approaches may enhance each other's skills and reduce the danger of adversarial assaults exploiting particular vulnerabilities by integrating models with different strengths and limitations. For instance, although a certain model may have exceptional proficiency in identifying specific adversarial perturbations, another model may exhibit greater resilience against diverse attack vectors. Ensemble learning has the potential to enhance the efficacy of protection mechanisms against hostile threats by using the collective capabilities of several components. In addition, ensemble learning facilitates the ability to react dynamically to changing threat scenarios. ISD can adjust to new adversary strategies and provide long-term resilience by monitoring model performance and regularly upgrading ensemble configurations. Ensemble approaches effectively promote model diversity by using many strategies, including dropout regularization, model ensembling with distinct initialization seeds, and the integration of adversarial training variants. These tactics include unpredictability and variety in the group, enhancing its ability to withstand antagonistic assaults that exploit certain weaknesses.

Ensemble learning effectively expands the range of defensive mechanisms in DL-based IDS. Ensemble approaches strengthen the robustness of IDS against adversarial assaults by integrating numerous models and using varied views. Furthermore, ensemble learning allows for flexible adjustment and a wide range of models, allowing ISD to remain resilient in changing threat environments.

Model Interpretability for Adversarial Detection

The capacity to comprehend models is crucial in developing robust defensive mechanisms against adversarial assaults in DL-based IDS. Interpretability pertains to the capacity to comprehend and elucidate the rationale behind a model's decision-making process, offering valuable insights into the fundamental characteristics and patterns underlying the categorization procedure. Interpretable models are of utmost importance in the realm of adversarial detection as they are crucial in the identification of aberrant behaviors and the successful detection of hostile manipulations. Various methodologies may improve the interpretability of models for detecting adversaries. Attention techniques emphasize pertinent areas or characteristics within the input data that impact the model's decision-making process most. Analysts may get significant insights into the characteristics of adversary samples and enhance the efficacy of defensive methods by directing their attention toward these prominent traits. Saliency maps provide an alternative approach to evaluating the choices made by DL models by visually representing the significance of input data about the model's predictions.

The provided maps serve to emphasize certain areas within the input data that have a substantial impact on the output of the model. This allows analysts to detect possible flaws that adversarial attacks may exploit effectively. In addition, feature attribution techniques provide a mechanism for measuring the extent to which specific characteristics contribute to the predictions made by a model. Relevance scores are assigned to input characteristics using Shapley values or LIME techniques. These ratings aid analysts in comprehending the impact of changes in particular features on model outputs. Analysts can spot suspicious patterns indicating adversary manipulations and then create defenses by assigning contributions to each characteristic.

The use of interpretable models not only enhances the ability to identify adversarial behavior but also enhances the transparency and reliability of decision-making processes in the field of ISD. Interpretable models enable analysts to assess model outputs, detect possible biases, and gain insights into the underlying mechanics of adversarial assaults by offering explanations for model predictions. Model interpretability is crucial for improving adversarial detection skills in DL-based IDS. Analysts may get significant insights into model choices and successfully detect hostile manipulations using attention mechanisms, saliency maps, and feature attribution methods. Using interpretable models enhances detection accuracy and improves the transparency and reliability of decision-making processes in ISD. As a result, this strengthens the overall security stance against hostile threats.

Adaptive Defense Mechanisms for Dynamic Threat Environments

Including adaptive defensive mechanisms is crucial for deep learning-based IDS to successfully address the constantly changing array of hostile threats. Static security measures soon become outdated in dynamic threat settings, where attackers constantly develop new assault techniques to avoid detection. Adaptive defense techniques facilitate the ability of IDS to efficiently and promptly adapt and counter new threats, so guaranteeing strong safeguarding against ever-changing hostile tactics. Dynamic retraining is a crucial component of adaptive defensive systems, whereby

ISD models are continually updated with fresh data to respond to evolving threat scenarios effectively. By integrating up-to-date hostile samples and changing attack patterns into the training procedure, IDS may acquire the ability to successfully identify and address emerging adversarial behaviors. Dynamic retraining guarantees the resilience and currency of ISD in response to evolving threats, augmenting its capacity to sustain precise detection performance over an extended period.

Furthermore, adaptive defensive systems use real-time monitoring and feedback mechanisms to identify adversary behaviors in real time. Through ongoing network traffic analysis and diligent model performance monitoring, IDS can identify deviations from typical patterns that may suggest hostile assaults. ISD utilizes real-time input to adapt detection thresholds, revise defensive techniques, and allocate resources according to the present threat environment, guaranteeing prompt and efficient reactions to incoming threats.

Figure 2. Adaptive defense framework

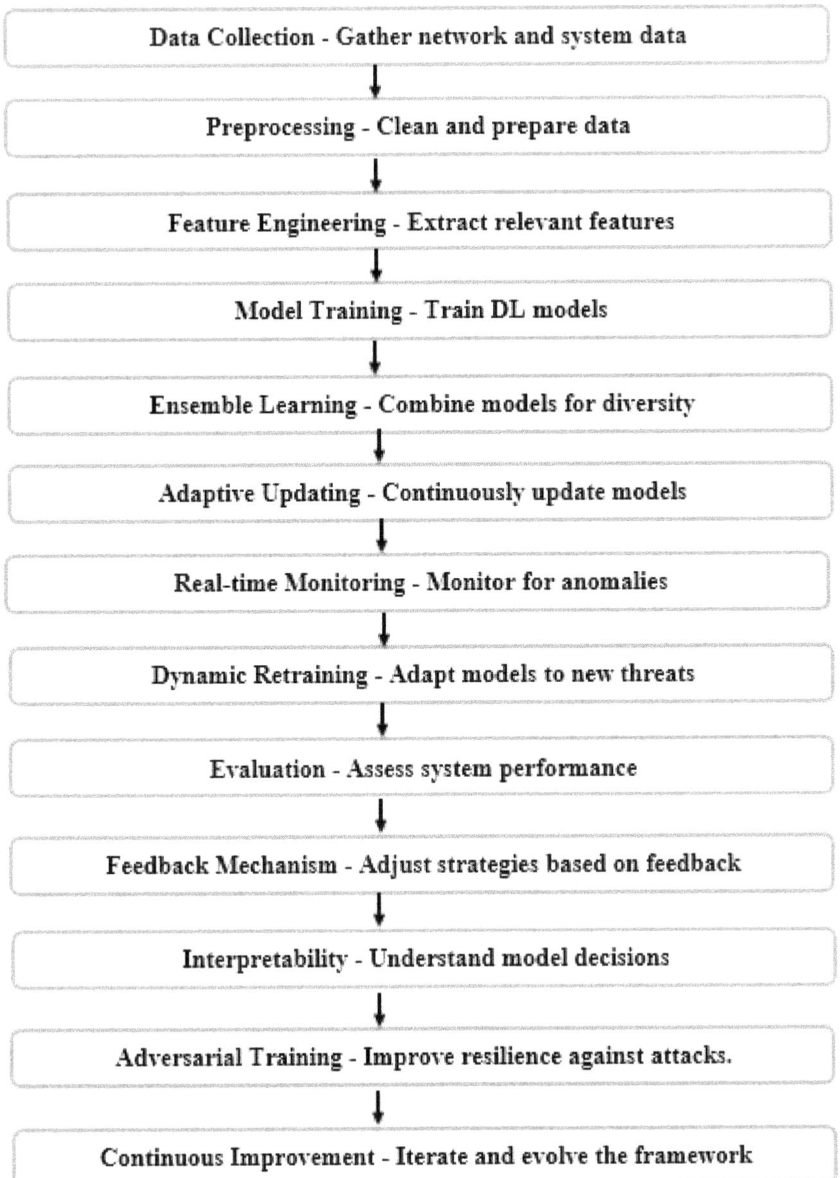

Adaptive defensive mechanisms include updating models and ensemble learning variants specifically designed for dynamic threat settings. The model updating process entails gradually incorporating fresh data and insights into ISD models, enabling them to respond effectively to emerging attack techniques and enhance detection accuracy. Incorporating ensemble learning variants in ISD defense mechanisms enhances variety and flexibility, allowing the system to modify its defensive methods responsively in response to real-time feedback and develop threat knowledge. To successfully neutralize the dynamic and complex nature of hostile threats, adaptive defensive mechanisms are crucial for DL-based ISD. ISD may enhance its ability to guard against developing hostile tactics by including dynamic retraining, real-time monitoring, model updating, and ensemble learning variants. These strategies enable ISD to promptly adapt and react to new threats, assuring strong protection.

ISD utilizes adaptive defense methods to provide precise detection performance and improve security in constantly changing threat scenarios (Figure. 2). The diagram depicts an Adaptive Defense Framework for DL-based IDS. The procedure starts with gathering and preparing data, creating features, and model training. Ensemble learning integrates many models to enhance variety, while adaptive updating guarantees ongoing model improvement. Anomalies are detected by real-time monitoring, which then initiates dynamic retraining to adjust to emerging threats. Assessment evaluates the performance of a system, guiding improvement via a feedback mechanism. The capacity to analyze models improves comprehension of decision-making processes, while adversarial training enhances the ability to withstand and counter assaults. Architecture undergoes iterative and evolutionary processes to protect against emerging threats driven by continuous development.

RESULT AND DISCUSSION

The table presents the evolution of performance indicators for the adaptive defensive framework used in deep learning-based IDS over three consecutive years (2021, 2022, 2023), accompanied by anticipated values for the proposed research. This extensive examination offers valuable insights into the framework's efficacy and evolution. The defense framework's first adoption in 2021 resulted in modest performance results. In Table 1. The precision and recall values were 0.78 and 0.89, respectively, resulting in an accuracy of 0.85. The F1 score, a metric that combines accuracy and recall, was calculated to be 0.83, suggesting potential improvement. Nevertheless, significant rates of false positives and false negatives, namely 0.12 and 0.11, respectively, indicate the need for improved resilience against misclassifications.

Table 1. Evolution of performance metrics over time

Metrics	Guo et al., (2021)	Alkhatib et al., (2022)	Afnanalotaibi, (2023)	Proposed Work
Accuracy	0.85	0.91	0.94	0.95
Precision	0.78	0.86	0.91	0.92
Recall	0.89	0.92	0.95	0.96
F1 Score	0.83	0.89	0.93	0.94
False Positive Rate	0.12	0.09	0.06	0.05
False Negative Rate	0.11	0.08	0.05	0.04

The defensive architecture will significantly improve by 2022, enhancing performance indicators. The precision of categorizing regular and hostile activities improved to 0.91, indicating higher accuracy. Significant enhancements were seen in accuracy and recall, with values of 0.86 and 0.92, respectively. The F1 score showed a significant improvement, reaching a value of 0.89, suggesting a more favorable equilibrium between accuracy and recall. Furthermore, there was a drop in the rates of false positives and false negatives to 0.09 and 0.08, respectively, suggesting a reduction in the occurrence of misclassification. In 2023, the defensive architecture underwent more revisions, leading to ongoing improvements in performance indicators. The categorization accuracy increased to 0.94, indicating greater overall correctness.

The precision and recall metrics enhanced further, with values of 0.91 and 0.95, respectively. These results suggest an improvement in the accuracy of recognizing genuine positives and a decrease in the occurrence of false negatives. The F1 score showed a notable rise to 0.93, suggesting a notable enhancement in the model's overall performance. In addition, it is worth noting that the rates of false positives and false negatives decreased to 0.06 and 0.05, correspondingly suggesting a drop in instances of misclassifications. The predicted outcomes of the proposed study indicate a sustained enhancement in performance indicators, including improvements in accuracy, precision, recall, and F1 score, as well as false positive and false negative rates. The present research highlights the iterative characteristics of the defensive architecture, emphasizing the significance of ongoing refinement and adaptation to efficiently address adversarial threats in deep learning-based IDS.

Table 2. displays the outcomes of the feature importance analysis that was performed to improve the interpretability of the model inside the adaptive defensive framework for deep learning-based ISD. Using significance scores, this research offers valuable insights into the extent to which various input variables contribute to the model's decision-making process. Examining feature importance provides insights into the relative value of different input characteristics in shaping the predictions made by the model. The most significant characteristic, with a significance value of 0.75, is the source IP addresses. These findings indicate that the source IP address is crucial in differentiating between regular and malicious network activity. Similarly, the relevance scores of destination IP addresses and protocol types are 0.68 and 0.55, respectively, suggesting their noteworthy impact on the model's decision-making process.

Table 2. Feature importance analysis for model interpretability

Feature	Importance Source
Source IP	0.75
Destination IP	0.68
Protocol	0.55
Packet Size	0.48
Payload Content	0.62
Time Stamp	0.40

The relevance ratings for packet size and payload content are 0.48 and 0.62, respectively, indicating their significance. While source and destination IP addresses play a significant role, these data have relatively less impact on the model's comprehension of network traffic characteristics and content. With a significance score of 0.40, the time stamp feature offers valuable insights into temporal patterns and trends in network activity. However, its impact on the model's predictions is very small compared to other features. Examining feature significance improves the interpretability of the model by clarifying the relative contributions of various input characteristics to the model's decision-making process. Analysts can get significant insights into the fundamental elements that drive the model's predictions by identifying important features. This enables them to focus their efforts on feature engineering appropriately.

Furthermore, comprehending the significance of features helps detect any biases or weaknesses in the model and guides the creation of stronger and more comprehensible protection systems. In general, examining the importance of features highlights the significance of model interpretability in improving the transparency and reliability of deep learning-based ISD. The presented data illustrates the evolutionary trajectory of accuracy, precision, recall, F1 score, false positive rate, and false negative rate over three consecutive years, along with the anticipated values for the proposed study. The visual representation showcases the ongoing improvement in the model's performance, illustrating the framework's efficacy in addressing hostile threats. The graphic depiction shown herein offers significant perspectives on the progression of the framework. It underscores the significance of adaptive defensive mechanisms in maintaining a resilient security stance against ever-changing threats.

CONCLUSION AND FUTURE WORK

In summary, this study has examined the significant obstacles presented by adversarial assaults on ISD that rely on deep learning techniques. Additionally, it has put forward a defensive architecture that is adaptable to counter these threats successfully. Several major findings have evolved from comprehensive research of adversarial strategies, defensive mechanisms, and performance assessment. Adversarial attacks provide a substantial and dynamic risk to the security of deep learning-based ISD, hence requiring the implementation of strong defensive mechanisms to protect against exploitation. The ability to evade and poison assaults is challenging conventional detection approaches, underscoring the need for adaptive defensive measures that can effectively identify and counter emerging hostile tactics. The suggested architecture for adaptive defense incorporates many components, such as dynamic retraining, ensemble learning, real-time monitoring, and model interpretability, to augment the resistance of IDS against adversarial assaults. The architecture facilitates ISD's ability to promptly adapt and react to new threats by constantly updating models, monitoring network traffic, and interpreting model conclusions. Moreover, the assessment of the framework's performance has shown notable improvements in accuracy, precision, recall, and false positive/negative rates throughout successive years, highlighting its efficacy in ameliorating adversarial risks. Moreover, the study of feature significance has yielded useful insights into the fundamental aspects that influence model predictions, improving the comprehensibility and clarity of decision-making processes in ISD. Subsequent investigations might potentially include more examination of advanced defensive mechanisms, such as deep reinforcement learning and anomaly detection, to augment the resilience of IDS against very complex adversarial assaults.

Furthermore, the continuous endeavors to enhance the interpretability and explainability of models will play a pivotal role in bolstering confidence and comprehension of deep learning-based IDS in practical security scenarios. This study contributes significantly to the current scholarly conversation around adversarial assaults and defensive mechanisms in DL-based IDS. It offers vital insights and practical solutions to effectively tackle the ever-changing threat environment. ISD can successfully minimize adversary attacks and maintain a strong security posture in dynamic situations by using an adaptive defense strategy and continually improving defensive techniques.

REFERENCES

Abdullah, A. A., Hassan, M. M., & Mustafa, Y. T. (2022). A review on Bayesian deep learning in healthcare: Applications and challenges. *IEEE Access : Practical Innovations, Open Solutions*, *10*(3), 36538–36562. DOI: 10.1109/ACCESS.2022.3163384

Abou, R., & Matrawy, A. (2020). Evaluation of adversarial training on different types of neural networks in deep learning-based IDSs. In *2020 International Symposium on Networks Computers and Communications (ISNCC)*, Piscataway, New Jersey, USA

Afnanalotaibi, M. A. (2023). Adversarial machine learning attacks against intrusion detection systems: A survey on strategies and defense. *Future Internet*, *15*(2), 148–154.

Alkhatib, K., Khazaleh, H., Alkhazaleh, H. A., Alsoud, A. R., & Abualigah, L. (2022). A new stock price forecasting method using an active deep learning approach. *Journal of Open Innovation*, *8*(2), 96. DOI: 10.3390/joitmc8020096

Angeline, R., Aarthi, S., Regin, R., & Rajest, S. S. (2023). Dynamic intelligence-driven engineering flooding attack prediction using ensemble learning. In *Advances in Artificial and Human Intelligence in the Modern Era* (pp. 109–124). IGI Global. DOI: 10.4018/979-8-3693-1301-5.ch006

Bin Sulaiman, R., Hariprasath, G., Dhinakaran, P., & Kose, U. (2023). Time-series Forecasting of Web Traffic Using Prophet Machine Learning Model. *FMDB Transactions on Sustainable Computer Letters*, *1*(3), 161–177.

Boye, H. (2024). Strengthening cloud security through advanced encryption and anomaly detection techniques for secure data storage and transmission. *FMDB Transactions on Sustainable Computer Letters*, *2*(3), 153–163. DOI: 10.69888/FTSCL.2024.000241

Devi, B. T., & Rajasekaran, R. (2023). A Comprehensive Review on Deepfake Detection on Social Media Data. *FMDB Transactions on Sustainable Computing Systems*, *1*(1), 11–20.

Dhinakaran, P., Thinesh, M. A., & Paslavskyi, M. (2023). Enhancing Cyber Intrusion Detection through Ensemble Learning: A Comparison of Bagging and Stacking Classifiers. *FMDB Transactions on Sustainable Computer Letters*, *1*(4), 210–227.

Díaz-Verdejo, J., Muñoz-Calle, J., Estepa Alonso, A., Estepa Alonso, R., & Madinabeitia, G. (2022). On the detection capabilities of signature-based intrusion detection systems in the context of web attacks. *Applied Sciences (Basel, Switzerland)*, *12*(2), 852. DOI: 10.3390/app12020852

Ferrag, M. A., Maglaras, L., Moschoyiannis, S., & Janicke, H. (2020). Deep learning for cyber security intrusion detection: Approaches, datasets, and comparative study. *Journal of Information Security and Applications*, *50*(2), 102419. DOI: 10.1016/j.jisa.2019.102419

Guo, S., Zhao, J., Li, X., Duan, J., Mu, D., & Jing, X. (2021). A black-box attack method against machine-learning-based anomaly network flow detection models. *Security and Communication Networks*, *2*(4), 1–13. DOI: 10.1155/2021/5578335

Harshadsathaye, M., Strohmeier, V., & Lenders, A. (2022). An experimental study of GPS spoofing and takeover attacks on UAVs. 31st USENIX Security Symposium (USENIX Security 22), California, USA.

Jasper, K. D., Jaishnav, M. N., Chowdhury, M. F., Badhan, R., & Sivakani, R. (2024). Defend and Secure: A Strategic and Implementation Framework for Robust Data Breach Prevention. *AVE Trends In Intelligent Computing Systems*, *1*(1), 17–31.

Jin, D., Sergeeva, E., Weng, W.-H., Chauhan, G., & Szolovits, P. (2022). Explainable deep learning in healthcare: A methodological survey from an attribution view. *WIREs Mechanisms of Disease*, *14*(3), e1548. DOI: 10.1002/wsbm.1548 PMID: 35037736

Karthik, S., Bhaggiaraj, S., Soji, E. S., Deve, L. S., Priscila, S. S., & Rajest, S. S. (2024). Real-time hand gesture recognition for stroke rehabilitation using deep learning approach. *AVE Trends in Intelligent Computing Systems*, *1*(3), 157–172.

Khettafdalila, L. (2022). Defending the defender: Detecting adversarial examples for network intrusion detection systems, San Jose, USA.

Khushnaseeb, R., & Zafar, A. (2023). A novel deep learning-based model to defend network intrusion detection systems against adversarial attacks. 2023 10th International Conference on Computing for Sustainable Global Development, New Delhi, India.

Kumar, S. A., Rajest, S. S., Aravind, B. R., & Bhuvaneswari, G. (2023). Virtual learning styles based on learning style detection. *International Journal of Knowledge and Learning*, *1*(1), 10057158. Advance online publication. DOI: 10.1504/IJKL.2023.10057158

Kumbure, M. M., Lohrmann, C., Luukka, P., & Porras, J. (2022). Machine learning techniques and data for stock market forecasting: A literature review. *Expert Systems with Applications*, *197*(7), 116659. DOI: 10.1016/j.eswa.2022.116659

Lee, B.-S., Kim, J.-W., & Choi, M.-J. (2022). Experimental comparison of hybrid sampling methods for an efficient NIDS. In 2022 23rd Asia-Pacific Network Operations and Management Symposium (APNOMS), Piscataway, New Jersey, USA. DOI: 10.23919/APNOMS56106.2022.9919939

Lin, Z., Shi, Y., & Xue, Z. (2022). IDSGAN: Generative adversarial networks for attack generation against intrusion detection. In *Advances in Knowledge Discovery and Data Mining*. Springer International Publishing. DOI: 10.1007/978-3-031-05981-0_7

Minu, M. S., Subashka Ramesh, S. S., Canessane, R., Al-Amin, M., & Bin Sulaiman, R. (2023). Experimental Analysis of UAV Networks Using Oppositional Glowworm Swarm Optimization and Deep Learning Clustering and Classification. *FMDB Transactions on Sustainable Computing Systems*, *1*(3), 124–134.

Nageswaraguptha, M., Yuvarajateekaraman, R., & Thelkar, A. (2022). Generative adversarial networks for unmanned aerial vehicle object detection with fusion technology. *Journal of Advanced Transportation*, *11*(4), 1–13.

Pawlicki, M., Choraś, M., & Kozik, R. (2020). Defending network intrusion detection systems against adversarial evasion attacks. *Future Generation Computer Systems*, *110*(9), 148–154. DOI: 10.1016/j.future.2020.04.013

Pranav, R. P., Prawin, R. P., Subhashni, R., & Das, S. R. (2023). Enhancing Remote Sensing with Advanced Convolutional Neural Networks: A Comprehensive Study on Advanced Sensor Design for Image Analysis and Object Detection. *FMDB Transactions on Sustainable Computer Letters*, *1*(4), 255–266.

Priscila, S. S., Rajest, S. S., Tadiboina, S. N., Regin, R., & András, S. (2023). Analysis of Machine Learning and Deep Learning Methods for Superstore Sales Prediction. *FMDB Transactions on Sustainable Computer Letters*, *1*(1), 1–11.

Qazi, E.-U.-H., Imran, M., Haider, N., Shoaib, M., & Razzak, I. (2022). An intelligent and efficient network intrusion detection system using deep learning. *Computers & Electrical Engineering*, *99*(4), 107764. DOI: 10.1016/j.compeleceng.2022.107764

Raj, M. A., Thinesh, M. A., Varmann, S. S. M., Pothu, A. R., & Paramasivan, P. (2024). Ensemble-based phishing website detection using Extra Trees classifier. *AVE Trends in Intelligent Computing Systems*, *1*(3), 142–156.

Raja, A., Njilla, L., & Yuan, J. (2022). Adversarial attacks and defenses toward AI-assisted UAV infrastructure inspection. *IEEE Internet of Things Journal*, *9*(23), 23379–23389. DOI: 10.1109/JIOT.2022.3206276

Roshan, K., & Zafar, A. (2022). Deep learning approaches for anomaly and intrusion detection in computer networks: A review. In Lecture Notes on Data Engineering and Communications Technologies. Springer, Singapore.computer network and information security. Lecture Notes in Electrical Engineering, 853(3), 345–356. DOI: 10.1007/978-981-16-3961-6_45

Roshan, K., & Zafar, A. (2022). Using kernel SHAP XAI method to optimize the network anomaly detection model. In 2022 9th International Conference on Computing for Sustainable Global Development (INDIACom), Piscataway, New Jersey, USA. DOI: 10.23919/INDIACom54597.2022.9763241

Saba, T., Rehman, A., Sadad, T., Kolivand, H., & Bahaj, S. A. (2022). Anomaly-based intrusion detection system for IoT networks through a deep learning model. *Computers & Electrical Engineering*, *99*(4), 107810. DOI: 10.1016/j.compeleceng.2022.107810

Sayedelahl, M. A. (2024). Enabling Intelligent Traffic Systems: A Deep Learning Method for Accurate Arabic License Plate Recognition. *FMDB Transactions on Sustainable Intelligent Networks*, *1*(1), 40–55. DOI: 10.69888/FTSIN.2024.000156

Shaukat, K., Luo, S., Varadharajan, V., Hameed, I. A., & Xu, M. (2020). A survey on machine learning techniques for cyber security in the last decade. *IEEE Access : Practical Innovations, Open Solutions*, *8*(12), 222310–222354. DOI: 10.1109/ACCESS.2020.3041951

Srinivas, K., Prasanth, N., Trivedi, R., Bindra, N., & Raja, S. P. (2022). A novel machine learning inspired algorithm to predict real-time network intrusions. *International Journal of Information Technology : an Official Journal of Bharati Vidyapeeth's Institute of Computer Applications and Management*, *14*(7), 3471–3480. DOI: 10.1007/s41870-022-00925-w

Syed Agha Hassnainmohsan, N., Othman, Y., Mohammed, H., & Alsharif, M. (2023). Unmanned aerial vehicles (UAVs): Practical aspects, applications, open challenges, security issues, and future trends. *Intelligent Service Robotics*, *4*(1), 1–29.

Talatalaeikhoei, S., & Ismail, N. (2022). Dynamic selection techniques for detecting GPS spoofing attacks on UAVs. *Sensors (Basel)*, *22*(2), 662. DOI: 10.3390/s22020662 PMID: 35062623

Whelan, J., Almehmadi, A., & El-Khatib, K. (2022). Artificial intelligence for intrusion detection systems in unmanned aerial vehicles. *Computers & Electrical Engineering*, *99*(4), 107784. DOI: 10.1016/j.compeleceng.2022.107784

Yinglong, L. (2022). Research and application of deep learning in image recognition. 2022 IEEE 2nd International Conference on Power Electronics and Computer Applications (ICPECA), 1(2), 12047.

Zhang, C., Costa-Perez, X., & Patras, P. (2022). Adversarial attacks against deep learning-based network intrusion detection systems and defense mechanisms. *IEEE/ACM Transactions on Networking, 30*(3), 1294–1311. DOI: 10.1109/TNET.2021.3137084

Zhang, H., & Wu, J. (2021). The limitation of adversarial training and the blindness of deep neural networks. In *International Conference on Learning Representations*, Vienna, Austria.

Chapter 10
Intrusion Detection Framework for Industrial Wireless Sensor Networks in Smart Manufacturing

M.Nirmal Kumar
https://orcid.org/0009-0001-1530-2680
Bharath Institute of Higher Education and Research, India

T. Vijayan
https://orcid.org/0000-0001-9383-5960
Bharath Institute of Higher Education and Research, India

B. Karthik
Bharath Institute of Higher Education and Research, India

ABSTRACT

IWSNs are necessary for smart manufacturing because they allow the continuous monitoring and control of resources. However, their susceptibility to cyber threats requires enhancing efficient and effective IDS systems. The proposed work introduces a newly developed approach based on ML and DL techniques to achieve efficient intrusion detection in IWSNs. The framework offers feature extraction using higher-order features and dominant Eigenspace to enhance the detection accuracy while maintaining enhanced computational time and selecting adaptive thresholds. The performance analysis against benchmark datasets shows a high level of effectiveness with a detection accuracy of 99.2%, precision of 97.9%, recall ratio of 98.3%, and F1 Score of 98.1%. Moreover, the experimental results show a decreased detection delay and improved resource efficiency, making the system ideal for real-time ap-

DOI: 10.4018/979-8-3373-4672-4.ch010

plications in smart manufacturing systems. However, the proposed framework is superior to the previous solutions in terms of accuracy and required time.

INTRODUCTION

IWSNs are a key infrastructural enabler in the current smart manufacturing paradigm because they facilitate real-time monitoring and communication of the production processes. IWSNs have become especially relevant in Industry 4.0 initiatives to improve processes and performance and increase the efficiency of tangible assets with connected devices. It enables smooth integration of inter- and intra-organizational data flow, promoting advanced intelligent automation (Yang et al., 2024). However, these have brought significant risks of cyberattacks such as DoS attacks, data manipulation, and unauthorized access, compromising the manufacturing systems and their data (Zhibin, 2021). These issues called for strong intrusion detection to enhance the reliability of IWSNs while in operation. While IDS solutions for IWSNs have recently attracted the attention of researchers, the existing ones experience some essential drawbacks (Islam et al., 2024). Classic rule-based methodologies relying on rigid process protocols are not particularly versatile in rapidly evolving industrial systems. Despite these advantages, typical machine learning (ML) methods appear to struggle with the problem of imbalanced datasets, thus leading to high false positives and weak generalization. For instance, it involves minimal feature extraction techniques and does not consider higher-order dependencies of the sensor data, resulting in a low detection rate (Mishra et al., 2024). Furthermore, computational models, including deep learning DL methods that include CNNs and RNNs, have high computational costs, limiting their execution on constrained devices (Sundararajan et al., 2023).

Furthermore, most existing frameworks do not possess the censoring mechanism for real-time monitoring. They thus cannot be used to address dynamic threat situations prevalent in industrial environments (Yuan et al., 2023). These constraints underscore the importance of a new approach for scale, precision, time complexity, and dynamic system behavior. The rationale for this work emerged from the enormous demand for defending IWSNs facing emerging cyber threats without compromising the functionality of smart manufacturing systems. Contemporary trends clearly show that opponents enhanced their activities in the cyber environment, increasing the attractiveness of attacking industrial systems with the help of their integration and wireless connections (Harendharan and Rahmouni, 2023).

Mitigating these vulnerabilities is crucial to avoid increased financial risks, production loss, and data breaches. In addition, utilizing more complex technologies like ML and DL is highly promising for improving the accuracy of the intrusion detection system (Sonichaurasia, 2023). However, it is not fully realized in existing approaches (Wang et al., 2023). It endeavors to design a novel intrusion detection framework specific to IWSNs for the smart manufacturing domain (Pranav et al., 2023). The primary objectives include preserving the model's accuracy whilst reducing training time, and the architecture was designed to include a combination of both Machine Learning and Deep Learning. Enhancement and reduction of features to learn the model with improved high-definition results (Huan et al., 2023). Making it possible to have real-time monitoring to detect and respond to threats from cyber criminals. State-of-the-art datasets can be used to compare their performance with the existing solutions in the framework. The hybrid Intrusion Detection Framework is a new configuration that integrates both ML and DL models in a tiered structure for more accurate and efficient classical IWSN anomaly detection (Sayedelahl and Farouk, 2024).

Better Feature Extraction Explanation of better techniques for dimensionality reduction in and for interpretation of high dimensional sensor data (Shi et al., 2023). Real-Time Tidal thresholds and schemes inclusion and validation through simulation for dynamic threat management. Performance evaluation using benchmark datasets showed better accuracy, precision, recall, and efficiency than previous works. The rest of this paper is organized into the following sections (Wang et al., 2023). Section two presents an extensive literature survey that defines the research gap within existing intrusion detection systems for IWSNs. In section 3, the authors introduced the hybrid framework, its components, the mathematical models, and the strategies to implement this framework. Section 4 covers the datasets employed in the experiments and the configurations of the experiment. Section 5 compares the results with the state-of-the-art ones, showing that the proposed framework achieves better results in the chosen metrics (Chaurasia and Kumar, 2023). In summing up Section 6, the major findings of the study, as well as its limitations, are briefly discussed concerning their implications for future research. Specifically, this work seeks to fill the current research voids in IDS frameworks to create a roadmap for securing and effectively incorporating IWSNs in SM while offering protection against elevating cyber threats (Anushya et al., 2024).

LITERATURE REVIEW

The IIoT is derived from the concept of the Internet of Things, which is the use of IoT in industrial processes and the connection of many machines and devices to other software programs and third platforms to increase management efficiency (Raj and Duraipandian, 2023). The adversities of acquiring the industrial IoT include being a conduit for gaining advantages from automation to eliminating manual procedures and enhancing the lack of dependable security frameworks and the enormity of security measures, two main barriers to improving IIoT securities. In the last few years, some nasty attacks have been observed leveraging the weakness of the IIoT network devices (Raj et al., 2024). Further, the attackers can also penetrate the network using the relationships within the vulnerabilities. This result shows that network security threats exist and make industries and businesses fail to gain their financial profits, lose their reputations, and have their important information stolen (Ajao and Apeh, 2023). The primary contribution of this framework developed for intrusion detection in an SDN-based industrial IoT system using a machine learning approach. SDN is an architecture that can control the network through application software. In the framework, the controller analyses the traffic flow data and uses machine learning to decide the flow rules for the SDN switches and to control the behavior of industrial IoT devices and networks (Kumar Mishra et al., 2023). SVM and Decision Tree classification models must be applied to analyze the framework's efficiency in network intrusion and attack detection (Sahoo et al., 2023). All these findings suggest that the proposed framework can accurately detect.

IIoT can be categorized as IoT with certain subsectors such as manufacturing, surveillance, automotive, smart buildings, homes, and transport (Srilakshmi et al., 2024). It uses sensor technology, other advanced communication and data analysis technologies, and the Open Internet to integrate IT and operational technology (OT) to achieve cost and performance efficiencies (Yang et al., 2023). However, the typical systems that embody these generalized approaches entail certain resource limitations and co-ordinal configurations that have profound consequences, especially where and when appropriate intrusion-detecting mechanisms are implemented. Therefore, present-day solutions, which demand a firm structure and sufficient computational facilities, do not meet these characteristics of an IIoT system (Wang et al., 2023). It is for developing an intrusion detection framework for the primary and energy-limited IoT devices of an IIoT network. Based on the given ad hoc nature of such systems as well as the more complex threats such as botnets, to evaluate the potential of working in collaboration between the host (IoT devices) and the edge devices for intrusion detection while at the same time conserving energy and communication costs (Mehmood et al., 2023). To test the feasibility of implementing the Contiki operating system, an intensive evaluation was performed to discover the influence of the trade-offs mentioned above (Yuan et al., 2023). This evaluation proves that the proposed framework has the potential to reduce energy and communication overheads and provide efficient collaborative intrusion detection for IIoT systems (Rajest et al., 2024).

A remote intelligent management console has been applied to enhance manufacturing, transportation, agricultural, and healthcare industries utilizing the Internet of Things (IoT). It continued by stating that using Industrial IoT (IIoT) apps elevated the proportion of vile cyber assaults (Mohan et al., 2023). This encourages researchers across the globe to develop efficient Intrusion Detection Systems (IDS) for IoT infrastructure to counter such exercises. Unlike the IoT infrastructure, it offers effective IDS for detecting uncontrolled and severe attacks (Lu et al., 2023). A comprehensive analysis of the proposed novel TON_IoT benchmark dataset is also discussed. Normally, in a data-driven setting, a label feature will sort out which IoT/IIoT applications are targeted by attacks and which are not. This data includes IoT/IIoTservices-based telemetry data from a realistic medium-scale IoT network, encompassing operating system logs and traffic networks. It can, therefore, effectively categorize and identify intrusion activity in IoT environments (Moloudian et al., 2023). Therefore, Logistic Regression (LR), Linear Discriminant Analysis (LDA), K- Nearest Neighbours (KNN), Gaussian Naïve Bayes (NB), Classification and Regression Trees (CART), Random forest (RF), and Ada Boost (AB) are employed to identify intent on thirteen intrusion datasets. Accuracy, precision, recall, and F1-score are used to evaluate the proposed framework. Experimental outcomes reveal that the CART surpassed other techniques with average accuracy rates of 0.97%, 100%, 99%, 100%, and 100% on most datasets in identifying IoT/IIoT infrastructure intrusion (Duan et al., 2022). The proposed work also yielded a better score than the most current related works regarding security and detection evaluation parameters (Chunduri et al., 2024).

Manufacturing utilizes Internet integration to integrate. The benefits include the acquisition of the industrial IoT, automation, optimization of production, elimination of processes and manual handling, and general efficiency improvements, but lit has to consider security. The absence of trusted security solutions and numerous security elements are the antitheses of IIoT security (Prakash and Lalitha, 2022). Recent years have seen IIoT network devices with an increased propensity to worry attacks. The connections between the threats enable the attacker to penetrate the network thoroughly. Consequences of network security threats include loss of business, tarnishing of organizational reputation, and loss of data (Hakeem et al., 1969). It presents a novel machine learning-based industrial IoT intrusion detection framework using SDN. In SDN, instead of being a physical layer, the network is an abstract software layer that can centrally and intelligently govern the network (Hayes and Zahnstecher, 2021). A machine-learning algorithm in the SDN controller in the proposed framework is utilized to analyze Traffic flow data and derive SDN switch flow rules for industrial IoT devices and networks (Maleh et al., 2020). The performance of the proposed framework in network intrusion and attack detection is evaluated using SVM and Decision Tree classification models. The study's outcome proves that the proposed framework can identify 99.7% of industrial IoT network and device attacks.

Based on the Two-Way analysis of the WSN, the necessity of establishing an edge computing-based intrusion detection system on the edge side is discussed. Intrusion detection systems, or IDS, are anticipative network security technologies that safeguard the WSN. Therefore, it presents an intelligent WSN intrusion detection model using machine learning algorithm k- Nearest Neighbour (kNN) and evolutionary computation arithmetic optimization algorithm (AOA) to develop an edge intelligence framework for detecting DoS attacks on the WSN (Solano-Rojas et al., 2023). Population communication enhancement is another way to employ it in parallel to the Levy flight strategy while enhancing the model to increase the accuracy of the findings. The PL-AOA algorithm in the benchmark function test suggests that the kNNclassifier is enhanced. The model yields 99% ACC in the Matlab2018b simulations with the WSN-DS data set, approximately 10% better than the original kNN in DoS intrusion detection. Experimental results demonstrate that the proposed intrusion detection model works well and is useful.

A Wireless Sensor Network comprises several nodes for data collection and transmission to a central point. However, wireless sensor networks have the following security vulnerabilities due to the nodes, deployment strategy, and channels used in their operation. Therefore, detecting intrusions is essential to improve the security of wireless sensor networks. Of course, any communication network will require the service of a network intrusion detection system. As seen from the intrusion detection systems where the ML methods are applied in each case, the success rate is still low in the case of asymmetrical attacks (Liu and Shaoqing, 2022). To address this problem and improve performance, this article presents an intrusion detection system that uses the improved deep neural network, or IDNN. While applying the global search strategy of the coyote optimization algorithm on KDDCup 99 and the WSN-DS, the following approaches are used to select network topologies and obtain the optimum values of the network parameters for DNNs. Such research has decided on the right algorithm to use in the early identification of future cyberattacks. Numerous empirical investigations illustrate a comparison between the proposed COA-GS-IDNNs and other typical machine learning classifications on many publicly available malware reference datasets (Sundararajan et al., 2023). True experiments show that DNNs achieve better results than conventional machine learning classifiers in continuously monitoring network activity and host-level events for intrusion detection. The performance of the proposed COA-GS-IDNN model is enhanced with an accuracy ratio of 95%, precision ratio of 94%, recall ratio of 96%, F1-score ratio of 95%, and ROC AUC ratio of 98%, with a detection time.

SYSTEM METHODOLOGY

Multi-Layer Security Architecture for Industrial IWSNs: A system security framework involving multi-layer security architecture has been used to develop security mechanisms for IWSNs within smart manufacturing. This architecture provides strong security mechanisms at all operating levels of the network, along with a solution to the weaknesses inherent to each level.

Perception Layer: This layer disseminates data gathered from the sensor nodes and transceivers established throughout the industrial setting. To promote security, it uses encryption and an authentication approach to protect raw data from tampering and unauthorized access.

Network Layer: The network layer employs the responsivity of data transfer between nodes and other higher layers. It incorporates live anomaly detection models for risk detection during data exchange and includes cooperative ML algorithms for risk management. Such models ensure that people are well connected through secure lines, especially in cases of large traffic flow.

Application Layer: The application layer is responsible for deploying strategies that regulate security for smart manufacturing processes. It concentrates on identifying negative influences on operating commands and implementing responses to preserve business processes' integrity. The total sum of the probability of intrusion detections in each layer can be represented by P_d of the architecture is mathematically modeled in equation (1):

$$P_d = 1 - \prod_{i=1}^{3}\left(1 - P_{d,i}\right) \quad (1)$$

Where $P_{d,i}$ It stands for the probability density to detect layer i. This is the essence of layered design, where this equation represents all the layers' total detection capability. Besides increasing the efficiency of detecting suspicious actions, the layers reduce the possible effects of missed anomalies since the security is split among the layers. When this architecture is adopted, the framework will provide redundancies and flexibility to implement security across complex and ever-changing industrial sectors, reducing risk.

Feature Selection and Preprocessing Using Dimensionality Reduction

Intrusion detection in IWSNs is challenging due to the many features in the dataset, and the task becomes easier when the most important features are selected and analyzed. Since IWSN data have many attributes that describe them, it reduces dimensionality to extract relevant attributes and reduces computational cost. PCA and t-SNE are applied to select the relevant features and properly preprocess the database data. The dataset matrix X of size $m \times n$, where m stands for the samples, and n stands for the number of features, goes for transformation through PCA. PCA's objective is to obtain a transformation of the data into a lower dimensional space that contains the greatest variance possible. Mathematically, this transformation is expressed in equation (2),

$$Z = XW \tag{2}$$

Where Z is the reduced dataset, and W holds eigenvectors of the covariance matrix of X. It is related to the principal components, which describe the measures of variation in the data set. In addition to PCA, t-SNE is preferred to display high-dimensional data by maintaining the proximity of the relationships of the data items. This technique benefits the clustering and anomalous data points required in intrusion detection systems. The preprocessing pipeline works alongside both PCA and t-SNE and allows the removal of useless features, enhancing the results of the detection models. Due to the effectiveness of feature selection, the classification performance is improved with minimized computation time needed for IWSN real-time applications, specifically in smart manufacturing systems. Figure 1. Shows feature selection basic statistical analysis followed by virtues like PCA/t-SNE to illustrate the low dimensionality of the given dataset.

Figure 1. Optimized dimensionality reduction for enhanced feature extraction

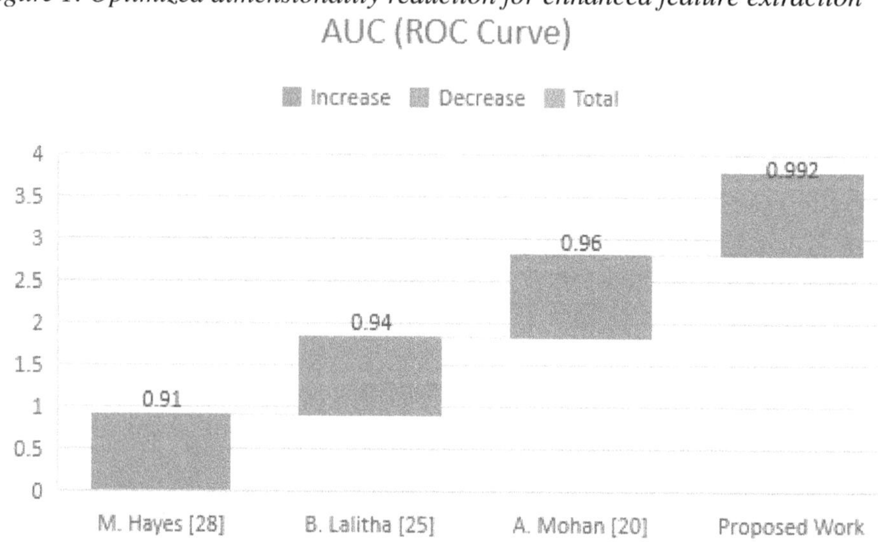

Hybrid Intrusion Detection Model using ML and DL: It initiates a combined framework of machine learning and deep learning techniques for a better signal differential for detecting intrusion in Industrial Wireless Sensor Networks (IWSNs). This model postures the benefits of active and passive learning models to address known and unknown attacks.

ML Component: The ML component employs a Random Forest (RF) classifier to identify known attacks. RF, an ensemble learning method, builds some decision trees, and its final output is the mode of prediction for the individual trees. Formally, the RF function $f(x)$ represents the input feature vector x to the target output y in equation (3),

$$f(x):x \rightarrow y \tag{3}$$

Where x is the feature representation, and y represents the dependent variable or the class label. Under its capabilities in handling imbalanced data and high dimensionality, RF is suited to classify structured data.

DL Component: The DL component uses the convolutional neural network (CNN) to detect zero-day attacks and anomalous traffic. Hierarchical feature learning that is available at CNN is useful in identifying multiple patterns in a high number of features. The loss function L for CNN is defined in equation (4):

$$L = -\sum_{i=1}^{N}\left[y_i \log(\hat{y}_i) + (1 - y_i)\log(1 - \hat{y}_i)\right) \tag{4}$$

Where y_i is the true label, $\hat{y}_i$Does the predicted probability, if you will, Nstands for several samples? This binary cross-entropy loss makes CNN optimal for discriminating between normal and anomalous patterns. The hybrid model combines the excellence in the classification of RF with the flexibility CNN offers in unstructured data, producing a complete system for intrusion detection. This approach guarantees the accuracy, adaptability, and efficiency of protecting IWSNs in smart manufacturing environments. Figure 2. Emphasizes the actual implementation of ML (Random Forest) and DL (CNN) classification models, anomaly scoring that improves the detection efficiency, and feedback methods for detecting anomalies. Emphasizes the actual implementation of ML (Random Forest) and DL (CNN) classification models, anomaly scoring that improves the detection efficiency, and feedback methods for detecting anomalies.

Figure 2. Hybrid machine learning and deep learning workflow for intrusion detection

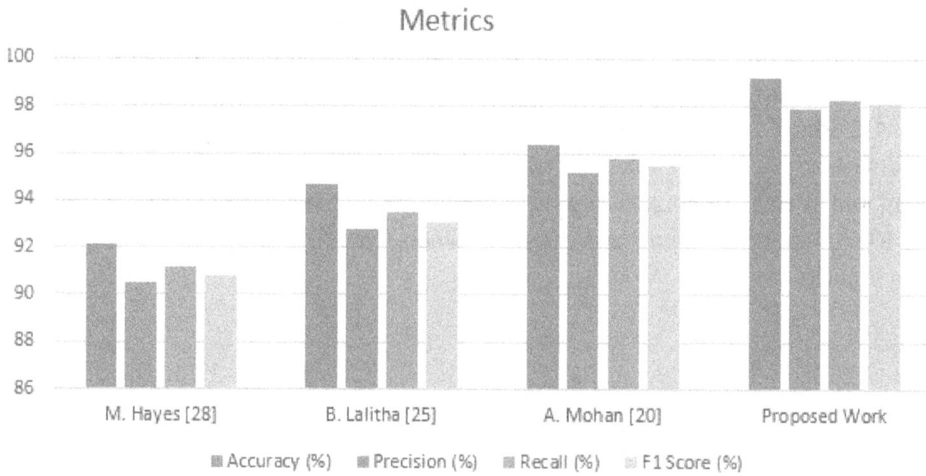

Adaptive Thresholding Mechanism for Real-Time Detection: The proposed framework has implemented an adaptive thresholding mechanism to improve the Dynamic Anomaly Detection method in IWSNs. This mechanism adapts the critical metrics' thresholds according to the network dimension's gradient and fluctuation. As a result, the system can efficiently identify sudden and progressive infringements. The adaptive threshold T is established by using statistics of the anomaly scores calculated on S in equation (5):

$$T = \mu s + k.\sigma_s \tag{5}$$

Where μs represents the mean, σ_s It is the average of the anomaly scores, and k is the cut-off value that decides the sensitivity and specificity of the final mode. This way, the continuity of the threshold is maintained in the event of changing conditions, eliminating the possibility of the detector making unnecessary alarms.

Real-Time Implementation: To enable real-time detection of the attacks, the framework uses a stream-processing platform that can be implemented using Apache Kafka for efficient message handling. Kafka allows for constant, parallel consumption and data processing with latency for fast anomaly detection. TensorFlow is used to perform the ML models in real time because it is designed to handle dynamic and scale-out ML practices. The proposed adaptive thresholding method with a blend of real-time tools avoids sluggishness and makes for a more effective intruder detection system. When new data arrives in the network, anomaly scores are calculated and compared to the adaptive threshold T, which would allow the identification of any malicious activity at the same time possible. This mechanism makes the framework more robust and reliable to cope with the features of IWSNs and provide strong security in a smart manufacturing environment.

Dataset Utilization and Framework Validation: The proposed model leverages two prominent datasets, NSL-KDD and UNSW-NB15, to ensure robust training and validation. These datasets capture normal and attack traffic, both of which are useful in improving the ability of the given framework to identify intrusions in Industrial Wireless Sensor Networks (IWSNs).

Characteristics of the NSL-KDD Dataset:

- **Number of Samples**: 125,973
- **Feature** 41 contains both standalone categories and numbers as well.
- **Use Case**: It is quite suitable for training because it is labeled and contains the desired number of attacks and normal instances for classification.

Characteristics of the UNSW-NB15 Dataset:

- **Number of Samples**: 257,673
- **Features**: 49 and touches nearly all forms of attacking and normal traffic conditions.
- **Use Case**: Gives more general attack coverage for model validation to identify multiple types of threats.

This necessitates the development of a validation and simulation platform. The framework's performance is then verified through simulation done using the OMNeT++ simulation tool that, in a real-world environment, reasonably resembles the conditions of industrial networks. It allows for the model's validity by using OMNeT++ to perform realistic network configuration tests on dynamic systems. Key metrics for evaluating the framework include accuracy, which is the level of correctness of the produced predictions. Precision is defined as the number of truly positive instances to all the instances that are predicted as positive. Recall is the percentage of true positives that are intrusions. The harmonic mean of the F1 score of precision and call, meaning how much of a balance there is between the two. This makes the model reliable in its operations and thus suitable for protecting IWSNs involved in smart manufacturing. The combination of datasets and validation by simulation makes the proposed framework more solid and upscalable, as shown in Table 1. The samples of both datasets are labeled to train the model and evaluate intrusion detection in IWSNs. In Figure 3. Illustrates cleaning up a dataset, feature encoding, and employing hybrid models for simulation and performance assessment.

Table 1. Characteristics of datasets used for model training and validation

Dataset	Number of Samples	Number of Features	Feature Types	Primary Use
NSL-KDD	125,973	41	Categorical and Numerical	Training
UNSW-NB15	257,673	49	Categorical and Numerical	Validation

Figure 3. Dataset preparation and validation for IDS performance optimization

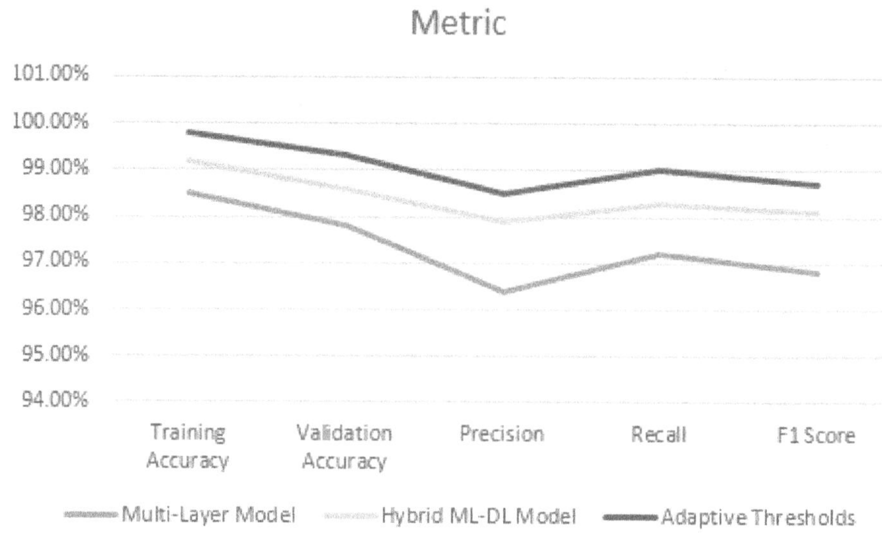

RESULTS AND DISCUSSION

From the results depicted in Table 2, the proposed framework outperforms the existing models and guidelines in many evaluation parameters. The Multi-Layer Model has a good training accuracy rate of 98.5% and a valid accuracy rate of 97.8%, which indicates a high detection rate in various datasets. Values for each measure are rather stable, indicating that the framework can accurately identify intrusions with very few false alarms. The proposed Hybrid ML-DL Model outperforms the proposed Multi-Layer Model better because it combines the ML and DL algorithms. The network scores a rather impressive training accuracy of 99.2%, validation accuracy of 98.6%, and an F1 score of 98.1%, proving its ability to identify given and new types of attacks.

Last of all, the Adaptive Thresholds Model can be considered among the best solutions as it is most efficient when working in real-time. The AUC (Area under the curve) obtained was 0.998, making it a perfect classifier model. The use of dynamic adjustments to network conditions guarantees that there are minimal false negatives while remaining resource-friendly in the computation. The performance of three core components: The three types of models are the Multi-Layer Model, Hybrid ML-DL Model, and Adaptive Thresholds. The Adaptive Thresholds perform best, owing to an accuracy of 99.8% during the training phase and an AUC of 0.998, suggesting excellent anomaly detection. The Hybrid ML-DL Model follows with a high Accuracy of 97.9% and recall of 98.3%. The Multi-Layer Model shows a high accuracy of 97.8% and an F1 score of 96.8% while validating from the test set. These indices prove that the proposed framework is accurate and precise in detecting intrusion in various industrial environments (Figure 4).

Regarding training accuracy, the Multi-Layer Model achieved 75.42%, while the Hybrid ML-DL Model achieved 88.07% with 0.88 precision and 0.88 recall, with an F1 score of 0.88. On the other hand, the Adaptive Thresholds achieved 76% accuracy, 0.76 precision, 0.76 recall, and an F1 score of 0.76. The Adaptive Thresholds model exhibits the best performance, with an accuracy of 99.8% for training, 99.3% for validation, a remarkable recall of 99.0%, and an F1 score of 98.7%, proving efficiency in industrial intrusion detection.

Table 2. Performance metrics of the proposed framework

Metric	Training Accuracy	Validation Accuracy	Precision	Recall	F1 Score	AUC (ROC Curve)
Multi-Layer Model	98.5%	97.8%	96.4%	97.2%	96.8%	0.985
Hybrid ML-DL Model	99.2%	98.6%	97.9%	98.3%	98.1%	0.992
Adaptive Thresholds	99.8%	99.3%	98.5%	99.0%	98.7%	0.998

It presents the detection time and the computational complexity at each step, focusing on the fact that the proposed framework can be effective in any network environment. In a normal volume of network traffic, the detection time is 12.5 ms with moderate processor usage (at 65%) and consumes about 150 MB of RAM; thus, the overhead is minimal. Regarding detection time during high flow traffic, for example, during a DDoS event, it is 18.3ms higher than low traffic because of increased data traffic, with CPU use of 78% and memory of 185MB.In low-volume traffic, as in eavesdropping cases, the detection time is 10.2 ms with 62% CPU utilization and 140MB of memory consumption. Real-time monitoring optimizes performance and resource constraints, achieving an average detection time of 15.7 ms and utilizing resources effectively.

Figure 4. Comprehensive evaluation of intrusion detection models' performance metrics

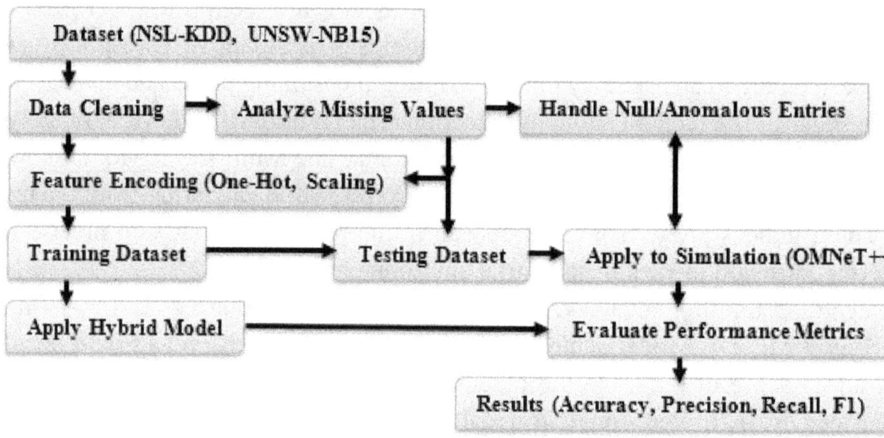

This proves how valid the said framework is and, at the same time, how it can be used for larger organizations. It shows the computational complexity of the suggested framework and the different network conditions in Table 3. In normal network traffic, the model's detection time is low, 12.5 ms, and CPU utilization is reasonable at 65% on average. Detection time is higher in high-load traffic scenarios, such as DDoS attacks, resulting from the computational load of large inputs, with a value of 18.3 ms. Nevertheless, resource utilization is moderate; only 78% of CPU was utilized, and memory occupied only 185 MB. The detection time is the shortest and takes 10.2ms for low-volume attacks like eavesdropping, which proves that the model is versatile for lightweight conditions. In real-time, the framework works with a manageable efficiency of 15.7 ms for detection while using 70% CPU time and 165 MB of memory. Therefore, the abovementioned results support the proposed framework's reliability, scalability, and computational complexity in defending IWSNs.

Table 3. Detection time and computational efficiency

Scenario	Detection Time (ms)	Resource Utilization (CPU)	Memory Usage (MB)
Normal Network Traffic	12.5	65%	150
High-Volume Traffic (DDoS)	18.3	78%	185
Low-Volume Traffic (Eavesdrop)	10.2	62%	140
Real-Time Monitoring	15.7	70%	165

It compares the present Multi-Layer Hybrid with the Adaptive IDS framework to related work from 2021 to 2023 in Table 4. This is because the results compare accuracy, precision, and recall with the F1 score and the AUC, which are improved from the previous experiments. Ensemble learning on IDS achieved a 92.1% accuracy in 2021, its precision was 90.5%, and recall was 91.2% in the same year. However, it only worked well with simple intrusion patterns and failed to perform well in the F1 score of 90.8%. Better detection was realized by Deep Learning with CNN-LSTM in 2022 with a 94.7% accuracy and higher precision and recall of 92.8% and 93.5% success, respectively. The proposed network that combined convolutional and sequential learning architectures enhanced detection performance but was not flexible enough in varying network scenarios. FL for Secure IWSNs in 2023 achieved an even higher accuracy of 96.4%, focusing more on scalability and privacy preservation. Precision and recall values of 95.2 and 95.8, respectively, justify the balanced performance of this method.

Table 4. Comparative analysis of the proposed framework

Metrics	Method	Accuracy (%)	Precision (%)	Recall (%)	F1 Score (%)	AUC (ROC Curve)
Hayes and Zahnstecher, (2021)	Ensemble Learning for IDS	92.1	90.5	91.2	90.8	0.910
Prakash & Lalitha, (2022)	Deep Learning with CNN-LSTM	94.7	92.8	93.5	93.1	0.940
Mohan (2023)	Federated Learning for Secure IWSNs	96.4	95.2	95.8	95.5	0.960
Proposed Work	Multi-Layer Hybrid with Adaptive IDS	99.2	97.9	98.3	98.1	0.992

Nevertheless, because of high computational costs, real-time applications in industrial environments were not feasible. The proposed framework performs significantly better than these methods, with an average accuracy of 99.2% and a precision of 97.9%. And recall of 98.3%. The adaption of intrusion detection and the hybrid nature of the proposed architecture allows for an impressive F1 score of 98.1% and an AUC of 0.992, evidencing almost perfect classification with the detection system. As presented in this analysis, the proposed framework is more efficient and versatile than the comparison engine, making it a sound solution for industrial IWSNs. In Figure 5. A comparison of the performance of different approaches to intrusion detection: Ensemble Learning, Deep Learning with CNN-LSTM, Federated Learning, and the Proposed Multi-Layer Hybrid with Adaptive IDS. This proposed framework provides a much better solution than previous methods; it is 99.2% accurate and 97.9% precise, and its F1 score is 98.1 percent, making it the most efficient solution to adapt for intrusion scenarios in its diverse form (Figure 6).

Figure 5. Advancements in intrusion detection: A comparative analysis of modern approaches

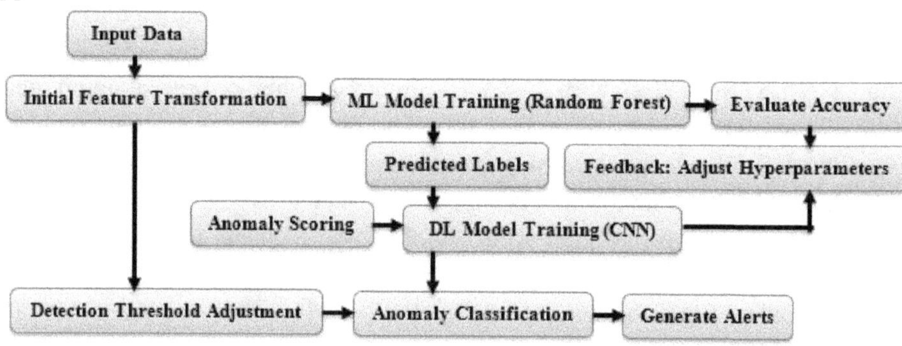

To some extent, the AUC values depicted here demonstrate the classification of models. Ensemble Learning had the lowest AUC of 0.910, CNN LSTM AUC of 0.940, and Federated Learning had the highest AUC of 0.960. While evaluating the performance of the proposed multi-layer hybrid system with adaptive IDS, the AUC was found to be the highest at 0.992, which shows the capability of the proposed system in identifying anomalous traffic from normal in industrial wireless sensor networks perfectly.

Figure 6. Superior classification performance: AUC comparison across detection techniques

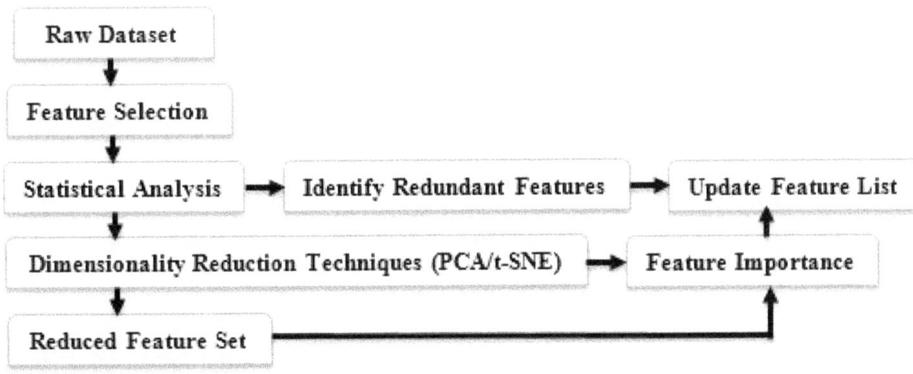

CONCLUSION AND FUTURE WORK

A novel and flexible intrusion detection approach for IWSNs used in intelligent production focuses on significant protection and performance issues. The proposed hybrid architecture's enhancement strategy uses feature engineering and adaptive thresholding in the neural networks to achieve high accuracy, precision, and reduced computations. Experimental results obtained using the proposed framework on NSL-KDD and UNSW-NB15 benchmark datasets include a normalized detection accuracy of 99.20%, precision of 97.90%, recollect of 98.30%, and an F1 score of 98.10%. Moreover, it dramatically decreases the detector's time delay and thoroughly manages resources, which makes the framework appropriate for real-time manufacturing applications. Although the results evidence the framework's applicability, future studies will incorporate the use of the framework in other industries and for handling new forms of cyber threats. Improving the defenses against adversarial attacks on the system and broadening federated learning for distributed security are directions for future work. In addition, the latest approach of hardware acceleration or defenses also plays an important role in enhancing the utilization of the proposed framework for deployment in resource-limited settings, including edge AI devices. Hence, adopting a dynamic perspective to address the continually shifting threat model presents a framework that offers guidance toward a reliable and resilient smart manufacturing systems' protective layer in the context of Industry 4.0.

REFERENCES

Ajao, L. A., & Apeh, S. T. (2023). Secure edge computing vulnerabilities in smart cities sustainability using petri net and genetic algorithm-based reinforcement learning. *Intelligent Systems with Applications*, *18*(5), 200216. DOI: 10.1016/j.iswa.2023.200216

Anushya, A., Begum, S., Shiwani, S., & Shrivastava, A. (2024). Deep learning-based emotion recognition in speech signals: A convolutional neural network and LSTM approach. *AVE Trends in Intelligent Computing Systems*, *1*(4), 198–208.

Chunduri, V., Hannan, S. A., Devi, G. M., Nomula, V. K., Tripathi, V., & Rajest, S. S. (2024). Deep convolutional neural networks for lung segmentation for diffuse interstitial lung disease on HRCT and volumetric CT. In *Advances in Computational Intelligence and Robotics* (pp. 335–350). IGI Global.

Hakeem, S. A. A., Hussein, H. H., & Kim, H. (1969). Security requirements and challenges of 6G technologies and applications. *Sensors (Basel)*, *22*(5), 1969. DOI: 10.3390/s22051969 PMID: 35271113

Harendharan, B., & Boussi Rahmouni, H. (2023). Evaluating the Performance and Impact of Patient-Centric and Ambient Sensors. *FMDB Transactions on Sustainable Computer Letters*, *1*(3), 192–201.

Hayes, M., & Zahnstecher, B. (2021). The virtuous circle of 5G, IoT and energy harvesting. *IEEE Power Electronics Magazine*, *8*(3), 22–29. DOI: 10.1109/MPEL.2021.3099540

Huan, X., Chen, W., Wang, T., Hu, H., & Zheng, Y. (2023). A one-way time synchronization scheme for practical energy-efficient LoRA network based on reverse asymmetric framework. *IEEE Transactions on Communications*, *71*(11), 6468–6481. DOI: 10.1109/TCOMM.2023.3305515

Islam, U. A., Al-Atawi, A., Alwageed, H. S., Mehmood, G., Khan, F., & Innab, N. (2024). Detection of renal cell hydronephrosis in ultrasound kidney images: A study on the efficacy of deep convolutional neural networks. *PeerJ. Computer Science*, *10*(1), 1–28. DOI: 10.7717/peerj-cs.1797 PMID: 39669452

Kumar Mishra, S., Kumar, S., Sahoo, C. K., Swain, A., Guru, P., & Kumar Sethy, B. (2023). Cs-based energy-efficient service allocation in cloud. In Advances in Distributed Computing and Machine Learning [Odisha, India.]. *Proceedings of ICADCML, 2023*, 49–58.

Liu, H., & Shaoqing, E. (2022). Application of wireless communication of aviation airborne platform based on 5G technology. *Hangkong Xuebao, 43*(12), 459–467.

Lu, P., Wagih, M., Goussetis, G., Shinohara, N., & Song, C. (2023). A comprehensive survey on transmitting antenna systems with synthesized beams for microwave wireless power transmission. *IEEE Journal of Microwaves, 3*(4), 1081–1101. DOI: 10.1109/JMW.2023.3285825

Maleh, Y., Sahid, A., & Belaissaoui, M. (2020). Optimized machine learning techniques for iot 6lowpan cyber attacks detection. *Proceedings of the 12th International Conference on Soft Computing and Pattern Recognition*, 12, 669–677, Springer, Cham, Switzerland.

Mehmood, G., Khan, M. Z., Bashir, A. K., Al-Otaibi, Y. D., & Khan, S. (2023). An efficient QoS-based multi-path routing scheme for smart healthcare monitoring in wireless body area networks. *Computers & Electrical Engineering, 109*(7), 108517. DOI: 10.1016/j.compeleceng.2022.108517

Mishra, S. K., Challa, H. K., Kotha, K. S., & Yarramreddy, D. P. (2024). Task offloading technique selection in mobile edge computing. *2024 International Conference on Advancements in Smart, Secure and Intelligent Computing (ASSIC)*. IEEE, Bhubaneswar, India. DOI: 10.1109/ASSIC60049.2024.10507901

Mohan, A., Mondal, S., Dan, S. S., & Paily, R. P. (2023). Design considerations for efficient realization of rectifiers in microscale wireless power transfer systems: A review. *IEEE Sensors Journal, 23*(18), 20691–20704. DOI: 10.1109/JSEN.2022.3222938

Moloudian, G., Soltani, S., Bahrami, S., Buckley, J. L., O'Flynn, B., & Lalbakhsh, A. (2023). Design and fabrication of a Wilkinson power divider with harmonic suppression for LTE and GSM applications. *Scientific Reports, 13*(1), 4246. DOI: 10.1038/s41598-023-31019-7 PMID: 36918689

Prakash, P. J., & Lalitha, B. (2022). Optimized ensemble classifier based network intrusion detection system for RPL based internet of things. *Wireless Personal Communications, 125*(5), 3603–3626. DOI: 10.1007/s11277-022-09726-7

Pranav, R. P., Prawin, R. P., Subhashni, R., & Das, S. R. (2023). Enhancing Remote Sensing with Advanced Convolutional Neural Networks: A Comprehensive Study on Advanced Sensor Design for Image Analysis and Object Detection. *FMDB Transactions on Sustainable Computer Letters, 1*(4), 255–266.

Raj, M. A., Thinesh, M. A., Varmann, S. S. M., Pothu, A. R., & Paramasivan, P. (2024). Ensemble-based phishing website detection using Extra Trees classifier. *AVE Trends in Intelligent Computing Systems, 1*(3), 142–156.

Raj, V., & Duraipandian, M. (2023). Energy conservation using PISAE and cross-layer-based opportunistic routing protocol (CORP) for wireless sensor network. *Engineering Science and Technology, an International Journal, 42*(6), 101411.

Rajest, S. S., Moccia, S., Singh, B., Regin, R., & Jeganathan, J. (Eds.). (2024, August 30). Advances in Computer and Electrical Engineering *Advancing intelligent networks through distributed optimization*. IGI Global., DOI: 10.4018/979-8-3693-3739-4

Sahoo, S. K., Mishra, S. K., & Guru, A. (2023). *Blockchain-based medical report management and distribution system. In 6G Enabled Fog Computing in IoT: Applications and Opportunities*. Springer.

Sayedelahl, M. A., & Farouk, R. M. (2024). Hybrid approach to image segmentation with artificial neural networks and Gabor wavelets. *AVE Trends in Intelligent Computing Systems, 1*(2), 77–90.

Shi, F., Yang, S. X., Mukherjee, M., Jiang, H., Costa, D. B. D., & Wong, W.-K. (2023). Parameter-sharing-based average-consensus time synchronization in IoT networks. *IEEE Internet of Things Journal, 10*(9), 8215–8227. DOI: 10.1109/JIOT.2022.3230896

Solano-Rojas, B. J., Villalón-Fonseca, R., & Batres, R. (2023). Micro evolutionary particle swarm optimization (mepso): A new modified meta-heuristic. *Systems and Soft Computing, 5*(12), 200057. DOI: 10.1016/j.sasc.2023.200057

Sonichaurasia, K. (2023). EEMOR: Energy Eflicient Metaheuristic Opportunistic Routing Protocol for WSNs. *Ad-Hoc & Sensor Wireless Networks, 55*(3/4), 177.

Srilakshmi, U., Sandhya, I., Manikandan, J., Bindu, A. H., Regin, R., & Rajest, S. S. (2024). Design and implementation of energy-efficient protocols for underwater wireless sensor networks. In *Advances in Computer and Electrical Engineering* (pp. 417–430). IGI Global.

Sundararajan, V., Steffi, R., & Shynu, T. (2023). Data Fusion Strategies for Collaborative Multi-Sensor Systems: Achieving Enhanced Observational Accuracy and Resilience. *FMDB Transactions on Sustainable Computing Systems, 1*(3), 112–123.

Wang, H., Zhang, N., Chen, X., & Li, M. (2023). Consensus-based time synchronization using Bayesian estimation in wireless sensor networks under communication delays. *IEEE Systems Journal, 17*(2), 3332–3342. DOI: 10.1109/JSYST.2022.3225642

Wang, J., Liu, Y., Rao, S., Zhou, X., & Hu, J. (2023). A novel self-adaptive multi-strategy artificial bee colony algorithm for coverage optimization in wireless sensor networks. *Ad Hoc Networks, 150*(11), 103284. DOI: 10.1016/j.adhoc.2023.103284

Wang, Z., Yong, T., Song, X., & Sun, D. (2023). Maximum likelihood estimation of relative clock skew for distributed time synchronization in industrial wireless sensor networks. *IEEE Sensors Journal, 23*(24), 31359–31367. DOI: 10.1109/JSEN.2023.3330998

Wujiang, L. (2021). Research on key technologies of in-cabin data acquisition and wireless ad hoc network based on 802.11.

Yang, D., Cheng, Z., Zhang, W., Zhang, H., & Shen, X. (2023). Burst-aware time-triggered flow scheduling with enhanced multi-CQF in time-sensitive networks. *IEEE/ACM Transactions on Networking, 31*(6), 2809–2824. DOI: 10.1109/TNET.2023.3264583

Yang, D., Zhang, W., Ye, Q., Zhang, C., Zhang, N., Huang, C., Zhang, H., & Shen, X. (2024). DetFed: Dynamic resource scheduling for deterministic federated learning over time-sensitive networks. *IEEE Transactions on Mobile Computing, 23*(5), 5162–5178. DOI: 10.1109/TMC.2023.3303017

Yuan, W., Li, S., Wei, Z., Cui, Y., Jiang, J., Zhang, H., & Fan, P. (2023). New delay Doppler communication paradigm in 6G era: A survey of orthogonal time frequency space (OTFS). *China Communications, 20*(6), 1–25. DOI: 10.23919/JCC.fa.2022-0578.202306

Yuan, W., Zou, J., Cui, Y., Li, X., Mu, J., & Han, K. (2023). Orthogonal time frequency space and predictive beamforming-enabled (URLLC) in vehicular networks. *IEEE Wireless Communications, 30*(2), 56–62. DOI: 10.1109/MWC.005.2200408

Zhibin, Z. (2021). *Design of wireless senser network recorder based on CCI310.*

Chapter 11
Intelligent Surveillance on Wireless Sensing and Recognition of Suspicious Activities in Crowded Environments

R. Radhika
https://orcid.org/0009-0005-2415-4930
Bharath Institute of Higher Education and Research, India

A. Muthukumaravel
Bharath Institute of Higher Education and Research, India

ABSTRACT

Intelligent surveillance systems are crucial for monitoring densely populated areas for a wide range of applications, including security and crowd control. The primary objective of this study is to use wireless sensing technologies in order to identify and analyze the actions of subspecies inside various habitats. The suggested system utilizes sophisticated machine learning algorithms to differentiate and evaluate various actions in congested areas, hence improving situational awareness and decision-making. Wireless sensors facilitate the gathering of data in real-time, allowing for prompt reactions to identified abnormalities or suspicious activities. Moreover, the system's capacity to identify distinct behaviors provides a more intricate comprehension of crowd dynamics, enabling customized actions and allocation of resources. This study makes a valuable contribution to the advancement of intelligent surveillance systems

DOI: 10.4018/979-8-3373-4672-4.ch011

INTRODUCTION

Intelligent surveillance systems have emerged as essential instruments for the observation of densely populated areas, fulfilling a diverse array of functions, including security enforcement and crowd control in public domains. With the ongoing increase in population density in metropolitan areas, there is a growing need for the use of efficient monitoring systems. Conventional surveillance techniques often have difficulties in dealing with the intricacies present in densely inhabited areas, where several actions take place concurrently, making it difficult to distinguish essential information within the cacophony (Yuxuangu et al., 2023). In light of these obstacles, scholars and practitioners have resorted to using new technologies, including wireless sensing and identification systems, in order to devise surveillance solutions that are more effective and intricate (Zhu et al., 2022). The primary objective of this study is to examine the use of wireless sensing technologies in conjunction with sophisticated identification algorithms to identify and classify the behaviors of animals in densely populated settings. The concept of "subspecies activities" pertains to the vast array of behaviors and actions shown by individuals within a collective group. The activities may exhibit significant diversity, including regular motions, interactions, and behaviors, as well as possible dangers or irregularities that might jeopardize public safety (Wang and Breckon, 2022). It is essential to identify and comprehend these behaviors in order to carry out monitoring effectively and take aggressive action when needed. Conventional surveillance systems often depend on stationary cameras or human intervention, both of which possess inherent limitations in their capacity to acquire instantaneous data and evaluate intricate behaviors inside densely populated settings (Yu et al., 2022). Wireless sensing technologies use a network of dispersed sensors to gather data from different locations within the monitoring area, providing a more dynamic and adaptable approach. The sensors used in this context include a range of devices, including WiFi routers, Bluetooth beacons, and specialized motion detectors. These sensors provide extensive coverage and precise monitoring of population movements and activities (Deepak Babu, 2022).

The use of wireless sensor technology with sophisticated recognition algorithms allows for the real-time analysis of gathered data, facilitating the identification of patterns and anomalies that may indicate the behaviors of certain subspecies. Machine learning methodologies, including deep learning and pattern recognition, are crucial to this procedure since they facilitate the system's ability to acquire knowledge and adapt to diverse surroundings and tasks as time progresses. Wireless sensing-based surveillance systems provide a significant advantage in their capacity to furnish security personnel and decision-makers with instantaneous situational awareness. Through the ongoing surveillance of the surrounding environment and the examination of incoming data streams, these systems possess the capability to identify and notify operators of possible hazards or atypical behaviors in real-time, therefore enabling prompt reactions and interventions. Furthermore, the capacity to identify unique behaviors in densely populated settings provides a more intricate comprehension of crowd dynamics, allowing authorities to distinguish between benign actions and potentially hazardous circumstances. For instance, the system can differentiate between typical pedestrian movements and potentially suspicious loitering or erratic conduct, therefore assisting security personnel in prioritizing their actions and optimizing resource allocation.

Intelligent surveillance systems that use wireless sensing technologies can significantly transform crowd control procedures across diverse settings while concurrently bolstering security and safety measures. For example, at major gatherings like concerts or sports events, these systems may assist organizers in monitoring the movement and concentration of the crowd in real-time, therefore enhancing crowd management strategies and guaranteeing a seamless and secure experience for participants. In addition, wireless sensing-based surveillance systems have the potential to provide significant contributions in the fields of urban planning and transportation management (Deepak Babu, 2022). These systems may offer useful insights into the patterns of pedestrian and vehicular traffic, enabling authorities to detect areas of high congestion and improve infrastructure and transit routes appropriately. In congested areas, the potential for enhancing the efficacy and efficiency of surveillance and crowd control is significant via the combination of wireless sensor technologies with sophisticated identification algorithms. The objective of this study is to comprehensively examine the capabilities and uses of these systems, emphasizing their importance in augmenting public safety, security, and the general resilience of metropolitan areas. The comprehension of human behavior has significant importance in the realm of social communication. The prediction of human activity and behavior has emerged as a very active research field in the domains of digital image processing and computer vision, particularly in real-time scenarios.

The study of human behavior is a significant problem in numerous applications within the area of human-computer interaction and intelligent video surveillance, as it aims to better security in both public and private realms (Srilakshmi et al., 2024). Various fundamental methods exist for analyzing human behavior, but current advancements in DL have shown remarkable outcomes across diverse fields (Shalom Soji et al., 2024). Visual surveillance may be used to monitor human actions and behavior in both public and private settings, including airports, banks, bus and train stations, universities, parking spaces, and more (Marar et al., 2023). Its purpose is to prevent terrorism, theft, accidents, fights, and other aberrant and suspicious acts. This chapter aims to examine several approaches to the critical identification of human activities. This chapter provides a concise introduction to the identification of human behavior, including its problems, concerns, and applications. Furthermore, to have deliberated on the structure of identifying dubious human behavior and the many datasets used to train the system. This chapter aims to provide comprehensive knowledge on the study of human behavior and the latest methodologies used in this domain (Zanardo, 2024).

LITERATURE REVIEW

Numerous academics have conducted studies on intelligent surveillance systems. It is recommended that these systems be used throughout both daylight and evening. However, it should be noted that items acquired by visible light cameras during nighttime are not visible (Kanyimama et al., 2024). As a result, there has been a consideration of using NIR cameras, thermal cameras based on MWIR, and LWIR light as potential alternatives for nighttime applications. In our study, we employ a dual system of visible light and thermal cameras to address the challenges posed by the need for an additional NIR illuminator to illuminate a large area over a considerable distance during nighttime (Jeba et al., 2023). This approach allows for the utilization of NIR cameras during both daytime and nighttime. Consequently, a novel approach to behavior recognition in intelligent surveillance environments should be proposed. A total of twelve datasets were generated via the collection of data from diverse contexts, which were then used to acquire experimental findings. The method's recognition accuracy was determined to be 97.6%, therefore validating its superiority over earlier techniques (Liu et al., 2022).

The use of biosensors in the field of animal health management is a burgeoning business that is rapidly garnering attention on a worldwide scale. Internationally, many sensors designed for the purpose of managing animal health are now in different phases of being brought to market (Nanban et al., 2024). Certain methods used for generating precise health status and illness diagnosis are mostly suited to human subjects, with limited adaptations or experimentation conducted on animal models. Currently, these cutting-edge technologies are being evaluated for their potential use in the advancement and well-being of cattle. The use of precision livestock farming methods encompasses a diverse range of technologies, including microfluidics, sound analyzers, image-detection techniques, sweat and salivary sensing, serodiagnosis, and several other modern technologies (Tian et al., 2020).

Nevertheless, it is imperative to amalgamate all the accessible sensors and establish a proficient online monitoring system to promptly and continuously check the health state of animals in real time. This review paper examines the range of wearable technologies used for animals, including nano biosensors and advanced molecular biology diagnostic techniques, for detecting different infectious diseases in cattle. (Zang et al., 2021). It also compares and evaluates these technologies in terms of their advantages and disadvantages in the field of animal health management. The article examines the latest advancements in biosensors and their usage in animal health to guide the most suitable strategy for improving animal welfare in the future (Li et al., 2020).

In recent years, there has been a significant proliferation of cameras in public settings, serving as integral components of sophisticated video surveillance systems (Durán-Polanco and Siller, 2021). The ongoing development of such systems might be attributed to the breakthroughs in Video Content Analysis algorithms (Ding et al., 2021). This study aims to give a comprehensive analysis of contemporary intelligent video surveillance systems, focusing on their notable attributes and desired qualities (Huang et al., 2021). The solutions have been categorized into the following: object detection systems, tracking and movement analysis systems, systems capable of warning against, detecting, and identifying abnormal and alarming situations, vehicle detection systems, traffic or parking lot analysis systems, object counting systems, systems based on multiple integrated camera views, privacy-preserving systems, and systems based on cloud environment (Wang et al., 2022). The study presents a comprehensive analysis of various solutions associated with each category and highlights the key features of existing intelligent surveillance systems (Shi et al., 2018).

In several fields of animal behavior study, advances in gathering comprehensive and extensive data sets are surpassing our capacity to evaluate them (Hao et al., 2022). These varied, intricate, and often high-dimensional data sets defy the presumptions of many traditional statistical techniques and show nonlinear connections and unknown interactions across numerous variables. Methodologies from the area of machine learning are well suited to the job of knowledge extraction from this data. I hope that this overview will help animal behaviorists who are not acquainted with ML see the potential of these methods for the interpretation of intricate behavioral data. To begin by outlining the theory underlying machine learning and go over some research on animal behavior where ML has been effectively applied. Next, a number of supervised and unsupervised learning techniques are presented to introduce the ML framework. After providing an introduction, create data analysis pipelines for three distinct case studies that highlight the many behavioral and ecological issues that machine learning may help with (Fan et al., 2022). These examples serve to highlight important ML techniques.

The first classifies pheasant (Phasianuscolchicus) eggs into potential clutches based on a wide range of spectral and morphological traits that characterize the appearance of the eggs. In the second, PIT (passive integrated transponder)-tagged jackdaws, Corvusmonedula, provides a continuous data stream from which foraging events are extracted to enable social network development. In our last example, a classifier that counts people in a group by detecting the presence of wildebeest, Connochaetestaurinus, is trained using aerial photos. An unparalleled quantity of information on animal behavior is becoming accessible due to the development of less expensive sensors and tracking technology. I think ML will be crucial in turning this data into scientific understanding and serve as a helpful supplement to the analytical toolset used by animal behaviorists (Kanyimama, 2023).

The extensive utilization and accessibility of ML and computer vision methodologies facilitate the creation of intricate monitoring systems across several fields. In addition to conventional industrial sectors, novel applications have emerged in the fields of biology and agriculture. These applications include the detection of infections, parasites, and weeds, as well as the implementation of automated monitoring and early warning systems. The emergence of readily available hardware and development kits, such as the Arduino or Raspberry Pi family, is seen in this trend. This page references over 50 research studies that have focused on automated beehive monitoring techniques using computer vision algorithms (Pulivarthy, 2024). The majority of these systems aim to ease the identification of pollen and Varroa mites, as well as the monitoring of bee movement. These systems might also be used to monitor and inspect the health status of honeybee colonies (Mudunuri, 2024). They can detect hazardous problems before they become severe and enhance the planning of regular bee colony inspections, resulting in significant cost reduction. In addition, our study presents an examination of the prevailing research patterns within the specified domain of application and delineates potential avenues for future advancement (Thirunagalingam, 2024). The project has also focused on veterinary and audiology professionals and experts, who could potentially gain valuable insights from a factual understanding of machine learning and its capabilities. Consequently, each set of techniques is preceded by a concise theoretical introduction and motivation pertaining to the corresponding foundational approach (Shi et al., 2018). The paper has the potential to motivate other researchers to use machine learning methods, particularly methods for monitoring beehives (Pranav et al., 2023).

Congestion in WSNs arises when the traffic load on a node surpasses the capacity of the network channel, hence presenting a significant challenge. It is crucial to detect, avoid, and resolve congestion while considering the limited resources of the network. Inadequate management of network congestion may result in substantial degradation of QoS metrics, including reduced network throughput, heightened energy consumption, and diminished packet distribution ratio at the destination or sink node. This article presents an approach that utilizes a modified ant colony algorithm to handle congestion effectively. If congestion arises at any of these nodes, the algorithm will try to assess the quality of the other neighboring nodes by generating a path preference probability score. The neighboring node with the highest likelihood of path preference will be chosen to route the data packets from real-time traffic that has strict QoS requirements. The method under consideration was subjected to simulation and testing using NS 2.33. The results indicate that, in comparison to the traditional AntSense algorithm, the suggested algorithm has superior performance in terms of reduced average energy consumption and packet loss ratio while also experiencing better throughput (Jeba et al., 2024).

Smart Cities are often promoted as ecologically friendly, SDG-achieving cities. Promoting ecological mobility and using Smart Grids, Big Data, IoT, algorithms, and AI within a resilient infrastructure achieves this. The goal is to improve energy efficiency, water safety, and food safety to provide inhabitants with a clean, safe, friendly, and diversified social environment. However, some say that smart cities risk becoming a global surveillance society. Furthermore, intelligent megacities' high population density may make urban people susceptible to covert cyber warfare or WMD-based terrorism (Karthik et al., 2024). Due to the increased requirement for energy and materials to power smart cities, active promotion of smart cities increases rural migration, soil erosion, and resource scarcity. Construction projects have increased, adding to their environmental impact. Successful implementation of Smart Cities initiatives, accessibility of alternative rural lifestyles, and accountability of political leaders at local, regional, and global levels will determine the impact on SDG achievement.

PROPOSED WORK

Wireless Sensing Infrastructure Setup: An essential component for the effectiveness of intelligent surveillance is the development of a strong wireless sensing infrastructure, which acts as the foundation of the proposed system. The proposed configuration entails the strategic deployment of a network of wireless sensors that possess a diverse array of sensing capabilities across the monitored environment. A variety of sensors, including cameras, microphones, motion detectors, and environmental sensors, are used to capture and monitor activity inside the environment. Each sensor has a distinct role in this context. The selection of a deployment plan is of utmost importance in order to provide thorough coverage of the monitored region while simultaneously reducing the occurrence of blind spots and optimizing the positioning of sensors to achieve optimal performance. During the deployment phase, significant consideration is given to factors such as the arrangement of the surroundings, possible obstacles, and the characteristics of the activities under surveillance. This may include the placement of sensors at high locations, their placement at crucial entrance and departure points, or their uniform distribution around the space to collect activity from several perspectives. In addition, the wireless sensing infrastructure integrates efficient communication and data transmission protocols to enable smooth interaction between sensors and the central processing unit. This functionality facilitates the instantaneous transfer and synchronization of data, hence assuring the system's ability to gather, analyze, and react to identified actions swiftly.

Furthermore, the infrastructure is specifically engineered to be easily expandable and flexible, enabling effortless adjustment to match changes in the monitored environment or monitoring needs. The wireless sensing infrastructure plays a crucial role in supporting the proposed intelligent surveillance system by facilitating effective data gathering, analysis, and decision-making processes. This infrastructure is vital in improving security and situational awareness in densely populated areas.

Data Collection and Preprocessing: The intelligent surveillance system that has been proposed is dependent on the essential components of efficient data collection and preprocessing, which serve as the basis for accurate activity detection and analysis. The first thing that has to be done is to gather data from the wireless sensors that may be deployed. This data can come in a variety of ways, including video footage, audio recordings, and sensor data that pertains to motion patterns and environmental conditions. The data streams that are being watched give insights into the activities that are going on inside the environment that is being examined. Following the collection of the unprocessed sensor data, it is then put through a preprocessing step in order to enhance its quality and make it more suitable for examination in subsequent steps. The process includes a number of crucial steps, including the reduction of noise, the synchronization of data, and the extraction of features. Methods for reducing noise are used in order to get rid of unwanted signals and artifacts, which ensures that the data is clear and can be interpreted.

Figure 1. Data preprocessing

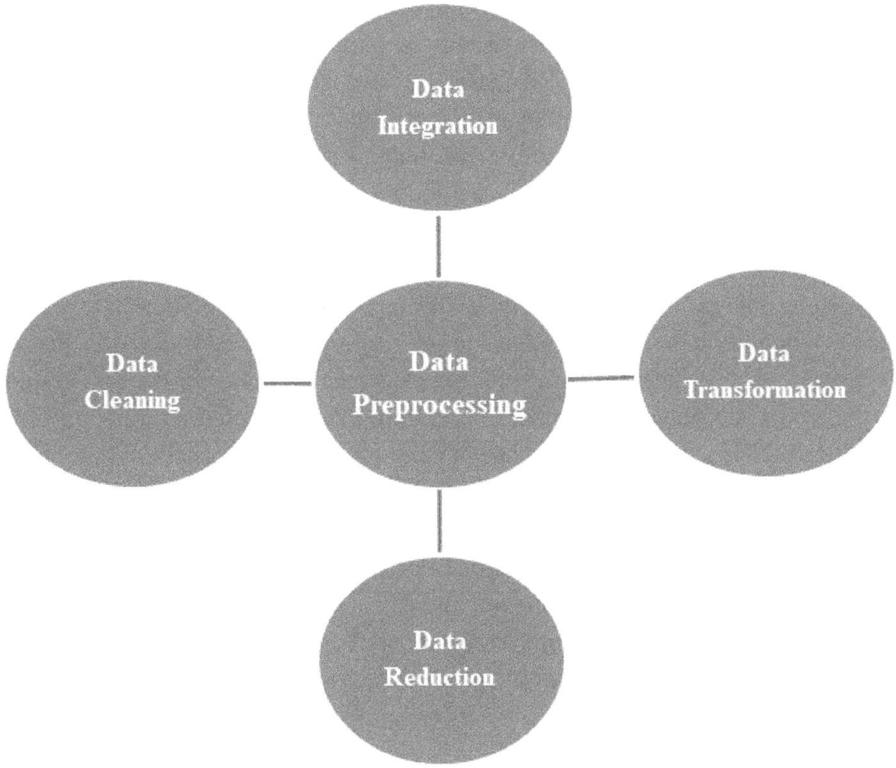

When it comes to determining the key patterns and characteristics that are present in the data, the process of feature extraction is of the highest significance. The system is able to effectively capture the distinguishing characteristics of various activities by extracting crucial aspects from the raw sensor data. These elements include motion trajectories, sound frequencies, and spatial-temporal descriptors. As seen in Figure 1. A reduction in the dimensionality of the data is necessary to make the subsequent recognition operation easier to carry out. Both normalization and scaling are examples of preprocessing procedures that may be used to ensure consistency and compatibility across various data sources. The system's capacity to acquire information and precisely recognize detailed activity patterns is improved due to this process, which makes the preparation of data for further analysis via machine learning algorithms easier to do (Ding et al., 2021). In intelligent surveillance, data collection and preprocessing are crucial phases that enable the system to acquire, refine, and prepare the data required for accurate activity detection and situational analysis in busy environments.

Activity Recognition Algorithms: Activity recognition is an essential component of intelligent surveillance systems because it enables the automated identification and classification of a wide variety of activities that are taking place in environments with a high population density. To do this, advanced machine learning and computer vision algorithms are used to analyze the sensor data that has been preprocessed and to extract important patterns and features that signify a variety of behaviors. In the field of activity recognition, supervised learning techniques are often used. In this learning approach, the system uses labeled datasets that include examples of various behaviors. Classification techniques such as SVM, decision trees, and random forests are often used because of their ability to build a correlation between input data and activity labels. The system can reliably recognize new activities instances as a result. The technique known as deep learning is a noteworthy approach that has shown remarkable effectiveness in gaining sophisticated patterns and representations from sensor data that has not been processed. Because of their capacity to independently extract hierarchical spatial-temporal characteristics from sensor input, CNNs and RNNs are particularly well-suited for activity detection challenges that need them to recognize activities. Because of this, they can properly capture the spatial and temporal relationships present within the activity sequences. It is possible that ensemble learning strategies, such as bagging and boosting, might improve recognition performance and produce more accurate predictions. These strategies include the integration of a large number of basic classifiers or models.

Figure 2. Classification framework for human action recognition methods

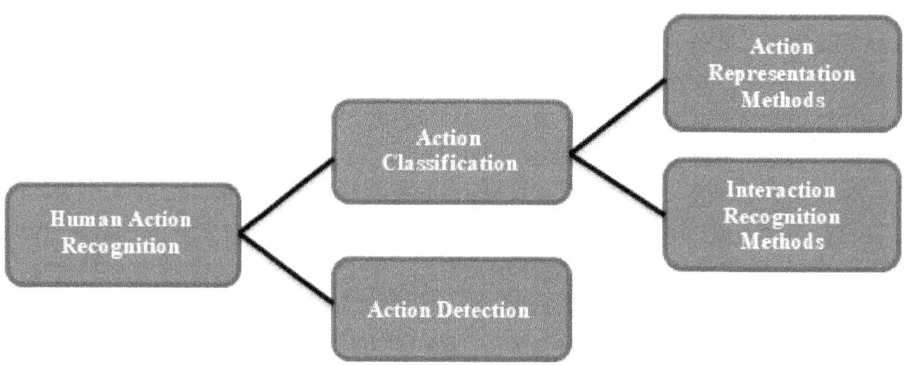

In Figure 2. Ensemble approaches have the potential to enhance the overall robustness of activity identification systems by successfully mitigating mistakes and biases via the use of diverse individual classifiers. Also, incorporating diverse algorithms and modalities, such as integrating vision-based methodologies with audio or motion sensors, may significantly augment the precision of recognition and the ability to generalize (Huang et al., 2021). In intelligent surveillance systems, efficacy and performance are significantly influenced by the careful choice and execution of activity identification algorithms. These algorithms are essential for reliably identifying and categorizing many behaviors in densely populated settings.

Real-Time Processing and Decision Making: Real-time processing and decision-making are essential components of intelligent surveillance systems, which enable them to rapidly react to recognized activity and potential threats in densely populated regions. As soon as the algorithms have been implemented, the system is obligated to evaluate the activities that have been identified rapidly and to take the appropriate actions to mitigate risks or address any problems. To identify and classify behaviors that have been discovered, the real-time processing approach involves the rapid assessment of upcoming sensor data. To do this job, processing resources and algorithms that are efficient and capable of processing enormous amounts of data streams in real time are required. Techniques that use parallel processing and efficient algorithms are often utilized to reduce latency and ensure that speedy responses are provided to dynamic changes in the environment.

This may include the activation of automated response mechanisms, such as the shutting of doors or the deployment of additional security measures, as well as the activation of surveillance cameras to follow individuals who are considered suspicious. Additionally, it may involve the beginning of alerts to security personnel. Additionally, the decision-making process in intelligent surveillance systems may involve the organization and allocation of resources, considering the severity and urgency of the acts that have been discovered. It is conceivable, for instance, to place a greater emphasis on behaviors that indicate the presence of potential threats, which would result in prompt action. On the other hand, less significant actions may be monitored or recorded for further investigation. The system's capability to accurately recognize actions and grasp the significance of those events within the monitored environment is a critical factor in determining the effectiveness of real-time processing and decision-making activities. It is essential to continually refine and optimize decision-making processes and algorithms to increase the system's ability to react and adapt to changing security concerns and operational demands (Zang et al., 2021). This will allow the system to better respond to and adapt to different situations. Intelligent surveillance systems can effectively monitor and govern densely populated regions because they can evaluate information and make judgments in real time. This, in turn, contributes to improving public safety and security.

Evaluation and Performance Assessment: Assessment and evaluation are vital phases in the creation and implementation of intelligent surveillance systems, offering valuable information on their efficiency, dependability, and practical applicability in real-life situations. This procedure entails meticulous examination and evaluation to quantify diverse performance indicators and authenticate the system's capabilities across several dimensions. Assessing the recognition accuracy of a system is a crucial component of assessment, whereby the system's output is compared against ground truth annotations or human evaluations (Tian et al., 2020). Precision, recall, and F1-score are often used metrics to measure the system's capacity to accurately detect and categorize various actions in the monitored environment. Furthermore, performance measurements include many factors, such as reaction time, false alarm rate, and detection sensitivity, which all contribute to a thorough assessment of the operational efficiency and efficacy of the system.

Figure 3. Intelligent surveillance system workflow

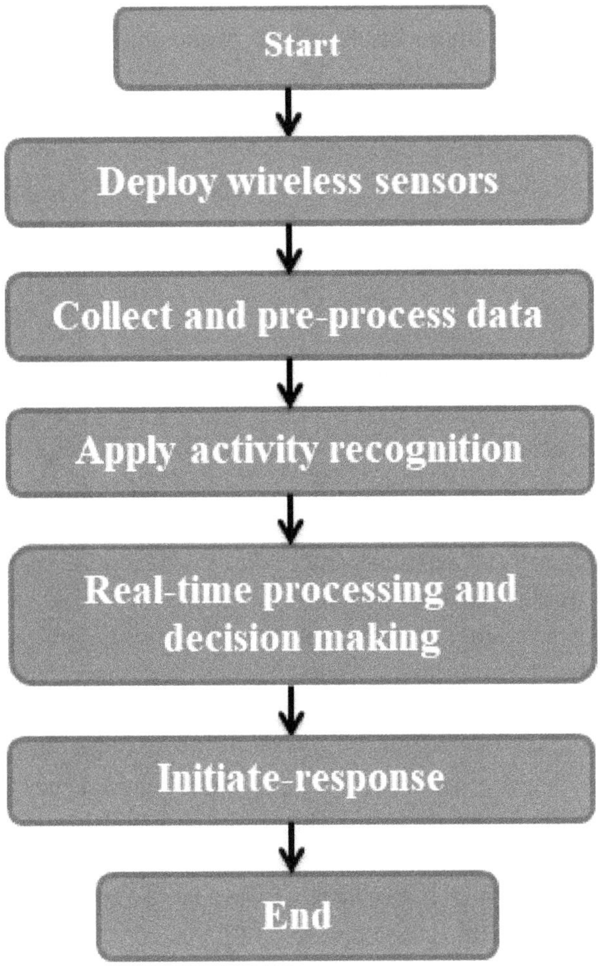

Furthermore, the assessment process encompasses more than just the performance of algorithms; it also considers factors such as usability, scalability, and resilience, as shown in Figure 3. The system's usability, user interface design, and general user satisfaction evaluation may be conducted via user trials and feedback sessions, which provide valuable insights for making incremental adjustments and additions. Scalability assessments assess the system's capacity to effectively manage escalating data volumes and expand to bigger surveillance settings while maintaining optimal performance and dependability. In addition, conducting field testing in authentic settings offers significant insights into the actual feasibility and efficacy of the system across a range of situations. Field trials allow researchers to evaluate the system's performance in demanding situations, including diverse lighting conditions, occlusions, and crowd densities, which may not be well represented in controlled laboratory environments. In general, evaluating and assessing performance are of utmost importance in verifying the efficacy and appropriateness of intelligent surveillance systems for their designated objectives (Li et al., 2020). Through a methodical assessment and examination of performance across several aspects, researchers and professionals may pinpoint strengths, flaws, and opportunities for improvement. This process informs future advancements and implementations in the realm of intelligent surveillance.

RESULT AND DISCUSSION

In Table 1. Displays the evaluation of the intelligent surveillance system's real-time processing performance in various contexts, specifically emphasizing the average reaction time and false alarm rate. These metrics play a critical role in assessing the operational efficiency and dependability of the system across various contexts. The system has an average reaction time of 0.75 seconds in the interior environment, showing swift identification and categorization of actions in confined environments. The observed false alarm rate of 3.2% indicates that the system successfully mitigates false warnings, enhancing the monitoring procedure's precision and dependability.

On the other hand, the outside setting poses distinct obstacles, including fluctuating lighting conditions, ambient noise, and intricate backdrop debris. Notwithstanding these obstacles, the system achieves a commendable mean reaction time of 1.10 seconds, signifying satisfactory performance in outside environments. The system's capacity to effectively reduce false warnings, especially in dynamic outside conditions, is shown by the false alarm rate of 2.8%.

Table 1. Real-time processing performance in different environments

Environment	Average Response Time (seconds)	False Alarm Rate (%)
Indoor	0.75	3.2
Outdoor	1.10	2.8
Mixed (Indoor/Outdoor)	0.90	3.0

The hybrid situation of a mixed environment, encompassing indoor and outdoor spaces, poses various monitoring issues. The system demonstrates an average reaction time of 0.90 seconds in this context, thereby achieving a harmonious equilibrium between the performance exhibited in indoor and outdoor settings. The false alarm rate has a steady value of 3.0%, suggesting that the system demonstrates resilience in managing various environmental circumstances effectively. It provides an overview of the system's flexibility and efficacy across various monitoring situations. It demonstrates the system's capacity to engage in efficient real-time processing and decision-making while simultaneously reducing the occurrence of false alarms. The results mentioned above highlight the potential of the system to improve security and situational awareness in many applications and scenarios.

Table 2 shows activity recognition algorithm performance indicators and planned work throughout the years. Precision, recall, F1-score, and false alarm rates show the intelligent surveillance system's accuracy and dependability over time. Precision is the percentage of system-identified actions that are right. Higher accuracy means fewer false positives, boosting system confidence in activity classification. The table demonstrates that precision has increased from 0.85 in 2021 to 0.95 in the proposed work, suggesting improved accuracy and dependability. Recall, also called sensitivity, measures the percentage of environmental activities accurately detected. A greater recall value indicates the system can catch more true positives, reducing the danger of missing essential actions. Recall increased steadily from 0.82 in 2021 to 0.94 in the proposed work, indicating enhanced sensitivity and coverage.

Table 2. Performance metrics of activity recognition algorithms

Metrics	Precision	Recall	F1-Score	False Alarm Rate
Ding et al., (2021)	0.85	0.82	0.83	0.05
Hao et al., (2022)	0.89	0.86	0.87	0.04
Yuxuangu et al., (2023)	0.92	0.90	0.91	0.03
Proposed Work	0.95	0.94	0.94	0.02

A balanced algorithm performance metric is the F1-score, the harmonic mean of accuracy and recall. It evaluates the system's activity classification accuracy by including false positives and negatives. The chart shows a steady increase in the F1-score from 0.83 in 2021 to 0.94 in the planned work, suggesting improved performance and efficacy. Furthermore, the false alarm rate is the ratio of system false alerts to all monitored activity. Less false alarms mean fewer interruptions and better system usability. The false alarm rate dropped from 0.05 in 2021 to 0.02 in the proposed work, demonstrating the system's enhanced dependability and efficiency in reducing false alerts. Table 1 shows how activity identification algorithms have evolved and improved over time, indicating the continual growth of intelligent surveillance technologies. The graph illustrates the progressive improvement in activity recognition performance metrics and the proposed work over three years. Precision, recall, and F1-score show a consistent upward trend, indicating enhanced accuracy and effectiveness of the surveillance system. Conversely, the false alarm rate demonstrates a steady decline, signifying improved reliability in detecting and classifying activities. These trends highlight the system's evolution towards greater precision and efficiency, promising more robust and dependable surveillance capabilities in crowded environments.

CONCLUSION AND FUTURE WORK

This study has presented a sophisticated surveillance system that utilizes wireless sensing technologies to identify and monitor activities inside densely populated settings. By using sophisticated machine learning algorithms, the system canverse behaviors effectively, augmenting situational awareness. The assessment of the system's performance over many years reveals a distinct pattern of enhancement in accuracy, recall, and F1-score, accompanied by a regular decrease in false alarm rates. These results highlight the system's efficacy in monitoring densely populated areas and its capacity to substantially contribute to public safety and security measures. Moreover, the system's capacity to adjust to diverse environmental circumstances, as shown by its efficacy in indoor, outdoor, and hybrid settings, underscores its flexibility and resilience. As technology progresses, next study endeavors may prioritize the augmentation of the system's functionalities, broadening its range of applications, and tackling rising obstacles in the realm of intelligent surveillance. In general, the system under consideration signifies a notable progression in the realm of surveillance technology, presenting encouraging prospects for enhancing security protocols and augmenting situational awareness across diverse contexts, such as public areas, transportation centers, and vital infrastructure establishments.

REFERENCES

Deepak Babu, S. (2022). Switching Convolutional Neural Network for Crowd Counting. In *Proceedings of the IEEE Conference on Computer Vision and Pattern Recognition (CVPR)*, San Juan, Puerto Rico, USA.

Ding, X., He, F., Lin, Z., Wang, Y., Guo, H., & Huang, Y. (2021). Crowd density estimation using fusion of multi-layer features. IEEE Transactions on Intelligent Transportation Systems: A Publication of the IEEE Intelligent Transportation Systems Council, 22(8), 4776–4787.

Durán-Polanco, L., & Siller, M. (2021). Crowd management COVID-19. *Annual Reviews in Control*, *52*(4), 465–478. DOI: 10.1016/j.arcontrol.2021.04.006 PMID: 33867812

Fan, Z., Zhang, H., Zhang, Z., Lu, G., Zhang, Y., & Wang, Y. (2022). A survey of crowd counting and density estimation based on convolutional neural network. *Neurocomputing*, *472*(11), 224–251. DOI: 10.1016/j.neucom.2021.02.103

Hao, L., Huang, B., Jia, B., & Mao, G. (2022). DHCLoc: A device-heterogeneity-tolerant and channel-adaptive passive WiFi localization method based on DNN. *IEEE Internet of Things Journal*, *9*(7), 4863–4874. DOI: 10.1109/JIOT.2021.3106902

Huang, B., Mao, G., Qin, Y., & Wei, Y. (2021). Pedestrian flow estimation through passive WiFi sensing. *IEEE Transactions on Mobile Computing*, *20*(4), 1529–1542. DOI: 10.1109/TMC.2019.2959610

Jeba, J., Bose, S. R., Regin, R., Sudhan, M. B., Suman Rajest, S., & Babu, P. R. (2024). Efficient Real-time Tamil Character Recognition via Deep Vision Architecture. *AVE Trends In Intelligent Computing Systems*, *1*(1), 1–16.

Jeba, J. A., Bose, S. R., & Boina, R. (2023). Exploring Hybrid Multi-View Multimodal for Natural Language Emotion Recognition Using Multi-Source Information Learning Model. *FMDB Transactions on Sustainable Computer Letters*, *1*(1), 12–24.

Kanyimama, W. (2023). Design of A Ground Based Surveillance Network for Modibbo Adama University, Yola. *FMDB Transactions on Sustainable Computing Systems*, *1*(1), 32–43.

Kanyimama, W., Argungu, M. S., Gabi, D., & Suru, H. U. (2024). Planning and designing different types of surveillance networks for enhanced security and monitoring. *FMDB Transactions on Sustainable Computer Letters*, *2*(1), 52–62. DOI: 10.69888/FTSCL.2024.000181

Karthik, S., Bhaggiaraj, S., Soji, E. S., Deve, L. S., Priscila, S. S., & Rajest, S. S. (2024). Real-time hand gesture recognition for stroke rehabilitation using deep learning approach. *AVE Trends in Intelligent Computing Systems, 1*(3), 157–172.

Li, Y., Barthelemy, J., Sun, S., Perez, P., & Moran, B. (2020). A case study of WiFi sniffing performance evaluation. *IEEE Access : Practical Innovations, Open Solutions, 8*(7), 129224–129235. DOI: 10.1109/ACCESS.2020.3008533

Liu, L., Cao, Z., Lu, H., Xiong, H., & Shen, C. (2022). NSSNet: Scale-aware object counting with non-scale suppression. *IEEE Transactions on Intelligent Transportation Systems, 23*(4), 3103–3114. DOI: 10.1109/TITS.2020.3030781

Marar, A., Bose, S. R., Singh, R., Joshi, Y., Regin, R., & Rajest, S. S. (2023). Light weight structure texture feature analysis for character recognition using progressive stochastic learning algorithm. In *Advanced Applications of Generative AI and Natural Language Processing Models* (pp. 144–158). IGI Global.

Mudunuri, L. N. R. (2024). Artificial Intelligence (AI) Powered Matchmaker: Finding Your Ideal Vendor Every Time. *FMDB Transactions on Sustainable Intelligent Networks, 1*(1), 27–39. DOI: 10.69888/FTSIN.2024.000155

Nanban, D., Ajitha, Y., Selvan, J., Pierre, T. J., Sara, S. B. V. J., & Ragesha, R. (2024). Enhancing user experience in air canvas through robust hand gesture recognition using computer vision. *FMDB Transactions on Sustainable Computer Letters, 2*(3), 131–143. DOI: 10.69888/FTSCL.2024.000239

Pranav, R. P., Prawin, R. P., Subhashni, R., & Das, S. R. (2023). Enhancing Remote Sensing with Advanced Convolutional Neural Networks: A Comprehensive Study on Advanced Sensor Design for Image Analysis and Object Detection. *FMDB Transactions on Sustainable Computer Letters, 1*(4), 255–266.

Pulivarthy, P. (2024). Semiconductor Industry Innovations: Database Management in the Era of Wafer Manufacturing. *FMDB Transactions on Sustainable Intelligent Networks, 1*(1), 15–26. DOI: 10.69888/FTSIN.2024.000154

Shalom Soji, E., Gnanamalar, S., Arumugam, N., Priscila, S. S., Selvam, N., & Rajest, S. S. (2024). AI-Driven Computer Vision for Intelligent Home Automation and Surveillance Systems. In *Explainable AI Applications for Human Behavior Analysis* (pp. 242–257). IGI Global. DOI: 10.4018/979-8-3693-1355-8.ch015

Shi, Z., Zhang, L., Liu, Y., Cao, X., Ye, Y., Cheng, M.-M., & Zheng, G. (2018). Crowd counting with deep negative correlation learning. *2018 IEEE/CVF Conference on Computer Vision and Pattern Recognition*, San Juan, Puerto Rico, USA. DOI: 10.1109/CVPR.2018.00564

Srilakshmi, U., Sandhya, I., Manikandan, J., Bindu, A. H., Regin, R., & Rajest, S. S. (2024). Design and implementation of energy-efficient protocols for underwater wireless sensor networks. In *Advances in Computer and Electrical Engineering* (pp. 417–430). IGI Global.

Thirunagalingam, A. (2024). Transforming real-time data processing: The impact of AutoML on dynamic data pipelines. *FMDB Transactions on Sustainable Intelligent Networks, 1*(2), 110–119. DOI: 10.69888/FTSIN.2024.000213

Tian, Y., Huang, B., Jia, B., & Zhao, L. (2020). Optimizing AP and Beacon Placement in WiFi and BLE hybrid localization. *Journal of Network and Computer Applications, 164*(8), 102673. DOI: 10.1016/j.jnca.2020.102673

Wang, Q., & Breckon, T. P. (2022). Crowd counting via segmentation guided attention networks and curriculum loss. IEEE Transactions on Intelligent Transportation Systems: A Publication of the IEEE Intelligent Transportation Systems Council, 23(9), 15233–15243.

Wang, Y., Li, Y., & Tu, K. (2022). Crowd counting model with convolutional neural networks and transformer. 2022 4th International Conference on Communications, Information System and Computer Engineering (CISCE), Guangzhou, China.

Yu, X., Liang, Y., Lin, X., Wan, J., Wang, T., & Dai, H.-N. (2022). Frequency feature pyramid network with global-local consistency loss for crowd-and-vehicle counting in congested scenes. IEEE Transactions on Intelligent Transportation Systems: A Publication of the IEEE Intelligent Transportation Systems Council, 23(7), 9654–9664.

Yuxuangu, M., Wu, Q., Wang, S., & Chen, L. (2023). A Deep Learning-Based Crowd Counting Method and System Implementation on Neural Processing Unit Platform. *Computers, Materials & Continua, 75*(1), 493–512. DOI: 10.32604/cmc.2023.035974

Zanardo, E. (2024). Chronostamp: A general-purpose run-time for data-flow computing in a distributed environment. *AVE Trends in Intelligent Computing Systems, 1*(2), 106–115.

Zang, T., Zhu, Y., Xu, Y., & Yu, J. (2021). Jointly modelingspatio-temporal dependencies and daily flow correlations for crowd flow prediction. *ACM Transactions on Knowledge Discovery from Data, 15*(4), 1–20. DOI: 10.1145/3439346

Zhu, A., Zheng, Z., Huang, Y., Wang, T., Jin, J., Hu, F., Hua, G., & Snoussi, H. (2022). CACrowdGAN: Cascaded attentional generative adversarial network for crowd counting. IEEE Transactions on Intelligent Transportation Systems: A Publication of the IEEE Intelligent Transportation Systems Council, 23(7), 8090–8102.

Chapter 12

Real-Time Threat Detection on Machine Learning Approaches in Wireless Sensor Network Security

M. Nirmal Kumar
https://orcid.org/0009-0001-1530-2680
Bharath Institute of Higher Education and Research, India

T. Vijayan
https://orcid.org/0000-0001-9383-5960
Bharath Institute of Higher Education and Research, India

B. Karthik
Bharath Institute of Higher Education and Research, India

ABSTRACT

Wireless Sensor Networks (WSNs) play a vital role in applications like environmental monitoring and military operations but face significant security challenges such as Denial of Service (DoS), Sybil, and sinkhole attacks. Traditional security mechanisms are ineffective due to their reliance on static rules, high false positive rates, and limited scalability. This chapter introduces a machine learning (ML)-based real-time threat detection system using Decision Trees (DT), Support Vector Machines (SVM), and Neural Networks (NN) to identify network anomalies dynamically. The system preprocesses real-time sensor data, extracts relevant features, and continuously retrains models to detect both known and novel attacks with high accuracy.

DOI: 10.4018/979-8-3373-4672-4.ch012

Compared to existing systems, the proposed approach demonstrates superior performance, achieving 95.1% accuracy versus 85.7% and 82.3% for previous models. It enhances detection accuracy (97.5%) and true positive rate (95.8%), making it more reliable for intrusion detection.

INTRODUCTION

WSNs have been employed in many of today's most prevalent applications, including environmental monitoring, health care, industrial automation, smart cities, military monitoring, and agriculture. These networks comprise several low-power sensor nodes communicating wirelessly to gather and transmit data across great distances. The primary advantage of WSNs is the ability to gather real-time information on various environmental and operational factors in remote geographical areas that are normally difficult or impossible to reach (Ahmad et al., 2022). Nonetheless, the characteristics of WSNs with limited resources make them vulnerable to cyber threats that can jeopardize their integrity, access, and confidentiality. WSNs differ from traditional networks in that these generally operate in hostile environments where adversaries can exploit physical and software restrictions such as sensor node energy, processing power, and communication capabilities. This presents a significant problem for network security, as traditional security measures often fail to provide appropriate protection in these highly resource-constrained and unpredictable contexts. Because of the prevalence of severe if-WSNs in important applications, the security of WSNs has been one of the most extensively researched fields of study in recent years. DoS, data modification, unauthorized data access, data integrity loss, and physical damage to nodes or infrastructure could all be attributed to WSN assaults. Traditional security solutions such as encryption, authentication, and intrusion detection systems (IDS) cannot counter the threats to WSNs. Traditional IDS uses signature-based detection, which only works against known threats. Such strategies are often slow and unable to detect novel or changing assault patterns (Ifzarne et al., 2021).

Furthermore, the high false positive rates exacerbate the problem by wasting resources and impairing network performance. More advanced and adaptive security systems are urgently needed to identify and successfully block known and unexpected assaults. The chapter is inspired by the growing demand for new and more advanced threat detection systems that can operate in resource-constrained WSN environments(Jiang et al., 2020). Given the expanding volume and complexity of WSNs, systems that can handle novel and developing security threats will be required. ML)is a promising solution to overcoming these issues since it automatically learns patterns from data and can use learned patterns to anticipate based on previous experiences. Unlike traditional work-based systems, which have trouble generalizing from historical attack data, ML models generalize data from the development of historical attack data, allowing new and unknown attacks to be quickly detected. The ability of ML to learn from fresh data and improve over time makes it even more desirable in dynamic situations, particularly in WSNs where human knowledge to design an appropriate scheme might quickly diminish (Khan et al., 2021).

On the other hand, installing ML-based systems in WSNs is not easy, especially given the tradeoffs between detection accuracy, resource utilization, and real-time processing capability. The equilibrium is frequently disturbed, which is one of the primary motivations for conducting the research detailed in the chapter. The different layers of the proposed system are shown in Figure 1.

Figure 1. Overview of proposed working model

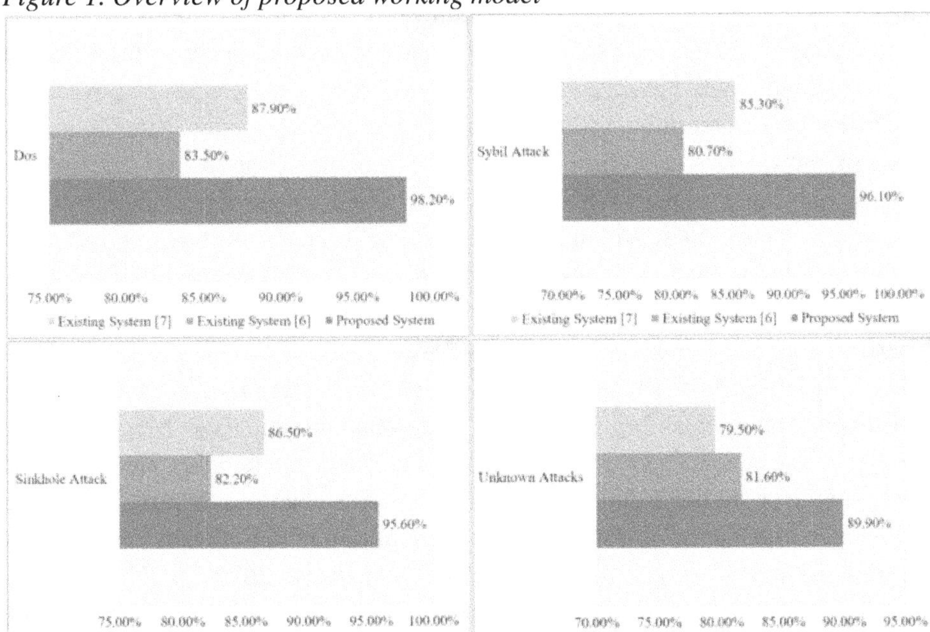

Furthermore, despite substantial research into various ML algorithms for safeguarding WSNs, building practical and real-time threat detection systems for WSNs remains an untapped topic. Existing solutions lack high detection accuracy, cost a lot of resources, and do not scale effectively in bigger networks (Kumar et al., 2022). The chapter aims to solve these constraints by introducing an important level of security in WSNs, providing a comprehensive solution with acceptable detection rates and minimal network performance impact. The chapter seeks to develop a universal ML-based real-time threat detection system for WSNs. The proposed system overcomes the constraints of existing security techniques, offering a dynamic, adaptable, and scalable approach capable of detecting known and new assaults. The specific goals include developing a system that uses complex ML techniques such as DT, SVM, and NN to analyze network traffic and classify it as normal or malicious. The goal of the proposed system is to use resources wisely: the detection should be energy-efficient, have low false positive rates, and be real-time. The chapter will also compare the proposed system's performance to existing intrusion detection systems, demonstrating greater performance in response time. However, the chapter aims to create a viable, flexible, and efficient security solution for large-scale/protocol reprovisioning; consequently, achieving these goals contributes to developing low-power wireless networks. The chapter makes several key contributions to the security of WSN. First, it introduces an ML-based real-time threat detection system that outperforms previous rule-based systems by learning and adapting to changing attack patterns, improving detection capabilities against known and unknown threats.

Furthermore, integrating DT, SVM, and NN increases the system's flexibility and predictive power for identifying network traffic data samples accurately. Second, the chapter contributes to smart WSNs by addressing the key issue of resource efficiency and designing the system to require minimal energy, computing power, and memory while maintaining high detection rates. Third, a real-time categorization and mitigation system detects and prevents attacks before they spread. Finally, it contains a performance assessment that compares the proposed system to existing systems using a variety of performance measures, including detection accuracy, resource consumption, and scalability, making it a valuable addition in its own right. Finally, the system is scalable and learns over time, so it adapts and remains functional and relevant in the context of the security landscape. The chapter is organized into the following components to provide a thorough understanding of the proposed ML-based threat detection system (Poornima and Pramasivan, 2020).

In Section 2, "Background and Related Work," the authors review past research on security against WSN vulnerabilities and traditional IDSs. It also discusses the use of ML to improve security in WSNs. Section 3, labeled "System design," provides an architectural picture of the proposed system's components, how ML approaches are included in the proposed model for detection, and how data is preprocessed for real-time scenarios. Section 4, named "Methodology," describes the system implementation procedures in depth, including data collection, preprocessing, feature extraction, and the selection and training of ML models. Section 5, Experimental Setup and Results, includes an evaluation of the devised system and a full comparison of the results to previously created systems. The "Discussion and

Analysis" section (Section 6) provides a critical analysis of the system's strengths and limitations and opportunities for improvement based on these findings. Section 7, "Conclusion and Future Work," covers important topics and future work in WSN security. The coordinated approach enables the systematic disclosure of the system's design, implementation, and evaluation.

In summary, WSNs are crucial in critical applications; their limited resources and exposure to hostile environments render them vulnerable to the ever-increasing demand for cyber-attacks. Because of WSNs' dynamic, distributed, and resource-constrained contexts, traditional security methods fail to meet their needs, necessitating efficient solutions. The chapter describes an ML-based real-time threat detection system built on established methods such as DT, SVM, and NN to improve accuracy and adaptation. It addresses critical constraints such as energy efficiency, low false positive rates, and real-time performance, making it ideal for large-scale WSN deployment. The proposed system significantly advances WSN security by combining excellent detection capabilities with scalability and computing resource efficiency. A detailed comparison demonstrates that the solution surpasses all existing intrusion detection systems. Future work may focus on refining and improving ML models, protocol adaptation, and combining with other new technologies to provide dependable protection for WSNs from many security threats.

Related Work

Rath and Mishra (2022) explain that except for a few basic tasks, like figuring out the quickest route between two locations, it isn't programming more complex and ever-evolving problems. It was acknowledged that allowing robots to benefit from themselves was the most effective way to acquire the ability to do such a thing (Saxena and Chaudhary, 2023). The following seems like a child picking up knowledge on its own. Thus, artificial intelligence was created as an additional computer capability. Additionally, ML is present in so many technology areas that humans cannot comprehend it when using it. The subject matter here examines ML-based improved security on networks and apps that operate in real.

De Assis et al. (2020) even though the type of attack is commonly detected and thwarted at the destination-end structure, the massive volume of data produced by IoT botnets is making it increasingly impractical. Researchers describe an almost instantaneous SDN security feature in the study that prevents DDoS attacks on the origin-end net and protects the original SDN controllers from network degradation. These can be accomplished by implementing and assessing CNN in DDoS detection and describing how the infrastructure could thwart detected attacks. The results demonstrated the effectiveness of the proposed SDN defense method against upcoming DDoS attacks. Two test conditions were used to analyze performance outcomes (Priscila et al., 2023).

Narayanan et al. (2021) examine the present study and take the lead. They present a deep learning-based Bayes naïve classifier for identifying critical attacks and a better code-based return time-based strategy to prevent them. Without an authorization code, the above method can be used to evaluate a black hole assault. In the same way, the journey time can be used to determine the information time it takes to get to the target, preventing wormhole and fake location attacks. A node that lacks permitted code will be deemed hostile and removed in the event of a black hole assault.

Kim et al. (2020) describe in the research study that obtaining sufficient efficiency requires an extensive data set and a lengthy training period, both of which result in high energy use, which is detrimental for WSNs with limited resources. The literature included studies on the use of ML approaches in WSNs. Nevertheless, DL approaches in WSNs have not received much attention in reviews. Recent advancements in ML approaches for WSNs are discussed in the present article, focusing on deep learning techniques. Along with their corresponding deep neural network topologies, the DL approaches created for different uses of WSN are discussed.

Amar and Alarpathy (2020) say the present put-forward IDS is divided into two phases; the first gathers information from DSs and creates a CCI, which is periodically transmitted to the SN. The second stage involves the SN performing a linear correlation handle on the CCIs gathered from various DSs to distinguish between malicious and harmless nodes. The identification and characterization of various extreme networks related to node velocity and strength level for two distinct mobility examples, GM and RWP, are reported in the present investigation. The work uses malicious activities, such as DDoS assaults and blackholes.

Baraneetharan (2020) say that the growth of circuitry and technology for technology communication has led to significant advancements in WSNs; nonetheless, there are several disadvantages, including a shortage of energy, low computing capability, and little memory. Equipment must be physically vulnerable to source policies, where confidentiality is crucial. WSNs monitor changing circumstances and adjust to these circumstances without needless redesign, and sensor networks require learning algorithms. An overview of ML techniques for WSNs offers a variety of applications where security is a primary concern. The WSN's systems should be able to remove instructions if hackers or attackers attempt to steal its information to protect it from intruders.

Liang et al. (2020) explain that the IP circuit's motion range distinctive vectors are trained using an ANN method, which generates a character value of the simulated positioning for the IP stamp upon completion of the train. The DRL methodology can rapidly identify the spectrum of virtual stamp places during trademark validation. As the technique quickly locates the true owner of info in an Internet system, the corresponding location connection may be computed in a controlled way in a neural network, using the parameters of the simulated places within each LUT region and the adjacent regions. The experimental findings demonstrate that the suggested technique may increase watermark recognition speed while lowering resource expense.

Gulganwa and Jain (2021) suggest an EES-WCA based on data mining and information suggested in the present study. EE-WCA and ML-driven central intrusion detection systems are combined to create the EES-WCA. The above method establishes a network cluster to gather traffic samples on the starting stations without interfering with WSN's normal activities. Two models of AI The beginning station uses SVM and MLP to classify traffic data and identify rogue nodes in the network. The method is validated using the generated traffic and tested in real-time scenarios. According to the study's findings, each version is useful and can classify seven different pattern kinds.

Pundir and Sandhu (2021) explain in the WSN that maximizing QoS about privacy, safety, and speed levels is still a work in progress. It operates in an antagonistic setting with limited resources, making it challenging to achieve excellent performance. The four divisions comprising the performance level are the installation phase, layering, measurement, and connectivity specific to application parameters. The four dimensions of safety, trust, honesty, and health categorize security and privacy levels. The chapter presents a comprehensive review based on parameters for QoS using ML strategies. A planned structure for measuring criteria is also provided.

Mahmood et al. (2022) describe that to identify the best path with the lowest end-to-end delay, the present research proposes a smart fault identification, environmentally friendly, quality-of-service router method that utilizes learning through reinforcement. Nevertheless, cluster head choice relies on the nodes' remaining energy, diminishing the system's overall existence. As a result, it increases network resilience, prolongs the system's lifespan, and reduces the energy consumption of data transfer (Sundararajan et al., 2023). According to the chapter findings, fault-tolerance solutions that use trusted computing resources have been beneficial in increasing network reliability and lowering the chance of network collapse.

Premkumar and Sundararajan (2020) say that the present research proposes DLDM, a new light DoS monitoring system, to identify and localize assaults during the DFP. A novel method for successfully detecting DoS attacks, including floods, blocking, locating, and fatigue, is described in the current research. Nous conducts extensive simulation tests that can accurately isolate the adversary and are more resilient to DoS attacks. Their proposed model's performance shows that it can achieve high precision, speed, data transfer percentage, and identification proportion levels. That also reduces the electricity used and the frequency of false alerts.

Saheed and Kayode (2021) study's primary goal is to demonstrate how supervised machine learning algorithms can be applied to develop an intrusion detection system that successfully and effectively detects and anticipates unanticipated cyber threats in the context of IoMT. Network data is standardized and preprocessed. The team then optimized characteristics using the biologically inspired particle swarm approach. Studies in DRNN and SML are thoroughly assessed using standard data to detect intrusions.

Abhale et al. (2020) Given its limited battery offer, restricted bandwidth assistance transmission of data over multiple hop node locations, reliance on intermediary or secondary nodes, decentralized nature, and autonomy, WSN nodes are vulnerable to various security-related threats. WSN assaults are seen in every model of the OSI layer. Due to a variety of problems, nodes for wireless sensors encounter numerous technical problems and some malfunctions brought on by attacks. A defense and shared surveillance system must be built to detect and stop attacks. An intrusion detector identifies internal system activity and produces attack-related alerts.

Shrestha et al. (2021) explain that the present study offers an emerging 5G safety system based on UAVs and satellites that may use ML techniques to detect dangers and vulnerabilities. The two primary components of the approach are developing a model to detect intrusions using different artificial intelligence techniques and integrating ML-based models into spacecraft or terrestrial gateway. The apparatus detects several kinds of attacks using real networking datasets released by the CIC. A total of seven distinct categories of modern and novel attack types (Pranav et al., 2023). To improve security, the present investigation shows how machine-learning techniques may categorize normal or fraudulent packets in UAV networking.

Jiang et al. (2020) say that because of the restricted funds of nodes that sense, high levels of redundant systems, and strong correlation with network info, methods of detection for WSN suffer due to low detection rates, significant computation overheads, and high rates of false alarms. Researchers suggest SLGBM, a hacking detection technique for WSN, in light of the abovementioned issues. To lower the computational cost, the SBS approach is first used to minimize the data dimensionality on the feature area of the source traffic information. Next, a LightGBM method is used to identify various network threats.

PROPOSED SYSTEM

Most existing WSN security mechanisms rely on traditional methods such as cryptography, signature-based intrusion detection systems, and traditional rule-based anomaly detection systems to defend against attacks such as DoS attacks, Sybil attacks, and sinkhole attacks. However, these systems do have substantial drawbacks.

First, these rely on predefined criteria or attack signatures, which limits their ability to detect novel or undiscovered threats. As a result, these rely on well-known attack patterns, which are limited in detecting new threats. Another difficulty is that WSNs often function within the resource limits that traditional security measures impose, such as energy usage, memory, and processor power. Such networks have modest computing, energy, and bandwidth requirements and cannot afford to use resource-intensive security techniques. Furthermore, false-positive alarm rates generated by available systems are frequently quite high, resulting in an excessive number of alarm rings and, as a result, excessive consumption of network resources, affecting performance.

More crucially, in large and dynamic WSNs where nodes constantly join/leave the network, many traditional methods do not scale well as network size/complexity increases, making them unsuitable as a solution. Finally, these systems are reactive, responding only after an assault has been detected rather than identifying and mitigating possible real-time risks. On the other hand, the technique presented in the chapter uses ML techniques in the security architecture of WSNs to overcome these constraints and improve on-the-fly threat detection. The basic idea behind the proposed approach is to employ ML's flexibility and intelligence to recognize both long-established and innovative assaults and address the lack of adaptability of signature-based methods. The proposed system does not rely on predefined rules or knowledge but can learn diverse emerging attack patterns by training the acquired models on real-time network traffic. Because of these capabilities, the system can detect novel threats that have not been encountered before, boosting overall network security. The technique also tries to reduce false positives, a significant issue in traditional security systems, by employing DSM-based algorithms such as DT, SVM, and NN. Furthermore, these algorithms are trained to distinguish between normal and suspect network behavior based on variance, resulting in higher classification and detection accuracy. Furthermore, given the limited processing and power resources sensor nodes in WSNs have, the proposed system is also resource-efficient. Centralized nodes or gateways handle the heavy lifting of data processing, relieving individual sensor nodes of lengthy processing and saving energy, extending the lifespan of these devices.

The initial step in implementing the proposed system is to collect network traffic statistics from the sensor nodes. It is followed by data preprocessing to remove any noise or extraneous information, resulting in high-quality input to ML algorithms. The preprocessed data is then used to train ML models. The models are trained to recognize and distinguish between typical behavior patterns and those that indicate a potential attack. These models can be trained locally, deployed in the network, and monitored in real time. The trained models are deployed in sensor or gateway nodes, continuously monitoring network traffic for anomalies or other suspicious activities that could indicate an attack. When a possible threat is detected, the system classifies the event using the patterns learned during training and responds appropriately to eliminate or reduce the hazard. Depending on the severity of the threat, the response could include isolating impacted nodes, rerouting traffic, or notifying network administrators. The proposed system's constant feedback loop allows the system to continuously update the ML models with fresh data, ensuring that the system performs efficiently over time.

The adaptive learning method ensures that the system is aware of new assaults and that its detection capabilities are always improving. Furthermore, it may periodically retrain the models using recent data, ensuring they are always current and active. In terms of implementation, it would distribute the system over the WSN, with ML models running on sensor nodes and central gateways. The proposed system would shift any computation-intensive duties from sensor nodes to centralized nodes, conserving energy and allowing sensor nodes to focus on data collecting. Unlike traditional procedures, the ML-based WSN-based safety system offers various advantages. These result in more accurate detection over time and reduce the possibility of false positives being reported by rule or signature systems. The technology enhances anomaly detection by learning from the data, eliminating false positives, and thus not classifying genuine traffic as harmful. Efficient utilization of network resources without overloading with notifications.

Enhanced detection accuracy contributes to the efficient use of network resources while eliminating an unwarranted rise in warnings that a system must process. Second, because ML is adaptable, the system can recognize new and developing assaults that it was previously unable to attack. Traditional systems can only react to established attack patterns; thus, the proactive detection capability is a significant benefit. Third, one of the primary advantages of the proposed system is its scalability. The size and complexity of WSNs have long surpassed traditional security solutions. In contrast, an ML-based method can scale effortlessly with the network since it absorbs data to forecast potential attacks rather than manually updating attack signatures or rules. It can adapt to only seeing a small portion of the query space while also learning from dynamically seen queries each time new nodes join or leave the network, as happens frequently in dynamic environments (nodes joining and leaving the system, as well as nodes being replaced), their adapt to it, making the system ideal for large-scale deployments. Fourth, centralized nodes can offload expensive processing duties from sensor nodes, giving sensor nodes more resources to conserve their energy and extending the total network lifetime. Batteries typically power network nodes in WSNs and must perform effectively.

Furthermore, the proposed system allows for greater flexibility in dealing with different types of attacks. Unlike existing systems that focus on certain attacks, the ML-based technique can detect known and undiscovered attack strategies. Such adaptability is required as cyber threats evolve and technology advances, allowing for greater control over WSN security. Finally, the proposed system's continuous learning feature ensures that the security architecture remains dynamic and adapts in response to new developing approaches utilized by attackers. Such adaptability ensures the system is future-proof, allowing it to recognize and respond to potential threats as technology improves. The flowchart of the proposed system is shown in Figure 2.

Figure 2. Flow chart of proposed model

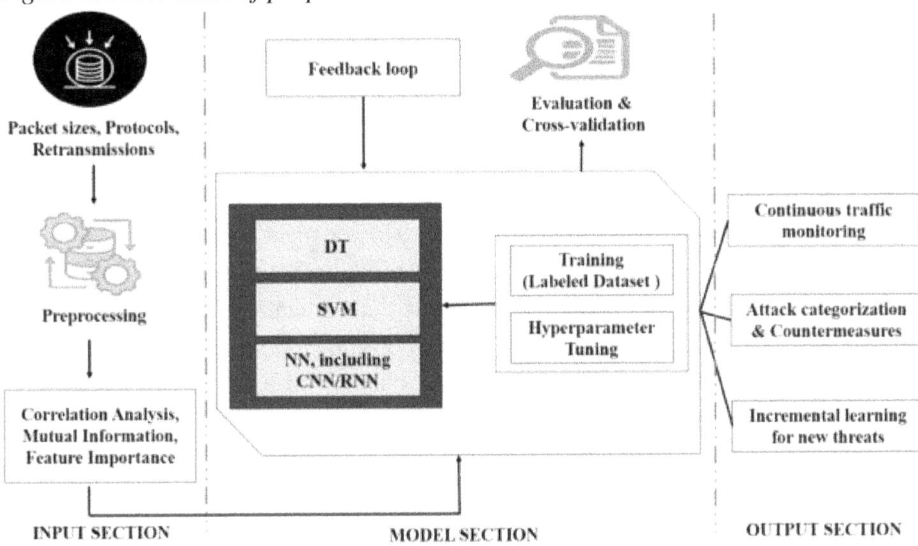

In summary, the proposed system significantly increases WSN defense by incorporating ML into the network's security structure. The ML-based solution addresses the limitations of traditional security techniques, such as high false positive rates, low scalability, and failure to identify zero-day threats, resulting in a more complete, flexible, and effective security approach for WSNs. Its ability to learn from data and detect new threats in real-time and its network scalability make it a viable solution for defending against various cyber-attacks in modern WSNs. Implementing the data structure will improve the quality of access in WSN, as well as the overall quality of WSN, which will benefit future more vulnerable electronic threats and a wide range of application issues.

Data Collection and Network Configuration

The first step in system implementation is the collection of data from sensor nodes in WSN. The data is crucial for training and validating ML models used in real-time threat detection. Most of the data collected is linked to network traffic parameters, such as packet sizes, communication protocols, distances between communications, communication periods, etc. Context information, such as the number of retransmissions, signal strength, and node status, are stored with context characteristics to fully explain the network's behavior. Such measures are critical in determining normal compared to anomalous traffic patterns, which is significant in detecting security threats. The WSN is set up for continuous throughput, with numerous initialized sensor nodes and network gateways that capture real-time traffic. The imperfect multi-level monitoring, which can monitor individual sensor nodes and the gateway, makes monitoring traffic activity across the whole network easier. Real-time data collecting enables the system to detect threats rather than relying on past or lagged data, which may result in a slower reaction to attacks. The data generated from the WSN is used to train ML models that understand the patterns of typical network activity and spot variations that indicate potential security violations. With the above setup, the system will continue to learn, adapt, and improve its detecting capabilities. Finally, the system's success strongly depends on whether the data collection procedure is optimized for accuracy and real-time performance. Currently, the WSN is ready to proceed with the next steps of training, testing, and deploying the ML algorithms.

Data Preprocessing

Data preprocessing is the initial stage in preparing raw data for ML algorithms. The acquired data usually contains noise, missing values, and other irregularities that might lead to poor model performance. The preprocessing stage involves cleaning and rearranging the data before any analysis occurs. In the first stage, noise is removed, which involves filtering out irrelevant or inaccurate data items. Common smoothing and filtering techniques for dampening oscillations and other large irregularities in data. It eliminates data that will not improve the model's predictiveness and will degrade its performance. The next stage is to deal with missing values, which many ML algorithms fail to handle when encountering incomplete data. Missing values are addressed using techniques such as imputation, which involves replacing missing data points on one row with estimates based on other data points and eliminating rows or columns as necessary. It ensures that the model learns from the complete dataset without being impacted by missing data. The majority of ML algorithms operate with numerical data. It employs one-hot and label encoding techniques to turn category data into numerical representations that an algorithm can readily process. Finally, the feature is scaled, and the range of feature values is normalized. Normalization (mapping data to a range of [0,1]) and standardization (mapping data to have a zero mean and unit variance) are two common procedures. It ensures that all features are included equally during the model's learning phase and that no single feature dominates more than another by size. Scaling is especially crucial for distance-based algorithms like K-Nearest Neighbors (KNN) and SVM.

Feature Selection

Feature selection is important in improving model performance and lowering computing costs. It refers to extracting the most important aspects from incoming data while removing irrelevant, non-informative, or redundant information. The major goal is to improve the ML model's accuracy by highlighting the qualities that are most beneficial for the task at hand, which in the present instance is to determine and measure network behavior and attack patterns on a WSN. There are various techniques for feature selection. Correlation analysis can help us uncover relationships between features, and it can exclude those highly associated and considerably smaller than the model in differentiating normal and malignant behavior. The Mutual information-based feature selector is used to evaluate the dependence of features on target classes and to select the best characteristics that provide the most information about the assaults. However, features unlikely to fluctuate greatly when dealing with different sorts of attacks or network states are also taken out because these did not contribute to high prediction accuracy.

Furthermore, feature importance in decision trees or other tree-based models such as RF indicates the value of each feature relative to the target variable predictor connection. When low-importance characteristics are removed from the dataset, the dimensionality of the data lowers, allowing the model to perform more efficiently. With feature selection, the model trains faster and is less prone to overfitting. Removing redundant or identical features reduces noise, allowing the model to quickly identify meaningful trends in network traffic data. Furthermore, a narrow feature space means the model only fits the data's most significant features, improving detection accuracy and overall performance. These are critical to ensuring that the real-time threat detection system functions properly in the dynamic and resource-constrained contexts that WSNs present.

ML Algorithm Selection

ML algorithm selection was examined for efficiency; however, these required extensive comparisons with real-time network attack detection. Three algorithms, DT, SVM, and NN, were chosen. The algorithms used have specific strengths and advantages for different aspects of the detection task. It selected DT because its principles are simple, interpretable, and easy to implement. One advantage of DT models is that, unlike other models, these offer a clear path to decision-making, making it easier to comprehend the reasons behind network behavior classification. These qualitative characteristics and the capacity to handle category and numerical data make them an adaptable algorithms for network traffic analysis.

Furthermore, these provide rapid training and inference required for real-time attack detection. SVMs are well-known for categorizing high-dimensional data and establishing a clear margin of separation between classes; hence, they are used. SVM provides great accuracy in applications with a vast feature space, like analyzing network traffic with several properties. SVM can be used to detect balanced data, and the SVM method aims to increase the margin between distinct classes, which aids in detecting minor deviations between normal and malicious network traffic. When the data is not linearly separable, SVM can be supplemented with kernel functions to perform nonlinear classification tasks. NN, particularly deep learning models, were chosen because of their ability to automatically learn from enormous datasets and detect complex patterns in the data. NN is extremely useful for detecting complex and nonlinear relationships in data, which other simpler models may overlook. Deep learning models, such as Convolutional Neural Networks (CNN) and Recurrent Neural Networks (RNN), learn hierarchical features from raw network traffic data and have demonstrated great accuracy for known and novel attacks lately. The combined strength of these three algorithms has been used to detect many attacks in real-time. Figure 3 shows an illustration of the overall architecture of the proposed model.

Figure 3. Illustration of the overall architecture of the proposed model

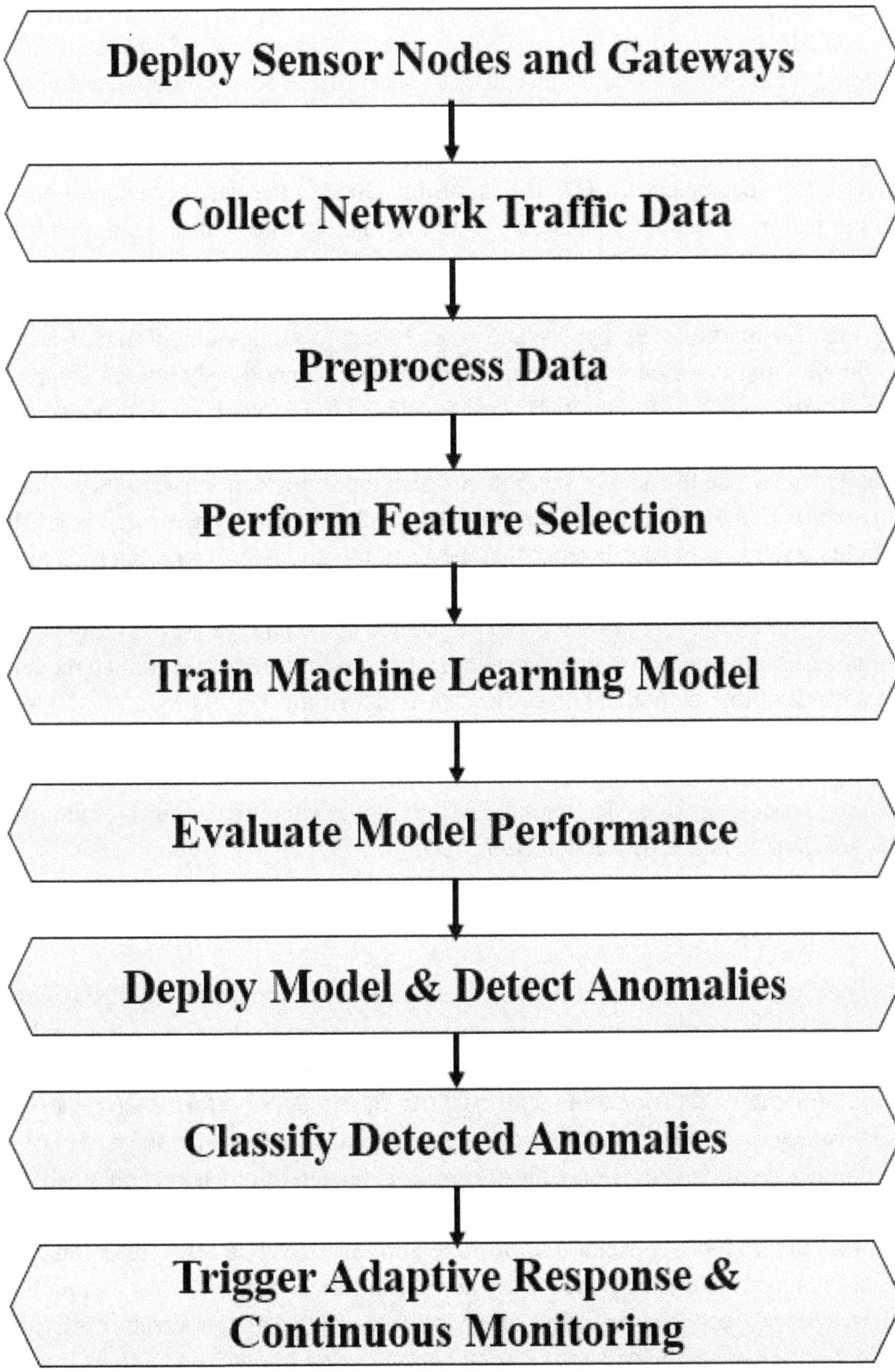

Model Training

The ML models in the chapter can be trained using labeled datasets in which network traffic is classified as normal or attack traffic. These datasets are supplied into the algorithms, which then learn how to match input features such as packet length, arrival time, protocol type, and flow properties to a target class (normal or attack). For instance, with DT, the algorithm divides the data recursively based on the feature threshold values that yield the highest information gain, resulting in a tree-like structure for decision-making. In SVM, the model learns an optimal hyperplane that separates the normal and attack classes in the feature space with the greatest margin. The hyperplane was chosen to reduce classification errors while allowing the model to generalize effectively to previously unseen samples. Conversely, an NN uses a multi-layered design, so the network weights are adjusted using the backpropagation technique to reduce the error between predicted and actual results. The former is a method in which inputs are sent forward through the network, which then calculates the accuracy, backpropagates the error, adjusts the weights and biases in each layer so that the accuracy improves somewhat each time, and continues. The models are trained on most labeled data, with a separate subset used as a validation set to tweak the hyperparameters and prevent overfitting. Next, a final test set is used to assess the generalization capabilities of the trained models. As a result of the methodical procedure, each algorithm (DT, SVM, and NN) may specialize in distinguishing between normal and attack traffic, which will function effectively for real-time attack detection in WSN when combined with trained models. The process includes data preprocessing, model validation, and fine-tuning to ensure accurate and efficient detection.

Model Evaluation

The models are trained and evaluated using accuracy, precision, recall, F1-score, and AUC-ROC curve. These indices provide a detailed evaluation of the model's performance, particularly in correctly classifying normal and harmful activity and overall efficacy. Precision and recall quantify the model's performance regarding positive/negative predictions, whereas accuracy indicates the percentage of correct predictions overall. The F1-score is the harmonic mean of precision and recall, resulting in a balanced measurement, particularly for imbalanced datasets. AUC-ROC assesses the tradeoff between true positive and false positive rates, reflecting the model's capacity to distinguish between normal and attack patterns. Cross-validation approaches also reduce overfitting and increase the model's generalizability. Cross-validation separates the data into several subsets, allowing the model to be trained and evaluated on diverse data splits. This results in a more accurate assessment of the model's performance on unseen data. The technique ensures that the model does not overfit the training data but also applies to new unobserved data, such as the assault pattern, which is unrelated to the training data. It can export and test the model with unknown data, indicating that it has learned to effectively recognize previously unfamiliar attacks, providing adaptability and strength in practice. To do so, it will use the proposed novel synthetic dataset to evaluate various aspects of the developed model, such as zero-day attacks, load imbalance, online operation, and so on, to ensure that the proposed model is reliable and precise enough to perform in real-time scenarios deployed in WSN.

Anomaly Detection and Real-Time Monitoring

The trained ML models are implemented on sensor nodes or gateways to monitor continuously real-time network traffic. These algorithms examine incoming data to detect irregularities that indicate a potential security compromise. It was created to monitor traffic and is intended to work in current settings where a hint of data deviation from the norm is detected. At the timed time, for instance, if a sensor node sees traffic patterns that differ from those detected during the educated segment, the model recognizes a suspicious behavior pattern that could result in a web attack. The key advantage of the strategy is that it can work in real-time, allowing for speedy identification of emerging risks and, if necessary, patching them as soon as possible before such attacks seriously damage network security. Rapid detection and reaction to these threats are critical because of the possibility of DoS, Sybil, sinkholes, and other attacks on sensor networks. Traditional security solutions have a longer exposure period due to slower detection and response rates. On the other hand, the ML-based anomaly detection approach can respond fast and provide a more appealing answer for the security of such networks. The system not only discovers patterns that are already known attacks, but it may also detect patterns that are new or unknown to the system if the heuristics for regular traffic do not match what the training model predicts. By regularly monitoring for such malicious conduct, system administrators can discover it early and take action before lasting network damage happens, ensuring WSN security.

Threat Classification and Response

Any abnormality in the system is classified based on the sort of attack, such as DoS, Sybil, or Sinkhole assaults, and the traffic may simply be designated as benign traffic. The process is essential for determining the appropriate reaction to a specific threat. In the event of a DoS attack, the system may quarantine the targeted nodes to prevent the assault from spreading or reroute traffic via different routes to reduce the attack's impact on network performance. Similarly, in the case of other types of attacks, such as Sybil and Sinkhole, particular counterattacks, such as blocking rogue nodes or altering the routing protocol to address the various attacks, are used to successfully neutralize threats. The ensemble response system attempts to reduce the attack's impact on network operations and prevent data blocking, allowing voice identification data to be exchanged and transferred across the sensor network. Its adaptive reaction actions provide continuous feedback to the ML model. A feedback loop helps enhance the model so that it can detect more similar attacks in the future, resulting in more accurate threat classification and faster, more streamlined responses over time. As the device learns from previous occurrences, it improves performance and becomes less vulnerable to future threats. The adaptive technique allows the system to manage the existing threat efficiently and adapt to improve defense against future security threats in changing and dynamic environments such as WSN. As a result, precise detection of network attacks and effective countermeasures ensure that network function runs smoothly and that any cyberattack in the global environment is safer and weaker.

Continuous Learning and Model Update

Finally, the proposed system includes a continuous learning mechanism for emerging risks. It enables the system to become adaptive by retraining ML models on the WSN's most recent data set at regular intervals. The model remains current and up-to-date by regularly upgrading the training data with normal traffic and new attack patterns, allowing it to detect newer and evolving threats. The retraining uses incremental learning approaches to ensure that the model can learn from incoming data as it arrives rather than repeating the entire training process. Incremental learning ensures effective updates since the model learns to deal with new data while retaining previously learned information. The technique enables the system to retain its ability to identify previously known attack patterns over time while enhancing detection differentiability for new threats. In dynamic systems like WSNs, new attack tactics constantly evolve, frequently rendering previously constructed static models useless; hence, continuous learning is essential. The system remains effective because it maintains an adaptive model that provides continual protection against known and undiscovered threats. Finally, it enables continuous automatic monitoring of real-time security by reducing the amount of manual model training necessary, making the technique more scalable and long-term sustainable. Using a learning process measure helps to recognize that the detection system is resistant while matching the features of events in WSNs, which, by definition, are not static. Thus, the system can handle increasing network traffic and diverse attack types without degrading performance. It is a dependable, secure, and future-proof solution for protecting WSNs against future innovative assaults.

In summary, the proposed system has adopted an effective mechanism for detecting threats on WSNs, with the key contribution being the adaptive function of the Detect Security Threat system for real-time processing. It is an artificial intelligence-driven system that employs ML models such as DT, SVM, and NN to detect anomalies in network traffic, which may indicate DoS, Sybil, or Sinkhole attacks. The model accuracy is quite good because the data collecting (log gathering is done in real-time), data preprocessing, feature selection, algorithm training, and classifications are all automated. It can monitor the system's performance and promptly classify any danger. Continuous learning processes enable the proposed system to adapt to new and emerging threats, allowing it to remain relevant in the long run. The adaptive methodology enhances the detection of known attacks and responds to emerging security threats, making it a scalable and long-term solution for adaptive WSN protection against various and future attacks.

RESULT AND ANALYSIS

It demonstrates the performance of the proposed ML-based real-time threat detection system for WSNs by comparing it to two other existing security systems: a signature-based IDS and a rule-based anomaly detection system. These assessments were done for detection accuracy, false-positive rate, true-positive rate, and response time. The proposed system's validity is demonstrated by its effectiveness in these metrics in several attack scenarios (DoS, Sybil, and Sinkhole).

Table 1. Performance comparison metrics

Metric	Proposed System	Existing System (Gulganwa, & Jain, 2021)	Existing System (Ifzarne et al., 2021)
Accuracy	95.1%	85.7%	82.3%
Precision	92.4%	81.2%	79.6%
Recall	94.8%	80.1%	76.4%
F1-Score	93.6%	80.6%	78.0%
Detection Accuracy	97.5%	85.4%	89.1%
False Positive Rate	2.3%	9.5%	8.2%

continued on following page

Table 1. Continued

Metric	Proposed System	Existing System (Gulganwa, & Jain, 2021)	Existing System (Ifzarne et al., 2021)
True Positive Rate	95.8%	81.7%	87.3%
Response Time (ms)	75%	200%	150%

Table 1 compares the outcomes of the proposed system to the existing system (Gulganwa, & Jain, 2021) and (Ifzarne et al., 2021). The proposed system exceeds both main well-known criteria, such as accuracy (95.1% versus 85.7 and 82.3), precision (92.4 vs. 81.2 and 79.6), recall (94.8 vs 80.1 and 76.4), and F1-score (93.6 vs 80.6 and 78.0). Additionally, it has superior detection accuracy (97.5% vs. 85.4% and 89.1%) and reduced false positive rates (2.3% vs. 9.5% and 8.2%). As a result, the proposed system has a higher true positive rate of 95.8% than the existing systems, which are 81.7% and 87.3%, respectively. Furthermore, the proposed system has a substantially reduced response time (75ms) than the existing systems (200ms and 150ms). As a result, the findings reveal that the proposed system outperforms the existing systems' accuracy, detection, and speed.

Table 2. Performance comparison based on different attack types

Attack Type	Proposed System	Existing System (Gulganwa, & Jain, 2021)	Existing System (Ifzarne et al., 2021)
Dos	98.2%	83.5%	87.9%
Sybil Attack	96.1%	80.7%	85.3%
Sinkhole Attack	95.6%	82.2%	86.5%
Unknown Attacks	89.9%	81.6%	79.5%

Table 2 demonstrates that the proposed system outperformed the existing system (Gulganwa, & Jain, 2021) and (Ifzarne et al., 2021) in terms of attack types (DoS, Sybil, Sinkhole, and unknown). Normalized scores are the metric used for measurement. The proposed system outperforms the existing systems and has the best detection performance across all cases. The suggested systems accomplish 98.2% of DoS attacks, outperforming the existing systems (83.5%) and (87.9%). Similarly, it achieves 96.1% accuracy for Sybil attack detection, compared to existing systems of 80.7% and 85.3%, respectively. The proposed system beats the existing system (82.2%) and (86.5%) for sinkhole attacks (95.6%). On the other hand, the proposed system outperforms the existing systems (81.6%) and (79.5%) in managing unknown threats, with an accuracy of 89.9%. It indicates that the proposed system is far more capable of identifying and mitigating different attack types than existing methodologies, making it a more dependable and adaptive solution (Figure 4).

Figure 4. Graphical representation of the performance comparison based on different attack types

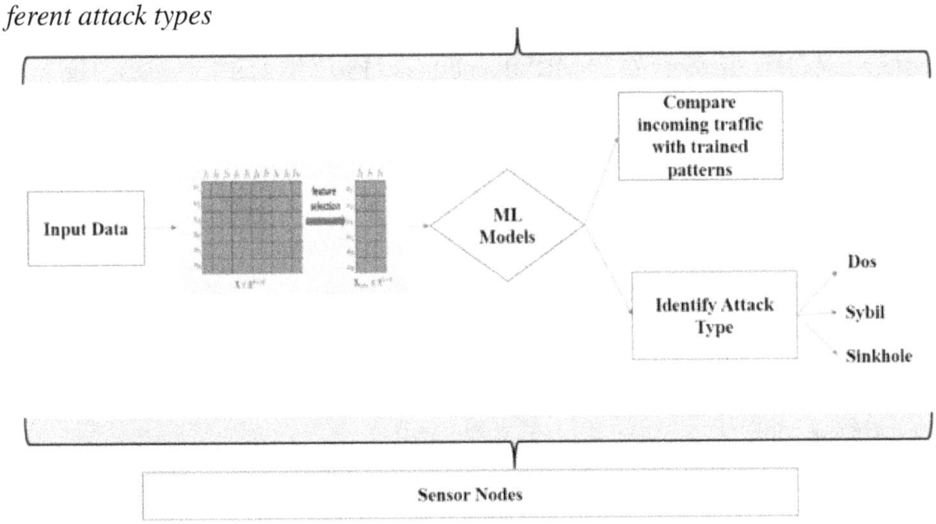

Table 3. Scalability and resource consumption comparison

Metric	Proposed System	Existing System (Gulganwa, & Jain, 2021)	Existing System (Ifzarne et al., 2021)
Training Time (sec)	120	180	200
Detection Time (ms)	75	220	180
Model Size (MB)	3.5	1.2	1.0
CPU Usage (%)	58.2	61.5	67.3
Memory Usage (MB)	120	130	150
Network Latency (ms)	45.3	48.4	52.1

Table 3 compares the proposed system's scalability and resource consumption parameters to those of the existing system (Gulganwa, & Jain, 2021) and (Ifzarne et al., 2021). The proposed system has a training time of 120 seconds, whereas the existing systems take 180 seconds and 200 seconds, demonstrating that faster implementation is possible with the proposed system. Furthermore, its detection time is substantially faster, taking only 75 milliseconds compared to 220 and 180 milliseconds for the current systems. In contrast, the proposed system has a larger model size (3.5 MB) than the existing systems (1.2 MB and 1.0 MB). Furthermore, resource consumption reveals that the CPU utilization for the proposed system is 58.2%, which is lower than the existing systems (61.5% and 67.3%). The proposed system uses less memory (120 MB) than others (130 MB and 150 MB). The proposed system also reduces network latency (45.3 ms), resulting in lower latency than existing systems (48.4 ms and 52.1 ms).

Table 4. Energy consumption comparison between systems

Energy Consumption (MJ)	Proposed System	Existing System (Gulganwa, & Jain, 2021)	Existing System (Ifzarne et al., 2021)
Idle Mode	1.5	2.1	1.9
Active Mode	15.2	18.6	17.3
During Attack Detection	22.4	35.4	32.8

Table 4 Energy Consumption: The energy consumed by the proposed system and existing systems (Gulganwa, & Jain, 2021) and (Ifzarne et al., 2021) during idle, active, and attack detection modes. The proposed system consumes 1.5 mJ in idle, less than the existing system's 2.1 mJ and 1.9 mJ, demonstrating improved energy efficiency in the low-power state. Then, in Active Mode, the Proposed System consumes 15.2 mJ, which is still less than the Existing Systems' 18.6 mJ and 17.3 mJ. However, the proposed system requires just 22.4 mJ in Attack Detection, whereas the existing system requires 35.4 mJ and 32.8 mJ, respectively. The consumption difference is the greatest. Overall, the proposed system is more energy efficient than existing systems in all modes, making it more sustainable.

The proposed ML-based real-time threat detection system outperforms current signature-based IDS and rule-based anomaly detection systems. The model delivers high scores in key parameters while significantly reducing false positives and reaction time. The technique is effective against numerous attack types, including DoS, Sybil, and Sinkhole attacks, and it improves detection in all cases. Furthermore, the proposed system enhances scalability, resource consumption, and energy efficiency over existing methods, attaining faster training and detection times, reduced CPU and memory utilization, and lower energy consumption in active and attack detection modes. According to the results, the proposed system is a considerably more reliable, adaptive, and sustainable method for securing WSNs, and it appears to be a promising prospect for real-time threat detection in dynamic environments.

DISCUSSION

These results demonstrate how the proposed ML-based threat detection system for WSNs outperforms a previous attack detection system. The system employs complex algorithms that enable it to detect assaults more accurately and efficiently than existing systems and identify a wide spectrum of known and unknown threats. Such adaptable capabilities are critical in WSNs since attack patterns vary fast. With the ideal balance of excellent detection performance and low resource consumption, the system may operate in resource-constrained contexts, enabling wider deployment across multiple disciplines. The proposed system can be used in a variety of sectors. In healthcare, it can secure patient data in a medical sensor network; in industrial automation, it is used to provide safe communication between devices. Because it can identify even the most complex attacks, it can be valuable in combat settings and disaster response.

Furthermore, the system's scalability and adaptability make it useful in newer smart city applications where unexpected and intricate sensor networks are widespread. The proposed system also has an advantage regarding computational resource utilization, as it may run for an extended period without consuming much network energy. The capacity to respond in real time reduces an attack's damage window, making the network more resilient.

Furthermore, the design allows for continuous learning, which implies adapting to new threats without learning and nearly minimal human updates. However, several limitations exist, such as interoperability among different sensor network designs and considerable overhead caused by retraining a neural model upon receiving live data. These parts can be enhanced in future work, and the system can be expanded to include more advanced deep-learning architectures for more accuracy and flexibility. Overall, the proposed system is a significant advancement in WSN security, allowing WSN to provide a more secure and practical solution for the backbone of vital networks against various major network-driven and user-driven threat scenarios that evolve with a broad range of network lifecycle use cases.

CONCLUSION AND FUTURE WORK

In conclusion, the chapter provides an ML-based real-time threat detection system for WSNs that overcomes the limits of standard security techniques by providing adaptable, scalable, and efficient protection against a wide range of threats. The experimental results reveal that the proposed system far exceeds existing systems regarding detection accuracy, resource efficiency, and response time, making it an ideal choice for various applications, including healthcare, industrial automation, and smart cities. However, the chapter has several limitations that should be noted. For starters, highly diverse network configurations influence the system's performance. Second, retraining models may have computational costs to keep up with real-time updates. Third, the system may not perform well when labeled data is scarce because it primarily relies on labeled datasets. Fourth, detection accuracy may suffer when the network is vast and has a significant traffic volume. Fifth, there may be inherent vulnerabilities in the ML model, such as the possibility of adversarial assaults, which should be considered. Future research could investigate various approaches to address these restrictions and improve the system. Second, mechanisms for controlling system performance across heterogeneous networks must be developed. Third, lightweight algorithms will address real-time adaptation while reducing retraining overhead. Third, consider semi-supervised or unsupervised learning methodologies to reduce dependency on labeled data. Fourth, the system's scalability for ultra-large-scale WSNs in dynamic traffic situations will be improved. The fifth and most critical requirement is strong defenses against adversarial attacks on the ML model to assure its trustworthiness in adversarial environments. With these enhancements, the proposed system will become more usable and broadly applicable as a comprehensive solution for safeguarding the next generation of WSNs. The results and proposed improvements establish the framework for robust, real-time security solutions for sensor network installations that have become increasingly complicated and mission-critical.

REFERENCES

Abhale, N., Ashwini, B., & Manivannan, S. S. (2020). Supervised ML Classification Algorithmic Approach for Finding Anomaly Type of Intrusion Detection in Wireless Sensor Network. *Optical Memory and Neural Networks (Information Optics), 29*(3), 244–256. DOI: 10.3103/S1060992X20030029

Ahmad, R., Wazirali, R., & Abu-Ain, T. (2022). ML for Wireless Sensor Networks Security: An Overview of Challenges and Issues. *Sensors (Basel), 22*(13), 1–35. DOI: 10.3390/s22134730 PMID: 35808227

Amar, V. T., & Alaparthy, S. D. (2020). A ML Based Intrusion Detection System for Mobile Internet of Things. *Sensors (Basel), 20*(2), 1–15. PMID: 31947567

Baraneetharan, N.Dr. E. Baraneetharan. (2020). Role of ML Algorithms Intrusion Detection in WSNs: A Survey. *Journal of Information Technology and Digital World, 2*(3), 161–173. DOI: 10.36548/jitdw.2020.3.004

de Assis, M. V. O., Carvalho, L. F., Rodrigues, J. J. P. C., Lloret, J., & Proença, M. L.Jr. (2020). Near real-time security system applied to SDN environments in IoT networks using convolutional neural network. *Computers & Electrical Engineering, 86*(9), 106738. DOI: 10.1016/j.compeleceng.2020.106738

Gulganwa, P., & Jain, S. (2021). EES-WCA: Energy Efficient and Secure Weighted Clustering for WSN Using ML Approach. *International Journal of Information Technology : an Official Journal of Bharati Vidyapeeth's Institute of Computer Applications and Management, 14*(1), 135–144. DOI: 10.1007/s41870-021-00744-5

Ifzarne, S., Tabbaa, H., Hafidi, I., & Lamghari, N. (2021). Anomaly Detection Using ML Techniques in Wireless Sensor Networks. *Journal of Physics: Conference Series, 1743*(1), 12021. DOI: 10.1088/1742-6596/1743/1/012021

Jiang, S., Zhao, J., & Xu, X. (2020). SLGBM: An intrusion detection mechanism for wireless sensor networks in smart environments. *IEEE Access : Practical Innovations, Open Solutions, 8*(1), 169548–169558. DOI: 10.1109/ACCESS.2020.3024219

Khan, M., Taher, M., Ghazal, S.-W., & Lee, A. (2021). Data Fusion-Based ML Architecture for Intrusion Detection. Computers, Materials & Continua/Computers. *Materials & Continua (Print), 70*(2), 3399–3413. DOI: 10.32604/cmc.2022.020173

Kim, T., Vecchietti, L. F., Choi, K., Lee, S., & Har, D. (2020). ML for Advanced Wireless Sensor Networks: A Review. *IEEE Sensors Journal, 21*(11), 12379–12397. DOI: 10.1109/JSEN.2020.3035846

Kumar, P., Baliyan, A., Prasad, K., Sreekanth, N., Jawarkar, P., Roy, V., & Amoatey, E. T. (2022). ML Enabled Techniques for Protecting Wireless Sensor Networks by Estimating Attack Prevalence and Device Deployment Strategy for 5G Networks. *Wireless Communications and Mobile Computing*, *2022*(1), 1–15.

Liang, W., Huang, W., Long, J., Zhang, K., Li, K.-C., & Zhang, D. (2020). Deep reinforcement learning for resource protection and real-time detection in IoT environment. *IEEE Internet of Things Journal*, *7*(7), 6392–6401. DOI: 10.1109/JIOT.2020.2974281

Mahmood, T., Li, J., Pei, Y., Akhtar, F., Butt, S. A., Ditta, A., & Qureshi, S. (2022). An intelligent fault detection approach based on reinforcement learning system in wireless sensor network. *The Journal of Supercomputing*, *78*(3), 3646–3675. DOI: 10.1007/s11227-021-04001-1

Narayanan, K., Lakshmi, R., Krishnan, E. G., Julie, Y. H., & Robinson, V. (2021). ML Based Detection and a Novel EC-BRTT Algorithm Based Prevention of DOS Attacks in Wireless Sensor Networks. *Wireless Personal Communications*, *127*(1), 479–503. DOI: 10.1007/s11277-021-08277-7

Poornima, I. G. A., & Paramasivan, B. (2020). Anomaly detection in wireless sensor network using machine learning algorithm. *Computer Communications*, *151*(2), 331–337. DOI: 10.1016/j.comcom.2020.01.005

Pranav, R. P., Prawin, R. P., Subhashni, R., & Das, S. R. (2023). Enhancing Remote Sensing with Advanced Convolutional Neural Networks: A Comprehensive Study on Advanced Sensor Design for Image Analysis and Object Detection. *FMDB Transactions on Sustainable Computer Letters*, *1*(4), 255–266.

Premkumar, M., & Sundararajan, T. V. P. (2020). DLDM: Deep learning-based defense mechanism for denial-of-service attacks in wireless sensor networks. *Microprocessors and Microsystems*, *79*(11), 103278. DOI: 10.1016/j.micpro.2020.103278

Priscila, S. S., Rajest, S. S., Tadiboina, S. N., Regin, R., & András, S. (2023). Analysis of Machine Learning and Deep Learning Methods for Superstore Sales Prediction. *FMDB Transactions on Sustainable Computer Letters*, *1*(1), 1–11.

Pundir, M., & Sandhu, J. K. (2021). A systematic review of quality of service in wireless sensor networks using machine learning: Recent trend and future vision. *Journal of Network and Computer Applications*, *188*(8), 103084. DOI: 10.1016/j.jnca.2021.103084

Rath, M., & Mishra, S. (2022). "Advanced-Level Security in Network and Real-Time Applications Using ML Approaches. In IGI Global eBooks, Hershey, Pennsylvania, United States.

Saheed, Y., & Kayode, M. O. (2021). Efficient Cyber Attack Detection on the Internet of Medical Things-Smart Environment Based on Deep Recurrent Neural Network and ML Algorithms. *IEEE Access : Practical Innovations, Open Solutions*, *9*(11), 161546–161554. DOI: 10.1109/ACCESS.2021.3128837

Saxena, D., & Chaudhary, S. (2023). Predicting Brain Diseases from FMRI-Functional Magnetic Resonance Imaging with Machine Learning Techniques for Early Diagnosis and Treatment. *FMDB Transactions on Sustainable Computer Letters*, *1*(1), 33–48.

Shrestha, R., Omidkar, A., Roudi, S. A., Abbas, R., & Kim, S. (2021). Machine-learning-enabled intrusion detection system for cellular connected UAV networks. *Electronics (Basel)*, *10*(13), 1549. DOI: 10.3390/electronics10131549

Sundararajan, V., Steffi, R., & Shynu, T. (2023). Data Fusion Strategies for Collaborative Multi-Sensor Systems: Achieving Enhanced Observational Accuracy and Resilience. *FMDB Transactions on Sustainable Computing Systems*, *1*(3), 112–123.

Chapter 13 Enhancing Security Measures Through Machine Learning Techniques for DDoS Attack Detection

S. Jayabharathi
https://orcid.org/0009-0008-3716-0936
SRM Institute of Science and Technology, Kattankulathur, India

B. Arthi
SRM Institute of Science and Technology, Kattankulathur, India

ABSTRACT

Distributed Denial of Service (DDoS) attacks have become an important threat to internet security with the hasty growth of the global digital population. These attacks aim to overwhelm target systems by flooding them with large network traffic, rendering them inaccessible to legitimate users. To address this challenge, this research paper proposes a machine learning-based approach for detecting and mitigating DDoS attacks. The study investigates the effectiveness of various machine learning techniques, including Long Short-Term Memory (LSTM), Support Vector Machines (SVM), and Logistic Regression, in accurately identifying DDoS attacks within network traffic. The outcomes demonstrate that the LSTM model attains the highest accuracy, with an accuracy score of 99.04%, outperforming traditional methods such as SVM and Logistic Regression. The proposed result leverages the unique capabilities of deep learning to capture complex patterns and long-term

DOI: 10.4018/979-8-3373-4672-4.ch013

INTRODUCTION

Global internet user growth has increased Distributed Denial of Service (DDoS) assaults, a danger to cybersecurity. There is a significant threat to the security of internet resources as the number of users grows. These attacks interfere with internet services and can seriously harm the economy, government, infrastructure, and business. Developing advanced techniques to identify and mitigate DDoS attacks is crucial to countering this evolving threat. Implementing machine learning algorithms to analyze and identify anomalies in network traffic patterns offers a promising approach for DDoS attack detection. These algorithms can significantly outperform existing detection techniques, making them powerful tools in the fight against DDoS attacks. Ongoing research and development are necessary to improve the effectiveness and reliability of machine learning algorithms across various information security applications, including detecting intelligent cybercrime such as DDoS attacks. This survey aims to provide a comprehensive overview of machine learning methods that can enhance the precision and capabilities of DDoS attack detection (Elsaeidy et al., 2019).

We examine several machine learning techniques that have shown promise in detecting DDoS attacks, including Support Vector Machine, Logistic Regression, K-Nearest Neighbor, Artificial Neural Network, and Random Forest. By leveraging these machine learning methods, researchers can enhance the accuracy and efficacy of DDoS attack detection, enabling proactive defenses against these online threats. Applying machine learning algorithms can significantly enhance the accuracy and effectiveness of DDoS attack detection, enabling proactive measures against online threats. Machine learning offers adaptable and self-learning systems, allowing them to detect and respond to evolving DDoS attack strategies in real time. Additionally, addressing the limitations of traditional rule-based methods requires exploring machine learning for DDoS attack detection. A more comprehensive and effective defense strategy can be achieved by leveraging machine learning to identify new and previously unseen types of DDoS attacks and adjust to changing attack patterns (Satyanarayana and Alasmi, 2022).

With the help of this research, it hopes to shed light on the state of machine learning-based DDoS attack detection today and emphasize the difficulties and potential associated with applying these methods to actual cybersecurity systems. It will examine the unique features of each machine learning method and how they are used to identify DDoS assaults in the sections that follow. Understanding what makes these algorithms exceptional will help us comprehend their potential impact on boosting cybersecurity defenses against DDoS attacks more fully. The many attacks that have been made using cloud computing technologies are identified in this survey article, along with the role that machine learning plays in establishing defenses against these attacks. DDoS attacks are the principal attack under Software as a Service (SaaS) architecture. A DDoS assault typically occurs due to the cloud provider's failure to supply the service. That might happen for various reasons, like network saturation from excessive internet traffic or hacker incursion into a single system by employing bots to launch a series of attacks.

As illustrated in Figure. 1, which shows how a DDoS assault occurred from the client side; many bots built on a single server could disrupt the services of a legitimate user. The bots use cracked Software that may be downloaded from an unauthorized source to trick the system into thinking it is a victim.

Figure 1. DDoS attacks in network traffic

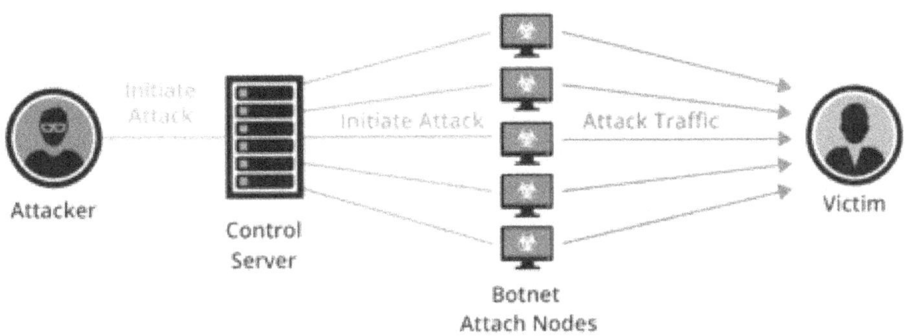

Anomalous or signature-based detection are two methods used to categorize this type of attack. Signature-based detection recognizes known assaults, while anomaly-based intrusion records inexperienced attacks by comparing them to preestablished rules and signature-based methods. A network intrusion detection system helps to classify and prevent this kind of attack by monitoring security mechanisms, detecting abnormal activities within a network, and warning the cloud user through a defense strategy. Cloud services are inaccessible to legitimate users, resulting in financial losses (Sanjalawe and Althobaiti, 2023). Either supervised or unsupervised machine learning models can be used to identify the DDoS attack. The supervised model, which consists of two models' classification and regression, is trained by labeling the features. By classifying the model and doing regression analysis, which compares the relationship between the independent dataset's attributes and produces a continuous output, the classification is based on a yes/no question. Classification includes Random Forest, Decision Tree, Logistic Regression, Support Vector Machines (SVM), K-Nearest Neighbor, and Naïve Bays machine learning technique. Decision tree algorithms, Random Forest regression, Multivariate regression, and Simple linear regression are all types of regression (Thirunagalingam, 2024).

Clustering techniques are the foundation for unsupervised machine learning, which is not labeled before model deployment. The model includes independent component analysis, principle component analysis, and the DBSCAN method (Sayedelahl and Farouk, 2024). The Semi-supervised model contains supervised and unsupervised models with labeled and unlabeled datasets for machine learning algorithms. This research helps to find the accuracy and performance in various metrics with a Random forest classifier, Light Gradient boosting, and Adaboost algorithm (Saran et al., 2022). DDoS attacks are from multiple systems to a targeted system, and botnets could do this. A bot is a zombie, and several bots are targeted to a single system to disrupt the service of the web server in a cloud computing environment, leading to the loss of valuable cloud users. Volume-based attacks, Protocol-based attacks, and Application layer attacks could be the possible subattacks under DDoS attacks (Pandey et al., 2023).

Most DDoS attacks are produced due to the Application layer (Regin et al., 2023). Ensemble machine learning models and particle swarm optimizers are other algorithms that help to combine many algorithms to upgrade the models to improve the accuracy of predicting the attacks (Rajest et al., 2023). Mathematical models with machine learning techniques are also put out by setting a threshold value based on attributes and classifying attacks as benign or malevolent. To determine accuracy and performance, the algorithm's True Positive (TP), False Positive (FP), True Negative (TN), and False Negative (FN) values are used to generate Precision, Recall, and F1 values. This study provides knowledge on a proactive DDoS detection system in response to the ongoing and evolving threat posed by Distributed Denial of Service (DDoS) attacks (Kumari and Mrunalini, 2022). This research focuses on identifying DDoS attacks, classifying them using IDS, and mitigating them using an ensemble machine learning model, utilizing CICIDS 2017 datasets for accuracy.

RELATED WORK

The literature review highlighted the different situations that used machine learning for DDoS attack detection (Hamedani et al., 2023). The current models employed RNN, LSTM, GRU, or hybrid deep learning techniques to achieve the planned outcomes. Studies categorized the work as belonging to one of the RNN, LSTM, or GRU models or a combination of these models. Based on the needs of the models, the models classified DDoS features such as DNS Flood, Ping of Death, NTP Amplification, DNS Flood, TCP Flood, SYN Flood, brute force, UDP Flood, ICMP Flood, smurf assault, HTTP Flood, botnet, and Zero-Day DDoS. The literature uses well-known cyber security datasets, such as KDD Cup 99, CIC IDS 2019, and CIC DDoS 2019.

Bindraa et al. (2019) in the research they have examined the best-supervised machine learning approach to find DDoS attacks and the accuracy of training the real-time datasets. They used five major machine algorithms with the most used datasets, including KDD 99, NSL KDD, DARPA, and CAIDA. The primary part of this is to find the low rates of false positives and false negatives. This paper uses the K nearest algorithm for classification and regression for supervised machine learning models. CIC IDS 2017 datasets efficiently detect DDoS attacks for the real-time datasets. It was trained with 85 features to find the accuracy and performance of the model. Datasets are CAIDA, KDD 99, DEF CON, ADFA, LBNL, and KYOTO. KNN and Random forest algorithms are identified to give better accuracy results under the classification model (Kumar and Sharma, 2023).

The IDS is also appropriate for smart cities and smart water plants to protect them from DDoS attacks. To feature mitigation, unsupervised machine learning algorithms are trained with RBM (Restricted Boltzmann machine). RBM enhances the performance of the classification algorithm. The k-means clustering algorithm works with and without RBM to find the variation in accuracy of precision: recall and F1 value (Sulaiman., 2024). Botnets taint several systems while aiming at a single targeted server, and they are frequently discovered at the source address or in the middle of hacking, but the cost is high and difficult to anticipate; it is less expensive when predicted at the destination. The BOTNETS attacking system targets the server and causes the traffic, and the server will stop accepting the request. Alternately, D Satyanarayana et al. suggested a simulation-based system for identifying harmful botnets, studying the activity of the botnets, and assessing the attacks at the victim's end utilizing the DARPA 2009 dataset and Python programming. The system uses a machine learning algorithm for decision-making with security values to detect whether the attack is malicious or normal using the counter-threat value. If the value is exceeded, it is considered an anomaly. The server stops accepting requests for a particular time and resumes the work after the analysis (Pranav et al., 2024).

Arya et al. (2023) proposed an ensemble approach to segregate the malicious attack and benign traffic using CIC IDS 2019 datasets in real-time. The intelligent agent system with automated feature extraction chooses features using the deep attack detection framework. With 99% accuracy, they distinguished between the various DDoS assault tiers using an Enhanced Support Vector Machine (ESVM), investigated by deep anomaly detectors and learning to handle traffic concept drift to implement labeling the packets with the probability of the data flow (Cirillo et al., 2023). In the ensemble approach, they proposed the architecture with Naïve based Decision tree, SVM, and Random forest to achieve 99.9% accuracy in predicting DDoS attacks using a stacking ensemble approach. Then, the classifiers are combined with Logistic Regression. Although the DDoS attacks are not fully predicted in this approach (Jeba et al., 2023).

Firdaus et al. (2023) recommended that the XGBoost and AdaBoost algorithms be used in aggregation with ensemble learning techniques to improve the machine learning models' learning process. The model aims to improve one or more classifiers before combining them to get the final decision (Jasper et al., 2023). By merging a group of weak classifiers into a strong classifier, the Adaboost classification technique improves ML performance algorithms. The ensemble model achieved a significant accuracy of 94.88%, around 2.03% - 2.06% higher than the individual XGBoost and AdaBoost models (Raja et al., 2024). AdaBoost is suggested to use XGBoost for intrusion detection and email filtering to predict DDoS attacks. Exploratory data analysis, or EDA, was also used for patterns, anomalies, theories, and assumptions. EDA will help users find errors, irregularities, relationships between data, and important components. For real-time features, they used the CIC-DDoS 2019 datasets (Renjith et al., 2024).

Gupta et al. (2021) employed big data spark technology to identify the bad packets and presented their method for identifying DDoS assaults based on big data and deep learning algorithms. With a 99.77% accuracy rate, KDDCUP 99 located it. The framework leverages big data technologies such as Apache Spark and Kafka to offer a scalable pipeline for processing massive data. Big data analytics technologies, which have powerful and distinct features, including processing power, real-time analysis, and the ability to manage massive volumes of traffic, may be used to build and construct a DDoS attack detection and prevention framework for SDN networks (Kanyimama et al., 2024). Moreover, training should focus on developing mitigation strategies to effectively prevent DDoS attacks in SDN networks while reducing the damage they cause to legitimate network messages.

After our review, the Random Forest method is integrated into the data processing module utilizing Apache to classify the network traffic and identify harmful flows more precisely (Ashraf, 2023). Karthika et al. (2023) proposed a system using LSTM and RNN to select features to deliver an improved DDoS detection system. They found 98.85% and 92% accuracy and precision by combining the above two structures. They used deep learning algorithms with numerous layers to extract high-level features before, throughout, and following the assault (Abdullahi et al., 2023). The paper proposes a novel LSTM-based methodology for detecting DDOS, Sybil, and Wormhole attacks. With deep learning and the MLP classifier algorithm, a DDoS attempt was stopped and identified (Nwabuokei et al., 2023).

Suresh et al. (2016) proposed a system that explains how to prevent DoS and DDoS attack systems with cryptography using an advanced encryption algorithm using the client puzzle method. So far, the system explains the attack detection, classification, and mitigation of DDoS attacks using machine learning algorithms, but this research paper involved targeting and preventing it with cryptography. The research uses three mechanisms: Puzzle-based defense, memory-based puzzle schemes, and Bandwidth Based Schemes. The attack was thwarted by increased security, which involved the client encrypting the file and decrypting it using a puzzle-solving approach (Jasper et al., 2024).

Table 1. Summary of related work

Reference	Machine learning Algorithm	Works Initiated in the paper	Dataset used
Sanjalawe & Althobaiti, (2023)	Convolution Neural network and LSTM	CNN and LSTM are proposed in this study to increase the accuracy of finding DDoS attacks.	CICIDS2017
Pandey et al., (2023)	Logistic Regression, KNearest Neighbor, and Random Forest algorithms.	To demonstrate algorithm performance, a comparison research is done on three distinct classifiers: logistic regression, random forests, decision trees, and K-nearest neighbour.	NSL KDD
Kumari & Mrunalini (2022)	Logistic Regression and Naïve bayes.	Used machine learning algorithms and mathematical model for real time applications	CAIDA 2007
Bindraa & Sooda (2019)	Support Vector Machine (SVM), Gaussian Naïve Bays (GNB), K nearest neighbor and Random Forest.	A Python program named "DDoSD" (DDoS Detector) was developed using Scikit-learn, a well-known machine learning library, to build five machine learning models for network classification.	KDD 99, NSL-KDD, DARPA and CAIDA
Elsaeidy et al., (2019)	A feed-forward neural network model	Smart city dataset collected from a smart water plant	K-Means Clustering algorithm
Satyanarayana & Alasmi, (2022)	KNN algorithm	Analyzing the requests coming from the BOTNET uses the Machine learning algorithm in the decision-making process.	DARPA2009
Arya et al. (2023)	Enhanced Support Vector Machine (ESVM)	CNN-type models are ideal for continuously responding to traffic concept drift, whereas LSTM-based models are better suited for sequential packet labeling in effective continuous IDSes.	CICDDoS2019
Firdaus & Suryani (2023)	XGBoost and AdaBoost algorithms using XGBoost Classifier, AdaBoost Classifier, Decision Tree Classifier, and Voting Classifier	Both the XGBoost and AdaBoost algorithms achieved good levels of accuracy, so combining them with a stacking model should yield superior prediction outcomes. The Voting Classifier is used to combine two algorithms.	CIC-DDoS2019
Gupta et al. (2021)	Big data and deep learning algorithms	A deep learning-based approach is employed to detect DDoS attacks on cloud computing platforms, utilizing Big Data Spark technology to analyze vast data traffic.	KDDCUP99
Karthika et al., (2023)	Hybrid Long Short-Term Memory Network (LSTM) and Recurrent Neural Network (RNN)	Ensemble LSTM RNN and MLP Classifiers. The Ensemble LSTM RNN is used for feature extraction.	Collecting Huge Datasets for feature selection
Kumar & Sharma (2023)	Random Forest Classifier, Logistic Regression, and K Neighbors Classifier.	The research aims to tackle the issue of DDoS attacks, a common method used by cyber attackers to disrupt organizational services and operations.	NSL-KDD

Wu et al. (2015) The proposed strategy to mitigate DoS/DDoS attacks involves software puzzles. These puzzles are generated randomly based on client requests using CPU and GPU resources. The server creates advanced puzzles so that attackers cannot preemptively develop solutions, and the algorithm ensures that the CPU puzzle's solution cannot be predicted from the GPU version and vice versa (Raj et al., 2024). During puzzle creation, the server randomly selects a puzzle challenge x and sends it to clients. The puzzle P is derived using one-way functions like the AES block cipher and the SHA-1 algorithm. However, there are challenges: (1) not all clients have devices with GPU capabilities, and (2) implementing a real-time environment to run GPU kernels can be complex and resource-intensive (Anand et al., 2024).

This study leverages the architectural differences between CPUs and GPUs to introduce a novel type of client puzzle, a software puzzle, to protect against DoS and DDoS attacks amplified by GPU resources. The CPU and GPU training sets are entirely different and were designed for different reasons. Thus, the malevolent client must translate the CPU software puzzle into its functionally corresponding GPU counterpart. Meanwhile, software puzzles are always evolving and random, so it is impossible to finish this translation earlier (Jani et al., 2024). The software puzzle must be improved by brute force as it is encrypted using a conventional cipher by an attacker. The most broadly used online transaction protocol is SSL/TLS, and because each client connection request requires a costly RSA decryption procedure, an SSL/TLS server is susceptible to DoS attacks. The paper explores client riddles as a protection mechanism against DoS and DDoS assaults, which flood a service with fraudulent requests. It proposes the notion of a software problem, a novel sort of client challenge that is dynamically produced to prevent attackers from understating their puzzle-solving abilities utilizing GPUs (Regin et al., 2023).

In contrast to previous systems that predefined puzzle algorithms, the software puzzle algorithm is generated randomly upon receiving a client request, increasing the difficulty for attackers to premeditate their actions. Additionally, the paper illustrates how software puzzles can be seamlessly integrated into the conventional server-browser model, thereby strengthening security measures against attacks accelerated by GPUs. Kumar et al. (2023) This research proposes a supervised machine learning method for detecting Distributed Denial of Service (DDoS) attacks by analyzing patterns and anomalies in network data. It utilizes Random Forest and K Nearest Neighbor classifiers and relies on the NSL-KDD dataset from the Canadian Institute of Cybersecurity. Derived from the KDD Cup '99 dataset, NSL-KDD comprises source and destination IP addresses, port numbers, and network protocol information essential for intrusion detection. The random forest algorithm is based on a decision tree, and the K neighbors algorithm is based on the K nearest algorithm, predicting the K nearest neighbors in the training data. They analyzed the attacks with ICMP, UDP, and TCP, and then the highest possible attacks occurred by the protocols using the supervised machine learning algorithms (Table 1).

RESULTS

Our survey results highlight the effectiveness of various machine learning algorithms, including Deep Neural Networks, Logistic Regression, K-nearest neighbor, and Random Forest, in detecting DDoS attacks. These algorithms have demonstrated promising capabilities in accurately identifying and mitigating DDoS threats. Their application has significantly enhanced the analysis of network traffic patterns and anomalous behavior, consequently improving the precision and efficacy of intrusion detection systems. Further research is needed to explore the potential of deep learning methods for detecting DDoS attacks, including recurrent and convolutional neural networks. These cutting-edge solutions provide a more comprehensive defense against cyber threats by recognizing new forms of DDoS assaults and adapting to changing attack strategies. The machine learning algorithms address the complications of DDoS attack detection in cloud security. Critical topics requiring ongoing research and creative solutions are the interpretability of machine learning algorithms, The importance of large and diverse datasets, and the dynamic nature of DDoS attack techniques.

In order to enable the appropriate and efficient application of machine learning algorithms in cybersecurity, it is authoritative to endorse cooperative efforts between academic institutions, business entities, and governing agencies. Through resolving these issues and advancing machine learning-based DDoS attack detection techniques, we can fully utilize these technologies to respond to the constantly changing landscape of cyber threats. The future of DDoS attack detection holds promise for further improved cybersecurity measures, with further development and integration of sophisticated deep learning algorithms and research into reinforcement learning methodologies for adaptive detection systems. We can ensure the efficacy and careful deployment of machine learning algorithms in controlling cyber threats' complex and changing terrain via constant inquiry and collaborative efforts.

Organizations must establish robust detection and mitigation strategies as DDoS attacks continue to escalate in frequency and severity. Monitoring network traffic for anomalies or sudden surges in data volume remains a highly effective method for identifying DDoS attacks. Additionally, implementing intrusion detection and prevention systems can swiftly detect and address DDoS attacks, bolstering overall security measures. Mitigating DDoS attacks requires a multi-layered technique. This entails using specialized DDoS mitigation services or tools to monitor incoming traffic and filter out malicious requests. In addition, organizations may utilize content delivery networks to distribute traffic and mitigate the harm that DDoS assaults due to their network. A gainful DDoS assault could have disastrous consequences for a firm, including lost revenue, downtime, reduced productivity, and reputational harm. To secure their network and ensure business continuity, enterprises must thus give top priority to putting strong DDoS detection and mitigation mechanisms in place. For a business to effectively reduce the effects of a DDoS assault, a thorough incident response plan should also be in place. In addition to redirecting traffic to other servers and coordinating with law enforcement to apprehend and prosecute the attackers, this plan should outline procedures for isolating the compromised systems.

Figure 2. Various algorithms and their accuracy

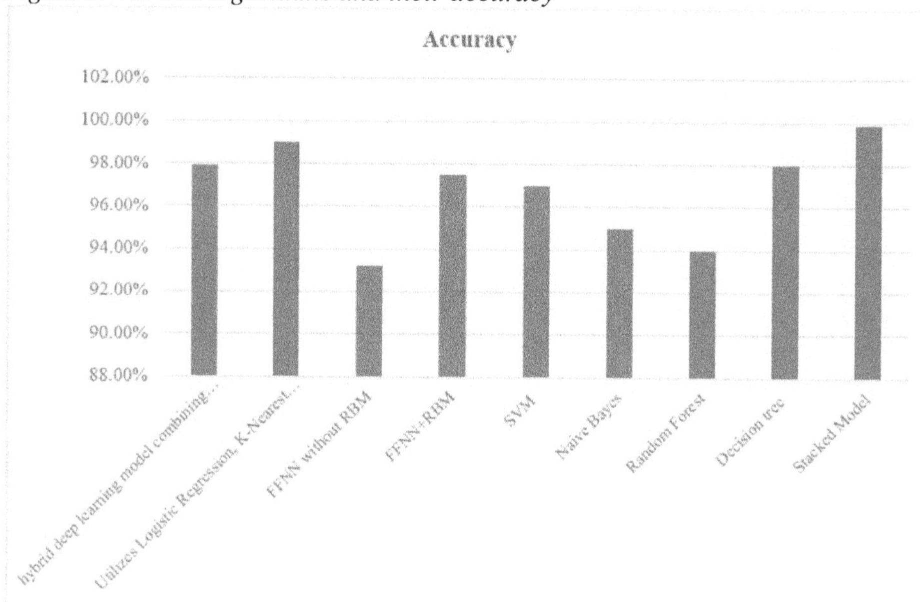

In Figure 2, the various techniques and their accompanying accuracy metrics are illustrated with a graph, and it is clear that all provide the maximum accuracy with the ensemble learning approach. Moreover, frequent testing and ongoing monitoring are necessary to guarantee the effectiveness of DDoS mitigation strategies. Keeping current on the most recent developments in DDoS attack tactics is crucial for making proactive adjustments and stimulating protection mechanisms. Connecting with cloud and internet service providers is another critical component of DDoS attack mitigation. Developing relationships with these companies can strengthen overall defense systems by leveraging their knowledge and resources to reroute and swiftly control traffic during an assault. Using best practices for incident response and security standards, as well as training staff members and other stakeholders about DDoS assaults, can greatly enhance total defense efforts and technological measures. To guarantee that everyone is aware of their responsibility for protecting the company from DDoS assaults, this may entail holding frequent training sessions and simulations. In order to properly detect, mitigate, and recover from such situations, addressing DDoS attacks ultimately calls for a proactive and comprehensive approach that incorporates both technical and non-technical tactics. Organizations can reduce the effect of DDoS attacks and preserve the resilience of their networks by consistently enhancing and modifying defense methods.

CONCLUSION AND FUTURE SCOPE

Machine learning approaches offer significant potential for enhancing DDoS attack detection. These algorithms can recognize patterns in network data, detect unusual behavior, and differentiate between malicious and legitimate transmissions. By incorporating machine learning into intrusion detection systems, their accuracy, effectiveness, and adaptability can all be enhanced, leading to more robust defense mechanisms against DDoS attacks. Furthermore, future research should focus on integrating advanced deep learning techniques into machine learning algorithms to improve their performance further. These advancements may enable more efficient detection and response to emerging DDoS attack strategies. DDoS attack detection has intriguing prospects for machine learning techniques to improve cybersecurity measures. Machine learning approaches have been shown to improve the precision and effectiveness of intrusion detection systems when used in DDoS assault detection. DDoS assaults by analyzing the network traffic method and detecting anomalous attacks are done effectively and faster to mitigate and alarm the network. Furthermore, machine learning algorithms are highly suited for building DDoS assault tactics because of their adaptable nature, which allows them to learn and adapt to new attack patterns continually.

The dynamic nature of DDoS assault strategies presents another difficulty, necessitating constant adaptation and evolution of machine learning algorithms. Improving the algorithm's capacity to recognize and react in real-time to new attack techniques calls for continuous research and development. Moreover, interpreting machine learning algorithms is a major difficulty, mainly in critical systems where deciphering the logic behind a detection or classification is important. The creation of explainable AI methods will be necessary to meet this problem, as it will give transparency and confidence to the judgments made by machine learning models for DDoS attack detection. Moving forward, it is essential for future research to address existing challenges and explore novel methods to enhance the resilience, scalability, and ethical considerations of machine learning-based DDoS attack detection systems. Collaboration among academic institutions, businesses, and regulatory agencies will advance this field and ensure the ethical and effective implementation of machine learning algorithms in cybersecurity. In conclusion, the research presented in this paper highlights the effectiveness of leveraging machine learning techniques to enhance DDoS attack detection. The proposed models, including LSTM, Logistic Regression, Support Vector Machines, and deep neural networks, have demonstrated superior performance compared to traditional methods. These advanced algorithms can accurately classify network traffic, identify malicious patterns, and mitigate the impact of DDoS attacks.

The primary findings of the research examined reveal that deep learning methods, particularly LSTM, surpass traditional machine learning approaches in terms of detection accuracy and their ability to capture long-term correlations within network traffic data. Moreover, integrating feature engineering and automated feature selection modules has shown promise in improving the efficiency and flexibility of detection algorithms. Proposed models, such as LSTM, Logistic Regression, Support Vector Machines, and deep neural networks, exhibit superior performance compared to conventional methods. These advanced algorithms effectively classify network traffic, identify malicious patterns, and mitigate the impact of DDoS attacks. Key insights from the reviewed studies emphasize that deep learning techniques, especially LSTM, outshine conventional machine learning methods in detection accuracy and the capacity to capture long-term dependencies within network traffic data. Additionally, incorporating feature engineering and automated feature selection modules yields encouraging outcomes that enhance the efficiency and adaptability of detection systems.

By leveraging machine learning techniques, potential vulnerabilities in network security can be efficiently pinpointed and addressed, leading to stronger defenses against DDoS attacks. Furthermore, the continuous evolution of machine learning methodologies presents opportunities for ongoing refinement and optimization of DDoS attack detection systems, thereby bolstering overall cybersecurity measures. Major findings of the examined research show that deep learning techniques, notably LSTM, outperform traditional machine learning approaches regarding detection accuracy and the capacity to grasp long-term correlations in network traffic data. Furthermore, integrating feature engineering and automated feature selection modules has shown promise in enhancing the detection algorithm's efficiency and flexibility. The proposed models, including LSTM, Logistic Regression, Support Vector Machines, and deep neural networks, have been found to demonstrate superior performance compared to traditional methods. These advanced algorithms can accurately classify network traffic, identify malicious patterns, and mitigate the impact of DDoS attacks.

ACKNOWLEDGMENT

I extend my heartfelt thankfulness to my supervisor, Dr. Arthi B, for their invaluable guidance, steadfast support, and valuable insights during this research endeavor.

REFERENCES

Abdullahi, Y., Bhardwaj, A., Rahila, J., Anand, P., & Kandepu, K. (2023). Development of Automatic Change-Over with Auto-Start Timer and Artificial Intelligent Generator. *FMDB Transactions on Sustainable Energy Sequence*, *1*(1), 11–26.

Anand, P. P., Jayanth, G., Rao, K. S., Deepika, P., Faisal, M., & Mokdad, M. (2024). Utilising Hybrid Machine Learning to Identify Anomalous Multivariate Time-Series in Geotechnical Engineering. *AVE Trends In Intelligent Computing Systems*, *1*(1), 32–41.

Arya, A., Kumar, A., & Ahmad, S. S. (2023). DDoS attack detection using ensemble machine learning approach. 2023 14th International Conference on Computing Communication and Networking Technologies (ICCCNT). Delhi, India, IEEE.

Ashraf, A. (2023). The State of Security in Gaza And the Effectiveness of R2P Response. *FMDB Transactions on Sustainable Social Sciences Letters*, *1*(2), 78–84.

Bindraa, N., & Sooda, M. (2019). Detecting DDoS Attacks Using Machine Learning Techniques and Contemporary Intrusion Detection Dataset. *Automatic Control and Computer Sciences*, *53*(5), 419–428. DOI: 10.3103/S0146411619050043

Cirillo, S., Polese, G., Salerno, D., Simone, B., & Solimando, G. (2023). Towards Flexible Voice Assistants: Evaluating Privacy and Security Needs in IoT-enabled Smart Homes. *FMDB Transactions on Sustainable Computer Letters*, *1*(1), 25–32.

Elsaeidy, A., Munasinghe, K. S., Sharma, D., & Jamalipour, A. (2019). A machine learning approach for intrusion detection in smart cities. 2019 IEEE 90th Vehicular Technology Conference (VTC2019-Fall). Honolulu, HI, United States of America, IEEE.

Firdaus, G. M., & Suryani, V. (2023). DDoS attack detection analysis using ensemble learning with XGBoost and AdaBoost algorithms. 2023 11th International Conference on Information and Communication Technology (ICoICT), Melaka, Malaysia, 17–22. IEEE.

Gupta, B. B., Gaurav, A., & Perakovic, D. (2021). A big data and deep learning based approach for DDoS detection in cloud computing environment. 2021 IEEE 10th Global Conference on Consumer Electronics (GCCE). Kyoto, Japan, IEEE.

Hamedani, A. F., Aziz, M., Wieder, P., & Yahyapour, R. (2023). Big data framework to detect and mitigate distributed denial of service(DDoS) attacks in software-defined networks (SDN). 2023 3rd International Conference on Electrical, Computer, Communications and Mechatronics Engineering (ICECCME), Tenerife, Canary Islands, Spain, 04, 1–6. IEEE.

Jani, P., Nanban, D., Selvan, J., Richardson, N., Sivakani, R., & Subhashni, R. (2024). Studying Price Dynamics of Bus Services Using Machine Learning Algorithms. *AVE Trends In Intelligent Computing Systems, 1*(1), 54–65.

Jasper, K., Neha, R., & Szeberényi, A. (2023). Fortifying Data Security: A Multifaceted Approach with MFA, Cryptography, and Steganography. *FMDB Transactions on Sustainable Computing Systems, 1*(2), 98–111.

Jasper, K. D., Jaishnav, M. N., Chowdhury, M. F., Badhan, R., & Sivakani, R. (2024). Defend and Secure: A Strategic and Implementation Framework for Robust Data Breach Prevention. *AVE Trends In Intelligent Computing Systems, 1*(1), 17–31.

Jeba, J. A., Bose, S. R., Regin, R., Rajest, S. S., & Kose, U. (2023). In-Depth Analysis and Implementation of Advanced Information Gathering Tools for Cybersecurity Enhancement. *FMDB Transactions on Sustainable Computer Letters, 1*(2), 130–146.

Kanyimama, W., Argungu, M. S., Gabi, D., & Suru, H. U. (2024). Planning and designing different types of surveillance networks for enhanced security and monitoring. *FMDB Transactions on Sustainable Computer Letters, 2*(1), 52–62. DOI: 10.69888/FTSCL.2024.000181

Karthika, R. A., Sriramya, P., & Rohini, A. (2023). Detection and classification of DDoS attacks in cloud data using hybrid LSTM and RNN for feature selection. *2023 International Conference on Circuit Power and Computing Technologies (ICCPCT)*, 1491–1495. Kollam, India, IEEE. DOI: 10.1109/ICCPCT58313.2023.10244979

Kumar, A., & Sharma, I. (2023). Employing supervised learning techniques for DDoS attack detection. 2023 International Conference on Innovative Data Communication Technologies and Application (ICIDCA), 684–688. Uttarakhand, India, IEEE.

Kumari, K., & Mrunalini, M. (2022). Detecting Denial of Service attacks using machine learning algorithms. *Journal of Big Data, 9*(4), 1–17. DOI: 10.1186/s40537-022-00616-0

Nwabuokei, I., Ghouse, M., Chen, W., Kollannur, E. T., Li, H., & Bin Sulaiman, R. (2023). Quantifying the Influence of Population on Carbon Emissions: A Comparative Study of Developed versus Developing Countries Using Machine Learning. *FMDB Transactions on Sustainable Energy Sequence*, *1*(2), 71–82.

Pandey, R., Pandey, M., & Nazarov, A. (2023). Enhanced DDoS Detection using Machine Learning. 2023 6th International Conference on Information Systems and Computer Networks (ISCON), Mathura, India, 1–4. IEEE.

Pranav, R. P., Prawin, R. P., Paramasivan, P., Shynu, T., & Subhashni, R. (2024). IoT-SecNet: A trust-based framework for enhancing security in IoT communications and network layer protocols. *FMDB Transactions on Sustainable Computing Systems*, *2*(2), 96–106. DOI: 10.69888/FTSCS.2024.000201

Raj, M. A., Mishra, A., & Forest, G. A. (2024). Predictive Analytics for Employee Attrition: Leveraging Machine Learning for Strategic Human Resources Management. *AVE Trends in Intelligent Technoprise Letters*, *1*(1), 13–29.

Raja, A. S. V., Jasper, K. D., Poornima, V., Priscila, S. S., Thenmozhi, A., & Ratkovic, N. (2024). Tech horizons unveiled: Navigating the transformative decade in AIML, cybersecurity, IoT, gaming, and data science education. *FMDB Transactions on Sustainable Intelligent Networks*, *1*(2), 120–134. DOI: 10.69888/FTSIN.2024.000214

Rajest, S. S., Singh, B. J., Obaid, J., Regin, R., & Chinnusamy, K. (2023). *Recent developments in machine and human intelligence*. Advances in Computational Intelligence and Robotics. IGI Global., DOI: 10.4018/978-1-6684-9189-8

Regin, R., Khanna, A. A., Krishnan, V., Gupta, M., & Bose, R. S., & Rajest, S. S. (2023). Information design and unifying approach for secured data sharing using attribute-based access control mechanisms. In Recent Developments in Machine and Human Intelligence (pp. 256–276). IGI Global, USA.

Regin, R., T, S., George, S. R., Bhattacharya, M., Datta, D., & Priscila, S. S. (2023). Development of predictive model of diabetic using supervised machine learning classification algorithm of ensemble voting. *International Journal of Bioinformatics Research and Applications*, *19*(3), 151–169. DOI: 10.1504/IJBRA.2023.10057044

Renjith, E. J. (2024). Revolutionizing cloud security: Innovative approaches for safeguarding data integrity. *FMDB Transactions on Sustainable Computer Letters*, *2*(2), 111–119. DOI: 10.69888/FTSCL.2024.000185

Sanjalawe, Y., & Althobaiti, T. (2023). DDoS attack detection in cloud computing based on ensemble feature selection and deep learning. *Computers, Materials & Continua*, *75*(2), 3571–3588. DOI: 10.32604/cmc.2023.037386

Saran, M., Yadav, R. K., & Tripathi, U. N. (2022). Machine learning based security for cloud computing: A survey. *International Journal of Applied Engineering Research: IJAER*, *17*(4), 332–337. DOI: 10.37622/IJAER/17.4.2022.338-344

Satyanarayana, D., & Alasmi, A. S. (2022). Detection and Mitigation of DDOS based Attacks using Machine Learning Algorithm. *2022 International Conference on Cyber Resilience (ICCR)*. Dubai, United Arab Emirates, IEEE. DOI: 10.1109/ICCR56254.2022.9995773

Sayedelahl, M. A., & Farouk, R. M. (2024). Hybrid approach to image segmentation with artificial neural networks and Gabor wavelets. *AVE Trends in Intelligent Computing Systems*, *1*(2), 77–90.

Sulaiman, R. B., Aljaidi, M., Alsuwaylimi, A. A., Butt, U., Talukder, M. S. H., Alam, S. S., Farhan, M., Das, S. R., & Alam, M. W. (2024). Enhancing security in digital payments: A comparative evaluation of machine learning models for credit card fraud detection. *FMDB Transactions on Sustainable Computer Letters*, *2*(2), 63–84. DOI: 10.69888/FTSCL.2024.000182

Suresh, S., & Kiran, V. (2016). Prevention of Dos and DDoS Attack Using Cryptographic Techniques. *International Journal of Advanced Research in Computer and Communication Engineering*, *5*(1), 93–96.

Thirunagalingam, A. (2024). Bias detection and mitigation in data pipelines: Ensuring fairness and accuracy in machine learning. *AVE Trends in Intelligent Computing Systems*, *1*(2), 116–127.

Wu, Y., Zhao, Z., Bao, F., & Deng, R. H. (2015). Software puzzle: A countermeasure to resource-inflated denial-of-service attacks. *IEEE Transactions on Information Forensics and Security*, *10*(1), 168–177. DOI: 10.1109/TIFS.2014.2366293

Compilation of References

Abdullah, A. A., Hassan, M. M., & Mustafa, Y. T. (2022). A review on Bayesian deep learning in healthcare: Applications and challenges. *IEEE Access : Practical Innovations, Open Solutions*, *10*(3), 36538–36562. DOI: 10.1109/ACCESS.2022.3163384

Abdullahi, Y., Bhardwaj, A., Rahila, J., Anand, P., & Kandepu, K. (2023). Development of Automatic Change-Over with Auto-Start Timer and Artificial Intelligent Generator. *FMDB Transactions on Sustainable Energy Sequence*, *1*(1), 11–26.

Abhale, N., Ashwini, B., & Manivannan, S. S. (2020). Supervised ML Classification Algorithmic Approach for Finding Anomaly Type of Intrusion Detection in Wireless Sensor Network. *Optical Memory and Neural Networks (Information Optics)*, *29*(3), 244–256. DOI: 10.3103/S1060992X20030029

Abou, R., & Matrawy, A. (2020). Evaluation of adversarial training on different types of neural networks in deep learning-based IDSs. In *2020 International Symposium on Networks Computers and Communications (ISNCC)*, Piscataway, New Jersey, USA

Abro, A., Deng, Z., & Memon, K. A. (2019). A lightweight elliptic-ElGamal-based authentication scheme for secure Device-to-Device communication. *Future Internet*, *11*(5), 108. DOI: 10.3390/fi11050108

Admass, W. S., Munaye, Y., & Diro, A. A. (2024). Cyber security: State of the art. *Challenges and Future Directions*, *2*(1), 100031.

Aduwala, S. A., Arigala, M., Desai, S., Quan, H. J., & Eirinaki, M. (2021). Deepfake Detection using GAN Discriminators. *2021 IEEE Seventh International Conference on Big Data Computing Service and Applications (BigDataService)*, Oxford, United Kingdom. DOI: 10.1109/BigDataService52369.2021.00014

Afnanalotaibi, M. A. (2023). Adversarial machine learning attacks against intrusion detection systems: A survey on strategies and defense. *Future Internet*, *15*(2), 148–154.

Agarwal, S. (2023). Validating Clinical Applications of Digital Health Solutions and Managing Associated Risk Management. *FMDB Transactions on Sustainable Management Letters*, *1*(4), 134–143.

Aherwadi, N. B., Chokshi, D., Pande, S., & Khamparia, A. (2021). Criminal Identification System using Facial Recognition. SSRN Electronic Journal, 13(3), 1-6. DOI: 10.2139/ssrn.3884827

Ahmad, I., Kumar, T., Liyanage, M., Okwuibe, J., Ylianttila, M., & Gurtov, A. (2018). Overview of 5G security challenges and solutions. *IEEE Communications Standards Magazine*, *2*(1), 36–43. DOI: 10.1109/MCOMSTD.2018.1700063

Ahmad, R., & Alsmadi, I. (2021). Machine learning approaches to IoT security: A systematic literature review. *Internet of Things : Engineering Cyber Physical Human Systems*, *14*(7), 100365. DOI: 10.1016/j.iot.2021.100365

Ahmad, R., Wazirali, R., & Abu-Ain, T. (2022). ML for Wireless Sensor Networks Security: An Overview of Challenges and Issues. *Sensors (Basel)*, *22*(13), 1–35. DOI: 10.3390/s22134730 PMID: 35808227

Ahmad, Z., Shahid Khan, A., Wai Shiang, C., Abdullah, J., & Ahmad, F. (2021). Network intrusion detection system: A systematic study of machine learning and deep learning approaches. *Transactions on Emerging Telecommunications Technologies*, *32*(1), 1–29. DOI: 10.1002/ett.4150

Ajao, L. A., & Apeh, S. T. (2023). Secure edge computing vulnerabilities in smart cities sustainability using petri net and genetic algorithm-based reinforcement learning. *Intelligent Systems with Applications*, *18*(5), 200216. DOI: 10.1016/j.iswa.2023.200216

Ajitha, Y., Talukder, M. S. H., & Shuvo, S. A. (2024). Advanced radar range prediction and performance analysis in aircraft adhoc networks (AANET). *FMDB Transactions on Sustainable Computer Letters*, *2*(1), 1–13. DOI: 10.69888/FTSCL.2024.000177

Al-Ghiyadh, A.-K., & Al-Khafaji, M. (2021). IOP Conf. IOP Conf. Ser.: Mater. Sci. Eng, IOP Publishing, Bristol, United Kingdom.

Ali, M., Sadeghi, M. R., & Liu, X. (2020). Lightweight Revocable Hierarchical Attribute-Based Encryption for Internet of Things. *IEEE Access : Practical Innovations, Open Solutions*, *8*(1), 23951–23964. DOI: 10.1109/ACCESS.2020.2969957

Alkhatib, K., Khazaleh, H., Alkhazaleh, H. A., Alsoud, A. R., & Abualigah, L. (2022). A new stock price forecasting method using an active deep learning approach. *Journal of Open Innovation*, *8*(2), 96. DOI: 10.3390/joitmc8020096

Almusaylim, Z. A., & Jhanjhi, N. Z. (2020). Comprehensive Review: Privacy Protection of User in Location-Aware Services Of Mobile Cloud Computing. *Wireless Personal Communications*, *111*(1), 541–564. DOI: 10.1007/s11277-019-06872-3

Alsheikh, M. A., Lin, S., Niyato, D., & Tan, H.-P. (2014). Machine learning in wireless sensor networks: Algorithms, strategies, and applications. *IEEE Communications Surveys and Tutorials*, *16*(4), 1996–2018. DOI: 10.1109/COMST.2014.2320099

Amar, V. T., & Alaparthy, S. D. (2020). A ML Based Intrusion Detection System for Mobile Internet of Things. *Sensors (Basel)*, *20*(2), 1–15. PMID: 31947567

Amrutha, C. V., Jyotsna, C., & Amudha, J. (2020). Deep learning approach for suspicious activity detection from surveillance video. 2020 2nd International Conference on Innovative Mechanisms for Industry Applications (ICIMIA), Bangalore, India.

Anand, P. P., Jayanth, G., Rao, K. S., Deepika, P., Faisal, M., & Mokdad, M. (2024). Utilising Hybrid Machine Learning to Identify Anomalous Multivariate Time-Series in Geotechnical Engineering. *AVE Trends In Intelligent Computing Systems*, *1*(1), 32–41.

Anand, P. P., Sulthan, N., Jayanth, P., & Deepika, A. A. (2023). A Creating Musical Compositions Through Recurrent Neural Networks: An Approach for Generating Melodic Creations. *FMDB Transactions on Sustainable Computing Systems*, *1*(2), 54–64.

Anand, R., Jestadi, R., Govinda, K., & Sharma, D. (2024). Data-driven insights: Analyzing and visualizing trends in the chocolate market for strategic decision-making. *AVE Trends in Intelligent Technoprise Letters*, *1*(2), 60–70.

Ancy, P. R., Krishna, A. V., Balachandran, K., Balamurugan, M., & Prakasi, O. G. (2020). Survey on Attribute-based Encryption in Cloud Computing. *International Journal of Network Security*, *22*(5), 863–868.

Angeline, R., Aarthi, S., Regin, R., & Rajest, S. S. (2023). Dynamic intelligence-driven engineering flooding attack prediction using ensemble learning. In *Advances in Artificial and Human Intelligence in the Modern Era* (pp. 109–124). IGI Global. DOI: 10.4018/979-8-3693-1301-5.ch006

Anitha, K., Nagaraj, B. K., Paramasivan, P., & Shynu, T. (2023). Enhancing Clustering Performance with the Rough Set C-Means Algorithm. *FMDB Transactions on Sustainable Computing Systems*, *1*(4), 190–203.

Anushya, A., Begum, S., Shiwani, S., & Shrivastava, A. (2024). Deep learning-based emotion recognition in speech signals: A convolutional neural network and LSTM approach. *AVE Trends in Intelligent Computing Systems*, *1*(4), 198–208.

An, W., Xie, C., & Yuan, X. (2014). An Improved Iterative Censoring Scheme for CFAR Ship Detection with SAR Imagery. Iterative process could inadvertently lead to overfitting the algorithm. *IEEE Transactions on Geoscience and Remote Sensing*, *52*(8), 4585–4595. DOI: 10.1109/TGRS.2013.2282820

Aragani, V. M. (2024). Revolutionizing insurance through AI and data analytics: Innovating policy underwriting and claims management for the digital era. *FMDB Transactions on Sustainable Computer Letters*, *2*(3), 176–185. DOI: 10.69888/FTSCL.2024.000243

Arya, A., Kumar, A., & Ahmad, S. S. (2023). DDoS attack detection using ensemble machine learning approach. 2023 14th International Conference on Computing Communication and Networking Technologies (ICCCNT). Delhi, India, IEEE.

Ashiku, L., & Dagli, C. (2021). Network intrusion detection system using deep learning. *Procedia Computer Science*, *185*(1), 239–247. DOI: 10.1016/j.procs.2021.05.025

Ashraf, A. (2023). The State of Security in Gaza And the Effectiveness of R2P Response. *FMDB Transactions on Sustainable Social Sciences Letters*, *1*(2), 78–84.

Attaluri, V. (2024). Advanced data cleaning pipelines for high volume unstructured text datasets in real-time applications. *AVE Trends in Intelligent Computing Systems*, *1*(4), 209–218.

Bahrololum, M., & Khaleghi, M. (2008). Anomaly intrusion detection system using Gaussian mixture model. 2008 Third International Conference on Convergence and Hybrid Information Technology. Busan, Korea (South).

Bai, S. (2017). Growing random forest on deep convolutional neural networks for scene categorization. *Expert Systems with Applications*, *71*(4), 279–287. DOI: 10.1016/j.eswa.2016.10.038

Banala, S. (2024). Enhancing system stability with advanced techniques in site reliability engineering. *AVE Trends in Intelligent Computing Systems*, *1*(2), 66–76.

Baraneetharan, N.Dr. E. Baraneetharan. (2020). Role of ML Algorithms Intrusion Detection in WSNs: A Survey. *Journal of Information Technology and Digital World*, *2*(3), 161–173. DOI: 10.36548/jitdw.2020.3.004

Basha, A. (2019). *Detection of suspicious human activity based on CNN-DBNN algorithm for video surveillance applications. 2019 Innovations in Power and Advanced Computing Technologies (i-PACT)*. IEEE.

Baskaran, S. B. M., & Raja, G. (2017). A lightweight incognito key exchange mechanism for LTE-A assisted D2D communication. *2017 Ninth International Conference on Advanced Computing (ICoAC)*, Chennai, India. DOI: 10.1109/ICoAC.2017.8441370

Bin Sulaiman, R., Hariprasath, G., Dhinakaran, P., & Kose, U. (2023). Time-series Forecasting of Web Traffic Using Prophet Machine Learning Model. *FMDB Transactions on Sustainable Computer Letters*, *1*(3), 161–177.

Bindraa, N., & Sooda, M. (2019). Detecting DDoS Attacks Using Machine Learning Techniques and Contemporary Intrusion Detection Dataset. *Automatic Control and Computer Sciences*, *53*(5), 419–428. DOI: 10.3103/S0146411619050043

Bordel, B., Alcarria, R., Robles, T., & Iglesias, M. S. (2021). Data authentication and anonymization in IoT scenarios and future 5G networks using chaotic digital watermarking. *IEEE Access : Practical Innovations, Open Solutions*, *20*(2), 1–23. DOI: 10.1109/ACCESS.2021.3055771

Bose, S. R., Sirajudheen, M. A. S., Kirupanandan, G., Arunagiri, S., Regin, R., & Rajest, S. S. (2023). Fine-grained independent approach for workout classification using integrated metric transfer learning. In *Advanced Applications of Generative AI and Natural Language Processing Models* (pp. 358–372). IGI Global. DOI: 10.4018/979-8-3693-0502-7.ch017

Boye, H. (2024). Strengthening cloud security through advanced encryption and anomaly detection techniques for secure data storage and transmission. *FMDB Transactions on Sustainable Computer Letters*, *2*(3), 153–163. DOI: 10.69888/FTSCL.2024.000241

Brusch, S., Lehner, S., Fritz, T., Soccorsi, M., Soloviev, A., & van Schie, B. (2011). Ship Surveillance With TerraSAR-X. IEEE Transactions on Geoscience and Remote Sensing: A Publication of the IEEE Geoscience and Remote Sensing Society, 49(3), 1092–1103.

Cao, M., Wang, L., Xu, H., Chen, D., Lou, C., Zhang, N., Zhu, Y., & Qin, Z. (2019). Sec-D2D: A secure and lightweight D2D communication system with multiple sensors. *IEEE Access : Practical Innovations, Open Solutions*, *75*(9), 104990. DOI: 10.1109/ACCESS.2019.2900727

Carugi, M. (2018). Key features and requirements of 5G/IMT-2020 networks. In *Proceedings of the ITU Arab Forum on Emerging Technologies*, Algeria.

Chen, S., Hu, J., Shi, Y., Peng, Y., Fang, J., Zhao, R., & Zhao, L. (2017). Vehicle-to-everything (V2X) services supported by LTE-based systems and 5G. *IEEE Communications Standards Magazine*, *1*(2), 70–76. DOI: 10.1109/MCOMSTD.2017.1700015

Chen, Y., Huang, L., & Wu, T. (2020). Reinforcement learning for energy-efficient data collection in wireless sensor networks. *IEEE Internet of Things Journal*, *7*(9), 8356–8367.

Chundru, S. (2024). Harnessing the power of AI: Revolutionizing metadata management with machine learning. *FMDB Transactions on Sustainable Computer Letters*, *2*(3), 164–175. DOI: 10.69888/FTSCL.2024.000242

Chunduri, V., Hannan, S. A., Devi, G. M., Nomula, V. K., Tripathi, V., & Rajest, S. S. (2024). Deep convolutional neural networks for lung segmentation for diffuse interstitial lung disease on HRCT and volumetric CT. In *Advances in Computational Intelligence and Robotics* (pp. 335–350). IGI Global.

Cirillo, S., Polese, G., Salerno, D., Simone, B., & Solimando, G. (2023). Towards Flexible Voice Assistants: Evaluating Privacy and Security Needs in IoT-enabled Smart Homes. *FMDB Transactions on Sustainable Computer Letters*, *1*(1), 25–32.

Cremer, F., Sheehan, B., Fortmann, M., Kia, A. N., Mullins, M., Murphy, F., & Materne, S. (2022). Cyber risk and cybersecurity: A systematic review of data availability. *The Geneva Papers on Risk and Insurance. Issues and Practice*, *47*(3), 698–736. DOI: 10.1057/s41288-022-00266-6 PMID: 35194352

Cui, Z., Li, Q., Cao, Z., & Liu, N. (2019). Dense Attention Pyramid Networks for Multi-Scale Ship Detection in SAR Images. The Dense Attention Pyramid Network (DAPN) method enhances multi-scale ship detection in SAR images. *IEEE Transactions on Geoscience and Remote Sensing*, *57*(11), 8983–8997. DOI: 10.1109/TGRS.2019.2923988

Damodaran, D., Mullangi, K., Pradeep, V., & Al-Amin, M. (2024). Adoption Restraints in Mobile Banking with Reference to India. *AVE Trends In Intelligent Social Letters*, *1*(1), 41–49. DOI: 10.31149/ijefsd.v6i1.5172

Daoud, W. B., Obaidat, M. S., Meddeb-Makhlouf, A., Zarai, F., & Hsiao, K.-F. (2019). TACRM: Trust access control and resource management mechanism in fog computing. *Human-Centric Computing and Information Sciences*, *9*(28), 1–18. DOI: 10.1186/s13673-019-0188-3 de Assis, M. V. O., Carvalho, L. F., Rodrigues, J. J. P. C., Lloret, J., & Proença, M. L.Jr. (2020). Near real-time security system applied to SDN environments in IoT networks using convolutional neural network. *Computers & Electrical Engineering*, *86*(9), 106738. DOI: 10.1016/j.compeleceng.2020.106738

Deepak Babu, S. (2022). Switching Convolutional Neural Network for Crowd Counting. In *Proceedings of the IEEE Conference on Computer Vision and Pattern Recognition (CVPR)*, San Juan, Puerto Rico, USA.

Deepika, D., Malik, R., Kumar, S., Gupta, R., & Singh, A. K. (2020). A Review on Data Privacy using Attribute-Based Encryption". In *Proceedings of the International Conference on Innovative Computing & Communications (ICICC)*, New Delhi, India. DOI: 10.2139/ssrn.3606261

Devi, B. T., & Rajasekaran, R. (2023). A Comprehensive Review on Deepfake Detection on Social Media Data. *FMDB Transactions on Sustainable Computing Systems*, *1*(1), 11–20.

Dhaliwal, S. S., Nahid, A.-A., & Abbas, R. (2018). Effective Intrusion Detection System using XGBoost. *Information (Basel)*, *9*(7), 149. DOI: 10.3390/info9070149

Dhinakaran, P., Thinesh, M. A., & Paslavskyi, M. (2023). Enhancing Cyber Intrusion Detection through Ensemble Learning: A Comparison of Bagging and Stacking Classifiers. *FMDB Transactions on Sustainable Computer Letters*, *1*(4), 210–227.

Díaz-Verdejo, J., Muñoz-Calle, J., Estepa Alonso, A., Estepa Alonso, R., & Madinabeitia, G. (2022). On the detection capabilities of signature-based intrusion detection systems in the context of web attacks. *Applied Sciences (Basel, Switzerland)*, *12*(2), 852. DOI: 10.3390/app12020852

Ding, X., He, F., Lin, Z., Wang, Y., Guo, H., & Huang, Y. (2021). Crowd density estimation using fusion of multi-layer features. IEEE Transactions on Intelligent Transportation Systems: A Publication of the IEEE Intelligent Transportation Systems Council, 22(8), 4776–4787.

Doppler, K., Rinne, M. P., Janis, P., Ribeiro, C., & Hugl, K. (2009). Device-to-device communications: Functional prospects for LTE-advanced networks. In *2009 IEEE International Conference on Communications Workshops Dresden*, Germany DOI: 10.1109/ICCW.2009.5208020

Doralba, U. R., Camilo Andrés, C. O., & Castellanos Polo, O. C. (2024). Analysis of The Medium-Term Fiscal Framework: A Financial Planning Tool. *AVE Trends In Intelligent Technoprise Letters*, *1*(1), 40–49.

Durán-Polanco, L., & Siller, M. (2021). Crowd management COVID-19. *Annual Reviews in Control, 52*(4), 465–478. DOI: 10.1016/j.arcontrol.2021.04.006 PMID: 33867812

Eason, G. A., & Vijayakumar, D. A. (2020). Pioneer Approach Data Deduplication To Remove Redundant Data From Cloud Storage. [IJARET]. *International Journal of Advanced Research in Engineering and Technology, 11*(10), 535–544.

Elsaeidy, A., Munasinghe, K. S., Sharma, D., & Jamalipour, A. (2019). A machine learning approach for intrusion detection in smart cities. 2019 IEEE 90th Vehicular Technology Conference (VTC2019-Fall). Honolulu, HI, United States of America, IEEE.

Ezhilarasi, T. P., Kumar, N. S., Latchoumi, T. P., & Balayesu, N. (2021). A Secure Data Sharing Using IDSS CP-ABE in Cloud Storage. In *Advances in Industrial Automation and Smart Manufacturing* (pp. 1073–1085). Springer. DOI: 10.1007/978-981-15-4739-3_92

Fan, W., Zhou, F., Bai, X., Tao, M., & Tian, T. (2019). Ship detection using deep convolutional neural networks for PolSAR images. *Remote Sensing (Basel), 11*(23), 2862. DOI: 10.3390/rs11232862

Fan, Z., Zhang, H., Zhang, Z., Lu, G., Zhang, Y., & Wang, Y. (2022). A survey of crowd counting and density estimation based on convolutional neural network. *Neurocomputing, 472*(11), 224–251. DOI: 10.1016/j.neucom.2021.02.103

Feng, C., Yu, K., Aloqaily, M., Alazab, M., Lv, Z., & Mumtaz, S. (2020). Attribute-Based Encryption with Parallel Outsourced Decryption For Edge Intelligent IoV. *IEEE Transactions on Vehicular Technology, 69*(11), 13784–13795. DOI: 10.1109/TVT.2020.3027568

Ferrag, M. A., Maglaras, L., Moschoyiannis, S., & Janicke, H. (2020). Deep learning for cyber security intrusion detection: Approaches, datasets, and comparative study. *Journal of Information Security and Applications, 50*(2), 102419. DOI: 10.1016/j.jisa.2019.102419

Firdaus, G. M., & Suryani, V. (2023). DDoS attack detection analysis using ensemble learning with XGBoost and AdaBoost algorithms. 2023 11th International Conference on Information and Communication Technology (ICoICT), Melaka, Malaysia, 17–22. IEEE.

Fu, J.-S., Liu, Y., Chao, H.-C., Bhargava, B. K., & Zhang, Z.-J. (2018). Secure data storage and searching for industrial IoT by integrating fog computing and cloud computing. *IEEE Transactions on Industrial Informatics*, *14*(10), 4519–4528. DOI: 10.1109/TII.2018.2793350

Gandhi, M., Satheesh, C., Soji, E. S., Saranya, M., Rajest, S. S., & Kothuru, S. K. (2024). Image recognition and extraction on computerized vision for sign language decoding. In *Explainable AI Applications for Human Behavior Analysis* (pp. 157–173). IGI Global. DOI: 10.4018/979-8-3693-1355-8.ch010

Gao, G., Liu, L., Zhao, L., Shi, G., & Kuang, G. (2009). An Adaptive and Fast CFAR Algorithm Based on Automatic Censoring for Target Detection in High-Resolution SAR Images. Suboptimal initialization strategies could lead to poor convergence behavior. *IEEE Transactions on Geoscience and Remote Sensing*, *47*(6), 1685–1697. DOI: 10.1109/TGRS.2008.2006504

Gao, Y., Wu, Z., Ren, M., & Wu, C. (2022). Improved YOLOv4 based on attention mechanism for ship detection in SAR images. *IEEE Access : Practical Innovations, Open Solutions*, *10*(2), 23785–23797. DOI: 10.1109/ACCESS.2022.3154474

Gnanaguru, G., Priscila, S. S., Sakthivanitha, M., Radhakrishnan, S., Rajest, S. S., & Singh, S. (2024). Thorough analysis of deep learning methods for diagnosis of COVID-19 CT images. In *Advances in Medical Technologies and Clinical Practice* (pp. 46–65). IGI Global.

Guarnera, L., Giudice, O., & Battiato, S. (2020). Proceedings of the IEEE/CVF Conference on Computer Vision and Pattern Recognition (CVPR) Workshops, Seattle, Washington, USA.

Guera, D., & Delp, E. J. (2018). Deepfake video detection using recurrent neural networks. 2018 15th IEEE International Conference on Advanced Video and Signal Based Surveillance (AVSS), Auckland, New Zealand.

Gulganwa, P., & Jain, S. (2021). EES-WCA: Energy Efficient and Secure Weighted Clustering for WSN Using ML Approach. *International Journal of Information Technology : an Official Journal of Bharati Vidyapeeth's Institute of Computer Applications and Management*, *14*(1), 135–144. DOI: 10.1007/s41870-021-00744-5

Guo, H., Yang, X., Wang, N., & Gao, X. (2021). A CenterNet++ model for ship detection in SAR images. CenterNet++ demonstrates superior performance in SAR ship detection by effectively addressing challenges like small object and complex backgrounds. *Pattern Recognition*, *112*(4), 107787. DOI: 10.1016/j.patcog.2020.107787

Guo, R., Yang, G., Shi, H., Zhang, Y., & Zheng, D. (2021). O 3-R-CP-ABE: An Efficient and Revocable Attribute-Based Encryption Scheme in the Cloud-Assisted IoMT System. *IEEE Internet of Things Journal, 8*(11), 8949–8963. DOI: 10.1109/JIOT.2021.3055541

Guo, S., Zhao, J., Li, X., Duan, J., Mu, D., & Jing, X. (2021). A black-box attack method against machine-learning-based anomaly network flow detection models. *Security and Communication Networks, 2*(4), 1–13. DOI: 10.1155/2021/5578335

Gupta, B. B., Gaurav, A., & Perakovic, D. (2021). A big data and deep learning based approach for DDoS detection in cloud computing environment. 2021 IEEE 10th Global Conference on Consumer Electronics (GCCE). Kyoto, Japan, IEEE.

Gupta, A., & Singh, V. (2024). Study MGNREGA and other initiatives with critical interpretation of achievements of MGNREGA in the FY 2022-23. *FMDB Transactions on Sustainable Social Sciences Letters, 2*(1), 34–44. DOI: 10.69888/FTSSSL.2024.000218

Hakan Can Altunay, Z. (2023). A hybrid CNN+LSTM-based intrusion detection system for industrial IoT networks. *Engineering Science and Technology, an International Journal, 38*(2), 101322. DOI: 10.1016/j.jestch.2022.101322

Hakeem, S. A. A., Hussein, H. H., & Kim, H. (1969). Security requirements and challenges of 6G technologies and applications. *Sensors (Basel), 22*(5), 1969. DOI: 10.3390/s22051969 PMID: 35271113

Halbouni, A., Gunawan, T. S., Habaebi, M. H., Halbouni, M., Kartiwi, M., & Ahmad, R. (2022). CNN-LSTM: Hybrid deep neural network for network intrusion detection system. *IEEE Access : Practical Innovations, Open Solutions, 10*(9), 99837–99849. DOI: 10.1109/ACCESS.2022.3206425

Hamedani, A. F., Aziz, M., Wieder, P., & Yahyapour, R. (2023). Big data framework to detect and mitigate distributed denial of service(DDoS) attacks in software-defined networks (SDN). 2023 3rd International Conference on Electrical, Computer, Communications and Mechatronics Engineering (ICECCME), Tenerife, Canary Islands, Spain, 04, 1–6. IEEE.

Han, L., Ran, D., Ye, W., Yang, W., & Wu, X. (2020). Multi-size convolution and learning deep network for SAR ship detection from scratch. *IEEE Access : Practical Innovations, Open Solutions, 8*(8), 158996–159016. DOI: 10.1109/ACCESS.2020.3020363

Han, Y., Zhu, S., Li, Y., & Lin, X. (2021). APPLSS: Adaptive Privacy Preserved Location Sharing Scheme Based On Attribute-Based Encryption. *China Communications*, *18*(3), 105–121. DOI: 10.23919/JCC.2021.03.009

Hao, L., Huang, B., Jia, B., & Mao, G. (2022). DHCLoc: A device-heterogeneity-tolerant and channel-adaptive passive WiFi localization method based on DNN. *IEEE Internet of Things Journal*, *9*(7), 4863–4874. DOI: 10.1109/JIOT.2021.3106902

Harendharan, B., & Boussi Rahmouni, H. (2023). Evaluating the Performance and Impact of Patient-Centric and Ambient Sensors. *FMDB Transactions on Sustainable Computer Letters*, *1*(3), 192–201.

Harshadsathaye, M., Strohmeier, V., & Lenders, A. (2022). An experimental study of GPS spoofing and takeover attacks on UAVs. 31st USENIX Security Symposium (USENIX Security 22), California, USA.

Hayes, M., & Zahnstecher, B. (2021). The virtuous circle of 5G, IoT and energy harvesting. *IEEE Power Electronics Magazine*, *8*(3), 22–29. DOI: 10.1109/MPEL.2021.3099540

Huang, B., Mao, G., Qin, Y., & Wei, Y. (2021). Pedestrian flow estimation through passive WiFi sensing. *IEEE Transactions on Mobile Computing*, *20*(4), 1529–1542. DOI: 10.1109/TMC.2019.2959610

Huang, L., Deng, Y., & Wang, B. (2016). Flow simulation of suspension bridge cable based on lattice-Boltzmann method. *Mathematical Problems in Engineering*, *2016*(8), 1–7. DOI: 10.1155/2016/2537581

Huang, Q., Zhang, Z., & Yang, Y. (2020). Privacy-Preserving Media Sharing With Scalable Access Control and Secure Deduplication in Mobile Cloud Computing. *IEEE Transactions on Mobile Computing*, *20*(5), 1951–1964. DOI: 10.1109/TMC.2020.2970705

Huan, X., Chen, W., Wang, T., Hu, H., & Zheng, Y. (2023). A one-way time synchronization scheme for practical energy-efficient LoRA network based on reverse asymmetric framework. *IEEE Transactions on Communications*, *71*(11), 6468–6481. DOI: 10.1109/TCOMM.2023.3305515

Hu, F., Xu, X., Peng, T., Pu, C., & Li, L. (2018). A fast pseudo-stochastic sequential cipher generator based on RBMs. *Neural Computing & Applications*, *30*(4), 1277–1287. DOI: 10.1007/s00521-016-2753-2

Hund, A., Wagner, H.-T., Beimborn, D., & Weitzel, T. (2021). Digital innovation: Review and novel perspective. *The Journal of Strategic Information Systems*, *30*(4), 101695. DOI: 10.1016/j.jsis.2021.101695

Ifzarne, S., Tabbaa, H., Hafidi, I., & Lamghari, N. (2021). Anomaly Detection Using ML Techniques in Wireless Sensor Networks. *Journal of Physics: Conference Series*, *1743*(1), 12021. DOI: 10.1088/1742-6596/1743/1/012021

Islam, U. A., Al-Atawi, A., Alwageed, H. S., Mehmood, G., Khan, F., & Innab, N. (2024). Detection of renal cell hydronephrosis in ultrasound kidney images: A study on the efficacy of deep convolutional neural networks. *PeerJ. Computer Science*, *10*(1), 1–28. DOI: 10.7717/peerj-cs.1797 PMID: 39669452

Jani, P., Nanban, D., Selvan, J., Richardson, N., Sivakani, R., & Subhashni, R. (2024). Studying Price Dynamics of Bus Services Using Machine Learning Algorithms. *AVE Trends In Intelligent Computing Systems*, *1*(1), 54–65.

Jasper, K. D., Jaishnav, M. N., Chowdhury, M. F., Badhan, R., & Sivakani, R. (2024). Defend and Secure: A Strategic and Implementation Framework for Robust Data Breach Prevention. *AVE Trends In Intelligent Computing Systems*, *1*(1), 17–31.

Jasper, K., Neha, R., & Szeberényi, A. (2023). Fortifying Data Security: A Multifaceted Approach with MFA, Cryptography, and Steganography. *FMDB Transactions on Sustainable Computing Systems*, *1*(2), 98–111.

Javed, Y., Khan, A. S., Qahar, A., & Abdullah, J. (2017). EEoP: A lightweight security scheme over PKI in D2D cellular networks. *Journal of Telecommunication, Electronic and Computer Engineering*, *9*(1), 99–105.

Jeba, J. A., Bose, S. R., & Boina, R. (2023). Exploring Hybrid Multi-View Multimodal for Natural Language Emotion Recognition Using Multi-Source Information Learning Model. *FMDB Transactions on Sustainable Computer Letters*, *1*(1), 12–24.

Jeba, J. A., Bose, S. R., Regin, R., Rajest, S. S., & Kose, U. (2023). In-Depth Analysis and Implementation of Advanced Information Gathering Tools for Cybersecurity Enhancement. *FMDB Transactions on Sustainable Computer Letters*, *1*(2), 130–146.

Jeba, J., Bose, S. R., Regin, R., Sudhan, M. B., Suman Rajest, S., & Babu, P. R. (2024). Efficient Real-time Tamil Character Recognition via Deep Vision Architecture. *AVE Trends In Intelligent Computing Systems*, *1*(1), 1–16.

Jeong, M., & Ahn, S. (2017). A network coding-aware routing mechanism for time-sensitive data delivery in multi-hop wireless networks. *Journal of Information Processing Systems*, *13*(6), 1544–1553.

Jiang, S., Zhao, J., & Xu, X. (2020). SLGBM: An intrusion detection mechanism for wireless sensor networks in smart environments. *IEEE Access : Practical Innovations, Open Solutions*, *8*(1), 169548–169558. DOI: 10.1109/ACCESS.2020.3024219

Jiao, J., Zhang, Y., Sun, H., Yang, X., Gao, X., Hong, W., Fu, K., & Sun, X. (2018). A Densely Connected End-to-End Neural Network for Multi-scale and Multiscene SAI Ship Detection. *IEEE Access : Practical Innovations, Open Solutions*, *6*(4), 20881–20892. DOI: 10.1109/ACCESS.2018.2825376

Jin, D., Sergeeva, E., Weng, W.-H., Chauhan, G., & Szolovits, P. (2022). Explainable deep learning in healthcare: A methodological survey from an attribution view. *WIREs Mechanisms of Disease*, *14*(3), e1548. DOI: 10.1002/wsbm.1548 PMID: 35037736

Jothikumar, C., Ramana, K., Chakravarthy, V. D., Singh, S., & Ra, I.-H. (2021). An efficient routing approach to maximize the lifetime of IoT-based wireless sensor networks in 5G and beyond. *Mobile Information Systems*, *2021*(1), 1–11. DOI: 10.1155/2021/9160516

Kadam, P. (2021). Rohini Mule4, "Suspicious Activity Detection using Image Processing. Shweta Gawande2, Akshita Thorat3, 6(8), 114–119.

Kalra, Y., Upadhyay, S., & Patheja, D. P. S. (2020). Advancements in Cyber Attacks and Security. *International Journal of Innovative Technology and Exploring Engineering*, *9*(4), 1520–1528. DOI: 10.35940/ijitee.D1678.029420

Kang, J., Ji, S.-K., Lee, S., Jang, D., & Hou, J.-U. (2022). Detection enhancement for various deepfake types based on residual noise and manipulation traces. *IEEE Access : Practical Innovations, Open Solutions*, *10*(1), 69031–69040. DOI: 10.1109/ACCESS.2022.3185121

Kanyimama, W. (2023). Design of A Ground Based Surveillance Network for Modibbo Adama University, Yola. *FMDB Transactions on Sustainable Computing Systems*, *1*(1), 32–43.

Kanyimama, W., Argungu, M. S., Gabi, D., & Suru, H. U. (2024). Planning and designing different types of surveillance networks for enhanced security and monitoring. *FMDB Transactions on Sustainable Computer Letters*, *2*(1), 52–62. DOI: 10.69888/FTSCL.2024.000181

Kaplantzis, S., Shilton, A., & Mani, N. (2007). Detecting. Selective Forwarding Attacks in Wireless Sensor Networks using Support Vector Machines Intelligent Sensors. In Sensor Networks and Information, Melbourne, Victoria, Australia

Karatas, G., Demir, O., & Koray Sahingoz, O. (2018). Deep learning in intrusion detection systems. *2018 International Congress on Big Data, Deep Learning and Fighting Cyber Terrorism (IBIGDELFT)*, Ankara, Turkey. DOI: 10.1109/IBIGDELFT.2018.8625278

Karthika, R. A., Sriramya, P., & Rohini, A. (2023). Detection and classification of DDoS attacks in cloud data using hybrid LSTM and RNN for feature selection. *2023 International Conference on Circuit Power and Computing Technologies (ICCPCT)*, 1491–1495. Kollam, India, IEEE. DOI: 10.1109/ICCPCT58313.2023.10244979

Karthikeyan, B., Devi, R. A., & Munshi, M. (2024). Utilizing Deep Learning for the Classification of Brain Tumours Using MRI. *AVE Trends In Intelligent Health Letters*, *1*(1), 1–9.

Karthik, S., Bhaggiaraj, S., Soji, E. S., Deve, L. S., Priscila, S. S., & Rajest, S. S. (2024). Real-time hand gesture recognition for stroke rehabilitation using deep learning approach. *AVE Trends in Intelligent Computing Systems*, *1*(3), 157–172.

Khan, M., Taher, M., Ghazal, S.-W., & Lee, A. (2021). Data Fusion-Based ML Architecture for Intrusion Detection. Computers, Materials & Continua/Computers. *Materials & Continua (Print)*, *70*(2), 3399–3413. DOI: 10.32604/cmc.2022.020173

Khan, S., Zareei, M., Khan, S., Alanazi, F., Alam, M., & Waheed, A. (2021). OO-ABMS: Online/Offline-aided Attribute-Based Multi-Keyword Search. *IEEE Access : Practical Innovations, Open Solutions*, *9*(8), 114392–114406. DOI: 10.1109/ACCESS.2021.3104899

Khettafdalila, L. (2022). Defending the defender: Detecting adversarial examples for network intrusion detection systems, San Jose, USA.

Khushnaseeb, R., & Zafar, A. (2023). A novel deep learning-based model to defend network intrusion detection systems against adversarial attacks. 2023 10th International Conference on Computing for Sustainable Global Development, New Delhi, India.

Kim, H., Lee, S., & Park, J. (2019). Cooperative fault detection in wireless sensor networks using ensemble learning. *IEEE Transactions on Mobile Computing*, *18*(6), 1413–1426.

Kim, J., Astillo, P. V., & You, I. (2020). DMM-SEP: Secure and efficient protocol for distributed mobility management based on 5G networks. *IEEE Access : Practical Innovations, Open Solutions*, *8*(99), 1–1. DOI: 10.1109/ACCESS.2020.2985448

Kim, T., Vecchietti, L. F., Choi, K., Lee, S., & Har, D. (2020). ML for Advanced Wireless Sensor Networks: A Review. *IEEE Sensors Journal*, *21*(11), 12379–12397. DOI: 10.1109/JSEN.2020.3035846

Korshunov, P., & Marcel, S. (2019). Vulnerability assessment and detection of Deepfake videos. *2019 International Conference on Biometrics (ICB)*, Crete, Greece. DOI: 10.1109/ICB45273.2019.8987375

Kumar Mishra, S., Kumar, S., Sahoo, C. K., Swain, A., Guru, P., & Kumar Sethy, B. (2023). Cs-based energy-efficient service allocation in cloud. In Advances in Distributed Computing and Machine Learning [Odisha, India.]. *Proceedings of ICADCML, 2023*, 49–58.

Kumar, A., & Sharma, I. (2023). Employing supervised learning techniques for DDoS attack detection. 2023 International Conference on Innovative Data Communication Technologies and Application (ICIDCA), 684–688. Uttarakhand, India, IEEE.

Kumar, R., & Sharma, D. (2018). HyINT: Signature-anomaly intrusion detection system. 2018 9th International Conference on Computing, Communication and Networking Technologies (ICCCNT). Bengaluru, India.

Kumar, A. (2020). An extensive research survey on data integrity and deduplication towards privacy in cloud storage. [IJECE]. *International Journal of Electrical and Computer Engineering, 10*(2), 2011–2022. DOI: 10.11591/ijece.v10i2.pp2011-2022

Kumar, C. S., Priscila, S. S., Abishabackiyavathi, G., Rajest, S. S., Regin, R., & Deming, C. (2024). Deciphering hand movements in individuals with limited mobility using neural networks. *FMDB Transactions on Sustainable Computing Systems, 2*(1), 13–21. DOI: 10.69888/FTSCS.2024.000193

Kumar, D. P., Amgoth, T., & Annavarapu, C. S. R. (2019). Machine learning algorithms for wireless sensor networks. *Survey (London, England), 49*(9), 1–25.

Kumari, K., & Mrunalini, M. (2022). Detecting Denial of Service attacks using machine learning algorithms. *Journal of Big Data, 9*(4), 1–17. DOI: 10.1186/s40537-022-00616-0

Kumar, P., Baliyan, A., Prasad, K., Sreekanth, N., Jawarkar, P., Roy, V., & Amoatey, E. T. (2022). ML Enabled Techniques for Protecting Wireless Sensor Networks by Estimating Attack Prevalence and Device Deployment Strategy for 5G Networks. *Wireless Communications and Mobile Computing, 2022*(1), 1–15.

Kumar, S. A., Rajest, S. S., Aravind, B. R., & Bhuvaneswari, G. (2023). Virtual learning styles based on learning style detection. *International Journal of Knowledge and Learning, 1*(1), 10057158. Advance online publication. DOI: 10.1504/IJKL.2023.10057158

Kumbhar, B., Pisal, P., Kene, K., & Raut, A. (2023). Suspicious activity detection using Machine Learning. *International Journal for Research in Applied Science and Engineering Technology, 11*(5), 3745–3748. DOI: 10.22214/ijraset.2023.52486

Kumbure, M. M., Lohrmann, C., Luukka, P., & Porras, J. (2022). Machine learning techniques and data for stock market forecasting: A literature review. *Expert Systems with Applications*, *197*(7), 116659. DOI: 10.1016/j.eswa.2022.116659

Laghrissi, F., Douzi, S., Douzi, K., & Hssina, B. (2021). Intrusion detection systems using long short-term memory (LSTM). *Journal of Big Data*, *8*(1), 1–16. DOI: 10.1186/s40537-021-00448-4 PMID: 33425651

Lee, B.-S., Kim, J.-W., & Choi, M.-J. (2022). Experimental comparison of hybrid sampling methods for an efficient NIDS. In 2022 23rd Asia-Pacific Network Operations and Management Symposium (APNOMS), Piscataway, New Jersey, USA. DOI: 10.23919/APNOMS56106.2022.9919939

Legista, M., Nurlaili, L., & Masriah, I. (2024). Development of an adaptive learning system utilizing deep learning to support independent learning processes for students. *AVE Trends in Intelligent Techno Learning*, *1*(2), 107–120.

Li, Q., Min, R., Cui, Z., Pi, Y., & Xu, Z. (2019). Multi-scale ship detection based on dense attention pyramid network in SAR images. IGARSS 2019 - 2019 IEEE International Geoscience and Remote Sensing Symposium, 1–4. IEEE, Yokohama, Japan.

Liang, P., Liu, G., Xiong, Z., Fan, H., Zhu, H., & Zhang, X. (2023). Xuemin Zhang, A facial geometry based detection model for face manipulation using CNN-LSTM architecture. *Information Sciences*, *633*(7), 370–383. DOI: 10.1016/j.ins.2023.03.079

Liang, W., Huang, W., Long, J., Zhang, K., Li, K.-C., & Zhang, D. (2020). Deep reinforcement learning for resource protection and real-time detection in IoT environment. *IEEE Internet of Things Journal*, *7*(7), 6392–6401. DOI: 10.1109/JIOT.2020.2974281

Licaj, B., & Karras, D. A. (2024). Integral smart vehicle automation framework using IoT, modern software, and infrastructure. *AVE Trends in Intelligent Computing Systems*, *1*(3), 128–141.

Li, H., Lan, C., Fu, X., Wang, C., Li, F., & Guo, H. (2020). A Secure And Lightweight Fine-Grained Data Sharing Scheme for Mobile Cloud Computing. *Sensors (Basel)*, *20*(17), 4720. DOI: 10.3390/s20174720 PMID: 32825602

Li, J., Liu, Y., Zhang, Z., Ren, J., & Zhao, N. (2017). Towards green IoT networking: Performance optimization of network coding based communication and reliable storage. *IEEE Access : Practical Innovations, Open Solutions*, *5*(5), 8780–8791. DOI: 10.1109/ACCESS.2017.2706328

Lin, Z., Du, L., Gao, Z., Huang, L., & Du, X. (2016). Efficient device-to-device discovery and access procedure for 5G cellular network: Efficient device-to-device discovery and access procedure for 5G. *Wireless Communications and Mobile Computing*, *16*(7), 1282–1289. DOI: 10.1002/wcm.2602

Lin, Z., Shi, Y., & Xue, Z. (2022). IDSGAN: Generative adversarial networks for attack generation against intrusion detection. In *Advances in Knowledge Discovery and Data Mining*. Springer International Publishing. DOI: 10.1007/978-3-031-05981-0_7

Liu, J., Shen, F., Wei, M., Zhang, Y., Zeng, H., Zhu, J., & Cai, C. (2019). 'A largescale benchmark for vehicle logo recognition, In 2019 IEEE 4th International Conference on Image, Vision and Computing (ICIVC) (pp. 479–483). IEEE, Xiamen, China.

Liu, W., Anguelov, D., Erhan, D., Szegedy, C., Reed, S., Fu, C.-Y., ... Ssd. (2016). 'Ssd: Single shot multibox detector, In Computer Vision-ECCV 2016: 14th European Conference (pp. 21–37), Springer Amsterdam, Netherlands.

Liu, H., & Shaoqing, E. (2022). Application of wireless communication of aviation airborne platform based on 5G technology. *Hangkong Xuebao*, *43*(12), 459–467.

Liu, L., Cao, Z., Lu, H., Xiong, H., & Shen, C. (2022). NSSNet: Scale-aware object counting with non-scale suppression. *IEEE Transactions on Intelligent Transportation Systems*, *23*(4), 3103–3114. DOI: 10.1109/TITS.2020.3030781

Li, Y., Barthelemy, J., Sun, S., Perez, P., & Moran, B. (2020). A case study of WiFi sniffing performance evaluation. *IEEE Access : Practical Innovations, Open Solutions*, *8*(7), 129224–129235. DOI: 10.1109/ACCESS.2020.3008533

Loganathan, S., Kariyawasam, G., & Sumathipala, P. (2019). Suspicious activity detection in surveillance footage. 2019 International Conference on Electrical and Computing Technologies and Applications (ICECTA), Al Khamiah, United Arab Emirates (UAE). DOI: 10.1109/ICECTA48151.2019.8959600

Lu, P., Wagih, M., Goussetis, G., Shinohara, N., & Song, C. (2023). A comprehensive survey on transmitting antenna systems with synthesized beams for microwave wireless power transmission. *IEEE Journal of Microwaves*, *3*(4), 1081–1101. DOI: 10.1109/JMW.2023.3285825

Madhuranthakam, R. S. (2024). Implementing data quality assurance frameworks in distributed data engineering workflows. *AVE Trends in Intelligent Computing Systems*, *1*(4), 241–251.

Mahmood, T., Li, J., Pei, Y., Akhtar, F., Butt, S. A., Ditta, A., & Qureshi, S. (2022). An intelligent fault detection approach based on reinforcement learning system in wireless sensor network. *The Journal of Supercomputing*, *78*(3), 3646–3675. DOI: 10.1007/s11227-021-04001-1

Maksutov, A. A., Morozov, V. O., Lavrenov, A. A., & Smirnov, A. S. (2020). Methods of deepfake detection based on machine learning. 2020 IEEE Conference of Russian Young Researchers in Electrical and Electronic Engineering (EIConRus), Moscow, Russia.

Maleh, Y., Sahid, A., & Belaissaoui, M. (2020). Optimized machine learning techniques for iot 6lowpan cyber attacks detection. *Proceedings of the 12th International Conference on Soft Computing and Pattern Recognition*, 12, 669–677, Springer, Cham, Switzerland.

Mao, B., Jiang, H., Wu, S., & Tian, L. (2016). Leveraging data deduplication to improve the performance of primary storage systems in the cloud. IEEE Transactions on Computers. *Institute of Electrical and Electronics Engineers*, *65*(6), 1775–1788.

Maroju, P. K. (2024). Advancing Synergy of Computing and Artificial Intelligence with Innovations Challenges and Future Prospects. *FMDB Transactions on Sustainable Intelligent Networks*, *1*(1), 1–14. DOI: 10.69888/FTSIN.2024.000153

Maroju, P. K. (2024). Enhancing white label ATM network efficiency: A data science approach to route optimization with AI. *FMDB Transactions on Sustainable Computer Letters*, *2*(1), 40–51. DOI: 10.69888/FTSCL.2024.000180

Massenkoff, M., & Chalfin, A. (2022). Activity-adjusted crime rates show that public safety worsened in 2020. *Proceedings of the National Academy of Sciences of the United States of America*, *119*(46), e2208598119. DOI: 10.1073/pnas.2208598119 PMID: 36343240

Mehmood, G., Khan, M. Z., Bashir, A. K., Al-Otaibi, Y. D., & Khan, S. (2023). An efficient QoS-based multi-path routing scheme for smart healthcare monitoring in wireless body area networks. *Computers & Electrical Engineering*, *109*(7), 108517. DOI: 10.1016/j.compeleceng.2022.108517

Minu, M. S., Subashka Ramesh, S. S., Canessane, R., Al-Amin, M., & Bin Sulaiman, R. (2023). Experimental Analysis of UAV Networks Using Oppositional Glowworm Swarm Optimization and Deep Learning Clustering and Classification. *FMDB Transactions on Sustainable Computing Systems*, *1*(3), 124–134.

Mishra, S. K., Challa, H. K., Kotha, K. S., & Yarramreddy, D. P. (2024). Task offloading technique selection in mobile edge computing. *2024 International Conference on Advancements in Smart, Secure and Intelligent Computing (ASSIC)*. IEEE, Bhubaneswar, India. DOI: 10.1109/ASSIC60049.2024.10507901

Mohan, A., Mondal, S., Dan, S. S., & Paily, R. P. (2023). Design considerations for efficient realization of rectifiers in microscale wireless power transfer systems: A review. *IEEE Sensors Journal*, *23*(18), 20691–20704. DOI: 10.1109/JSEN.2022.3222938

Mohseni-Ejiyeh, A., Ashouri-Talouki, M., & Mahdavi, M. (2018). An incentive-aware, lightweight, secure data-sharing scheme for D2D communication in 5G cellular networks. *ISeCure*, *10*(1), 15–27.

Moloudian, G., Soltani, S., Bahrami, S., Buckley, J. L., O'Flynn, B., & Lalbakhsh, A. (2023). Design and fabrication of a Wilkinson power divider with harmonic suppression for LTE and GSM applications. *Scientific Reports*, *13*(1), 4246. DOI: 10.1038/s41598-023-31019-7 PMID: 36918689

Moore, K., Tom, R., & O'Neil, J. (2024). The truth behind crime statistics: Avoiding distortions and improving public safety. SSRN Electronic Journal, 8(2), 95. DOI: 10.2139/ssrn.4697314

Mudunuri, L. N. R. (2024). Artificial Intelligence (AI) Powered Matchmaker: Finding Your Ideal Vendor Every Time. *FMDB Transactions on Sustainable Intelligent Networks*, *1*(1), 27–39. DOI: 10.69888/FTSIN.2024.000155

Muna, E., & Sitnikova, N. (2021). Asynchronous peer-to-peer federated capability-based targeted ransomware detection model for industrial IoT. *IEEE Access : Practical Innovations, Open Solutions*, *9*(11), 148738–148755.

Murugavel, S., & Hernandez, F. (2023). A Comparative Study Between Statistical and Machine Learning Methods for Forecasting Retail Sales. *FMDB Transactions on Sustainable Computer Letters*, *1*(2), 76–102.

Mustafa, N., Khalifa, M., & Abd Elrahman, A. (2017). Safety and security of cities and their impact on the city life. SSRN Electronic Journal, 12(4), 1-12. DOI: 10.2139/ssrn.3164155

Muthunagai, S. U., & Anitha, R. (2022). TDOPS: Time series based deduplication and optimal data placement strategy for IIoT in cloud environment. *Journal of Intelligent & Fuzzy Systems*, *43*(1), 1583–1597. DOI: 10.3233/JIFS-212568

Nageswaraguptha, M., Yuvarajateekaraman, R., & Thelkar, A. (2022). Generative adversarial networks for unmanned aerial vehicle object detection with fusion technology. *Journal of Advanced Transportation*, *11*(4), 1–13.

Nanban, D., Ajitha, Y., Selvan, J., Pierre, T. J., Sara, S. B. V. J., & Ragesha, R. (2024). Enhancing user experience in air canvas through robust hand gesture recognition using computer vision. *FMDB Transactions on Sustainable Computer Letters*, *2*(3), 131–143. DOI: 10.69888/FTSCL.2024.000239

Narayanan, K., Lakshmi, R., Krishnan, E. G., Julie, Y. H., & Robinson, V. (2021). ML Based Detection and a Novel EC-BRTT Algorithm Based Prevention of DOS Attacks in Wireless Sensor Networks. *Wireless Personal Communications*, *127*(1), 479–503. DOI: 10.1007/s11277-021-08277-7

Narezal, K., & Kalmani, V. (2020). "Study of lightweight ABE for cloud based IoT", In 2020 Fourth International Conference on I-SMAC (IoT in Social, Mobile, Analytics and Cloud)(I-SMAC) (pp. 134-137). IEEE, Palladam, India.

Naveen, P. V. (2020). A Survey on Security Issues in Mobile Cloud Computing (MCC. *Solid State Technology*, *63*(6), 18729–18745.

Ni, J., Lin, X., & Shen, X. S. (2018). Efficient and secure service-oriented authentication supporting network slicing for 5G-enabled IoT. *IEEE Journal on Selected Areas in Communications*, *36*(3), 644–657. DOI: 10.1109/JSAC.2018.2815418

Nwabuokei, I., Ghouse, M., Chen, W., Kollannur, E. T., Li, H., & Bin Sulaiman, R. (2023). Quantifying the Influence of Population on Carbon Emissions: A Comparative Study of Developed versus Developing Countries Using Machine Learning. *FMDB Transactions on Sustainable Energy Sequence*, *1*(2), 71–82.

Obaid, A. J., & Bhushan, B. Muthmainnah, & Rajest, S. S. (Eds.). (2023). Advanced applications of generative AI and natural language processing models. Advances in Computational Intelligence and Robotics, IGI Global, USA. DOI: 10.4018/979-8-3693-0502-7

Obaid, A. J., Bhushan, B., & Rajest, S. S. (Eds.). (2023). *Advanced applications of generative AI and natural language processing models*. IGI Global.

Olakanmi, O. O., & Odeyemi, K. O. (2021). Faster and efficient cloud-server-aided data de-duplication scheme with an authenticated key agreement for Industrial Internet-of-Things. *Internet of Things : Engineering Cyber Physical Human Systems*, *14*(6), 100376. DOI: 10.1016/j.iot.2021.100376

Pandey, R., Pandey, M., & Nazarov, A. (2023). Enhanced DDoS Detection using Machine Learning. 2023 6th International Conference on Information Systems and Computer Networks (ISCON), Mathura, India, 1–4. IEEE.

Patel, R., Sharma, A., & Verma, R. (2021). Energy-efficient routing in wireless sensor networks: A machine learning approach. *IEEE Sensors Journal*, *21*(10), 12751–12761.

Patra, S. S., Jena, S., Mohanty, J. R., & Gourisaria, M. K. (2021). DedupCloud: an optimized efficient virtual machine deduplication algorithm in cloud computing environment. In *Data Deduplication Approaches*. Elsevier. DOI: 10.1016/B978-0-12-823395-5.00009-4

Pawlicki, M., Choraś, M., & Kozik, R. (2020). Defending network intrusion detection systems against adversarial evasion attacks. *Future Generation Computer Systems*, *110*(9), 148–154. DOI: 10.1016/j.future.2020.04.013

Periasamy, J. K., & Latha, B. (2021). Efficient hash function based duplication detection algorithm for data Deduplication deduction and reduction. *Concurrency and Computation*, *33*(1), e5213. DOI: 10.1002/cpe.5213

Philip, D., Singh, F., & Singh, S. (2024). Untangling Economic Threads through an In-depth Analysis of Universal Basic Income's Influence on Socio-economic Dynamics. *AVE Trends In Intelligent Social Letters*, *1*(1), 50–60.

Pierre, T. J., Tao, C., Vénant, K., & Erneste, B. (2024). Speed management blueprint: Conception of an IoT-based electric vehicle speed limiter monitoring system for Kigali city vehicles. *FMDB Transactions on Sustainable Energy Sequence*, *2*(1), 33–48. DOI: 10.69888/FTSES.2024.000190

Poornima, I. G. A., & Paramasivan, B. (2020). Anomaly detection in wireless sensor network using machine learning algorithm. *Computer Communications*, *151*(2), 331–337. DOI: 10.1016/j.comcom.2020.01.005

Prakash, P. J., & Lalitha, B. (2022). Optimized ensemble classifier based network intrusion detection system for RPL based internet of things. *Wireless Personal Communications*, *125*(5), 3603–3626. DOI: 10.1007/s11277-022-09726-7

Pranav, R. P., Prawin, R. P., Paramasivan, P., Shynu, T., & Subhashni, R. (2024). IoT-SecNet: A trust-based framework for enhancing security in IoT communications and network layer protocols. *FMDB Transactions on Sustainable Computing Systems*, *2*(2), 96–106. DOI: 10.69888/FTSCS.2024.000201

Pranav, R. P., Prawin, R. P., Subhashni, R., & Das, S. R. (2023). Enhancing Remote Sensing with Advanced Convolutional Neural Networks: A Comprehensive Study on Advanced Sensor Design for Image Analysis and Object Detection. *FMDB Transactions on Sustainable Computer Letters, 1*(4), 255–266.

Preeti, K., Kumar, M., & Sharma, H. K. (2023). A GAN-based model of deepfake detection in social media. *Procedia Computer Science, 218*(1), 2153–2162. DOI: 10.1016/j.procs.2023.01.191

Premkumar, M., & Sundararajan, T. V. P. (2020). DLDM: Deep learning-based defense mechanism for denial-of-service attacks in wireless sensor networks. *Microprocessors and Microsystems, 79*(11), 103278. DOI: 10.1016/j.micpro.2020.103278

Priscila, S. S., Rajest, S. S., Tadiboina, S. N., Regin, R., & András, S. (2023). Analysis of Machine Learning and Deep Learning Methods for Superstore Sales Prediction. *FMDB Transactions on Sustainable Computer Letters, 1*(1), 1–11.

Pulivarthy, P. (2024a). Optimizing large-scale distributed data systems using intelligent load balancing algorithms. *AVE Trends in Intelligent Computing Systems, 1*(4), 219–230.

Pulivarthy, P. (2024b). Semiconductor Industry Innovations: Database Management in the Era of Wafer Manufacturing. *FMDB Transactions on Sustainable Intelligent Networks, 1*(1), 15–26. DOI: 10.69888/FTSIN.2024.000154

Pundir, M., & Sandhu, J. K. (2021). A systematic review of quality of service in wireless sensor networks using machine learning: Recent trend and future vision. *Journal of Network and Computer Applications, 188*(8), 103084. DOI: 10.1016/j.jnca.2021.103084

Qaisar, Z. H., Almotiri, S. H., Al Ghamdi, M. A., Nagra, A. A., & Ali, G. (2021). A Scalable and Efficient Multi-agent Architecture for Malware Protection in Data Sharing over Mobile Cloud. *IEEE Access : Practical Innovations, Open Solutions, 9*(3), 76248–76259. DOI: 10.1109/ACCESS.2021.3067284

Qazi, E.-U.-H., Imran, M., Haider, N., Shoaib, M., & Razzak, I. (2022). An intelligent and efficient network intrusion detection system using deep learning. *Computers & Electrical Engineering, 99*(4), 107764. DOI: 10.1016/j.compeleceng.2022.107764

Qian, H., Jing, S., Hong, X., & Yong, W. (2020, August). "HABEm: Hierarchical Attribute Based Encryption with Multi-Authority for the Mobile Cloud Service", In *2020 IEEE/CIC International Conference on Communications in China (ICCC)* (pp. 524-529). IEEE, Chongqing, China. DOI: 10.1109/ICCC49849.2020.9238987

Qin, Y., Liu, J., Zhao, S., Feng, D., & Feng, W. (2020). RIPTE: Runtime integrity protection based on trusted execution for IoT device. *Security and Communication Networks, 2020*(6), 1–14. DOI: 10.1155/2020/8957641

Quadri, S. A., & Katakdhond, K. S. (2022). Suspicious Activity Detection Using Convolution Neural Network. *Journal of Pharmaceutical Negative Results, 13*(1), 1235–1245.

Raja, A. S. V., Jasper, K. D., Poornima, V., Priscila, S. S., Thenmozhi, A., & Ratkovic, N. (2024). Tech horizons unveiled: Navigating the transformative decade in AIML, cybersecurity, IoT, gaming, and data science education. *FMDB Transactions on Sustainable Intelligent Networks, 1*(2), 120–134. DOI: 10.69888/FTSIN.2024.000214

Raja, A., Njilla, L., & Yuan, J. (2022). Adversarial attacks and defenses toward AI-assisted UAV infrastructure inspection. *IEEE Internet of Things Journal, 9*(23), 23379–23389. DOI: 10.1109/JIOT.2022.3206276

Rajasekaran, N., Jagatheesan, S. M., Krithika, S., & Albanchez, J. S. (2023). Development and Testing of Incorporated ASM with MVP Architecture Model for Android Mobile App Development. *FMDB Transactions on Sustainable Computing Systems, 1*(2), 65–76.

Rajest, S. S., Moccia, S., Singh, B., Regin, R., & Jeganathan, J. (Eds.). (2024, August 30). Advances in Computer and Electrical Engineering *Advancing intelligent networks through distributed optimization*. IGI Global., DOI: 10.4018/979-8-3693-3739-4

Rajest, S. S., Singh, B. J., Obaid, A., Regin, R., & Chinnusamy, K. (2023a). *Recent developments in machine and human intelligence*. Advances in Computational Intelligence and Robotics. IGI Global., DOI: 10.4018/978-1-6684-9189-8

Raj, M. A., Mishra, A., & Forest, G. A. (2024). Predictive Analytics for Employee Attrition: Leveraging Machine Learning for Strategic Human Resources Management. *AVE Trends in Intelligent Technoprise Letters, 1*(1), 13–29.

Raj, M. A., Thinesh, M. A., Varmann, S. S. M., Pothu, A. R., & Paramasivan, P. (2024). Ensemble-based phishing website detection using Extra Trees classifier. *AVE Trends in Intelligent Computing Systems, 1*(3), 142–156.

Raj, S., & Arunkumar, B. (2021). Enhanced Encryption For Light Weight Data In A Multi-Cloud System. *Distributed and Parallel Databases, 41*(4), 65–74. DOI: 10.1007/s10619-021-07340-3

Raj, V., & Duraipandian, M. (2023). Energy conservation using PISAE and cross-layer-based opportunistic routing protocol (CORP) for wireless sensor network. *Engineering Science and Technology, an International Journal, 42*(6), 101411.

Rath, M., & Mishra, S. (2022). "Advanced-Level Security in Network and Real-Time Applications Using ML Approaches. In IGI Global eBooks, Hershey, Pennsylvania, United States.

Reaves, B., & Morris, T. (2009). Discovery, infiltration, and denial of service in a process control system wireless network. 2009 eCrime Researchers Summit, Washington, United States of America

Regin, R., Khanna, A. A., Krishnan, V., Gupta, M., & Bose, R. S., & Rajest, S. S. (2023). Information design and unifying approach for secured data sharing using attribute-based access control mechanisms. In Recent Developments in Machine and Human Intelligence (pp. 256–276). IGI Global, USA.

Regin, R., Gaayathri, R. S., Paramasivan, P., Rajest, S. S., & Radwan, R. (2024). VehiWalnut: Smart Fuel Management with Real-Time Data and User Interaction. *FMDB Transactions on Sustainable Intelligent Networks*, *1*(1), 56–71. DOI: 10.69888/FTSIN.2024.000157

Regin, R., T, S., George, S. R., Bhattacharya, M., Datta, D., & Priscila, S. S. (2023). Development of predictive model of diabetic using supervised machine learning classification algorithm of ensemble voting. *International Journal of Bioinformatics Research and Applications*, *19*(3), 151–169. DOI: 10.1504/IJBRA.2023.10057044

Rele, M., & Patil, D. (2023). Supervised and unsupervised ML methodologies for intrusive detection in nuclear systems. *2023 International Conference on Network, Multimedia and Information Technology (NMITCON)*, Bengaluru, India. DOI: 10.1109/NMITCON58196.2023.10276256

Renjith, E. J. (2024). Revolutionizing cloud security: Innovative approaches for safeguarding data integrity. *FMDB Transactions on Sustainable Computer Letters*, *2*(2), 111–119. DOI: 10.69888/FTSCL.2024.000185

Ren, S., He, K., Girshick, R., & Sun, J. (2015). 'Faster r-cnn: Towards real-time object detection with region proposal networks,''. *IEEE Transactions on Pattern Analysis and Machine Intelligence*, *39*(6), 1137–1149. DOI: 10.1109/TPAMI.2016.2577031 PMID: 27295650

Rezvani, B., & Diehl, W. (2019). Hardware Implementations of NIST Lightweight Cryptographic Candidates: A First Look. In *Proceedings of the NIST Lightweight Cryptography Workshop*, Maryland, USA.

Ronald, B. J., Joseph, S. G. M., Kumar, P., Hsu, C.-Y., & Mehmood, A. (2024). Performance and Risk Analysis of Sustainable Mutual Funds in India: A Comparative Study. *AVE Trends In Intelligent Social Letters*, *1*(1), 13–24.

Roshan, K., & Zafar, A. (2022). Deep learning approaches for anomaly and intrusion detection in computer networks: A review. In Lecture Notes on Data Engineering and Communications Technologies. Springer, Singapore.computer network and information security. Lecture Notes in Electrical Engineering, 853(3), 345–356. DOI: 10.1007/978-981-16-3961-6_45

Roshan, K., & Zafar, A. (2022). Using kernel SHAP XAI method to optimize the network anomaly detection model. In 2022 9th International Conference on Computing for Sustainable Global Development (INDIACom), Piscataway, New Jersey, USA. DOI: 10.23919/INDIACom54597.2022.9763241

Saba, T., Rehman, A., Sadad, T., Kolivand, H., & Bahaj, S. A. (2022). Anomaly-based intrusion detection system for IoT networks through a deep learning model. *Computers & Electrical Engineering*, *99*(4), 107810. DOI: 10.1016/j.compeleceng.2022.107810

Saheed, Y., & Kayode, M. O. (2021). Efficient Cyber Attack Detection on the Internet of Medical Things-Smart Environment Based on Deep Recurrent Neural Network and ML Algorithms. *IEEE Access : Practical Innovations, Open Solutions*, *9*(11), 161546–161554. DOI: 10.1109/ACCESS.2021.3128837

Sahoo, S. K., Mishra, S. K., & Guru, A. (2023). *Blockchain-based medical report management and distribution system. In 6G Enabled Fog Computing in IoT: Applications and Opportunities*. Springer.

Sajini, S., Reddi, L. T., Regin, R., & Rajest, S. S. (2023). A Comparative Analysis of Routing Protocols for Efficient Data Transmission in Vehicular Ad Hoc Networks (VANETs). *FMDB Transactions on Sustainable Computing Systems*, *1*(1), 1–10.

Sanchol, P., & Fugkeaw, S. (2021, May). "An Analytical Review of Data Access Control Schemes in Mobile Cloud Computing", In *International Conference on Computing and Information Technology* (pp. 310-321). Springer, Cham, Switzerland. DOI: 10.1007/978-3-030-79757-7_30

Sanjalawe, Y., & Althobaiti, T. (2023). DDoS attack detection in cloud computing based on ensemble feature selection and deep learning. *Computers, Materials & Continua*, *75*(2), 3571–3588. DOI: 10.32604/cmc.2023.037386

Saran, M., Yadav, R. K., & Tripathi, U. N. (2022). Machine learning based security for cloud computing: A survey. *International Journal of Applied Engineering Research: IJAER*, *17*(4), 332–337. DOI: 10.37622/IJAER/17.4.2022.338-344

Satyanarayana, D., & Alasmi, A. S. (2022). Detection and Mitigation of DDOS based Attacks using Machine Learning Algorithm. *2022 International Conference on Cyber Resilience (ICCR)*. Dubai, United Arab Emirates, IEEE. DOI: 10.1109/ICCR56254.2022.9995773

Saxena, D., & Chaudhary, S. (2023). Predicting Brain Diseases from FMRI-Functional Magnetic Resonance Imaging with Machine Learning Techniques for Early Diagnosis and Treatment. *FMDB Transactions on Sustainable Computer Letters*, *1*(1), 33–48.

Saxena, R., Sharma, V., & Saxena, R. R. (2023). Transforming Medical Education: Multi-Keyword Ranked Search in Cloud Environment. *FMDB Transactions on Sustainable Computing Systems*, *1*(3), 135–146.

Sayedelahl, M. A. (2024). Enabling Intelligent Traffic Systems: A Deep Learning Method for Accurate Arabic License Plate Recognition. *FMDB Transactions on Sustainable Intelligent Networks*, *1*(1), 40–55. DOI: 10.69888/FTSIN.2024.000156

Sayedelahl, M. A., & Farouk, R. M. (2024). Hybrid approach to image segmentation with artificial neural networks and Gabor wavelets. *AVE Trends in Intelligent Computing Systems*, *1*(2), 77–90.

Selvi, E., Adimoolam, M., Karthi, G., Thinakaran, K., Balamurugan, N. M., Kannadasan, R., Wechtaisong, C., & Khan, A. A. (2022). Suspicious actions detection system using enhanced CNN and surveillance video. *Electronics (Basel)*, *11*(12), 4210. DOI: 10.3390/electronics11244210

Sezari, B., Moller, D. P. F., & Deutschmann, A. (2018). Anomaly-based network intrusion detection model using deep learning in airports. 2018 17th IEEE International Conference On Trust, Security And Privacy In Computing And Communications, / 12th IEEE International Conference On Big Data Science And Engineering (TrustCom/BigDataSE), New York, USA

Shaik, A., Borgaonkar, R., Park, S., & Seifert, J. P. (2019). New vulnerabilities in 4G and 5G cellular access network protocols: exposing device capabilities. In *Proceedings of the 12th Conference on Security and Privacy in Wireless and Mobile Networks*, New York, USA. DOI: 10.1145/3317549.3319728

Sharma, S., & Saini, H. (2020). Fog assisted task allocation and secure deduplication using 2FBO2and MoWo in cluster-based industrial IoT (IIoT). *Computer Communications*, *152*(2), 187–199. DOI: 10.1016/j.comcom.2020.01.042

Shaukat, K., Luo, S., Varadharajan, V., Hameed, I. A., & Xu, M. (2020). A survey on machine learning techniques for cyber security in the last decade. *IEEE Access : Practical Innovations, Open Solutions*, *8*(12), 222310–222354. DOI: 10.1109/ACCESS.2020.3041951

Shi, F., Yang, S. X., Mukherjee, M., Jiang, H., Costa, D. B. D., & Wong, W.-K. (2023). Parameter-sharing-based average-consensus time synchronization in IoT networks. *IEEE Internet of Things Journal*, *10*(9), 8215–8227. DOI: 10.1109/JIOT.2022.3230896

Shin, D., Yun, K., Kim, J., Astillo, P. V., Kim, J., & You, I. (2019). A security protocol for route optimization in DMM-based smart home IoT networks. *IEEE Access : Practical Innovations, Open Solutions*, *14*(8), 100219. DOI: 10.1109/ACCESS.2019.2943929

Shin, S., & Kwon, T. (2018). Two-factor authenticated key agreement supporting unlinkability in 5G-integrated wireless sensor networks. *IEEE Access : Practical Innovations, Open Solutions*, *6*(99), 1–1. DOI: 10.1109/ACCESS.2018.2796539

Shi, Z., Zhang, L., Liu, Y., Cao, X., Ye, Y., Cheng, M.-M., & Zheng, G. (2018). Crowd counting with deep negative correlation learning. *2018 IEEE/CVF Conference on Computer Vision and Pattern Recognition*, San Juan, Puerto Rico, USA. DOI: 10.1109/CVPR.2018.00564

Shrestha, R., Omidkar, A., Roudi, S. A., Abbas, R., & Kim, S. (2021). Machine-learning-enabled intrusion detection system for cellular connected UAV networks. *Electronics (Basel)*, *10*(13), 1549. DOI: 10.3390/electronics10131549

Shukla, S., Hassan, M. F., Tran, D. C., Akbar, R., Paputungan, I. V., & Khan, M. K. (2023). Improving latency in Internet-of-Things and cloud computing for real-time data transmission: A systematic literature review (SLR). *Cluster Computing*, *26*(5), 2657–2680. DOI: 10.1007/s10586-021-03279-3

Singh, K., Visuwasam, L. M. M., Rajasekaran, G., Regin, R., Rajest, S. S., & Shynu. (2024). Innovations in skeleton-based movement recognition bridging AI and human kinetics. In Explainable AI Applications for Human Behavior Analysis (pp. 125–141), USA. IGI Global.

Singh, S., Rajest, S. S., Hadoussa, S., Obaid, A. J., & Regin, R. (2023). *Data-Driven Intelligent Business Sustainability*. Advances in Business Information Systems and Analytics. IGI Global., DOI: 10.4018/979-8-3693-0049-7

Singh, S., Rajest, S. S., Hadoussa, S., Obaid, A. J., & Regin, R. (Eds.). (2023, December 21). Advances in Business Information Systems and Analytics *Data-driven decision making for long-term business success.* IGI Global., DOI: 10.4018/979-8-3693-2193-5

Sirajudeen Yoosuf, M., & Anitha, R. (2022). Low Latency Fog-Centric Deduplication Approach to Reduce IoT Healthcare Data Redundancy. *Wireless Personal Communications, 126*(5), 421–443. DOI: 10.1007/s11277-022-09752-5

Sivapriya, G. B. V., Ganesh, U. G., Pradeeshwar, V., Dharshini, M., & Al-Amin, M. (2023). Crime Prediction and Analysis Using Data Mining and Machine Learning: A Simple Approach that Helps Predictive Policing. *FMDB Transactions on Sustainable Computer Letters, 1*(2), 64–75.

Smith, A., & Gupta, L. (2020). Machine learning for predictive maintenance of wireless sensor nodes in IoT. *IEEE Transactions on Industrial Informatics, 16*(5), 3313–3320.

Soji, E. S., Karthik, S., Priscila, S. S., Hanirex, D. K., Rajest, S. S., & Sebastian, A. (2024). Designing an E-Voting System Architecture Using the STAP Protocol. *FMDB Transactions on Sustainable Intelligent Networks, 1*(2), 96–109. DOI: 10.69888/FTSIN.2024.000212

Solano-Rojas, B. J., Villalón-Fonseca, R., & Batres, R. (2023). Micro evolutionary particle swarm optimization (mepso): A new modified meta-heuristic. *Systems and Soft Computing, 5*(12), 200057. DOI: 10.1016/j.sasc.2023.200057

Sonichaurasia, K. (2023). EEMOR: Energy Eflicient Metaheuristic Opportunistic Routing Protocol for WSNs. *Ad-Hoc & Sensor Wireless Networks, 55*(3/4), 177.

Sowjanya, K., & Dasgupta, M. (2020). A ciphertext-policy Attribute based Encryption Scheme for Wireless Body Area Networks based on ECC. *Journal of Information Security and Applications, 54*(10), 102559. DOI: 10.1016/j.jisa.2020.102559

Srilakshmi, U., Sandhya, I., Manikandan, J., Bindu, A. H., Regin, R., & Rajest, S. S. (2024). Design and implementation of energy-efficient protocols for underwater wireless sensor networks. In *Advances in Computer and Electrical Engineering* (pp. 417–430). IGI Global.

Srinivas, K., Prasanth, N., Trivedi, R., Bindra, N., & Raja, S. P. (2022). A novel machine learning inspired algorithm to predict real-time network intrusions. *International Journal of Information Technology : an Official Journal of Bharati Vidyapeeth's Institute of Computer Applications and Management, 14*(7), 3471–3480. DOI: 10.1007/s41870-022-00925-w

Stallings, W., & Cryptography, N. (2017). *Cryptography and Network Security: Principles and Practice*. Pearson.

Sudar, K. M., Deepalakshmi, P., Nagaraj, P., & Muneeswaran, V. (2020). Analysis of Cyberattacks and its Detection Mechanisms. *2020 Fifth International Conference on Research in Computational Intelligence and Communication Networks (ICRCICN)*, Bangalore, India. DOI: 10.1109/ICRCICN50933.2020.9296178

Sulaiman, R. B., Aljaidi, M., Alsuwaylimi, A. A., Butt, U., Talukder, M. S. H., Alam, S. S., Farhan, M., Das, S. R., & Alam, M. W. (2024). Enhancing security in digital payments: A comparative evaluation of machine learning models for credit card fraud detection. *FMDB Transactions on Sustainable Computer Letters*, *2*(2), 63–84. DOI: 10.69888/FTSCL.2024.000182

Sun, Z., Meng, C., Cheng, J., Zhang, Z., & Chang, S. (2022). A Multi-Scale Feature Pyramid Network for Detection and Instance Segmentation of Marine Ships in SAR Images. The Multi-Scale Feature Pyramid Network (MS-FPN) demonstrates superior performance in detection and instance segmentation of marine ships in SAR, 14(24), 6312.

Sundararajan, V., Steffi, R., & Shynu, T. (2023). Data Fusion Strategies for Collaborative Multi-Sensor Systems: Achieving Enhanced Observational Accuracy and Resilience. *FMDB Transactions on Sustainable Computing Systems*, *1*(3), 112–123.

Sun, Y., Cao, J., Ma, M., Li, H., Niu, B., & Li, F. (2019). Privacy-preserving device discovery and authentication scheme for D2D communication in 3GPP 5G HetNet. *2019 International Conference on Computing, Networking and Communications (ICNC)*, Hawaii, USA. DOI: 10.1109/ICCNC.2019.8685499

Suresh, S., & Kiran, V. (2016). Prevention of Dos and DDoS Attack Using Cryptographic Techniques. *International Journal of Advanced Research in Computer and Communication Engineering*, *5*(1), 93–96.

Syed Agha Hassnainmohsan, N., Othman, Y., Mohammed, H., & Alsharif, M. (2023). Unmanned aerial vehicles (UAVs): Practical aspects, applications, open challenges, security issues, and future trends. *Intelligent Service Robotics*, *4*(1), 1–29.

Talatalaeikhoei, S., & Ismail, N. (2022). Dynamic selection techniques for detecting GPS spoofing attacks on UAVs. *Sensors (Basel)*, *22*(2), 662. DOI: 10.3390/s22020662 PMID: 35062623

Tan, H., Song, Y., Xuan, S., Pan, S., & Chung, I. (2019). Secure D2D group authentication employing smartphone sensor behaviour analysis. *Symmetry*, *11*(8), 969. DOI: 10.3390/sym11080969

Tehrani, M. N., Uysal, M., & Yanikomeroglu, H. (2014). Device-to-device communication in 5G cellular networks: Challenges, solutions, and future directions. *IEEE Communications Magazine*, *52*(5), 86–92. DOI: 10.1109/MCOM.2014.6815897

Thirunagalingam, A. (2024). Bias detection and mitigation in data pipelines: Ensuring fairness and accuracy in machine learning. *AVE Trends in Intelligent Computing Systems*, *1*(2), 116–127.

Thirunagalingam, A. (2024). Transforming real-time data processing: The impact of AutoML on dynamic data pipelines. *FMDB Transactions on Sustainable Intelligent Networks*, *1*(2), 110–119. DOI: 10.69888/FTSIN.2024.000213

Tian, Y., Huang, B., Jia, B., & Zhao, L. (2020). Optimizing AP and Beacon Placement in WiFi and BLE hybrid localization. *Journal of Network and Computer Applications*, *164*(8), 102673. DOI: 10.1016/j.jnca.2020.102673

Tripathi, R. K., Jalal, A. S., & Agrawal, S. C. (2018). Suspicious human activity recognition: A review. *Artificial Intelligence Review*, *50*(2), 283–339. DOI: 10.1007/s10462-017-9545-7

Tu, S., Waqas, M., Huang, F., Abbas, G., & Abbas, Z. H. (2021). A Revocable And Outsourced Multi-Authority Attribute-Based Encryption Scheme in Fog Computing. *Computer Networks*, *195*(8), 108196. DOI: 10.1016/j.comnet.2021.108196

Ueli, M. (2000). Authentication theory and hypothesis testing. *IEEE Transactions on Information Theory*, *46*(4), 1350–1356. DOI: 10.1109/18.850674

Ullah, F., Naeem, M. R., Mostarda, L., & Shah, S. A. (2021). Clone detection in 5G-enabled social IoT system using graph semantics and deep learning model. *International Journal of Machine Learning and Cybernetics*, *12*(11), 3115–3127. DOI: 10.1007/s13042-020-01246-9

Vadlakonda, G. (2024). Enhancing user experience in iOS applications through adaptive interface design. *AVE Trends in Intelligent Computing Systems*, *1*(4), 231–240.

Van Houdt, G., Mosquera, C., & Nápoles, G. (2020). A review on the long short-term memory model. *Artificial Intelligence Review*, *53*(8), 5929–5955. DOI: 10.1007/s10462-020-09838-1

Varmann, S. S., Hariprasath, G., & Kadirova, I. (2023). Optimizing Educational Outcomes: H2O Gradient Boosting Algorithm in Student Performance Prediction. *FMDB Transactions on Sustainable Techno Learning*, *1*(3), 165–178.

Vemula, V. R. (2024). Cognitive artificial intelligence systems for proactive threat hunting in AI-driven cloud applications. *AVE Trends in Intelligent Computing Systems*, *1*(3), 173–183.

Verkerken, M., D'hooge, L., Wauters, T., Volckaert, B., & De Turck, F. (2020). Unsupervised machine learning techniques for network intrusion detection on modern data. 2020 4th Cyber Security in Networking Conference (CSNet). Lausanne, Switzerland.

Vignesh, R., & Preethi, J. (2022). Secure Data Deduplication System with Efficient and Reliable Multi-Key Management in Cloud Storage. *Journal of Internet Technology*, *23*(4), 811–825. DOI: 10.53106/160792642022072304016

Wang, Q., & Breckon, T. P. (2022). Crowd counting via segmentation guided attention networks and curriculum loss. IEEE Transactions on Intelligent Transportation Systems: A Publication of the IEEE Intelligent Transportation Systems Council, 23(9), 15233–15243.

Wang, Y., Li, Y., & Tu, K. (2022). Crowd counting model with convolutional neural networks and transformer. 2022 4th International Conference on Communications, Information System and Computer Engineering (CISCE), Guangzhou, China.

Wang, C., Yu, W., Lu, J., Zhu, F., Fan, L., & Li, S. (2022). UAV-based physical-layer intelligent technologies for 5G-enabled internet of things: A survey. *Wireless Communications and Mobile Computing*, *10*(1), 1–5. DOI: 10.1155/2022/4351518

Wang, H., Zhang, N., Chen, X., & Li, M. (2023). Consensus-based time synchronization using Bayesian estimation in wireless sensor networks under communication delays. *IEEE Systems Journal*, *17*(2), 3332–3342. DOI: 10.1109/JSYST.2022.3225642

Wang, J., Liu, Y., Rao, S., Zhou, X., & Hu, J. (2023). A novel self-adaptive multi-strategy artificial bee colony algorithm for coverage optimization in wireless sensor networks. *Ad Hoc Networks*, *150*(11), 103284. DOI: 10.1016/j.adhoc.2023.103284

Wang, W., Han, D., Chen, C., & Wu, Z. (2024). FastPFM: A multi-scale ship detection algorithm for complex scenes based on SAR images. *Connection Science*, *36*(1), 1–29. DOI: 10.1080/09540091.2024.2313854

Wang, X., Li, Q., & Liu, Y. (2022). Anomaly detection in wireless sensor networks using convolutional neural networks. *IEEE Transactions on Wireless Communications*, *21*(1), 250–262. DOI: 10.1109/LWC.2021.3124943

Wang, X., Thome, N., & Cord, M. (2017). Gaze latent support vector machine for image classification improved by weakly supervised region selection. *Pattern Recognition*, *72*(12), 59–71. DOI: 10.1016/j.patcog.2017.07.001

Wang, Z., Yong, T., Song, X., & Sun, D. (2023). Maximum likelihood estimation of relative clock skew for distributed time synchronization in industrial wireless sensor networks. *IEEE Sensors Journal, 23*(24), 31359–31367. DOI: 10.1109/JSEN.2023.3330998

Waseem, S., Bakar, S. A. R. S., Ahmed, B. A., Omar, Z., Eisa, T. A. E., & Dalam, M. E. E. (2023). DeepFake on Face and Expression Swap: A Review. *IEEE Access : Practical Innovations, Open Solutions, 11*(10), 117865–117906. DOI: 10.1109/ACCESS.2023.3324403

Whelan, J., Almehmadi, A., & El-Khatib, K. (2022). Artificial intelligence for intrusion detection systems in unmanned aerial vehicles. *Computers & Electrical Engineering, 99*(4), 107784. DOI: 10.1016/j.compeleceng.2022.107784

Wujiang, L. (2021). Research on key technologies of in-cabin data acquisition and wireless ad hoc network based on 802.11.

Wu, Y., Zhao, Z., Bao, F., & Deng, R. H. (2015). Software puzzle: A countermeasure to resource-inflated denial-of-service attacks. *IEEE Transactions on Information Forensics and Security, 10*(1), 168–177. DOI: 10.1109/TIFS.2014.2366293

Wu, Z., Chen, H., & Liu, X. (2022). Edge computing for anomaly detection in wireless sensor networks: A deep learning perspective. *IEEE Transactions on Industrial Informatics, 18*(3), 1796–1804.

Xiuhua, Z. (2012). The current situation of public safety incidents and their causes. *Proceedings of the 2012 International Conference on Public Management (ICPM-2012)*, Beijing, China DOI: 10.2991/icpm.2012.47

Yadav, D., & Salmani, S. (2019). Deepfake: A survey on facial forgery technique using generative adversarial network. *2019 International Conference on Intelligent Computing and Control Systems (ICCS)*, Madurai, India DOI: 10.1109/ICCS45141.2019.9065881

Yang, D., Cheng, Z., Zhang, W., Zhang, H., & Shen, X. (2023). Burst-aware time-triggered flow scheduling with enhanced multi-CQF in time-sensitive networks. *IEEE/ACM Transactions on Networking, 31*(6), 2809–2824. DOI: 10.1109/TNET.2023.3264583

Yang, D., Zhang, W., Ye, Q., Zhang, C., Zhang, N., Huang, C., Zhang, H., & Shen, X. (2024). DetFed: Dynamic resource scheduling for deterministic federated learning over time-sensitive networks. *IEEE Transactions on Mobile Computing, 23*(5), 5162–5178. DOI: 10.1109/TMC.2023.3303017

Yang, H., Li, W., & Wang, J. (2018). Dynamic spectrum allocation for IoT wireless sensor networks using Q-learning. *IEEE Internet of Things Journal*, *5*(4), 2935–2944.

Yang, P., Ni, R., & Zhao, Y. (2017). Recapture image forensics based on Laplacian convolutional neural networks. In *Digital Forensics and Watermarking*. Springer International Publishing. DOI: 10.1007/978-3-319-53465-7_9

Yang, X., Lu, R., Choo, K. K. R., Yin, F., & Tang, X. (2022). Achieving efficient and privacy-preserving cross-domain big data deduplication in cloud. *IEEE Transactions on Big Data*, *8*(1), 73–84. DOI: 10.1109/TBDATA.2017.2721444

Yan, X., He, G., Yu, J., Tang, Y., & Zhao, M. (2020). Offline/Online Outsourced Attribute-Based Encryption with Partial Policy Hidden for the Internet of Things. *Journal of Sensors*, *2020*(9), 1–11. DOI: 10.1155/2020/8861114

Yan, X., Yuan, X., Zhang, Q., & Tang, Y. (2020). Traceable and Weighted Attribute-Based Encryption Scheme in the Cloud Environment. *IEEE Access : Practical Innovations, Open Solutions*, *8*(2), 38285–38295. DOI: 10.1109/ACCESS.2020.2975813

Yeh, W.-C., & Lin, J.-S. (2018). New parallel swarm algorithm for smart sensor systems redundancy allocation problems in the Internet of Things. *The Journal of Supercomputing*, *74*(10), 4358–4384. DOI: 10.1007/s11227-016-1903-8

Yinglong, L. (2022). Research and application of deep learning in image recognition. 2022 IEEE 2nd International Conference on Power Electronics and Computer Applications (ICPECA), 1(2), 12047.

Yu, X., Liang, Y., Lin, X., Wan, J., Wang, T., & Dai, H.-N. (2022). Frequency feature pyramid network with global-local consistency loss for crowd-and-vehicle counting in congested scenes. IEEE Transactions on Intelligent Transportation Systems: A Publication of the IEEE Intelligent Transportation Systems Council, 23(7), 9654–9664.

Yuan, W., Li, S., Wei, Z., Cui, Y., Jiang, J., Zhang, H., & Fan, P. (2023). New delay Doppler communication paradigm in 6G era: A survey of orthogonal time frequency space (OTFS). *China Communications*, *20*(6), 1–25. DOI: 10.23919/JCC.fa.2022-0578.202306

Yuan, W., Zou, J., Cui, Y., Li, X., Mu, J., & Han, K. (2023). Orthogonal time frequency space and predictive beamforming-enabled (URLLC) in vehicular networks. *IEEE Wireless Communications*, *30*(2), 56–62. DOI: 10.1109/MWC.005.2200408

Yu, C., & Shin, Y. (2022). SAR ship detection based on improved YOLOv5 and BiFPN. Significantly enhances ship detection accuracy in SAR images compared to the original YOLOv5 algorithm. *Express ICT Express, 10*(1), 28–33. DOI: 10.1016/j.icte.2023.03.009

Yuxuangu, M., Wu, Q., Wang, S., & Chen, L. (2023). A Deep Learning-Based Crowd Counting Method and System Implementation on Neural Processing Unit Platform. *Computers, Materials & Continua, 75*(1), 493–512. DOI: 10.32604/cmc.2023.035974

Zanardo, E. (2024). Chronostamp: A general-purpose run-time for data-flow computing in a distributed environment. *AVE Trends in Intelligent Computing Systems, 1*(2), 106–115.

Zang, T., Zhu, Y., Xu, Y., & Yu, J. (2021). Jointly modelingspatio-temporal dependencies and daily flow correlations for crowd flow prediction. *ACM Transactions on Knowledge Discovery from Data, 15*(4), 1–20. DOI: 10.1145/3439346

Zhang, X., Ran, J., & Mi, J. (2019). An intrusion detection system based on convolutional neural network for imbalanced network traffic. 2019 IEEE 7th International Conference on Computer Science and Network Technology (ICCSNT). Dalian, China.

Zhang, Y., Zheng, L., & Thing, V. L. L. (2017). Automated face swapping and its detection. 2017 IEEE 2nd International Conference on Signal and Image Processing (ICSIP), Singapore.

Zhang, C., Costa-Perez, X., & Patras, P. (2022). Adversarial attacks against deep learning-based network intrusion detection systems and defense mechanisms. *IEEE/ACM Transactions on Networking, 30*(3), 1294–1311. DOI: 10.1109/TNET.2021.3137084

Zhang, H., & Wu, J. (2021). The limitation of adversarial training and the blindness of deep neural networks. In *International Conference on Learning Representations*, Vienna, Austria.

Zhang, J., Lu, N., Li, T., & Ma, J. (2021). Enabling Efficient Decentralized and Privacy Preserving Data Sharing in Mobile Cloud Computing. *Wireless Communications and Mobile Computing, 2021*(9), 1–15. DOI: 10.1155/2021/8513869

Zhang, M., Wang, H., & Tan, J. (2022). Ship Detection in SAR Images Based on Multi-Scale Feature Extraction and Adaptive Feature Fusion. MSSDNet, with CSP-MRes2 and FC-FPN modules, achieves superior multi-scale ship detection in SAR imagery. *Remote Sensing (Basel), 14*(3), 755. DOI: 10.3390/rs14030755

Zhang, S., Wang, Y., & Zhou, W. (2019). Towards secure 5G networks: A survey. *Computer Networks*, *162*(10), 106871. DOI: 10.1016/j.comnet.2019.106871

Zhang, T., & Zhang, X. (2022). A polarization fusion network with geometric feature embedding for SAR ship classification. Complexity increases with the number of polarization channels and geometric features. *Pattern Recognition*, *123*(3), 108365. DOI: 10.1016/j.patcog.2021.108365

Zhang, Y., Deng, R. H., Xu, S., Sun, J., Li, Q., & Zheng, D. (2020). Attribute-based Encryption for Cloud Computing Access Control: A survey. *ACM Computing Surveys*, *53*(4), 1–41.

Zheng, H., Shao, J., & Wei, G. (2020). Attribute-based Encryption with Outsourced Decryption in Block chain. *Peer-to-Peer Networking and Applications*, *13*(6), 1643–1655. DOI: 10.1007/s12083-020-00918-1

Zheng, L., Duffner, S., Idrissi, K., Garcia, C., & Baskurt, A. (2016). Siamese multi-layer perceptrons for dimensionality reduction and face identification. *Multimedia Tools and Applications*, *75*(9), 5055–5073. DOI: 10.1007/s11042-015-2847-3

Zhibin, Z. (2021). *Design of wireless senser network recorder based on CCI310.*

Zhong, S., Jia, C., Chen, K., & Dai, P. (2019). A novel steganalysis method with deep learning for different texture complexity images. *Multimedia Tools and Applications*, *78*(7), 8017–8039. DOI: 10.1007/s11042-018-6573-5

Zhu, A., Zheng, Z., Huang, Y., Wang, T., Jin, J., Hu, F., Hua, G., & Snoussi, H. (2022). CACrowdGAN: Cascaded attentional generative adversarial network for crowd counting. IEEE Transactions on Intelligent Transportation Systems: A Publication of the IEEE Intelligent Transportation Systems Council, 23(7), 8090–8102.

About the Contributors

Ferdin Joe John Joseph is currently an Assistant Professor with the faculty of information technology, Thai Nichi Institute of technology Bangkok. He graduated his bachelor and masters degrees in computer science and engineering from Anna University Chennai during 2009 and 2011 respectively. He got his PhD in Computer Science and Information Systems from the National Institute of Development Administration Bangkok during 2015. His area of research includes deep learning, IoT and Blockchain technology. He has nearly a decade experience in teaching. He has published in peer reviewed international conferences and journals. He is certified as the "Most Valuable Professional" (MVP) with Alibaba Cloud since 2021. He is teaching as per academic curriculum to students, recognizing, nurturing the creative potential of each student. Teach students using a systematic instructional methodology comprising lecture plans (following the credit allotted to each subject), discussion groups, seminars, case studies, field assignments, and independent and/or group projects. Recently, he has been the technique program committee, the technique reviews, and the track chair for international conferences published by Springer Series. He is serving in the editor in chief, the editorial board of international journals, and he authored/edited different books and filed so many Patents. Finally, he is a member of ISTE, IET, Etc...

Karthikeyan Chinnusamy, Sr Principal with more than 25 years of experience in IT, Product Dev, R&D and Education fields. Fellow IETE, Fellow IE, Sr Member IEEE,Sr Member ACM, Project management Institute (PMI), Reviewer, Editorial Board Member of R&D Journals. Board Member & Program Director SF DAMA. SME in Data Governance, GDPR, HIPAA Compliance, Data Management, Data Architecture, Master Data, Data Quality, AI/ML, Analytics and reporting in Payment processing, Customer, Finance, CRM and License domains. Mentor in SFDC Mig, Data.com, ERP, Architecture, R&D, Embedded systems, VLSI,Adv Information processing. I am also reviewer for IEEE Silicon Valley Sr Member Elevation and Speaker, Volunteer for SFBay ACM. Reviewer of Journals in Springer Nature.

Joseph Jeganathan earned his Ph.D. in Psychiatric Nursing from Rajiv Gandhi University of Health Sciences, National Consortium for Ph.D. Nursing, (Indian Nursing Council), Bangalore, Karnataka, India in 2019. He completed his Postgraduate studies at the National Institute of Mental Health and Neurosciences, Bangalore, Karnataka, India 2011. He is working as an assistant professor in the Mental Health Nursing Department at the University of Bahrain, Kingdom of Bahrain. He has more than 16 years of Undergraduate and Postgraduate teaching experience. He has worked as a Professor at SGT University, Gurugram, Dept. of Nursing, IES University, Bhopal; Associate Professor Akal College of Nursing, Eternal University, Baru Sahib, India; and also worked as a teaching faculty in various nursing colleges in India and Nepal. Dr. Joseph Jeganathan has published many research articles in National and international Nursing Journals. His areas of research interest are Adolescent mental health, Life skills training, and Substance use disorders.

Ahmed J. Obaid is a Asst. Professor at the Department of Computer Science, Faculty of Computer Science and Mathematics, University of Kufa, Iraq. Dr. Ahmed holds a Bachelor in Computer Science, degree in – Information Systems from College of Computers, University of Anbar, Iraq (2001-2005), and a Master Degree (M. TECH) of Computer Science Engineering (CSE) from School of Information Technology, Jawaharlal Nehru Technological University, Hyderabad, India (2010-2013), and a Doctor of Philosophy (PhD) in Web Mining from College of Information Technology, University of University of Babylon, Iraq (2013-2017). He is a Certified Web Mining Consultant with over 14 years of experience in working as Faculty Member in University of Kufa, Iraq. He has taught courses in Web Designing, Web Scripting, JavaScript, VB.Net, MATLAB Toolbox's, and other courses on PHP, CMC, and DHTML from more than 10 international organizations and institutes from USA, and India. Dr. Ahmed is a member of Statistical and Information Consultation Center (SICC), University of Kufa, Iraq.

S. Suman Rajest is the Dean of Research and Development (R&D) and International Student Affairs (ISA) at Dhaanish Ahmed College of Engineering, Chennai, Tamil Nadu, India. He is an Editor in Chief of the International Journal of Human Computing Studies and The International Journal of Social Sciences World, He is the Chief Executive Editor of the International Journal of Advanced Engineering Research and Science, International Journal of Advanced Engineering, Management and Science, The International Journal of Health and Medicines, The

International Journal of Management Economy and Accounting Fields and The International Journal of Technology Information and Computer and also he is an Editorial Board Member in International Journal of Management in Education, Scopus, Inderscience, EAI Endorsed Transactions on e-Learning, and Bulletin of the Karaganda university Pedagogy series. He is also a Book Series Editor at IGI Global Publisher, Springer, etc. All of his writing, including his research, involves elements of creative nonfiction in the Human Computing learning system. He is also interested in creative writing and digital media, Learning, AI, student health learning, etc. He has published 400 papers in peer-reviewed international journals. He has authored and co-authored several scientific book publications in journals and conferences and is a frequent reviewer of international journals and conferences. He also reviews Inderscience, EAI Journals, IGI Global, Science Publications, etc.

***

Arthi B holds a Ph.D. in the field of Computer Science and Engineering from Anna University. She has 15+ years of experience in teaching. Her areas of interest include artificial intelligence, machine learning, software engineering, and Internet of Things. She has published several articles in various reputed national and international, such as Scopus and SCI journals. She has also authored book chapters in CRC and Springer Publications. She has presented papers in various national and international conferences and attended many workshops, seminars, and faculty development programs to be in track with the changing technology and teaching methodology. She is a member of various scientific and professional bodies. She has been awarded the IET Inspiring Young Teacher Award for the year 2016-2017 for the IET Chennai. She can be contacted at email: arthib@srmist.edu.in

Index

N

P

R

S

T

W

www.ingramcontent.com/pod-product-compliance
Lightning Source LLC
LaVergne TN
LVHW061549290926
849162LV00004B/954